Project
Management

Other Titles of Interest

Project Management

Strategic Design
and Implementation

David I. Cleland, Ph.D.

Ernest E. Roth Professor
and Professor of Engineering Management
University of Pittsburgh

Second Edition

Boston, Massachusetts   Burr Ridge, Illinois
Dubuque, Iowa   Madison, Wisconsin   New York, New York
San Francisco, California   St. Louis, Missouri

Library of Congress Cataloging-in-Publication Data

Cleland, David I.
    Project management : strategic design and implementation / David
I. Cleland—2nd ed.
       p.   cm.
    Includes index.
    ISBN 0-07-011351-3 (acid-free paper)
    1. Industrial project management. I. Title.
    HD69.P75C526 1994
    658.4'04—dc20
                                           93-44757
                                             CIP

McGraw-Hill

A Division of The McGraw·Hill Companies

6 7 8 9 10 11 12 13 14 BKMBKM 9 9 8 7

ISBN 0-07-011351-3

*The sponsoring editor for this book was Larry Hager, the editing super-
visor was Kimberly A. Goff, and the production supervisor was Donald
F. Schmidt. This book was set in Century Schoolbook. It was composed
by McGraw-Hill's Professional Book Group composition unit.*

This book is printed on acid-free paper.

Contents

Part 1 Introduction

Part 2 The Strategic Context of Projects

Part 3 Organizational Design for Project Management

Part 4 Project Operations

Preface

The typical organization today looks very different from its counterpart of 25 years ago. Organizational downsizing, restructuring, the impact of the computer and telecommunications, empowerment of employees, team management, deregulation, and global competition have set in motion a sea of changes that show no signs of abating. The changes occurring today are profound. These changes continue to herald the need for project management, particularly as contemporary organizational managers grope for ways to survive in the face of these changes.

Formal project or program management emerged in an unobtrusive manner in the late 1950s and began taking on the characteristics of a discipline in its own right. No one can claim to have invented project management. Its early beginnings are found in the construction industry and in more recent years in military weapons and systems development businesses. The origins of many of the techniques of project management can be found in the management of large-scale ad hoc endeavors such as the Manhattan Project, the Polaris submarine program, large construction projects, or the use of naval task forces. In the early 1960s we began to recognize project management for what it is: a philosophy and a process for the management of ad hoc activities in organizations, characterized by a distinct life cycle and integrated by a management system, consisting of a "matrix" organizational design supported by appropriate management activities such as planning, control, information support, and cultural facilitation. Specialized techniques such as PERT, CPM, and schedule-cost control systems have developed, facilitated by the growing use of computers in modern organizations. Professional societies, such as the Project Management Institute and INTERNET, have come into existence, greatly aiding the maturation of the theory and the practice of project management.

Project management is an idea whose time has come. It is a distinct discipline to be applied to the management of ad hoc activities in organizations. As a discipline, project management has become a key philosophy and process to contribute to the strategic management of organizations—the management of organizations as if their futures mattered.

Most of the books about project management today treat the discipline as if it were a nearly separate entity in the management discipline. Little is found in these books that puts project management into its proper place in the strategic management of organizations. This book tries to do just that. The first edition of this book had its genesis during my many consulting assignments with different organizations, starting or improving their use of project management. My study of these organizations' needs led me to believe that in spite of an abundance of literature dealing with project management per se, there was a serious lack of theoretical and practical literature that placed project management in the context of the design and execution of organizational strategies. As I studied the growing abundance of project management literature and observed its widespread practice, I became more convinced that strategic design and implementation of project management was a slowly but surely emerging area of contemporary practice requiring management and professional education and training. This study and observation provided the basis for the title of the book.

I also found that too many managers, particularly at senior levels, were inclined to view project management as a "special case" of management—a departure from the proper or expected courses of organizational leadership. Too often these managers failed to appreciate the strategic role that projects played in the long-term management of their organizations. Unfortunately, often project management was more tolerated than accepted, placing the project managers, functional managers, and project professionals in ambiguous roles in trying to support the project needs. Once these senior managers recognized the logic of the project as a building block in organizational strategy along with other elements such as functional strategies, policies, procedures, and action plans, then project management was accepted and supported more fully in the organization's strategic management.

My continued work as a consultant in the field of project management and strategic planning reinforces my belief that projects are truly building blocks in the design and execution of organizational strategies.

In the second edition of this book, care has been taken to strengthen the existing chapters by updating the theory of project management and to show how project management continues to move toward "institutionalization" in the sense of becoming a permanent feature in the strategic management of organizations. In addition, a chapter "Continuous Improvement Through Projects" has been added to the text to show how the application of project management has expanded.

Many examples have been given of the use of project management in different applications. For the most part, these examples have been drawn from the consulting experience of the author or from the current periodical literature. Those examples that have been drawn from the periodical literature reflect the current applications of project management and thus are believed to be of particular interest to the reader who can read the full article or report that is cited for reference. Of course, because of the time required to publish the book, the circumstances that have been cited in the periodical literature have changed. Nevertheless, the citation of these examples has value as a reminder to the reader that the material described in the book is strongly supported by current practices in the field of project management.

In the first edition of this book, the point was made—and emphasized at every opportunity—that projects were building blocks in the design and execution of organizational strategies. This unabashed emphasis continues in the second edition. The book pushes the state of the art of project management, as supported by strategic management, to put forth the important philosophy that project management is one of the cardinal strategies to follow in dealing with the inevitable national and global changes that face all organizations today.

This book is written for use in senior undergraduate or graduate programs within universities and colleges providing management instruction in the areas of business, engineering, education, public health, public administration, and law. At the undergraduate level, the book should have wide appeal for the young professional and manager-to-be who finds that project management of one form or another is a part of the management systems used by the organization she or he joins. At the graduate level, this book can provide the more mature student with an opportunity to develop an understanding of the lexicon, processes, techniques, and systems applications of a fascinating area of contemporary management.

Managers and professionals who attend continuing education short courses also should find the book useful for self-improvement in management and reference on how project management can and should be practiced.

The book is also written for the practitioner who needs a basic text that can provide a paradigm on how best to manage projects and other teams. The book provides an overview of the discipline. The reader who wishes to probe more deeply into such subjects as project planning, project software, scheduling techniques, information systems, and the like has an abundance of literature to draw upon. Project management has grown to the extent that specialized areas of knowledge, skills, and attitudes have been developed that provide the reader much more depth in processes and techniques than would be possible in a book of

Acknowledgments

My deep appreciation goes to many of my contemporaries in the Project Management Institute and INTERNET with whom the opportunity was provided to discuss, debate, and expound on some of the core ideas put forth in this book. Special thanks to my students in the School of Engineering at the University of Pittsburgh, who endured my lectures and seminars on project management and who helped me to finalize many of the concepts and processes put forth in the text.

I thank Dr. Harvey Wolfe, chairman of the Industrial Engineering Department, and Dr. Charles A. Sorber, former Dean of the School of Engineering, of the University of Pittsburgh, who continued to provide an environment and the resources that made the preparation of this book possible.

A special debt of gratitude to Ms. Claire Zubritzky whose unparalleled administrative skills have aided my work over the last 18 years. Without doubt, her dedication, candor, and encouragement contributed significantly to this book. I thank her for her unwavering and critical support.

Introduction

I believe that the manager or professional who assumes responsibility for some part of the practice of project management needs to develop a *philosophy* of project management as well as an understanding of the role that project management plays in the strategic management of organizations. I use the term *philosophy* in the sense of a body of thought—a way of thinking—that underlies the project management discipline.

There are three key attributes of a project management philosophy. First is *knowledge*—a familiarity with project management theory and practice applied to contemporary organizations. Second is *skill* in applying that knowledge to project management processes, techniques, and methodologies. Third is the development of a set of *attitudes*—values and aspirations—that facilitate both manager and professional leadership in project management.

Managers and professionals who aspire to be effective in project management need to develop knowledge, skills, and attitudes in the context of a project management philosophy that recognizes the role of project management by itself, and in the larger organizational context in which projects are designed, developed, and carried out.

The format for the book is adaptable to many different uses. The reader and the teacher may choose those sections and topics—and their order—which best suit their objectives.

"Part 1: Introduction" consists of two chapters which introduce project management and describe the process that is involved in the practice of that discipline.

"Part 2: The Strategic Context of Projects" deals with the strategic use of projects in managing organizations and when projects should be used. Project stakeholder management, strategic issue management, and the role of the board of directors also are described in this part.

"Part 3: Organizational Design for Project Management" considers in three chapters how projects can be organized, with supporting authority, responsibility, and accountability.

"Part 4: Project Operations" contains five chapters concerned with planning, information systems, control, contract management, and project termination.

"Part 5: Interpersonal Dynamics in the Management of Projects" looks at communication patterns, team building, and the important role of leadership in attaining project objectives.

"Part 6: The Cultural Elements" considers the use of project teams for continuous improvement. One of the chapters in this part also provides insight into the cultural ambience in which projects are best managed.

Throughout the text project management is described in the context of *products* and organizational *processes*. Organizational *services* are assumed to be included in those things of value that organizations offer their customers. In the interest of brevity, just organizational products and processes will be mentioned in the text.

Of course, the reader who wishes to do more reading about project management is encouraged to use the abundant current periodical references that are cited in the text.

Project
Management

Introduction

1

Why Project Management?

"There is nothing permanent except change."
HERACLITUS OF GREECE, 513 B.C.,
Rogers: Student's History of Philosophy

This is a book about project management, a "field of study" and practice that have evolved over decades and now promise to take the rightful place in the lexicon of management and in contemporary organizations. In this chapter the overall concept of a project will be presented along with some examples of contemporary projects.

Just what is a *project*? Two early definitions are helpful. For example, it is "any undertaking that has definite, final objectives representing specified values to be used in the satisfaction of some need or desire."[1]

Newman et al. defined a project and described its value as

> ...simply a cluster of activities that is relatively separate and clear cut. Building a plant, designing a new package, soliciting gifts of $500,000 for a men's dormitory are examples. A project typically has a distinct mission and a clear termination point.
>
> The task of management is eased when work can be set up in projects. The assignment of duties is sharpened, control is simplified, and the men who do the work can sense their accomplishment....
>
> [—A project might be part of a broader program, yet the] chief virtue of a project lies in identifying a nice, neat work package within a bewildering array of objectives, alternatives, and activities.[2]

---

[1]Ralph Currier Davis, *The Fundamentals of Top Management* (New York: Harper and Brothers, Publishers, 1951), p. 268.

[2]William H. Newman, E. Kirby Warren, and McGill, *The Process of Management: Strategy, Action, Results,* 6th ed. (Englewood Cliffs, N.J.: Prentice-Hall, Inc., © 1987), p. 140. Reprinted by permission of Prentice-Hall, Inc., Englewood Cliffs, N.J.

A project consists of a combination of organizational resources pulled together to create something that did not previously exist and that will provide a performance capability in the design and execution of organizational strategies. Projects have a distinct life cycle, starting with an idea and progressing through design, engineering, and manufacturing or construction, through use by a project owner.

Four key considerations always are involved in a project:

1. What will it cost?
2. What time is required?
3. What technical performance capability will it provide?
4. How will the project results fit into the design and execution of organizational strategies?

These project results take the form of a new product (new automobile), new service (air transportation), new process (manufacturing technology), or some other enhanced capability in an organization's operational business.

The Evolution

Formal project management emerged in a quiet manner in the late 1950s. Its emergence was stimulated by the need to develop and implement a management philosophy for the management of large military and support systems. Much of the early theory of project management was developed by military organizations working with defense contractors who were involved in supplying large, complex systems to military services. No one can claim to have invented project management. Its beginnings are found in the construction industry and in the engineering discipline. The use of task forces and other organizational teams contributed to the emergence of project management as an emerging management philosophy and process for the integration of ad hoc activities in organizations. Projects became characterized by a distinct life cycle and a management system which provided for a formal and legitimate integration of organizational resources across the existing line and staff organizational design. As project management matured, specialized planning, organization, motivation, leadership, and control techniques emerged to support the management of ad hoc activities from a focal point in the organizational structure. Professional societies, such as the Project Management Institute, developed to "transfer" the technology of project management. These societies greatly aided the growing maturation of the theory and practice of project management. Today, project management is recognized as having a rightful place in the continued emergence of the management discipline. Project management is practiced, to some degree, in all business industries and in educational, military, government, and ecclesiastical organizations—and even in our personal lives. Truly project management is an idea whose time has come. A body of knowledge has developed to describe the art and science of project management. This body of knowledge is changing the way that contemporary organizations are managed.

Projects are managed by project management techniques and processes. The Project Management Institute defines *project management* as

> ...the art of directing and coordinating human and material resources throughout the life of a project by using modern management techniques to achieve predetermined objectives of scope, cost, time, quality and participant satisfaction.[3]

Project management's origins are rooted in antiquity. The Egyptian pyramids, the Great Wall of China, the Panama Canal, Roman buildings and roads, and ship building are but a few of the examples where project management was used. In modern times, its origins can be traced to the management of large-scale ad hoc endeavors, such as the Manhattan Project, and on a smaller scale, to the practical models provided by project engineering. Although no one can claim credit for its invention, its actual formal beginnings often are cited in the U.S. ballistic missile program or the space program.

In 1961, Gerald Fisch, writing in the *Harvard Business Review,* spoke of the obsolescence of the line-staff concept and heralded a growing trend toward "functioning-teamwork" approaches to organization. Also in 1961, IBM established systems managers with overall responsibility for various computer models across functional division lines. In the 1960s and 1970s, a wide variety of organizations experimented with the use of alternative project management organizational forms. At present, project management has reached a high degree of maturity and is used widely in industrial, educational, government, and military circles. As a result, a distinctive field of literature has emerged dealing with project management endeavors in contemporary organizations.

The evolution of project management parallels the development of the project-oriented literature. By 1962 a substantial amount of literature had developed, principally prepared by practitioners who were immersed in ongoing projects and anxious to tell their stories about the new management concept of project management, which seemed to contradict many of the established ways of managing activities.

---

[3]Brochure, Project Management Institute, P.O. Box 43, Drexel Hill, PA 19026.

Since the early 1960s over 150 books have been published on the various aspects of project management. Hundreds of articles have appeared in management and technical publications. Professional associations such as the Project Management Institute (PMI) hold seminars and symposia each year where members present papers about their special areas of interest in project management.

Professional Societies

In 1969 the Project Management Institute was established. PMI's objectives are to

- Foster professionalism in the management of projects
- Identify and promote the fundamentals of project management and advance the body of knowledge for managing projects successfully
- Provide a recognized forum for the free exchange of ideas, applications, and solutions to project management challenges
- Stimulate the application of project management to the benefit of industry and the public
- Provide an interface between users and suppliers of hardware and software project management systems
- Collaborate with universities and other educational institutions to encourage appropriate educational and career development at all levels in project management
- Encourage academic and industrial research in the field of project management
- Foster contacts internationally with other public and private organizations, which relate to project management, and cooperate in matters of common interest.

PMI offers its current international membership of over 10,000 a full set of professional association benefits, including an annual symposium; publications, a professional publication, the *Project Management Journal*; PMNET; education and certification benefits; workshops; local chapter affiliation; and a code of ethics.[4]

INTERNET, another project management professional organization, is an international network of professionals having vested interests in the project management discipline. Members are found worldwide. In its early days, INTERNET was a professional association whose members were primarily interested in project management

---

[4]Ibid.

networks and techniques; at present, the interests of the membership have moved to promoting project management as having an integral role in management itself.

INTERNET is supported by over 18 national associations which are currently members of INTERNET. As the countries in Eastern Europe continue their political and economic advances, there will be more national government and project management associations. INTERNET's focus now is to coordinate, stimulate, and facilitate cooperation among national project management associations. Indeed, to highlight this, the emerging strategy and theme of INTERNET for the 1990s are "Project management without boundaries"— and the use of project management as a general management tool— as an approach to the management of change.[5]

Impact on history

Projects change the course of history. The opening of the first fixed link between England and France in the form of the Channel Tunnel will start a change in affecting the course of human development in Europe well into the next century. The Channel Tunnel will shorten the lines of communication for large numbers of people. Thirty million people are expected to use the tunnel each year; about 100 million tons of freight will move between the continent and England. Like the Panama Canal, the Channel Tunnel will be a significant transportation link.

The Channel Tunnel project required awesome inputs of technology, finance, human resources, and management skill. Some 13,000 people from France and the United Kingdom as well as representatives from a large part of the rest of the world took part in the development of the project's objective: to deliver an efficient, reliable, and safe transportation system. The Channel Tunnel has been called the *chantier du siecle,* the project of the century.[6]

An important and exciting project that captured the attention and emotions of millions of people around the world occurred in the form of *Desert Storm,* a military project that changed the world and the use of military forces to bring about political change. Max Wideman, a Fellow of the Project Management Institute, described this extraordinary project as follows:

---

[5]"Project Management without Boundaries," *Project Management Monthly,* October 1991, pp. 16–22.

[6]Philippe Essiq and Jack Lemley, "Introduction," *Link Magazine,* Transmanche-Link, Special Edition, 1992, p. 2.

Project Desert Storm (July 2, 1991)

Projects come in all sizes and shapes, so they tell us. Whether differentiated by duration, complexity or area of application makes no difference. A project is a project. So a [military] project like Desert Storm lasting just 100 hours should be nothing out of the ordinary. Of course, that covered only the duration of the execution [battle] and completion [victory] phases. The prior phases and stages of concept, planning, design, and procurement of a complex set of commitments by a large diverse group of culturally different participants [the United Nations], plus preparation for execution [the prior air campaign] which preceded the project accomplishment phases, added considerably to the real overall project duration.

Nevertheless, the project was a managerial triumph of successful project management [resounding military victory] even though one of the potential deliverables [the opposing Commander in Chief] was not included. The project had some unique features. The location [miles of empty desert] was hardly one of the choicest. Project success would rely heavily on teamwork [joint military command], a decisive logistical achievement [assembling, supplying, and transporting over unheard-of-distances the most fearsome strike force in history] and innovation [military surprise]. The project manager [General Schwarzkopf] did well to give recognition to his logistics manager [General Pagonis] for a job well done [battlefield promotion].

The project was full of risk, and was opposed by a large number of stakeholders [both at home and overseas]. Once committed, success depended on utterly logical and overwhelmingly powerful and determined courses of action.

For example, Project Desert Storm was superbly equipped. Firstly, its technology was unsurpassed [world-beating] and state-of-the-art [high-technology], the product of intensive and highly successful R&D. Secondly, the human resources [troops] working with the equipment and materials [weaponry and firepower] were rigorously trained to the higher standards—that showed not only in their effectiveness but also in their morale. Thirdly, an able team of leaders, highly trained, experienced, qualified and selected, had only reached the top [through military promotion] after much education and training both technical and general.

Another equally important aspect was the organizational structure [army command] within which the team operated. The project manager had full delegated power to run the operation his way. His instructions from above [the President's office] were absolutely clear, and his immediate sponsors [such as General Powell] gave their total support. Authority and responsibility were passed down the organization structure in the same way. Once allotted their role by the project manager, work package managers [field commanders] made their own plans and executed them decisively.

It is true that the project team was not very keen when the project manager first proposed his outlandish and risky strategy [a mighty encircling sweep behind the Republican guard] to save man-hours [lives], time and, ultimately, cost [subsequent prolonged war effort]. His team [tactical commanders] gave the classical response "It can't be done" but that only made the project manager the more determined. After all, had he not found a very tempting market niche ignored by others? [Iraq's generals no doubt also thought that no army could drive their tanks over all that desert and that far without breaking down and going to ruin.] "They could never make it," they said.

That's what made the project so exciting. The project manager performed a crucial role of any project leader—he converted a tremendous risk into a tremendous opportunity by insisting that his team had to achieve the impossible. However, the team members only agreed to the course of action after the project manager had ordered his logistics manager [Paginos] to pledge in writing that everything would be in place by the scheduled deadline [February 21, 1991]. But that too is an elementary lesson of project management—give people the tools if you want them to do the job.

There's even more to it than that, of course. Project Desert Storm had an enormous supply of two vital elements: quality information and planning. They are necessary in that order because nothing can be effectively planned without solid information. But the planning and information experts were not an isolated function to satisfy some latest management theory whether in the design office [Washington] or in the field [war zone]. They were an integral part of the project process [war effort]. Line and staff relations were not an issue, the focus was on getting the job done [winning].

One advantage the project did enjoy, and that was it was not constrained by budget. Yet the very acts of determination, precision, and quality organization [to say nothing of superb timing and decision making by the Chief-Executive in the White House for launching the project] the project has proved to be highly cost-effective, compared to most similar ventures. It may even be a significant revenue generator when indirects are taken into account. All of this in a most unappetizing market [the Middle East], where competition at the outset appeared to be overwhelming [the fourth largest army in the world]. Indeed, the project represents a powerful argument in support of establishing highly selective strategic alliances in order to achieve project goals.

Surely this must be one of the best object lessons for any project manager today?[7]

Early Literature

One of the first comprehensive articles that caught the attention of the project management community was published by Paul O. Gaddis in the *Harvard Business Review* (May-June 1959). This article, titled "The Project Manager," describes the role of that individual in an advanced technology industry, the prerequisites for performing the

---

[7]With apologies to *Management Today*, British Institute of Management, May 1991, p. 34. Appreciation is extended to R. Max Wideman, P. Eng., MCSCE, FEIC, FICE, Fellow PMI for contributing the information on project *Desert Storm*.

project management job, and the type of training recommended to prepare an individual to management projects. Several basic notions put forth by Gaddis contributed to a conceptual framework for the management of projects that holds true today. These basic notions were:

- A project is an organizational unit dedicated to delivering a development project on time, within budget, and within predetermined technical performance specifications.
- The project team consists of specialists representing the disciplines needed to bring the project to a successful conclusion.
- Projects are organized by tasks requiring an integration across the traditional functional structure of the organization.
- The project manager manages a high proportion of professionals organized on a team basis.
- The superior/subordinate relationship is modified resulting in a unique set of authority, responsibility, and accountability relationships.
- The project is finite in duration.
- A clear delineation of authority and responsibility is essential.
- The project manager is a person of action, a person of thought, and a front person.
- Project planning is vital to project success.
- The project manager is the person between management and the technologist.
- The subject of communication deserves a great deal of attention in project management.
- Project teams will begin to break up when the members sense the project has started to end.
- The integrative function of the project manager should be emphasized.
- Status reporting is appropriate and valuable to management of the project.
- The role played by project management in the years ahead will be challenging, exciting, and crucial.

Project management, as an important and growing *philosophy of management,* came into its present conceptual framework as a culmination of experimentation with a variety of organizational liaison devices.

Organizational Liaison Devices

Project management evolved from a series of liaison devices that have been developed in contemporary organizations. These liaison devices, both formal and informal, have encouraged experimentation in integrating activities across organizational structures. Jay K. Galbraith is one of several researchers who have studied these liaison devices.[8] His research provides in part the basis for a description of the following types:

- Individual liaison
- Standing committees
- Product managers
- Managerial liaison
- Task forces
- Project engineer
- Liaison position

A brief discussion of these types follows.

Individual liaisons

The simplest and perhaps best form of liaison is that brought about by people who sense the need to work together and go about maintaining contact with others in the organization who have a vested interest in an activity under way. This liaison is usually self-motivated.

Standing committees

Standing committees are used extensively to integrate organizational activities. These committees are found at all levels in the organization. At the top level such committees are called *plural executives.* They bring about synergy in the making and execution of key operational and strategic decisions for the organization.

Product managers

Product managers usually are appointed to act as a focal point for the marketing and sales promotion of a product. Originating in the personal products area, the first product manager appeared before 1930. Persons occupying these positions usually were provided a small administrative staff and might have had profit/loss responsibility.

---

[8]Jay K. Galbraith, *Organization Design* (Reading, Mass.: Addison-Wesley, 1977).

They usually were not backed up by a specific team, but rather worked closely in a coordinating role with other key individuals.

Managerial liaisons

When a more formal linkage is needed, a manager or supervisor is appointed who is in charge of several people through setting direction for the organizational unit and providing supervisory jurisdiction over the people. This form is widely used in modern organizations. As the organization increases in size and the work becomes more complex, additional managers are added, resulting in the creation of a chain of command eventually leading to large management structures. Other liaison roles as described in this chapter deal with the organizational complexity and bureaucracy to encourage contacts between individuals and organizational units.

Task forces

Task forces often are used to bring a focus to organizational activities, usually those that are short-term. Members are appointed to the task force to work on an ad hoc problem or opportunity. During the time they are on the task force, members have a reporting relationship to their regular organizational unit and to the task force chairperson as well. When the purpose for which the task force was created is accomplished, the task force is dissolved.

Project engineers

Sometimes a liaison position evolves through practice. Such is the case of the project engineer, who is responsible for directing and integrating the technical aspects of the design/development process. These positions have evolved in contemporary organizations to the point where the project engineer manages a product through all its engineering steps, from initial design to manufacture or construction.

Liaison positions

When a significant amount of contact is required to coordinate the activities of two or more organizational entities, a liaison position is formally established to bring about synergy and communication between the units. Usually this position has no direct formal authority over the organizational units but is expected to communicate, coordinate, pull together, and informally integrate work among the organizational units. Examples of liaison roles are an engineering or construction liaison person and a production coordinator who mediates between the production control, product engineering, and manufacturing. A purchase engineer who sits between purchasing and engineering is another example.

Other liaison positions may join line and staff groups. In the military establishment, the position of military aide-de-camp, a military officer acting as a secretary and confidential assistant to the superior officer of general or flag rank, is a liaison role. Originating in the French Army, this position originally served as a camp assistant. The aide-de-camp carries out a coordinating and liaison role for his or her commanding officer; since the aide was close to the senior officer, there was a good deal of implied authority attached to the aide's role.

Teams

In modern organizations, teams are used to complement an existing organizational design. An overriding feature of the team design is a departure from the traditional form of management in favor of a team form in which there are multiple authority, responsibility, and accountability relationships, resulting in shared decisions, results, and rewards. These teams include some of the teams already mentioned—project teams, project engineering teams, and task forces—but also include production teams, quality circles, product design teams, and crisis management teams. The importance of the use of teams in contemporary organizations cannot be underestimated. Peters and Austin found that small-scale team organization and decentralized units are vital components of top performance.[9]

In contemporary organizations project teams are becoming popular as a strategy for dealing with ad hoc problems and opportunities. Some examples of project teams follow.

Some examples

Projects come in all sizes, shapes, and disciplines. Some large projects take years to complete; others can be done in a few hours.

1. At the riot-ravaged Taco Bell restaurant in Compton, California, a joint effort of the city of Compton and Taco Bell management launched a 48-hour rebuilding plan. Fluor Daniel, Inc., an international engineering, construction, maintenance, and technical services subsidiary of Fluor Corporation, was called in to plan for the new restaurant less than 3 weeks before the building was to begin. Taco Bell wanted everything done on site with nothing prefabricated and wanted to have the restaurant open and ready for business in 48 hours. Fluor Daniel used Primavera's Finest Hour software, which

---

[9]Tom Peters and Nancy Austin, "A Passion for Excellence," *Fortune*, May 13, 1985, pp. 20–32.

allows its users to schedule by 1-hour increments to handle the complexities of a short-term, intensive project. Fluor Daniel organized a dry run of everything 3 days before construction started to ensure that all team members knew the plan. Progress meetings were held every 3 hours to distribute the earned-value report, just one of the software's several productivity reports, comparing plans versus actuals in terms of both budget and work accomplished. At hour 46 the health inspector gave the okay, and at hour 47 the certificate of occupancy was signed. At hour 48 the first new tacos were served.[10]

2. At the Pennsylvania Electric Company's Generation Division (Penelec) project management is used as a "way of life." A centralized division planning group has been set up to link the different functional units required for a project and to integrate these units into a single project control system. Project teams are responsible for satisfying project objectives in the areas of life extension, maintenance, plant improvement, and the environment. On one project created to study turbine outage, the company estimated that the computerized project management system saved the company $300,000. Project management is recognized by senior division management as having credit to successfully allocate organizational resources to satisfy company objectives.[11]

3. At Johnson Controls Automotive Systems Group, product development activities are done by using a company-institutionalized project management system. Use of project management by the company has prompted an increase in the training of employees and the creation of a standard approach for project management. The use of a common approach in project management has facilitated the development of organizational strategies, policies, procedures, and other ways of working on projects. Employees are educated in the company's project management process; the improvement of the culture for project management—and the development of a common approach for the management of projects—has enabled the company to complete project development efforts in a timely and efficient manner.[12]

4. At MBI, Inc., a company that produces collectibles, such as porcelain birds and plates, program (project) managers are used, one for each series of collectibles. Two key objectives guide these program managers: Get new customers at the lowest possible cost, and retain

---

[10]"Riot-Ravaged Taco Bell Rebuilt in 48 Hours Using Project Planning Software," *Industrial Engineering*, September 1992, p. 18.

[11]Anthony J. Catanese, "At Penelec Project Management Is a Way of Life," *Project Management Journal*, December 1990, p. 7.

[12]W. D. Keith and D. B. Kandt, "Project Management as a Major Automotive Seating Supplier," *Project Management Journal*, September 1991, p. 28.

them for follow-on purchases. The company "piggybacks" on the Franklin Mint's product development costs and market research. Accordingly, industry observers believe that MBI, Inc.'s costs are much lower than its competitors.[13]

5. In Italy, a high-speed train project is under way that has an unusual approach—for Italy—of combining public and private sector effort in developing the train. The size of the project—some $23 billion—implies the potential for cost overruns and schedule slippages. The trains of this high-speed network are expected to be in operation in 5 to 7 years. What makes the project interesting is its size and the huge technical, economic, and financial leaps that are required to make the trains operational. The Italian government has agreed to fund 40 percent of the project and to pay interest on loans until the system becomes operational. Italian banks are seeking funds from international financial markets. Capital will be raised through a combination of equity and debt with a variety of instruments on international markets.[14]

6. At the Intel Corporation, project teams are used to develop new generation microprocessors. One such project, the 486 project, involves 1.2 million transistors which took more than $250 million and 450 work-years to develop. The technical performance objective for the 486 is far more formidable with 20 million instructions per second. Around the year 2000, Intel envisions a quantum leap to 100 million transistors divided into several independent chips for parallel processing. The overall chip will execute 2 billion instructions per second—supercomputer territory—and may be on desks by the turn of the century.

7. A central blood bank in a major U.S. city sees project management as a key management strategy in its world-class center for general support of the area hospitals' blood banks. Today over 400 staff members collect and test the units of over 152,000 donations, distributing more than 400,000 blood products per year for 22 member hospitals. In addition, the bank provides pretransfusion testing services to three hospitals, reference testing to all areas involving clotting and bleeding disorders, and outpatient transfusion services for patients not requiring hospitalization.

8. Nicolas G. Hayek and his colleagues at the Swiss Corporation for Microelectronics and Watchmaking have brought about one of the most spectacular industrial comebacks in the world—the revitaliza-

---

[13] Phyllis Berman with E. Lee Sullivan, "Getting Even," *Forbes*, August 31, 1992, pp. 54–55.

[14] *Wall Street Journal*, October 14, 1991.

tion of the Swiss watch industry. According to Hayek, "...we are big believers in project teams." He describes the use of project teams in the context of finding your best people, letting them take on a problem, disbanding them, and then moving on to the next problem. According to Hayek, the whole process of using projects works only if the whole management team focuses on developing products and improving operations—not fighting with each other.[15]

9. Project management is used in the U.S. Justice Department. In the early 1980s the Reagan administration came close to merging the Drug Enforcement Agency (DEA) and the Federal Bureau of Investigation (FBI)—a merger that was evaluated through the use of a project team. In 1984, over 56 separate projects were under way to integrate various functions of the two agencies. Only 9 of the 56 projects were completed; the others dropped into a state of bureaucratic limbo. An area that was successfully merged was training. But now the DEA has received $11 million to build its own training center in Quantico, Virginia—an effort that will use project management to design, construct, and start up this new facility.[16]

Two alternative uses of project management have recently emerged as key elements of contemporary strategy in dealing with global competitive challenges: simultaneous (or concurrent) engineering and strategic alliances.

Concurrent engineering or *simultaneous engineering* involves the organization of a product design team composed of individuals from design engineering, manufacturing engineering, marketing, procurement, quality, and after-sales service to work jointly on both product/ service and organizational process design and development. A body of literature is emerging on how the process of simultaneous engineering is carried out.[17] The Japanese have led the way in the use of simultaneous engineering. Computer and information technology, computer-aided design and manufacturing, and the use of telecommunications in transmitting engineering change information to global manufacturers have helped to make simultaneous engineering possible. Dramatic reductions in the cost and time to commercialize a product or service and at the same time improve quality have been realized. Some examples of the successful use of concurrent engineering include the following:

---

[15] Reported in William Taylor, "Message and Muscle," *Harvard Business Review*, March-April, 1993, pp. 99–110.

[16] Janet Novack, "How about a Little Restructuring?" *Forbes,* March 15, 1993, pp. 91–96.

[17] In this book the term *product* will include both *product* and *service* as appropriate.

1. Through the use of individual teams working in parallel from the start of a development project, Xerox has slashed its development time from 5 years to less than 2 years.[18]

2. A large electronics company uses product design teams in simultaneous engineering to ensure the right timing and integration required during product and process development. These teams provide a focus for bringing together the people on a product development activity to coordinate and integrate an effort to support the product and process synergy. A product design team might include design engineers, technical writers, customer support people, marketing representatives, regulator and legal experts, purchasing agents, human factors analysts, and representatives from manufacturing and quality. These team members, acting in concert, provide both a focus and the necessary cross-fertilization of information and strategies to reduce the time required to get the product developed, manufactured, and in the customer's hands.

3. In Romeo, Michigan, Ford Motor Company is completing a new engine manufacturing facility which promises to be a revolution in U.S. automobile engine manufacturing. This new flexible manufacturing plant is a billion-dollar gamble to design and build V-6 and V-8 engines on a basic building block—in this case a combustion chamber designed for maximum fuel economy. In this plant, the use of flexible manufacturing equipment will permit production of more than a dozen engine sizes and configurations on one line. The engines will share about 350 parts which will give the company freedom to match the plant's 500,000-engine capacity with customer demand. Manufacturing engineers traditionally have little to say over the engine design itself, but Ford has made them an integral part of the product design process in planning for this plant. These engineers have worked closely with product design engineers in designing the engines so that the engines are easy to assemble, and they have reduced the overall number of components by more than 25 percent. Although most of the engines will share 75 percent of their parts, important components such as cylinder heads and connecting rods may be different. The building of this plant is a response by the Ford Motor Company to the need to use modular design and flexible manufacturing to remain competitive in the industry.[19]

4. A large agricultural and industrial equipment manufacturer that does material, manufacturing, and product-applied research at the business unit level uses concurrent engineering to accelerate product and process product development cycles. Product development research

---

[18]"Another Day, Another Bright Idea," *The Economist*, April 16, 1988, pp. 82–84.

[19]David Woodruff, "A Dozen Motor Factories under One Roof," *Business Week*, November 20, 1989, pp. 90–94.

is not usually considered high-risk since it is primarily applied research. Few new product development efforts are carried out; rather the research is aimed at incremental product and process improvements. Product improvement includes the enhancement of the product's performance as well as cost reduction and improvement of product quality. The research follows product lines and is evolutionary.

5. The Ford Motor Company provides a more extensive example of concurrent engineering with its $3 billion development effort on the Taurus automobile. The development of this car included the design of the product and the processes by which it would be manufactured. It also included a change in the organizational design and management style used in managing this program. Ford's corporate culture was fundamentally altered for the future. The use of simultaneous engineering carried out within the focus of a product design team with representatives from the various organizational units such as design, marketing, manufacturing, procurement, service, spares, and documentation enabled the team to take on final responsibility for the development of the car. The concept of the product design team was a drastic break from tradition, requiring people to work together and communicate in a manner that was foreign to this automobile company.

Ford bet the family jewels on Taurus. Between 1980 and 1982, Ford lost a staggering $3.26 billion, and its factory sales had decreased from 2.63 million vehicles in 1978, to 1.27 million by 1982. Something had to be done—and the development of simultaneous engineering through product design teams is what happened. The basic idea behind Taurus was to get everyone involved in the project before any design work was done. In so doing, it was hoped that the "chimneys"—manufacturing, engineering, marketing, suppliers, and so on—culturally and historically attuned to an attitude of "Don't touch my field" would do away with their parochialism and work together cooperatively in a team effort to come up with a new automobile. Before the design was put together, a lot of time was spent talking about the car design and how it would be built, sold, and serviced. Many people were involved in these discussions, including workers and other production line people who were to make valuable suggestions on how things might be done differently and better.

Companies today, facing unprecedented global competition, are finding it advantageous to cooperate with partners around the world to share resources, risks, and rewards. These partnerships take the form of *strategic alliances* and are used for many purposes, such as sharing the design of products and processes, sharing manufacturing and marketing facilities, and sharing in the financial risk and rewards. Technology is changing so fast today that companies are finding it impossible to assemble the resources to keep ahead of the competition. Indeed, a form of "cooperative competition" is becoming the standard for success in the unforgiving global marketplace.

Once the opportunity for a strategic alliance has been established, a joint project team is often appointed to begin the analysis and work on the alliance. This project team establishes the rationale for the alliance, makes recommendations for the selection of the partner(s), and initiates the analysis required for the development of a suitable working agreement among the partners. Key matters considered by these teams include the mission, objectives, goals, and strategies for the alliance. The team develops the alliance performance standards and builds a recommended strategy for how the joint arrangement will be integrated and managed. A key responsibility of the joint project team is to prepare a strategy for and participate in the execution of the negotiations required to bring about a meeting of the minds on the partnership alliance.

Once the alliance is consummated, the project team that managed the alliance during its development can be disbanded. Then the alliance will start the process of becoming "institutionalized"—merged into the ongoing businesses of the partners. Something that did not previously exist has been created through the use of project management technologies. Sometimes the partners will continue the project teams' existence to oversee the alliance in its early period and until the alliance can be integrated into the ongoing operations of the partners.

Many projects are becoming global, in some cases coming forth out of strategic alliances that global partners have negotiated. Boeing Corporation, in the development of its twin-engine 777, has consummated an alliance with Mitsubishi, Kawasaki, and Fuji Heavy Industries. Selecting partners in the Pacific Rim by Boeing has overtones of marketing—an expectation of the large growth in that area for the airplane industry in the forthcoming decade. By building an alliance with Japanese companies, Boeing is well positioned to exploit a potentially lucrative market.[20]

The use of a strategic alliance by Apple Computer and Sony Corporation to manufacture Apple's highly successful Powerbook line of computers linked Apple's technology of easy-to-use products with Sony's miniaturization and manufacturing know-how necessary to make compact products.

IBM alone has joined in over 400 strategic alliances with various companies in the United States and abroad, reflecting the fact that alliances have become a part of strategic thinking.

The challenges in a strategic alliance lie in the comparative management of the business and in the personal relationships between

---

[20]James Flanigan, "Boeing Knows What It's Doing Overseas," *Los Angeles Times*, December 20, 1989, p. 21, D1.

managers from different organizational cultures—perhaps the biggest stumbling block to making an alliance work is the lack of trust among the partners.[21]

Global projects provide a focus for the transfer and integration of technologies through strategic alliances from around the world. One of the keys to global competitive survival is to be open to development, productive resources, and technology from anywhere in the world. Project management provides one universally appropriate and acceptable competitive methodology. *Global project management* may be defined as the application of project management techniques in order to successfully cooperate and compete in foreign countries. As the definition implies, global project management applies to not only expansion into foreign markets, but also for foreign companies to build strategic alliances which will give them access to U.S. technology, markets, and resources.

And more teams

Peter Drucker opines that organizations of the future will be "information-based, have reduced numbers of hierarchical levels, with much of the work being done in task-focused teams."[22] He further believes that these teams will work on new-product and process development from the concept of a product until it is established in the marketplace. Other authors have described these teams as a *product realization process,* which uses interdepartmental and interactive techniques to pull the organizational disciplines together to design, manufacture, market, and, in some cases, service the product. Figure 1.1 depicts the product realization process described by the National Academy of Engineering. Note that this process is similar to the process of concurrent engineering described earlier.

Tracy Kidder's book *The Soul of a New Machine* told how a team of hard-working inventors built a computer by teamwork. The key message in Kidder's story is that economic success comes through the motivation, talent, and commitment of a team of people seeking a common objective.

This team effort accounts for the act of taking a project from an idea through design and development and into successful production and marketing. Japan, for example, has developed and used effective teams of engineers, managers, production workers, marketeers, and

---

[21] Paraphrased from Ricardo Sookedeo, "Are Strategic Alliances Working?" *Fortune,* September 21, 1992, pp. 77–78.

[22] Peter F. Drucker, "The Coming of the New Organization," *Harvard Business Review,* January-February 1988, pp. 45–53.

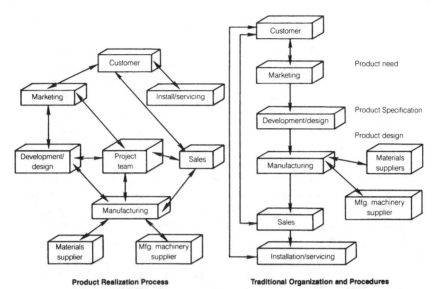

Product Realization Process   **Traditional Organization and Procedures**

The term "product realization process" denotes improved organizational arrangements and procedures to determine customer and market needs; translate these needs into designs suitable for manufacturing; produce a product that is introduced into the market; and make improvements that take advantage of better materials, processes, or equipment. The product realization process is interdepartmental and interactive. In contrast, traditional organization and procedures are compartmentalized and linear.

* *The Technological Dimensions of International Competitiveness* (Washington, D.C.: 1988), National Academy of Engineering, p. 28. Reprinted with permission of the National Academy Press, Washington, D.C.

Figure 1.1   Response to the global challenge.

salespeople to launch new products. Teams are a departure from the traditional idea of a lone entrepreneur producing an innovative, big, industry-making idea. Instead innovation today must "become both continuous and collective. And that requires embracing a new ideal: Collective entrepreneurship."[23] Reich further describes collective entrepreneurship as the use of individual skills in a group to provide a greater capacity to innovate because of the resulting synergy.

Some organizations are managed by formal teams organized for that purpose. For example, at Honeywell's Systems and Research Center, a large R&D center serving Honeywell's Aerospace and Defense Group, which employs 250 engineers and scientists plus support personnel, teams of managers make decisions by consensus in areas affecting the entire operation. Teams of managers oversee resource allocation, funds distribution, facility design, budgeting, hiring, and similar areas, subject to top management approval. Senior managers at this facility believe that this team effort yields better

[23] Robert B. Reich, "Entrepreneurship Reconsidered: The Team as Hero," *Harvard Business Review*, May-June 1987, pp. 77–83.

decisions, protects the unit from arbitrary or careless actions, and strengthens the team members' commitment to the center's goals.[24]

No one would doubt the impact that computer technology is having on today's organization. New computer programs which facilitate the exchange of information among managers, technicians, and other people working on team projects will give new impetus to team management. Programs currently under development will emerge as networks of computer workstations to guide teams of professionals through large shared databases. Such programs can help solve a major challenge of managing a team: human coordination.[25]

Dilenschneider and Hyde suggest the use of scenario teams for dealing with crisis situations. Such teams should be made up of senior managers or responsible professionals carefully chosen for their capabilities and status in the organization. Although such crises cannot be predetermined, there are some situations that can be expected to have a high potential to develop into a crisis. Labor contract negotiations, pollution control problems, plant accidents, product-related problems, and such matters, although not crises, do have the seeds for crises to develop and could be better "managed" by having a crisis team in existence. The team would be a "standing team" prepared to deal with the potential crisis by providing overall direction and counsel through management strategies. You cannot plan a crisis, but you can plan and manage the reaction of the organization to a potential crisis by using the basic principles of team management.[26]

In summary, project teams can be used for a wide variety of projects:

- Design, engineering, and construction of a civil engineering project such as a highway, bridge, building, dam, canal, etc.

- Design and production of a military project such as a submarine, fighter aircraft, tank, or military communications system

- Building of a nuclear power generating plant

- Research and development of a new machine tool

- Development of a new product or manufacturing process

- Reorganization of a corporation

---

[24] Tolly Kizilos and Robert P. Heinisch, "How a Management Team Selects Managers," *Harvard Business Review,* September-October 1986, pp. 6–12.

[25] Louis S. Richman, "Software Catches the Team Spirit," *Fortune,* June 8, 1987, pp. 125–126.

[26] R. L. Dilenschneider and Richard C. Hyde, "Crisis Communications: Planning for the Unplanned," *Business Horizons,* January-February 1985, pp. 35–39.

- Landing an astronaut on the moon and returning her or him safely to earth

Project work in the engineering, architecture, construction, defense, and manufacturing environments is easy to recognize. A new plant, bridge, building, aircraft, or product is something tangible; however, the project model applies to many fields, even to our personal lives.

These projects are the leading edge of change, in both our professional and our private lives. Change encourages—or may force—us to do something different, at some cost, and on some time or schedule basis. These changes often take the form of projects, such as:

- Writing a book or article
- Painting a picture
- Having a cocktail party and dinner
- Restoring an antique piece of furniture or an automobile
- Getting married or divorced
- Having children
- Adopting a child
- Designing and teaching a course
- Organizing and developing a sports team
- Building a house or modifying an existing house

Projects have an impact on all our lives, yet many of us fail to appreciate the influence that the results of project management can have. In the material that follows, additional examples of projects are given which affect our way of life.

Air travel

The prototype Boeing Dash 80 aircraft rolled out of the hangar of the Boeing facility in Renton, Washington, on May 14, 1954. At the time the plane represented a $16 million bid to capture the huge potential market for commercial and military jet planes. The plane was under development for 8 years by 300 of Boeing's top engineers. It represented a commitment to costly investment in jets for commercial services, even though the airlines had refused to place a single advance order. Boeing took the competitive gamble to develop the plane on its own and prove the case for future passenger jets everywhere. The project was a success and opened the way for commercial jet aviation in the United States.

Nuclear submarines

In the summer following World War II, the U.S. Navy's Bureau of Ships, sensing an opportunity to evaluate nuclear power for possible use in ship propulsion, assigned a captain and four young naval officers to the uranium reaction plant in Oak Ridge, Tennessee, to explore the technology for application of the Navy fleet. This project, under the leadership of a zealot, Captain Hyman George Rickover, led to the design and construction of the world's first nuclear submarine. The *Nautilus* put to sea from her home base in New London, Connecticut, on the 1381-mile shakedown cruise to San Juan, Puerto Rico. She performed perfectly, breaking most of the existing speed and endurance records for submarine performance. The vessel, longer than a football field, made the journey in 84 hours entirely under water, the longest time a submarine had ever remained submerged. Today nuclear submarines are an important part of the Navy's military force, and they are designed, engineered, and built by using a project management approach.

Law enforcement

In the U.S. Department of Justice, project management is used to deal with many changes in the department. For example, project management philosophies and techniques are used to

- Computerize alien files to eliminate 20 million paper folders
- Develop a computer system to manage information and statistics about the seizure and forfeiture of assets used during the commission of drug-related crimes
- Manage the Improved Automated Fingerprinting Reader System project to design, develop, and enhance new fingerprint scanners and readers for the FBI.

Motor sports

Motor sports may seem a curious opportunity to practice project management. However, the organization and staging of a car rally are a rational use of project management techniques.[27]

---

[27] Ian D. Muir, "Use of Project Management in the Organization of Major Sport Events," *International Journal of Project Management,* vol. 4, no. 2, May 1986, pp. 82–86.

Pipeline

The Trans-Alaska Pipeline System (TAPS) stretches 800 miles across Alaska. It was constructed between 1974 and 1976, at a cost of approximately $8 billion. TAPS started its life cycle in 1968, following the discovery of oil at Prudhoe Bay, Alaska. The owners of TAPS declared that it was the largest privately financed project of all time.

Canal

Some projects are a long time in the making. The Tennessee-Tombigbee (TENN-TOM) Waterway, the largest civil works project ever designed and built by the U.S. Army Corps of Engineers, cost $2 billion, is 234 miles long, and required the excavation of 40 percent more material than the Panama Canal.

More than 114 major contracts were awarded during the 14-year construction period. The TENN-TOM waterway was 175 years in the making. In 1810, the citizens of Knox County in eastern Tennessee asked Congress to provide a canal to Mobile Bay. The first congressional study was commissioned in 1874, but the project was delayed through 22 presidential administrations (beginning with the Grant administration), 55 terms of Congress, major studies and restudies, and two lawsuits.

On January 14, 1985, the first commercial tow moved northward on the waterway. The TENN-TOM was completed 18 months ahead of schedule and within the budget that was forecasted in 1973. The engineering design phase proceeded without any significant problems, and there were few construction surprises.

The project almost didn't make it. An environmental suit in 1971 delayed the start of construction, and another environmental suit in the late 1970s slowed the award of some construction contracts. President Carter blacklisted the TENN-TOM, but reversed his position under congressional pressure. The media chronically berated it. And it survived a critical vote in the U.S. Senate by only two votes in 1981, even though the entire waterway was under construction at that time. The TENN-TOM has been called the biggest boondoggle ever inflicted on the U.S. public.[28]

---

[28] Kenneth McIntyre, "The Tennessee-Tombigbee," *Large Scale Programs Institute Working Paper,* Colloquium on Research Priorities for Large Scale Programs, Austin, Tex. (March 1985).

Space travel

The Apollo space program achievement can be compared to Columbus' discovery of America, a monumental occurrence that set in motion enormous and far-reaching changes. Although project management played an important part in bringing about the success of the landing on the moon, the clear mandate given by President Kennedy provided the support to meet the moon landing challenge. President Kennedy's words in May of 1961 served as a rallying cry for the nation to provide the resources and sacrifices to make it happen. The President stated: "I believe this nation should commit itself to achieving the goal, before this decade is out, of landing a man on the moon and returning him safely to earth. No single space project in this period will be more impressive to mankind, or more important for the long-range exploration of space; and none will be so difficult or expensive to accomplish."

The success, and agony, of the U.S. space program is well known. Project management will continue to play a key role in future space explorations.

Competitive intelligence system

LaCasse describes the setting up of a *competitive intelligence system* (CIS) in a Canadian government agency. This project's goal was "...to have in place fully operational, within 2 years a complete CIS which would be at least as good as the best ones existing in the private sector." This system would contribute to the expansion of Canadian exports and would keep Canadian government officials informed of Canada's chief competitors for tourist dollars in promising markets. The project used to develop the CIS illustrates how project management can

- Be used where the work is not hardware-oriented and the project objectives are, at the outset, relatively nebulous
- Be used to track progress through the use of indicators that are management technology-related
- Emphasize the need to develop project success measurement methods for sharpening the planning and control processes.[29]

Performing arts

Wirth and deVries have introduced project management concepts and techniques into the production of performing arts. Their demonstra-

---

[29]François LaCasse, "Goal Definition and Performance Indicators in Soft Projects: Building a Competitive Intelligence System (CIS)," PMI Seminar/Symposium, *Proceedings,* Montreal, Canada, September 1986.

tion offers producers, directors, and other managers from the performing arts techniques previously unknown in that industry. A completed play or a movie, according to them, constitutes a unique, custom-made product which faces uncertainties, budgetary limitations, and rigorous scheduling, organizing, leadership, evaluation, and control during the life cycle of the play or exhibition.[30]

Storm barrier

A multibillion-dollar project by the Netherlands to construct an Eastern Scheldt Storm Surge Barrier will protect the southwestern part of the Netherlands by closing certain estuaries. It has changed hydraulic engineering from a traditional activity to a scientifically based discipline. Despite many uncertainties, including technical and environmental challenges, the time target on this project has been exceeded by less than 1 year in a total construction time of 10 years and has exceeded the budget by some 30 percent.[31]

Defense projects

Defense acquisition is the largest business in the world. Annual purchases by the U.S. Department of Defense (DOD) total almost $170 billion, spread over almost 15 million separate contracts per year. DOD uses program management to keep track of its military systems.

Once DOD defines its military requirements, it assembles a program team to define the weapon system and to "market" the system within the government to get funding support. Since many weapon systems are under development simultaneously, there is competition among the systems and the military departments that are developing a particular system. This competitive environment does not encourage realistic estimates of cost, schedule, and military requirements.

Once a list of potential bidders has been made and the program is launched, the DOD program manager sets out to manage the program—a program which usually has overly optimistic cost and schedule parameters and overstated requirements. Once funding is approved, the program team develops detailed specifications and sets out to complete the program. At this point, many "stakeholders" enter the program who have vested interests and who wish to influence the program. These stakeholders seek to ensure that the program complies

---

[30] Itzhak Wirth and Jack H. DeVries, "Project Management Techniques Implemented in the Performing Arts," *Project Management Institute Seminar/Symposium,* Denver, 1985.

[31] K. D'Angremond and D. Kooman, *INTERNET,* vol. 4, no. 3, August 1986, pp. 149–157.

with various standards for military specifications, reliability, maintainability, operability, small and minority business utilization, and competitive forces.

None of these vested interests, or *stakes,* is undesirable in itself, but the aggregate of these vested interests leaves little room for the program manager to manage the program with any reasonable freedom of decision making. Rather than a true program manager, he or she becomes one of the stakeholders who strive to influence the program. The manager has little room to balance the many demands of the other stakeholders, some of which are in conflict with each other and most of which are in conflict with the program's cost and schedule objectives. One serious outcome of this managerial ambience is an unreasonably long acquisition cycle—from 10 to 15 years—for major weapons systems. From this central problem other acquisition problems stem, such as unnecessarily high costs of development, obsolete technology because of the lead time to get technology from the laboratory to the field, and "gold plating" of the equipment because of the opportunity to submit engineering changes over the program's extended life cycle.

Recognizing the problems with the present system for managing programs, DOD undertook a study of several successful commercial programs to identify management features that they had in common and that could be incorporated into the defense acquisition process. In this study, six features typified the most successful programs:

1. *Clear command channels.* A commercial program manager has clear responsibility for her or his program and a short, unambiguous chain of command to the chief executive officer (CEO), group general manager, or some comparable decision maker. Corporate interest groups who wish to influence program actions must persuade the responsible program manager, who may accept or reject their proposals. Major unresolved issues are referred to the CEO, who has the clear authority to resolve any conflicts.

2. *Stability.* At the outset of a commercial program, a program manager enters into a fundamental agreement or "contract" with the CEO on the specifics of performance, schedule, and cost. So long as a program manager lives by this contract, the CEO provides strong management support throughout the life of the program. This gives a program manager maximum incentive to make realistic estimates and maximum support in achieving them. In turn, a CEO does not authorize full-scale development for a program until the board of directors is solidly behind it, prepared to fund the program fully and let the CEO run it within the agreed-to funding.

3. *Limited reporting requirements.* A commercial program manager reports only to his or her CEO. Typically, the program manager does

so on a "management by exception" basis, focusing on deviations from plan.

4. *Small, high-quality staffs.* Generally, commercial program management staffs are smaller than those in typical defense programs, but personnel are hand-selected by the program manager and are of very high quality. Program staff spend their time managing the program, not selling it or defending it.

5. *Communications with users.* A commercial program manager establishes a dialogue with the customer, or user, at the conception of the program when the initial tradeoffs are made and maintains that communication throughout the program. Generally, when developmental problems arise, performance tradeoffs are made—with the user's concurrence—in order to protect cost and schedule. As a result, a program manager is motivated to seek out and address problems, rather than hide them.

6. *Prototyping and testing.* In commercial programs, a system (or critical subsystem) involving unproven technology is realized in prototype hardware and is tested under simulated operational conditions before final design approval or authorization for production. In many cases, a program manager establishes a "red team," or devil's advocate, within the program office to seek out pitfalls—particularly those that might arise from operational problems or from an unexpected response by a competitor. Prototyping, early operational testing, and red teaming are used in concert for the timely identification and correction of problems unforeseen at a program's start.[32]

Education

Even students are feeling the impact of project management. In May 1985, the National Academy of Engineering held a symposium on U.S. industrial competitiveness. The symposium brought together some of the nation's leading industrial and academic technological leaders to discuss the industrial competitiveness challenge and how the National Academy of Engineering might formulate its programs to improve U.S. competitiveness. During the symposium's discussion of engineering education, it was recommended that the education of engineers for a future technological age require that the students develop the skills of leadership "for projects and programs...as well as technical leadership in their respective discipline."[33]

---

[32]*A Formula for Action,* A Report to the President of Defense. Acquisition, by the President's Blue Ribbon Commission on Defense Management, April 1986, pp. 12–13.

[33]*The Bridge,* Summer 1985, pp. 22–25.

Automated factories

In many U.S. factories, a change toward more automation is under way. Labor costs, foreign competition, demand for better quality, the need for increased productivity, and many other factors require the use of modern technologies to produce goods and services. These technologies include just-in-time inventory, group technology, product design teams, robotics, laser cutting, and flexible manufacturing systems. The introduction of these techniques requires mastery of complex new concepts and processes to bring about the change. Thus the conceptualization, design, introduction, and implementation of the change go far beyond the routine management of the production function. Meredith suggests the use of project management for factory automation projects.[34]

International projects

Project management is truly international in its application. Japan's Engineering Advancement Association (ENNA) has taken a lead in "exporting" U.S. know-how in project management to Japanese enterprises. As the government-sponsored agency responsible for improvement of Japanese engineering, ENNA has been heavily involved in the study of project management systems and strategies for developing and training project managers. ENNA has promoted studies and cooperative efforts to learn as much as possible about the state of the art of project management in other countries. The nonprofit organization was established in August 1974, under the umbrella of the Japanese Ministry of International Trade and Industry (MITI) and with the support of over a hundred enterprises in Japan. The Project Management Committee of ENNA conducted an analysis of the project directing function at Japanese companies as one of the main themes of its subcommittee dedicated to formulating the framework of Japanese project management.[35]

Water projects

The U.S. Army Corps of Engineers (COE) has used project management techniques for a long time. Recently COE created a new man-

---

[34] Jack R. Meredith, "Project Planning for Factory Automation," *Project Management Journal,* December 1986, pp. 56–62.

[35] An example of the work of this committee is contained in Sunao Shirouzu and Hiroshi Tanaka, "Project Management in Japan: An Analysis of Project Direction in the Japanese Context," Project Management Institute Proceedings, Denver, 1985. See also John R. Adams and William R. VanBuskirk, "An International Cooperative Study of Japanese and American Project Management Methodologies," *Project Management Institute Proceedings,* Denver, 1985.

agement system that promises to reduce the time it takes to bring water projects from feasibility study to construction. Revised project review and approval procedures, clearer designation of organizational roles, closer monitoring of project costs, new strategic planning, and concurrent handling of project authorizations are a few of the major innovations in the COE's new project management system.[36]

The Change Factor

Projects are found in all phases of modern life. They account for the way we live and the changes in society. Most of us accept the notion of projects in our personal lives as the opportunities and problems encountered in our daily living. For the organizations where we work, projects are important elements of change. Projects are conceptualized, designed, engineered, and produced (or constructed); something is created that did not previously exist. An organizational strategy has been executed to facilitate the support of ongoing organizational life. Projects therefore support the ongoing activities of a going concern. For example,

- An R&D project bridges the gap from an existing technology to a future technology.
- A pipeline moves oil, gas, or water.
- A canal provides a waterway over land.
- A new highway improves transportation systems in a geographical area.
- A new factory adds to the manufacturing capability of an industrial enterprise.
- A new building contributes to the infrastructure of a city.
- A new house improves the living standard of a family.

Projects are the leading edge of change in organizations; this change has to be managed, and that is where project management comes into play.

Yet today with projects playing a role in our changing world, there are still managers who find it difficult to accept project management as an integral part of a manager's philosophy. To some theorists and practitioners, project management is still a "special case" of management.

---

[36]"Corps Is Overhauling Management Systems," *Engineering Review*, September 8, 1988, pp. 9–10.

A Special Case of Management

The majority of the body of knowledge on *general management* today treats project management as if it were a nearly separate entity in the management of contemporary organizations. Little is found in this literature that puts project management in its larger, more important role as a philosophy and process for the management of change in organizations. Yet, in practice, projects have truly become building blocks in the strategic management of organizations. When project management is viewed in its strategic context as a means of dealing with change in the strategic management of organizations, it no longer is viewed as a special case of management, but rather as a means to survive and grow in today's changing and unforgiving competitive markets.

Today the political, social, economic, technological, legal, and competitive changes under way in the world are awesome, and they pose extraordinary challenges to contemporary managers. We are reminded of the inevitability of change. "There is nothing permanent except change."[37] Product and process technology is changing so fast that success in the marketplace is a fleeting opportunity. Product (and service) life cycles are getting shorter. New technologies such as the computer, information systems, flexible manufacturing systems, CAD, and CAM, to name a few, once developed and used, begin aging, soon to be threatened by an incremental advancement of technology offered by a competitor arising somewhere in the global marketplace. Product and process obsolescence is inevitable—it is only a matter of time before improved ways of developing products and processes begin to impact the marketplace. No organization can escape the relentless pace of change. Out of the threats and promises of such change takes project management from its "special case" of management to the objective of a rightful place as a *philosophy* in the strategic management of organizations.

A Philosophy

A philosophy is a synthesis of all the knowledge, skills, and attitudes that one has about a field of learning and practice, the critique and analysis of fundamental beliefs about a discipline. A philosophy is also the system of motivating concepts and principles surrounding a field of study and practice. A field of thought or, to put it into more pragmatic terms, a "way of thinking" about a field of learning and practices—is what a philosophy is all about. Anyone who has been

---

[37] Heraclitus of Greece, 513 B.C.

exposed to the field of management, as either a manager or the objective of management, has a philosophy or way of thinking about management. The study of the management discipline—and of project management in particular—enables one to broaden and sharpen the way one thinks about project management concepts and processes. Remember: To a large degree we participate on a project team, either as the team's leader or as a member of team, based on the way we think about the project management discipline. Although we may not recognize it, the philosophy that we hold about project management influences almost all the decisions that we make and implement in the project management way of doing things.

An Overview

A project manager is a manager in the truest sense of the word. In managing she or he operates as the "general manager" of the project as far as the organization is concerned. In executing the managerial task of providing leadership for the project, the project manager is concerned with several key elements of the project activities:

- Organizing the people and other resources to support the project objectives, goals, and strategies
- Planning for what resources are required to support the project objectives, goals, and strategy
- Identifying and using relevant information to manage the project
- Providing leadership for the project team members
- Conducting periodic evaluation of project results and redirecting or reprogramming resources as required to keep the project moving toward its goals and objectives
- Using modern tools and techniques to facilitate the project management process
- Maintaining an awareness of the influence of the organizational cultural ambience in which the project exists
- Keeping the customer informed and happy
- Keeping the project owner senior management informed of the status of the project so that they know how well the project fits into their organizational strategies

The basic idea behind building the organization around a project is to bring a focus for the planning and execution of an ad hoc specific work element without the restriction of the organizational structure and the policies and procedures of the existing organization.

Project management enables the senior managers to plan, organize, and control organizational strategic initiatives through ad hoc activity. As a management concept, project management involves the design and execution of the management functions of planning, organization, motivation, direction, and control through an organizational focal point. It includes the management of a project team and coordination with a variety of outside persons, agencies, institutions, and enterprises that have, or feel that they have, a vested interest in the project. The project owner and the organization that is putting up the money for the project and intends to use the project results in its operations retain the residual responsibility and accountability for project results.

Project management starts with identifying and selecting a project idea and developing that idea through feasibility, production (or construction), installation, and use. Project management permits a flexible use of organizational resources not possible in the traditional organizational approach.

Project management constitutes one of the main forms for converting an organization from one state to another. It might be called *transitional management*. It is the art and science of managing the conversion period from one organizational strategy to another, usually with a change in the products and services that the organization provides.

Summary

Project management is the creation and delivery of something that did not previously exist, on an ad hoc basis, so that the project meets cost and schedule objectives. Projects are building blocks in the strategic management of organizations which when conceptualized, designed, produced, and put into a customer's enterprise, facilitates that organization's growth and survival.

In reviewing the examples given in this chapter of the many different contexts in which project management is used, the reader should develop an appreciation of the role that project management plays in contemporary organizations. With such appreciation, the readers should be encouraged to read further in the book to increase their understanding of the theory and practice of project management.

Projects will continue to gain acceptance as building blocks in the design and execution of organizational strategies. Managers are finding that the development and implementation of projects can better position the organization for global competition, such as in the use of concurrent engineering. Projects also are an efficient way to bring a focus to the use of resources in the enterprise.

Project management can be used to circumvent a slow decision-making process through the functional and organizational hierarchies. Since the purpose of a project is to bring a synergy to the use of resources on a project, decisions can be made at that organizational focus without having to work through several organizational hierarchical units. Members of the project team can work with the project manager in making and designing those strategies which best promise to support the project's objectives.

More broadly, a project is something that brings about change in an organization and has

- Time, cost, and technical performance parameters (or objectives)
- Complexity, scope, or innovation beyond the operational work of the enterprise
- A key role in preparing the organization for its future
- Significant contributions by two or more functional units of the organization
- A direct contribution to the success or failure of the enterprise

Projects come in many different sizes, ranging from a small project such as the realignment of a manufacturing machine shop to a megaproject such as a nuclear power generation plant. Projects play a role in both our professional and our personal lives.

During organizational change, the use of project teams plays a key, if not dominant, role in preparing the organization for its future. Projects are used to capture opportunity in new product, service, and process development, leading to enhanced market competition and future growth and survival.

As a final note, the key to success in the 1990s will be to have new ideas and to develop those ideas through teams which will operate through a willingness to ignore traditional borders such as social, political, economic, and informational ones. Disparate empowered groups will participate to bring about change through the sharing of common ideas and actions. These groups will require someone to provide leadership, have a respect for market forces, sacrifice, and be willing to participate.[38]

Discussion Questions

1. Based on the descriptions and discussions in the chapter, how would you define project management?

2. Describe and discuss situations in your work or personal experience that fit the definition of a project. How were/are these managed?

---

[38]John Huey, "Finding New Hereos for a New Era," *Fortune,* January 25, 1992, pp. 62–69.

3. In what ways do the concepts of project management appear to violate traditional, established ways of managing?

4. How do the three parameters of a project—cost, time, and technical performance—interact?

5. What are the various roles that need to be accounted for on a project team?

6. How do the leader's and the project manager's styles affect how these roles are played?

7. List and discuss the various liaison devices described in the chapter.

8. What are some of the advantages of the use of teams in organizations?

9. Why is it important for project managers to adapt "synergistic thinking"?

10. Discuss the steps involved in the management of change. What additional steps can be taken?

11. How can a young professional's experience in working on small projects benefit his or her professional development?

12. Describe what is meant by *team management*.

User Checklist

1. Does your organization undertake activities on an ad hoc basis for a strategic change?

2. Does the management of your organization recognize projects and understand the concepts of project management?

3. How well does your organization use project management in dealing with change?

4. Are clear lines of authority, responsibility, and accountability defined for project team members?

5. How well are the liaison devices described in the chapter used to integrate activities across organizational lines?

6. Are cost, time, and technical performance objectives defined for each project? Are they properly managed?

7. Does your organization use teams to its advantage? In what ways?

8. Is your organization prepared for change? Is change being managed effectively?

9. Are young professionals being properly trained in the concepts of project management so that they are prepared to take on the responsibilities of a project or team manager?

10. Does top management provide support and opportunities for functional and project managers to plan, organize, motivate, direct, and control those project activities for which they are responsible?

11. Does the organization use contemporaneous, state-of-the-art project management techniques in the management of projects?

12. How is project management integrated into the strategic management philosophies of the organization?

2

The Project Management Process

*"The distance is nothing; it is only the first
step which counts."*
MADAME DUDEFFARD, *1697–1784*

Project management is a series of activities embodied in a process of getting things done on a project by working with members of the project team and with other people in order to reach the project schedule, cost, and technical performance objectives. This description helps to identify project management, but it does not tell too much about how a project manager reaches project goals and objectives. This chapter will describe the project management process along with the idea of the *life cycle*.

First, we review the management process.

The Management Process

A *process* may be defined as a system of operations in the production of something—a series of actions, changes, or functions that bring about an end result. Another way of describing a process is as a series of steps or procedures.

The management discipline is usually described as a *process* consisting of distinct yet overlapping major activities or functions. A simple yet important way of describing the management process through its major functions is indicated below:

- *Planning: What are we aiming for and why?* In the execution of this function, the organization's *mission, objectives, goals, and strategies* are determined.

- *Organizing: What's involved and why?* In carrying out the organizing function, a determination is made of the need for human and nonhuman resources—and how those resources will be aligned and used to accomplish the organization's mission. Authority, responsibility, and accountability are the "glue" that holds an organization together.

- *Motivation: What brings out the best performance of people in supporting the organization's purposes?*

- *Directing: Who decides what and when?* In the discharge of this management function, the manager provides the face-to-face leadership of the organizational members.

- *Controlling: Who judges results and by what standards?* In this function the manager monitors, evaluates, and controls the effectiveness and efficiency in the utilization of organizational resources.

There is much literature describing these management functions. Thousands of articles and hundreds of books are published every year about the management discipline. An early writer, Henri Fayol, captured the essence of the functions of the management discipline.

Henri Fayol's contribution

In the classic management book *General and Industrial Management,* originally published in French in 1916, Henri Fayol suggested that all activities to which industrial undertakings give rise can be divided into six groups:

1. Technical activities (production, manufacture, adaptation)

2. Commercial activities (buying and selling exchange)

3. Financial activities (search for and optimum use of capital)

4. Security activities (protection of property and persons)

5. Accounting activities (stock taking, balance sheet, costs, statistics)

6. Managerial activities (planning, organization, command, coordination, control)

Fayol's description of the major activities or functions of the manager as planning, organization, command, coordination, and control was one of the first times that the *management process* was put into the context of *major activities or functions.*[1]

The Project Management Process

In Table 2.1, the project management process is portrayed in terms of its major functions. The activities noted under each of these functions

---

[1] Henri Fayol, *General and Industrial Management,* Sir Isaac Pitman & Sons, Ltd., London, 1949, pp. 3–6.

TABLE 2.1   Representative Functions/Processes of Project Management

Planning (What are we aiming for and why?)

- Develop project objectives, goals, and strategies.
- Develop project work breakdown structure.
- Develop precedence diagrams to establish logical relationship of project activities and milestones.
- Develop time-based schedule for the project based on the time precedence diagram.
- Plan for the resource support of the project.

Organizing (What's involved and why?)

- Establish organizational structure for the team.
- Identify and assign project roles to members of the project team.
- Define project management policies, procedures, and techniques.
- Prepare project management charter and other delegation instruments.
- Establish standards for the authority, responsibility, and accountability of the project team.

Motivation (What motivates people to do their best work?)

- Determine project team member needs.
- Assess factors that motivate people to do their best work.
- Provide appropriate counseling and mentoring as required.
- Establish rewards program for project team members.
- Conduct initial study of impact of motivation on productivity.

Directing (Who decides what and when?)

- Establish "limits" of authority for decision making for the allocation of project resources.
- Develop leadership style.
- Enhance interpersonal skills.
- Prepare plan for increasing participative management techniques in managing the project team.
- Develop consensus decision-making techniques for the project team.

Control (Who judges results and by what standards?)

- Establish cost, schedule, and technical performance standards for the project.
- Prepare plans for the means to evaluate project progress.
- Establish a project management information system for the project.
- Prepare project review strategy.
- Evaluate project progress.

are only representative. Effective project management requires many more activities under each of these functions. More descriptions of these functions are found elsewhere in this book.

Project management is a continuing process. New demands always are put on the project team and have to be coordinated by the project manager through a process of planning, organizing, motivating, directing, and controlling. As new needs come up before the project, someone has to satisfy these needs, solve the problems, and exploit the opportunities. The project originates as an idea in someone's mind, takes a conceptual form, and eventually has enough substance that key decision makers in the organization select the project as a means of executing elements of strategy in the organization. In practice, the project manager must learn to deal with a wide range of problems and opportunities, each in a different stage of evolution and each having different relationships with the evolving project. This continuing flow of problems and opportunities underscores the need to comprehend a *project management process* which, if effectively and efficiently planned for and executed, results in the creation of project results which complement the organizational strategy.

Managing a large project is so complex that it is difficult to comprehend all the actions that have to be taken to successfully plan and execute the project. We need to divide the project into parts in order to grasp the full significance of each part and just where that part fits in the scheme of the project. We have to look at the project parts, its "work packages," its logical flow of activities, the phases that the project goes through in its evolution, growth, and decline.[2]

Using a model of the project's life cycle is useful in identifying and understanding the total breadth and longevity of the project and as a means to identify the management functions involved in the project life cycle.

The Project Life Cycle

A project's life cycle contains a series of major steps in the *process* of conceptualizing, designing, developing, and putting in operation the project's technical performance "deliverables." These major steps, usually called *work packages,* are the key work elements around which the project is managed. In this chapter the project management process will be described in the context of a *project life cycle*—and how the conceptualization and development of that life cycle provide a useful model for project management.

Many ways have been developed to describe the life cycle of projects. Organizations tend to develop their own peculiar ways of

---

[2]The "work package" concept is discussed in Chapter 11.

describing these life cycles. A generic way of describing a life cycle would include the following phases:

- *Insight*—discovery and acquisition of the knowledge
- *Conceptualization*—formulation of an intellectual model
- *Design*—demonstration of the configuration
- *Prototype*—building and testing of the first model
- *Production*—construction or production for markets
- *Operational*—customer use of the product or service
- *Phase-out*—product or service ceases to exist

Assad and Pelser[3] describe a project life cycle as having 12 phases:

- Concept
- Feasibility study
- Concept revision
- Project definition
- Tenders/quotations
- Final design
- Contracts
- Physical execution
- Product tests
- Final and integrating tests
- Project review
- Production/maintenance

Projects, like organizations, are always in motion as each proceeds along its life cycle. Projects go through a life cycle to completion, hopefully on time, within budget, and satisfying the technical performance objective. When completed, the project joins an inventory of capability provided by the organization that owns the project.

All projects—be they weapons systems, transportation systems, or new products—begin as a gleam in the eye of someone and undergo many different phases of development before being deployed, made operational, or marketed. For instance, the Department of Defense (DOD) uses a life-cycle concept in the management of the development of weapons systems and other defense systems. An early U.S.

---

[3] Michael G. Assad, and G. P. J. Pelser, "Project Management: A Goal-Directed Approach," *Project Management Quarterly*, June 1983, p. 49.

Air Force version of this life cycle identifies a number of phases, each with specific content and management approaches. Between the various phases are *decision points,* at which an explicit decision is made concerning whether the next phase should be undertaken, its timing, etc. Generically, these phases are as follows:

1. *The conceptual phase.*   During this phase, the technical, military, and economic bases are established, and the management approach is formulated.

2. *The validation phase.*   During this phase, major program characteristics are validated and refined, and program risks and costs are assessed, resolved, or minimized. An affirmative decision concerning further work is sought when the success and cost realism become sufficient to warrant progression to the next phase.

3. *The full-scale development phase.*   In the third phase, design, fabrication, and testing are completed. Costs are assessed to ensure that the program is ready for the production phase.

4. *The production phase.*   In this period, the system is produced and delivered as an effective, economical, and supportable weapons system. When this phase begins, the weapons system has reached its operational ready state and is turned over to the using command. During this period, responsibility for program management is transferred as an Air Force logistics supporting capability within the Air Force.

5. *The deployment phase.*   In this phase, the weapons system is actually deployed as an integral organizational combat unit somewhere within the Air Force.

The Pratt & Whitney Aircraft Group of the United Technologies Corporation uses a life-cycle approach in the design and development of its basic-product advanced-technology gas-turbine aircraft engines. Figure 2.1 illustrates six fundamental phases of this life cycle. If the scope of a project is less than the full development of an engine, only certain steps are applicable.

The project development life-cycle concept recognizes a natural order of thought and action pervasive in the development of many kinds of projects, whether commercial products, space exploration projects, or management projects.

New products, services, production processes, or roles for the organization have their genesis in ideas evolving within the organization. Typically, such ideas go through a distinct life cycle, i.e., a natural and pervasive order of thought and action. In each phase of this cycle, different levels and varieties of specific thought and action are required within the organization to assess the potential efficacy of the project.

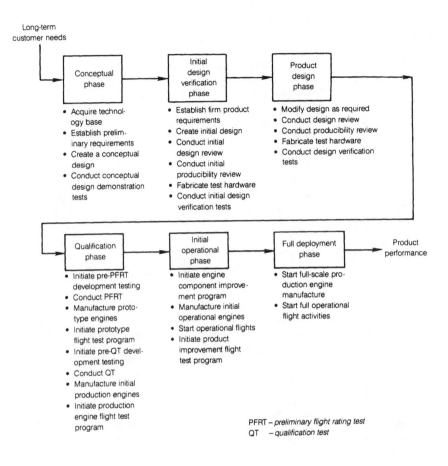

Source: Management Guide, Pratt & Whitney Aircraft Group Government Products Division, United Technologies, 39. Used with permission.

Figure 2.1   Flow of the design/development process.

Product Development

The National Society of Professional Engineers (NSPE) has developed a valuable and comprehensive document describing the new-product stages of development. These stages are defined, the objectives of the stage are presented, the engineering activities are described, and the information needed to communicate the actions and activities in each stage is provided.[4]

---

[4] See for example *Engineering Stages of New Product Development,* Publication 1018, pp. 16–23, National Society of Professional Engineers, 1420 King Street, Alexandria, VA 22314, undated.

Table 2.2   Managerial Actions by Project Phase

Phase 1: Conceptual	Phase 2: Planning	Phase 3: Execution	Phase 4: Termination
Determine that a project is needed.	Define the project organization approach.	Perform the work of the project, (i.e., design, construction, production, site activation, testing, delivery, etc.).	Assist in transfer of project product.
Establish goals.	Define project targets.		Transfer human and nonhuman resources to other organizations.
Estimate the resources that the organization is willing to commit.	Prepare schedule for execution phase.		
"Sell" the organization on the need for a project organization.	Define and allocate tasks and resources.		Transfer or complete commitments.
	Build the project team.		Terminate project.
Make key personnel appointments.			Reward personnel.

Managing the Life Cycle

One of the first undertakings in planning for a project is to develop a rough first estimate of the major tasks or work packages to be done in each phase.

There are many ways of looking at a project life cycle. Adams and Barndt suggest two ways of looking at the managerial actions by project phase and the tasks accomplished by project phase. See Table 2.2 and Fig. 2.2.

Once established, the life-cycle model should be updated as more is learned about the project. As the project progresses through its life cycle, the project exhibits ever-changing levels of cost, time, and performance. The project manager must make correspondingly dynamic responses by changing the mix of resources assigned to the project as a whole and to its various work packages. Thus, budgets will fluctuate substantially in total and in terms of the allocation to the various project work packages. The need for resources and various kinds of expertise will similarly fluctuate, as will virtually everything else. This is portrayed in Fig. 2.3, which shows changing levels of budget and of engineering and marketing personnel for various stages of the life cycle.

This constantly changing picture of the life cycle is an underlying structural rationale for project management. The traditional hierar-

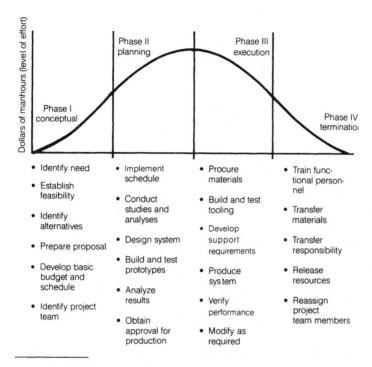

Source: John R. Adams and Stephen E. Barndt, "Behavioral Implications of the Project Life Cycle, David I. Cleland and William R. King (eds.), *Project Management Handbook*, (New York: © 1983 Van Nostrand Reinhold Co.: 227. All rights reserved.

Figure 2.2 Tasks accomplished by project phase.

chical organization is not fully designed to cope with managing such an always-changing mix of resources. Rather, it is designed to control and monitor a much more static entity that, day to day, involves stable levels of expenditures, numbers of persons, etc.

Project Life Cycles and Uncertainty

As the project life cycle progresses, the cost, time, and performance parameters must be "managed." This involves continuous replanning of the as yet undone phases in the light of emerging data on what has actually been accomplished.

The project team must rethink much during the project life cycle to modify and fine-tune the work packages for each phase. Archibald notes, "The area of uncertainty is reduced with each succeeding phase until the actual point of completion is reached."[5]

---

[5] Russell D. Archibald, *Managing High-Technology Programs and Projects* (New York: Wiley, 1976), p. 23.

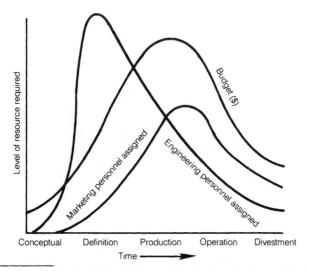

Figure 2.3   Changing resource requirements over the life cycle.

Many organizations can be characterized at any time by a "stream of projects" that place demands on its resources. The combined effect of all the projects facing an organization at any given time determines the overall *product* and *process* status of the organization at that time and gives insight into the organization's future.

The projects facing a given organization at a given time typically are diverse—some products are in various stages of their life cycles and embody different technologies, other products are in various stages of development. Management subsystems are undergoing development. Organizational units are in transition. And major decision problems, such as merger and plant location decisions, are usually studied as projects.

Moreover, at any given time, each of these projects usually will be in a different phase of its life cycle. For instance, one product may be in the conceptual phase undergoing feasibility study, another may be in the definition phase. Some might be in production. Others possibly are being phased out in favor of upcoming models.

The challenges associated with the overall management of an organization that is involved in a stream of projects are influenced by life cycles, just as are the challenges associated with managing individual projects. In project-driven organizations whose main business is management of the stream of projects passing through the organization, the mix of projects in their various phases is most challenging, particularly in allocating work force, funding resources, scheduling work loads, etc., to maintain a stable organizational effort.

Summary

This chapter dealt with the dynamic nature of projects and the project management process. Projects provide the link between what the organization is doing today and what it is likely to be doing in the future. Projects are like many other things in the world—they are created, they live, and they die—in other words go through a natural life cycle.

Several summary models and an extensive model of a project life cycle were offered in the text. The project life cycle, with its inherent work packages, provides a useful point of departure for the management of the project. Project management is an approach for responding to the dynamic nature of projects during their life cycle. Since projects are part of an organizational strategy to deal with the complex problems and opportunities facing an organization, their successful management is important to the future well-being of the enterprise. The project life cycle is a focus around which management processes and techniques can be used to bring the project results in on time and within the budget.

Discussion Questions

1. List and define the management functions discussed in the chapter.
2. Within the management function of planning, project managers and team members should settle on project objectives, goals, and strategies. How can this task help to define the "strategic fit" of the project to the organization?
3. Discuss the difference between organizational policies and procedures.
4. Project review meetings often are used as a tool for controlling projects. What kinds of questions should be addressed in these meetings?
5. List and briefly define the phases of the generic project life cycle.
6. What management functions are most important in the conceptual phase of the project life cycle?
7. During the definition phase of a project, it is important for management to design and develop the project management system to support the project. Discuss the importance of each system.
8. Discuss what is meant by the project "losing its identity" and being "assimilated into the ongoing 'business' of the user."

9. Discuss the importance of the divestment phase as a tool for avoiding technological obsolescence.

10. What is meant by the *phased/approach* for project development?

11. How can a project manager, by understanding the project life cycle, use the concepts of this chapter to help direct and control projects?

12. Discuss the challenge of managing a project-driven organization with ongoing projects at various stages in their life cycles.

User Checklist

1. Do the managers of your organization understand and use the management functions—planning, organizing, motivating, directing, and controlling?

2. Do the managers of your organization understand the project management process?

3. In the early stages of projects within your organization, are objectives, goals, and strategies clearly defined?

4. Are project management roles assigned? Are standards for responsibility and accountability established?

5. Does management consider the needs of individual team members in order to motivate people to do their best work?

6. How well does your organization use participative management techniques and consensus decision making in your project management work?

7. What techniques do project managers, within your organization, use to control projects?

8. Do your organization's managers truly understand the implications of the project life cycle?

9. Does your organization use a systematic approach for managing projects?

10. During the conceptual phase of a project, does the organization attempt to determine the strategic fit of the project?

11. Does the organization recognize the project management system and the accompanying subsystems?

12. Are projects purposely put through the divestment phase in order to avoid technical obsolescence?

The Strategic Context of Projects

3

When to Use Project Management[1]

*"I keep six honest serving-men (they taught
me all I knew); their names are What and
Why and When and How and Where and
Who."*
　　　　　　　RUDYARD KIPLING, 1865–1936

The primary reason for using project management is to provide an organizational design and a strategy to bring an organizational focus to those ad hoc activities needed to effect change in the organization. Modification of organizational products and processes is required to accommodate the inevitable changes that affect all enterprises today. Reaction to these changes usually requires an organized and focused use of resources to design new strategies to commit current organizational resources to prepare the enterprise for its future. An organization today that wants to remain competitive in providing its customers with continually improving products and services has no choice but to use project management concepts and processes.

In the development of new products and processes in organizations today—and in particular industrial organizations—there is the need to provide an organizational focal point through which resources can be directed to keep abreast—and even move beyond—changing technologies. A "champion," such as a project manager, is needed to provide the leadership and management skills to bring about the needed changes. Strategic alliances—a form of long-term partnerships being seen more

---

[1]Some material in this chapter has been paraphrased from D. I. Cleland and W. R. King, *Systems Analysis and Project Management,* 3d ed. (New York: McGraw-Hill, 1983).

and more in global competitive markets—are being conceptualized, developed, and managed through the use of project management.

Specific Uses

Project management concepts and processes can be used to support an organization's crisis management strategies. Crises can arise from such mishaps as plane crashes, toxic chemical spills, hostage taking, product liability lawsuits, poisoned products, natural disasters such as storms and earthquakes, and so forth. Sawle recommends the use of a crisis control model consisting of the logical steps in preparing for and resolving a major crisis. He believes that project management and crisis management skills can be combined to deal more effectively with crisis situations.[2]

Project management is being increasingly used to support a company's factory operations. The entire field of manufacturing systems technology is changing rapidly, Just-in-time (JIT) inventory management, materials requirements planning (MRP), total quality management, computer-integrated manufacturing, computer-aided design, and flexible manufacturing systems are some of the primary new technologies that have been developed to support manufacturing operations. No doubt the pace of technology in manufacturing systems will continue to advance, resulting in "systems" changes impacting manufacturing as well as the supporting functions in the enterprise such as R&D, marketing, finance, and after-sales maintenance and support. What all these changes have done is create an environment in the modern company that is too multidisciplinary to be organized solely along traditional functional entities. Contemporary factory managers need a management philosophy that allows them to bring an organizational focus to the management of resources in the factory that are dedicated to change—to the creation of something that does not currently exist but that is needed to remain competitive in the global manufacturing environment.

The factory manager has a wide range of options to consider in using resources to manufacture products and provide supporting resources. The "traditional" factory retains most of the basic functional characteristics tied together by hierarchical relationships where clearly established lines of command are exercised through authority and responsibility relationships. The functional subunits of the factory are headed by a department manager, along with a person designated to be in charge of the production workers—this individual is

---

[2]See W. Stephen Sawle, "Crisis Project Management," *pmNETwork,* January 1991, pp. 25–29.

traditionally called a *first-level supervisor, foreman, production boss,* or some such title. The role of this first-level supervisor has changed, and will continue to change, significantly. Peter Drucker has noted that no job is going to change more in the future than that of the first-level supervisor. The use of production teams, concurrent engineering teams, quality teams, task forces, and such organizational designs dedicated to managing change in today's factories—all draw heavily on the concepts and processes of project management to pull together resources across traditional factory operations.

The use of robots to perform simple, repetitive manufacturing tasks reliably at relatively low cost is another application of manufacturing systems technology facilitated by the use of project management concepts and processes. However, the use of robots has not become widespread in manufacturing operations; less than 10 percent of the industrial enterprises that could benefit from robots have even one. Part of the problem has been that in most companies the design process is not adequately integrated with manufacturing. The typical robot system takes up to 12 months or more to go through a life cycle of concept, design, fabrication, installation, debugging, and start-up. The use of a project manager, such as an industrial engineer, to define robot tasks establishes operating parameters; and the designing and interfacing of the human/material/robot system provide for a means to integrate different disciplines to support a common objective. A project team led by an industrial engineer, including representatives from engineering, maintenance, production control, manufacturing, management, safety, personnel, labor reporting, and accounting, can effectively address the issues involved in setting up robots for use in the factory. Other responsibilities of this project team include addressing the issues of what will happen to the employees who are displaced by robots and how the supporting functional elements of the factory will be realigned to support the use of robots in the changed factory operation.

An industrial engineer whose education and experience are in forecasting techniques, EOQ calculations, material requirements planning, flow process charts, human-machine charts, time and motion study, time balancing Gantt charts, from-to charts, queuing networks, computer simulation, and of course project management is well suited to perform the key role of a project manager in the factory environment.

More and more literature is coming forth that describes how project management can be applied to the factory. A typical contribution to the literature has been offered by Professor Hans Thamhain in his Chapter 5, "Project Management in the Factory," in *The Automated Factory Handbook,* edited by David I. Cleland and Bopaya Bidanda, Tab Professional and Reference Books, Division of McGraw-Hill, Blue Ridge Summit, Pa.

Projects and Strategic Planning

Strategic planning establishes the mission, objectives, goals, and strategies for where the organization wants to go in the future. *Strategic design and implementation* is concerned with how the organization is going to get there through the planned use of resources. *Strategies* include things such as short-term action plans, policies, procedures, resource allocation directions, programs, and projects. Of these, *programs* and *projects* are of special interest. *Programs* are resource-consuming sets of organizational resources which have a common purpose. For example, a productivity improvement program could be composed of the following projects:

- A participative management style training project
- Plant and equipment modernization projects
- Professional management development projects
- A project for development and use of autonomous production teams
- Use of computer-aided design and manufacturing

A principal reason to use project management is to facilitate the implementation of organizational strategy, although project management can be used effectively in other organizational contexts. Another reason for electing to manage things on a project basis is the fragmentation of functions and skills throughout the organizational structure. When an activity that is too large for any one functional department to manage is introduced into the organization, a single focal point must integrate the functional efforts through a matrix organizational design. The matrix organizational design is discussed in Chapter 8.

Davis and Lawrence insist that one should turn to a project "matrix" only when the following conditions exist simultaneously:

1. When outside pressures require that intensive attention be focused on two or more different kinds of organizational tasks simultaneously, e.g., functional groupings around technical specialties and project groupings around unique customer needs

2. When tasks become so uncertain, complex, and interdependent that the information-processing load threatens to overwhelm competent managers

3. When the organization must achieve economies of scale and high performance through the shared and flexible use of scarce human resources.[3]

---

[3]Stanley M. Davis and Paul R. Lawrence, *Matrix* (Reading, Mass.: Addison-Wesley, 1977).

Projects are resource-consuming activities used to implement organizational strategies, achieve goals, and contribute to the accomplishment of the organizational mission, all of which suggest that when an enterprise considers the use of project management in its strategy, it should first determine if the proposed projects could be associated with the following:

- The core "product line" business being pursued in the organization's market strategy

- A proposed new product, service, or process design and development effort

- The development of resources to support the enterprise's product lines, such as facilities construction, productivity improvement programs, quality assurance programs, and employee participation projects

The question of whether to use project management raises the fundamental question: How should we organize to implement our organizational strategy? For it is the strategy pursued by an organization that sets the organizational design that follows.

In some situations, the decision to use project management techniques is made by the customer. Companies that bid on government contracts will find that they are expected to establish a project management system as a prerequisite to winning a contract.

In general, project management can be applied effectively to any ad hoc undertaking. If such an undertaking is unique or unfamiliar, the need for project management is intensified. In some cases, such as that of an undertaking whose successful accomplishment involves complex and interdependent activities, a project manager can pull everything together to accomplish an organizational purpose.

When Is a Project Needed?

Basic to successful project management is recognizing when the project is needed—in other words, when to form a project as opposed to when to use another form of organization to do the job. At what time do the forces in the organization and its environment add up to project management? The senior executives must have a basis for identifying undertakings which the regular departments cannot manage. There are no simple rules to follow, but several general criteria can be applied in considering the use of project management:

- Size of the undertaking
- Unfamiliarity

- Market change
- Interdependence
- Resource sharing
- Importance of the effort
- Organizational reputation

In the material that follows, each of these criteria will be discussed.

Size of the undertaking

The question of size is difficult to pin down because size is a relative matter. When an undertaking requires substantially more resources (people, money, equipment) than are normally employed in the business, project techniques may be indicated. Even though the functional elements for the end product are discernible in the organization, the diversity and complexity of the task easily can overwhelm a department. In these cases, project management provides a logical approach to the organizational relationships and problems encountered in the integration of the work. For example, let us consider the move of a company from an eastern city to one in a southern state. This may appear to be a simple operation, but the complex development and correlation of plans, the coordination required in constructing the new site, and the task of answering numerous inquiries about the new site easily can swamp the existing organizational structure. These difficulties are compounded by the fact that the company must continue its normal operations during the period of the move. In such a situation, managing the move along traditional lines would be difficult, if not impossible.

The minimum magnitude of project-oriented effort depends on the basic strategy of the organization. A company engaged in routine manufacturing probably does not require much project management. However, if the company were to go through a major redesign of its product line which dictated significant special tooling and facility changes, project management could be set up to manage the change.

In the development and production of a weapons system or a nuclear power plant, an awesome inventory of human and nonhuman resources has to be synchronized and integrated into an operable system. The use of project management in these situations is clearly needed.

Indeed, the need for formal project management was realized during the early days of the large DOD-NASA awards for the design, development, and production of major systems. For in managing these programs, companies recognized that two or more functional elements of their organizations had to be pulled together in order to develop these systems. The U.S. Air Force provided a strong impetus for the use of project management in the early 1950s. At that time it became clear to the USAF and the aerospace industry that a key point in the selection of system contractors would be whether the contractor had a project-driven organizational structure where work on a project could be centralized. By late 1958 and early 1959, aerospace companies had begun to establish project-driven organizations that cut across functional lines in order to accomplish project objectives. Factors that emerged in this period to account for the trend to centralize the management of projects within these organizations were as follows:

- A rapid technical advance in U.S. Air Force weaponry that had led to the demand for minimum lead time in developing an operational system

- A change in technology that had fostered new doctrines for the employment of costly weapons systems, along with the urgent need to produce project results at a minimum cost

- In the development of long-range ballistic missile systems, the motivation that arose from the management of the technology rather than the technology itself

- The extremely tight schedules, limited funding, state-of-the-art pressures, and increasingly complex procurement regulations that provided an unparalleled challenge to the aerospace industry

The current reduction of the DOD budget and the conversion to nondefense products by defense contractors will also provide ample opportunity for the use of project management.

Unfamiliarity

An *ad hoc undertaking* is a project out of the ordinary, something different from a normal, routine affair in the organization. But the degree of unfamiliarity also must be considered. For example, the redesign of a major product would require project management. An engineering change to an existing product, however, could be conducted without setting up a project, although there might be a loss of overall efficiency in accomplishing the objective. In the first instance, the changes in cost, schedule, and technology would require a central management point to bring together the functional activities required and relate them to compatibility. In the second case, each of the functional managers could draw on experience to accomplish the work.

Unique opportunities or problems are generally project-oriented. Work on these opportunities is usually scattered in the organization, yet it is all interrelated, for various functional groups have to provide different disciplines to support the undertaking. Project management handles such opportunities well.

At NCR a corporate project manager was made responsible for overseeing all activities relating to a postmerger integration of AT&T's computer systems with those of NCR. The use of project management techniques helped to reduce the time-consuming and complicated process of integrating the AT&T's worldwide computer services division with NCR, without interrupting business as usual.[4]

There are other important and unfamiliar activities in an organization that require a management focus so that resources can be marshaled and closely controlled. Some of the particular problems or opportunities that fit into the category of the "unfamiliar" are

- A major reorganization
- A takeover threat by an unfriendly suitor
- A crisis, such as a serious product failure, legal action, or other nonroutine occurrence, that seriously threatens the integrity of the enterprise
- Any unfamiliar undertaking that is of critical importance to the enterprise, such as new product or market development, new business venture, or acquisition of another company

In these ad hoc situations, management may not know how to integrate many different profit centers in the corporate structure. To meet this problem, one large corporation created a Projects Division as a profit center to enhance its capabilities in competing for projects business in its industry products business unit. The mission of this profit center was to act as the project management arm of the corporation for those jobs that required teamwork among the corporate divisions that produced the products, the various sales organizations, and the supporting corporate staff. This Projects Division was chartered to handle projects

- Of $1 million or more in the industrial products province
- With products from two or more divisions
- Managed under one contract
- Either domestic or international in scope
- Without any other appropriate lead division

---

[4]Eva Hofstadter, "The Science of the Deal: Project Management Needs Wall Street," *pmNETwork,* November 1992, pp. 11–19.

This division acts as a "strike force" to develop project markets in a market segment for the overall benefit of the corporation. This division also organizes, coordinates, delivers, and installs the electrical equipment package for large industrial projects. Here, project management is used for the advantage of single-source responsibility for all stages of a project, including

- Up-front studies and analyses
- A single, coordinated proposal
- A single contract covering all products and services
- An interface with customers, or with other contractors as required by the contract
- Large and complex projects packaged from smaller pieces
- Integrated equipment design and installation
- Stringent control of scheduling, shipping, and installation
- A single point of contact for problem resolution
- Centralized invoicing

In this corporation, project management is carried out by a team composed of representatives from the participating profit centers. The team is formed during proposal development and has responsibility through the warranty period. In addition to the design, development, and production phases of a project, the team manages installation, erection, and equipment start-ups (all integrated into the overall project) as well as support activities such as personnel training and start-up engineering. Some projects include field service and contract maintenance and repairs.

It took many years for this "interdivisional project management" to evolve, principally because of the territorial restrictions of the divisional charters that existed within the product group structure of the corporation. As the market for industrial equipment systems emerged, it became clear that no single division had the familiarity with the "systems" capability to serve the industry/construction project needs. What was needed was an organizational design to facilitate strategy across the many corporate profit centers that produced product components.

Market change

Many firms and organizations operate in a turbulent market that is characterized by continually changing products, rapid technological innovations, and rapid changes in the values and behavior of customers and competitors. Such conditions place a premium on innovation, creativity, rapid response, and flexibility. Heterogeneous, changing markets require a management system that can flourish in the ambiguity of changing objectives and goals with the life cycle of many projects placing varying demands on managerial and professional support. These rapid market changes require an organizational approach that permits flexibility in the use of resources.

One company whose products are well known throughout America's kitchens uses project management as part of its competitive strategy.

Wooster, Ohio-based Rubbermaid Company's products exhibit such high quality that they rarely need replacing. So this company must depend on new products and new markets for growth. The company's CEO wants to add a new market segment every 12 to 18 months. In the design of new products, the company depends heavily on a new generation of computer-aided design (CAD) workstations—so advanced that they reduce new-product design time from months to days. These workstations enable Rubbermaid to go directly from rough sketches to finished products in weeks rather than months. The company is moving from sequential to simultaneous design through the use of project teams—and in so doing is able to reduce cycle time, duplication of effort, and errors. In their markets, the reduction of cycle time is critical—to enable the company to have a market as long as possible and before cheaper versions appear. The company, to survive, has to "reinvent itself" continuously. Simultaneous engineering facilitated by CAD technology is critical to this reinvention.[5]

A senior executive in a project-driving organization comments on the flexibility that project management provides:

- In the short term, the matrix provides for flexible use of key technical resources, both people and facilities. (Functional "fiefdoms" don't have to be reorganized to move the talent from program to program to meet fluctuating demands.)

- For the long term, the matrix expands the avenues for business benefit from broadly applicable strategic investment. (A pattern of shared resources and shared responsibilities obviates the traditional "technology transfer" issue altogether.)

- Basically, through the program management dimension, the matrix establishes mini general managers who are extensions of the GM for a subset of the business, but without imposing the inflexibility and communication isolation of the functional resources that

---

[5]Seth Lubove, "Okay, Call Me a Predator," *Forbes,* February 15, 1993, pp. 150–153.

are characteristic of self-contained business segment departments.[6]

Interdependence

Another decision criterion for establishing a project is the degree of
interdependence between the departments of the organization. If the
effort calls for many functionally separated activities to be pulled
together and if these activities are so closely related that moving one
affects the others, project techniques clearly are needed.

Consider the development and introduction of a new product. The
early planning would require sales forecasts to be completed before
plans for manufacturing processes, industrial facilities, special tooling,
and marketing could be developed. Sales promotions cannot be completed before plans for manufacturing processes, industrial facilities, special tooling, and marketing. Sales promotions also cannot be completed
until the marketing research points the direction for the promotions.
Performance and technical specifications, as well as the many interdependencies between the production, marketing, finance, advertising,
and administration groups, must be resolved. Provincialism cannot be
tolerated. If no one agency can pull all the separate parts together, if
the functional groups fail to make credible estimates, or if the plans
submitted by the different departments cannot be reconciled, then the
activity needs the singleness of purpose of project management.

Sometimes project management comes about through a reorganization. In Norwalk, Connecticut, Perkin-Elmer Corporation recently
reorganized into a functional alignment from its former geographical
organization, one designed to compete in one global market. Project
teams composed of people from engineering, manufacturing, sales,
and services have the responsibility of developing new products.[7]

Product and service development projects are the lifeblood for success in the future. Manufacturing and marketing process development provide the basis for determining the resources needed to support the new product or service and the customer-related processes
that will be used to get the product or service to the customer. In such
situations, the interrelatedness factor in justifying a project is an
important consideration. The timing of the development of projects is
important as well.

---

[6]John W. Stuntz, "A General Manager Talks about Matrix Management," in David I.
Cleland (ed.), *Matrix Management Handbook* (New York: Van Nostrand Reinhold,
1984), p. 211. All rights reserved.

[7]Reed Abelson, "Getting Its Act Together," *Forbes,* August 31, 1992, pp. 44–45.

Sometimes the risks and costs of developing new technology dictate the use of project management. For example, a project team with IBM, Siemens, and Toshiba participation has been formed to design the first 256-Mbit memory chip and its fabrication process at an estimated cost of $1 billion. Factories to produce the chips in volume will run another billion each. These huge costs are the reason why such huge international alliances are likely to become the norm in the future.

The new project-process team is centered at IBM's new Advanced Semiconductor Technology Center in East Fishkill, New York, where a trilateral team of some 200 engineers will report to a Toshiba manager.[8]

World-class manufacturers are skillful at both product and process development and become expert in the design and manufacture of production equipment, either doing the work themselves or subcontracting the work to outside suppliers. Product development and process development are closely intertwined, usually through the use of a project team, often called a *product-process design team,* or *simultaneous engineering.* A brief continuing discussion of the subject of simultaneous engineering is presented here to demonstrate the project relevance of such engineering. This intertwining provides for the continual improvement of all the "systems" that support future organizational strategies.

Using project-process design teams in simultaneous engineering increases the probability of close interaction among engineering, marketing, and manufacturing groups. The teamwork across disciplines helps to ensure that everything that can influence the success of the new product or service in the marketplace is considered. With suitable senior management involvement and surveillance, a final core value is added to the development of new businesses.

The importance of interrelatedness is clearly demonstrated in the use of product-process design teams. Not only does the use of such teams provide the opportunity to get the product or service to the market sooner, but also it ensures more "systems" considerations in the strategic management of the enterprise. Other benefits include these:

1. Organizational resources are used more effectively and efficiently.

2. People working on the teams sense a higher degree of ownership with the product or process being developed.

---

[8]Otis Port, et al., "Talk about Your Dream Team," *Business Week,* July 27, 1992, pp. 59–60.

3. The composition of the team, with people having different backgrounds and coming from different disciplines in the organization, provides an enhanced "checks and balances" in the design and execution of strategies for the product, service, or process being developed.

4. Time is saved. Time represents money—and profit when the product or service is introduced into the market.

Figure 3.1 illustrates some of the key relationships in the product/service and process development processes.

When a large research laboratory must pull together many different specialties, that is another example of the importance of interrelatedness. The laboratory must establish criteria for the use of formal project management when research and/or development projects require assembling diverse technologies and when larger projects require an engineering/design output as well as advanced technology. Labora-

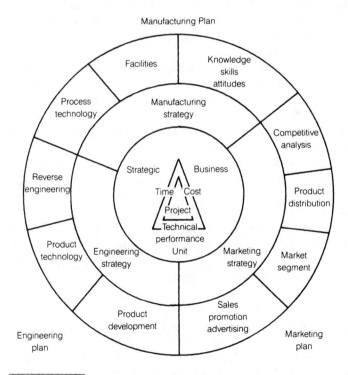

Source: Adapted with permission of The Free Press, a Division of Macmillan, Inc. from *Dynamic Manufacturing: Creating the Learning Organization* by Robert H. Hayes, Steven C. Wheelwright, Kim B. Clark ©1988 by The Free Press (New York 1988): 284.

Figure 3.1 Product/process development relationships.

tories use project management when a research project exhibits the following characteristics:

- A potential and significant long-range impact on the corporation
- The need to pinpoint corporate responsibility for the project
- The need for fast response
- The need for integrating widely varying disciplines, technical skills, backgrounds, and facilities
- The need for close coordination with corporate profit centers on product design, development, manufacturing equipment, and processes
- Significant size and duration
- Corporate technical and financial reporting requirements

Each year dozens of research projects are funded in a laboratory. A principal investigator or project manager provides the technical direction and integration of the project as well as accomplishing tasks on schedule and within budget. An informal project management system is used for small projects where only a few disciplines are required. For larger projects meeting the criteria just given, a formal project management system is used.

Projects are characterized by strong lateral working relationships requiring continuing coordination and decisions by many individuals, both within the parent organization and in outside companies. During the development of a major product, there is close collaboration between the process and design engineers, and even closer collaboration between the individuals of a single department. These horizontal relationships do not function to the exclusion of the vertical relationships. Resource sharing becomes common practice.

Successful project management was executed in a resourse-sharing partnership between General Electric and a group of Mexican appliance manufacturers to build a gas range manufacturing plant in San Luis Potosi in Mexico. GE management realized that the project's complexity was increased by working with a foreign partner in a foreign land. All members of the project team were given extensive Spanish instructions; Mexican members of the team were put through an extensive U.S. language and culture training program. Care was taken during the project to identify cultural, linguistic, and other related issues that were liable to create barriers to communication.[9]

---

[9]Robert J. Butler, "A Project Milestone Bonus Plan: Bringing a Plant Startup On-Line, On-Time, On-Cost," *National Productivity Series,* Winter 1991/1992, pp. 31–39.

Resource sharing

Project management makes sense when increasing professional specialization and its attendant higher costs lead to the need to share professional resources throughout the organization. It also makes sense when there are critical or scarce resources; or when, in the ebb and flow of the life cycles of modern business products and services, it is difficult to keep a professional work force fully and effectively employed; or when certain types of professional skills are in short supply. Project management techniques can be utilized to share resources, potentially reducing both direct and indirect costs and delivering needed services.

Importance of the project

Another reason for using project management techniques is the importance of the project to the company. Managers might not want to place it in the "bureaucracy" of the organization, where it might become lost in the daily operational workings. When an ad hoc activity has high risks and uncertainty factors, then the use of project management techniques may be required. If an emerging problem or project is viewed as a potential building block in the design and implementation of future strategies for the enterprise, then project management techniques are required.

A new product line requires financing, design, development, and production—clearly an opportunity for project management, particularly if the emerging opportunity constitutes an effort that is too large to manage in a "business as usual" approach or if the product is very important to the company's future business. If such an emerging product carries high risk and has an apparent direct relationship to the company's objectives, then project management is usually required.

An important part of an organization's policy should be a statement of the conditions under which project management will be used. Senior managers will develop these criteria when they realize the important role that projects can play in the management of the enterprise.

The important thing to remember is that a project, as an ad hoc activity, cannot stand on its own; it is interrelated to the strategic mission of the organization. A project contributes something to the ability of an organization to change to meet its future. A project is the opportunity for an enterprise to complete a goal that leads to accomplishing its objectives, and ultimately its mission. Thus the basic purpose for starting a project is to accomplish some goals that are held by the larger organizational unit—the department, the division, or the corporate entity. The reason for using a project is to provide a focus for organizational resources to be applied against the organizational problem or opportunity so that an enterprise goal can be attained.

Organizational reputation

The overall organizational stake in the undertaking is another crucial determinant in the decision of whether to use the project techniques. For instance, if a failure to complete a contract on time and within cost and performance limits would seriously damage the company's image and result in customer and stockholder dissatisfaction, then the case for using project management is strong. A company's financial position can be seriously damaged if its performance on a contract fails to meet standards. In the case of government contracting, the company faces a single, knowledgeable customer, and failure to perform successfully can be catastrophic in terms of obtaining further contracts with the government.

Project management is no panacea, but it does provide a means for effective use of resources in ad hoc efforts. Project managers who see their role as that of integrator-generalists, responsible for meeting time, cost, and performance objectives, can do much to lessen the dangers inherent in an ad hoc undertaking. Project management concentrates into one person the attention demanded by a complex and unique undertaking which will affect the enterprise's reputation.

Before a decision is made about whether to use project techniques, the effects of the company's environment on the project must be weighed and evaluated. The objective of the undertaking must be considered. Methodological improvements that might take some time to implement require considerable thought. The size and complexity of the project must be considered, since too much sophistication is also an ever-present danger. Other factors that merit consideration are the number of current projects in the company, the number in prospect, and the time remaining to complete the project. For example, establishing project management would be more appropriate at the start of an undertaking or at least early in its life, before large expenditures of work hours and resources are made. Each situation is unique, and the decision of whether to manage by a project or another approach should be made on the basis of specific problems expected as well as the concepts of organization presently used in the enterprise.

No company management takes a purely project-oriented or a purely functional approach. All companies combine the two, although one form may predominate.

The Coming of Teams

The introduction of teams into an existing traditional organizational structure changes the way in which the organizational processes are carried out. A process-oriented organizational design, rather than the traditional functional design, is suggested where the processes needed to produce a product or service become the focus and primary element of the organizational design. The organizational processes become the enterprise's main components, not the functional departments. Managers become *process owners.* Teams are built around the focus needed to capture the process flows for people to carry out their responsibilities and produce a quality product or service useful to someone else. For example, Eastman Kodak's black-and-white film manufacturing was reorganized around horizontal processes and now boasts about increased productivity, profitability, and morale. Hallmark uses "centers of excellence" for employees between projects for training and brief, special assignments.[10]

Another organizational design alternative is found at Texas Instruments' semiconductor group. A hierarchy of teams has been created within the existing hierarchy. A steering committee consisting of the plant manager and the heads of manufacturing, finance, engineering, and human resources has been formed. This steering committee provides key strategies and reviews and approves large projects. Below the steering committee three types of teams are provided: corrective-action teams, quality improvement teams, and effectiveness teams. The first two of these teams are cross-functional and consist primarily of middle managers and professionals; the effectiveness teams are principally blue-collar and professional people. The quality improvement teams work on long-range projects, such as the streamlining of the manufacturing processes. These teams are examples of the move toward more adaptive, dynamic organizational designs to accommodate self-managed teams.[11]

Promoting participative management

In some cases, project management is used to provide an opportunity for an individual to take an idea and see that idea through to a successful product or service. Some companies have recognized the value of individual initiative and have organized their corporate structure and management philosophy to accommodate the entrepreneurial abilities of individuals.

At Honda, a fixed percentage (approximately 10 percent) of the R&D budget is set aside to fund new-concept development. Anyone can propose a new concept. It is reviewed by a peer group. If it is accepted, Honda organizes a small project team and provides funds to develop the concept to the point of a formal evaluation by senior management.

Texas Instruments' IDEA Program has a small pool of funds, distributed by senior technical people, to pay for concept development.

---

[10]Thomas A. Stewart, "The Search for the Organization of Tomorrow," *Fortune,* May 18, 1992, pp. 92–98.

[11]Brian Dumaine, "Who Needs a Boss?" *Fortune,* May 7, 1990, pp. 52–60.

Anyone who can get a concept development idea funded can manage a small project. Some ideas have led to full-scale product development projects and even commercial products.

In 3M Company, anyone who invents a new product, or promotes an idea when others lose faith, or figures out how to mass-produce a product economically, has a chance to manage that product as though it were her or his own business, with a minimum of constraints from higher management. Called the process of *divide and grow,* the practice is aimed at keeping 3M a company of entrepreneurs. 3M's culture and its organizational structure are all directed to encouraging its people to take an idea and run with it. The new-product enterprises are broken out into self-sustaining units, each with considerable responsibility for its future. These ideas, developed into small projects managed by a team of professionals, may grow into departments and then into divisions within the corporate organizational structure. The depth of 3M's faith in allowing people to manage their ideas into projects was summed up by one manager at 3M, who stated:

> If you put fences around people, you get sheep. If you want the best from people, give them all the room they need to grow, and all the responsibility they can handle.[12]

3M's growth has been compared to cell mitosis because of the company's history of allowing small projects to grow and then dividing them. As described in a letter to the author:

> ...a product idea may emerge from a laboratory and link with a small amount of test-marketing assistance from a parent organization.
>
> This product moves into the marketplace and reaches a level where a project is created as a profit center having responsibility for creating additional business and products.
>
> The project succeeds and becomes a department. The department succeeds and becomes a division, which is the basic business unit at 3M.
>
> Divisions, in turn, are organized into product groups which themselves form business sectors.
>
> The "mitosis" usually occurs at the division level when a department achieves certain goals for profitability and sales. It is spun off from the parent division to create another, new division. Simplistically but accurately, a former board chairman once explained, "Split a $100 million division and you get two $60 million divisions."
>
> This process allows the product champions who have built a business to be rewarded without their having to wait for their bosses to retire or advance.
>
> For example: 1. In the 1950s, Lewis W. Lehr was working as a tape engineer when he had some contacts with physicians with an idea for a surgical tape. Lehr developed such a product, which languished. 3M

---

[12]*Getting to Know Us,* 3M Pamphlet (St. Paul, Minn.: 3M Center), undated.

wanted to drop the idea, but Lehr asked to buy the line, and 3M regained its interest. The product succeeded eventually. 2. Autoclave tapes and other medical products followed. 3. In 1960, Lehr was named manager (not even general manager) of a Medical Products Division. 4. Through new technologies and acquisitions, the Medical Products Division grew to become a group, with medical, surgical, orthopedic and dental products divisions. This group, Health Care Products and Services, is a significant portion of our Life Sciences Sector, one of four major business areas of the company.

As for Lehr, he moved with expanding business—becoming division general manager, division vice president and group vice president. He then became president of U.S. Operations and board chairman and CEO, retiring March 1.[13]

Truly, 3M's organizational design and operating philosophy emphasize project management which in turn supports their corporate mission: "We Are in the Business of Building Businesses."[14]

Senior management responsibility

Although it does not always happen, project management should be used only when senior management fully understands its own role in the strategic management of the enterprise and is fully committed to making it happen. The responsibilities of the senior managers of an organization and their willingness to provide an environment for the growth and propagation of project management depend on how well they establish an organizational culture for project management by doing the following:

- Maintaining the balance of power between the project office and the functional elements of the organization

- Providing facilitating services such as budget, finance, accounting, general administrative accommodation, etc., to the project

- Developing and promulgating a philosophy of how resource priorities will be determined in the organization's matrix and how conflict over these resources will be resolved

- Providing performance standards for both project success and adequacy of functional support

- Establishing criteria for performance evaluation and wage and salary classification schemes in the organization's matrix

- Acquainting key individuals with the theory of matrix organization

[13]Letter from H. G. Owen, 3M Center, St. Paul, Minn., to D. I. Cleland, March 20, 1986.

[14]3M 1985 Annual Report, title page.

and presenting a process model of how the organization is intended to operate

- Providing models of organizational interfaces—developing authority, responsibility, and accountability relationships

- Defining decision parameters within the matrix organization

- Providing the project manager and the functional manager with strategic direction

Project management is used in the design and execution of strategies for an organization. Both large and small projects require a rationalization for their use in organizational strategy. An important part of an organizational policy is a clear statement of when projects will be used in the organization and how the organizational managers will support the ensuing project management process.

Much of the material in this book provides guidance on how organizational senior managers can facilitate and grow in the use of project management in their organizations. In addition, senior management should recognize when project management is not required.

When Not to Use Project Management

Project management may not be required when

- The business products or services are highly standardized and the production processes are routine or seldom change. This condition is becoming more rare in today's world competition.

- Strategic and key operating decisions within the enterprise can be made within a standard organizational framework.

- The product or service technology is stable, well within the state of the art.

- The political, social, economic, technological, and competitive environments faced by the enterprise are stable.

- Projects are not integral building blocks of enterprise strategy, i.e., market strategy does not require the use of project management techniques.

- The organization is small, and the same results can be accomplished through the functional organization by using an informal liaison or coordinating function. Even then, "informal" project techniques will be used.

These conditions suggest a stable environment, something that very few organizations have today. Even under these conditions there may be opportunity in modern organizations to use teams on engineering projects, task force management, quality circles, and project management.

Summary

Perhaps the most basic reason for the need to develop a project-driven organizational approach is simply that the traditional ways of organizing—such as functional, process, geographical, and line-staff—do not provide the focus necessary to effectively manage interorganizational ad hoc work. The introduction of a project-driven organizational approach, while immediately setting in motion a new form of organization, soon creates the need for specialized planning and control systems. Information systems are required which are attuned to the project's functional and general management needs. Personnel assignments on project work tend to fluctuate, based, as each assignment must be, on the life cycle of a "stream of projects" flowing throughout the organization. This impermanence creates challenges for the traditionally oriented organization.

In general, project management techniques are called for when certain conditions exist. The reasons for using a project management approach are

- To share resources across organizational units
- To focus attention on specific customers in specific market segments
- To integrate systems and subsystems simultaneously or in parallel within independent organizations
- To manage focused interorganizational efforts from a profit-center perspective
- To deal with specific ad hoc problems and opportunities
- To expedite responses to new events in the organization or its environment
- To accommodate the inherent interdependency within an organizational system
- To combine several proven methods of organizational design, such as product, functional, and geographic
- To preserve unity of command, unity of direction, and parity of responsibility and authority for disparate activities
- To fix accountability within organizations
- To bring a wide range of experience and viewpoints into focus on tasks, opportunities, and problems
- To formalize an informal management process such as project engineering
- To establish a liaison role between organizational units or specialties
- To test a new organizational strategy without committing to a formal structural reorganization

- To deal with the magnitude of an undertaking requiring massive input of capital, technology, skills, and resources
- To manage unique or rare activity
- To focus effort to maintain an organizational reputation
- To keep a low-profile, long-term organizational effort alive while awaiting suitable competitive or environmental conditions
- To facilitate the participation of organizational members in the management process of the enterprise
- To deal with a new technology which requires pooling of existing resources and capacities
- To satisfy a customer's need for the unified management of a project-based contract in order to avoid having that customer work with many different functional organizations
- To meet competition
- To deal with a task that is bigger than anything the organization is accustomed to handling
- To promote participative and professional management

Project management meets the need for providing an organizational focus not found in the traditional form of organization. However justified, project management should not be used until the leaders of the organization are committed to its use and are willing to prepare a suitable culture for project management to germinate and grow.

Discussion Questions

1. What is involved in strategic planning? In strategic implementation?

2. How do projects become the driving force in determining how organizational resources are used?

3. What is meant by the sentence, "Projects are resource-consuming activities"?

4. List and describe some of the major reasons for the use of project management.

5. How does an organization know when the size of an undertaking suggests project management?

6. Discuss situations in your work or school experience that were permeated by unfamiliarity. Could project management have been used to address the unfamiliarity?

7. What kinds of industries experience "turbulent" markets?

8. Discuss the various interrelationships that can exist between the functional specialties within an organization.

9. What kinds of projects can be crucial to an organization's professional reputation?

10. What types of questions would a manager ask to determine the importance of a project?

11. How does the use of a project management structure affect the culture of a corporation?

12. What kinds of questions are important in determining whether a project supports an organization's strategies and its overall mission, objectives, and goals?

User Checklist

1. Is the use of project management in your organization driven by any outside forces?

2. Is your organization project-driven in any way?

3. Does your organization recognize when the need for project management arises?

4. Does the size of any of your current undertakings warrant project management?

5. Are any of the ad hoc projects currently being undertaken by your organization fraught with unfamiliarity?

6. Is your organization comfortable in understanding the competitive market in which it works? Is the market dictating the use of project management?

7. Does management recognize and control the large number of interrelationships that can exist between functional departments when each has some role in a project?

8. Are any of your organization's current undertakings crucial to its reputation?

9. How does your organization combine project and functional approaches to management?

10. Does your organization take advantage of emerging opportunities for new products by using a project management team to design and develop innovative ideas?

11. Does your organization promote individual entrepreneurship by supporting the development of creative ideas?

12. Does your organization recognize when not to use project management?

4

The Strategic Context of Projects[1]

*"It is much less what we do than what we
think, which fits us for the future."*
PHILLIP JAMES BAILEY, 1816–1902

The most dangerous time for an organization is when the old strategies are discarded and new ones are developed to respond to competitive opportunities. The changes that are appearing in the global marketplace have no precedence; survival in today's unforgiving global marketplace requires extraordinary changes in organizational products—and in the organizational processes needed to identify, conceptualize, develop, produce, and market something of value to the customers. Projects, as building blocks in the design and execution of organizational strategies, provide the means for bringing about realizable changes in products and processes. Senior managers, who have the residual responsibility for the strategic management of the enterprise, can gain valuable insights into both the trajectory of the enterprise and the speed with which the competitive position of the enterprise is being maintained and enhanced.

Implications of Technology

Management of an enterprise so that its future is ensured requires that the technology involved in products and/or services and organizational processes be approached from two principal directions: the strategic or long-term perspective and the systems viewpoint. In both

[1]Portions of this chapter have been taken from D. I. Cleland, "Measuring Success: The Owner's Viewpoint," *PMI Seminar/Symposium,* Montreal, Canada, September 20–25, 1986, and D. I. Cleland, "Project Owners: Beware," *Project Management Journal*, December 1986, pp. 83–93.

these directions, projects play a key role. In this chapter these two directions will be woven into a project management philosophy in which projects are building blocks in the design and execution of organizational strategies. A couple of examples of how contemporary organizations deal with projects make the point:

> At Banc One Corporation, one of the fastest-growing and most profitable banks in the United States, 3 percent of the profits has been dedicated to technology R&D. One of the bank's most important technology projects is the development of a new computer system that will dramatically alter the way Banc One branches operate to include the creation of a new credit card processing system. With the assistance of the Dallas-based Electronic Data Systems Corporation, the bank is moving from older mainframe systems to a distributed architecture.[2]

> Sony, which had nearly $26 billion in sales last year, is the most consistently inventive consumer electronics enterprise in the world. It has had hit after hit of high-technology products. Its products have created billion-dollar markets, designing and producing devices that have altered people's work and leisure. Sony's portfolio of products ranges from semiconductors, batteries, and recording tapes to video and audio gear for consumers, professionals, computers, communications equipment, and factory robots. Last year the company spent $1.5 billion on research and product development projects—roughly 5.6 percent of revenues. Each year the company sends out 1000 new products—an average of almost 4 a day. Some 200 of these new products are aimed at creating whole new markets, such as the Mini Disc portable digital stereo. Sony founder and honorary chairman Masaru says that the key to success at Sony—and to everything in business, science, and technology—is never to follow the others. In other words, innovation—the creation of something that does not currently exist. Product/project ideas come from many different organizational levels in the company, from the senior managers to the young engineers working in the product design department. Some of Sony's key philosophies are

> ■ An emphasis on making something out of nothing
> ■ People who are optimistic, open-minded, and wide-ranging in their interests, who move around a lot among product groups

---

[2]Alice LaPlante, "Shared Destinies: CEOs and CIOs," *Forbes ASAP*, December 7, 1992, pp. 32–42.

- A belief that having continuous success in the same area makes you believe too much in your own power, which harms your creativity
- A belief that new products come primarily out of a creator's imagination, not from a marketing study
- Occasional use of a "skunk works" project to circumvent the formal project approval process in the company
- Use of competing project teams to work on promising technologies[3]

Projects are essential to the survival and growth of organizations. Failure in project management in an enterprise can prevent the organization from accomplishing its mission. The greater the use of projects in accomplishing organizational purposes, the more dependent the organization is on the effect and efficient management of those projects. Projects are a direct means of creating value for the customer in terms of future products and services. The pathway to change will be through development and process projects. Future strategies will entail a portfolio of projects, some of which will survive and lead to new products and/or services and the manufacturing and marketing processes that will beat out the competition. With projects playing such a pivotal role in future strategies, senior managers must approve and maintain surveillance over these projects to determine which ones can make a contribution to the strategic survival of the company.

A product or process development project is a business venture—the creation of something that does not currently exist but which can provide support to the overall organizational strategy being developed to meet competition. Many projects are found in successful organizations.

A Stream of Projects

An enterprise that is successful has a "stream of projects" flowing through it at all times. When that stream of projects dries up, the organization has reached a stable condition in its competitive environment. In the face of the inevitable change facing the organization, the basis for the firm's decline in its products and processes is laid—and the firm will hobble on but ultimately face liquidation.

In the healthy firm, a variety of different product and process preliminary ideas are fermenting. As these ideas are evaluated, some will fall by the wayside for many reasons: lack of suitable organizational resources, unacceptable development costs, position too far behind the competition, lack of "strategic fit" with the enterprises

---

[3]Brenton R. Schlender, "How Sony Keeps the Magic Going," *Fortune*, February 24, 1992, pp. 75–82.

direction, and so on. There is a high mortality rate in these preliminary ideas. Only a small percentage will survive and will be given
additional resources for study and evaluation in later stages of their
life cycles. Senior managers need to ensure that evaluation techniques are made available and their use known to the people who
provide these preliminary innovative ideas. Essentially this means
that everyone in the organization needs to know the general basis on
which product and process ideas can survive and can be given additional resources for further study. Senior management must create a
balance between providing a cultural ambience in the enterprise that
encourages people to bring forth innovative product and process
ideas and an environment that ensures that rigorous strategic assessment will be done on these emerging ideas to determine their
likely strategic fit in the enterprise's future. For example, Elan Corporation, Plc. whose mission is the development of novel drug ab-
sorption systems for therapeutic compounds that provide distinctive
benefits for the physician and patient—carrying out all the necessary
clinical studies and regulatory work prior to market introduction—
follows a fundamental strategy called *mind to market.* To implement
this strategy which brings their products to market through the formulation, clinical testing, registration, and manufacturing phases,
project management is used. In the product development area, the
company is currently committed to 56 active projects, utilizing 9 specialized drug delivery technologies in 18 therapeutic categories
which range from cardiovascular and narcotic analgesics to anti-
emetics and neuropharmacological agents. Research and development is the very essence of the company's business. Its work in R&D
ensures a continuing stream of new products and technologies. In the
global marketplace, the company currently has new-drug applications or their equivalent filed for 20 products in 30 countries around
the world.[4]

Kmart Corporation's strategy in assessing strategic opportunities is
to jump-start a number of small projects at a relatively low cost and
then shift the money into the promising ideas as the development
work evolves. One example of such a promising project involves the
development of electronic shelf tags which would display pertinent
information about a product, including the unit price, price per ounce,
sales data, or whatever the company wanted to highlight. No longer
would the employees have to change the traditional shelf tags.
Another project is under development for a ceiling-mounted scanner
to track the number of customers entering and exiting a Kmart store,
thus alerting personnel that additional sales assistance is needed in

---

[4]*Annual Report,* Elan Corporation, Plc. 1992.

specific departments. Another project borrows from manufacturing just-in-time inventory management concepts and processes. Products are shipped to Kmart distribution centers only when needed, thus reducing inventory requirements. Suppliers under this new procedure would write their own purchase orders by looking into Kmart's inventory databases and would ship products in time to keep Kmart's shelves from becoming bare.[5]

Strategic Relationship of Projects

Organizational conceptual planning forms the basis for developing a project's scope in supporting the organizational mission.[6] For example, a project plan for facilities design and construction would be a series of engineering documents from which detailed design, estimating, scheduling, cost control, and effective project management will flow. Conceptual planning, while forming the framework of a successful project, is strategic in nature and forms the basis for

- Contributing, through the execution of strategies, to the organizational objectives, goals, and mission
- Standards by which the project can be managed
- Coping with the market and other environmental factors likely to have an impact on the project and the organization

Senior management deficiencies in the organization using project management will probably be echoed in the management of the projects. For example, an audit conducted in the early 1980s of a gas and electric utility that experienced problems with a major capital project found several key deficiencies in that utility, such as

1. Weak basic management processes
2. No implementation of the project management concept for major facilities
3. Fragmented and overlapping organizational functions
4. No focus of authority and accountability[7]

Thus the projects of an organization are interrelated with organizational strategies. The project selection framework therefore must

---

[5] LaPlante, op. cit.

[6] Project planning within the context of strategic organizational planning is discussed in Chapter 11.

[7] Cresap, McCormick, and Paget, Inc., *An Operational and Management Audit of PG&E, Executive Summary,* June 1980.

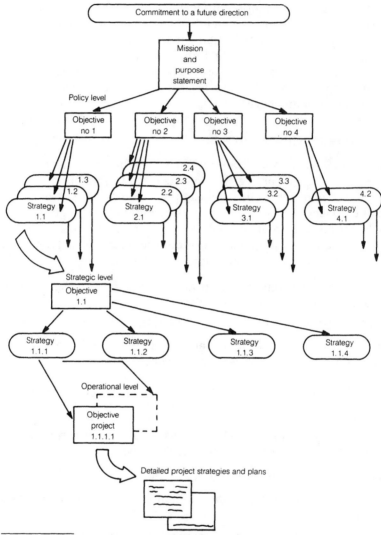

Figure 4.1 The hierarchy of objectives > strategies > projects.

itself be an integral part of the enterprise's strategic management.[8] Archibald envisions organizational objectives, strategies, and projects as fitting together in a hierarchical fashion as portrayed in Fig. 4.1. In his model, projects come into play at the operational level to

---

[8] Project selection techniques are discussed later in this chapter.

achieve operational objectives through the development of detailed projects and plans. In commenting on the importance of projects in the organization's portfolio of strategies, Archibald notes:

> Unless the higher level objectives and strategies are translated into actions through projects, they will simply sit unnoticed on the shelf in the corporate planner's office, waiting for the next annual planning exercise to generate a flurry of staff wheel-spinning amid great clouds of dust and debris. Far better for senior line managers to create their own strategies, with the implementing projects authorized through the organization's budgetary approval process. Then the strategies will become realities.[9]

Ford Motor Company is committed to the use of project management in its corporate strategy. To provide consistency in the use of project management, Ford realized during the 1980s that a *common* project management system was required. To bring about a consistent way to manage projects, a Ford corporate mainframe project management tool selection committee was created. Care was taken to ensure that users would be given a voice in the system selection process. Several key policies were established to both guide and motivate the committee to pursue its work. (1) There was agreement by senior management to accept the recommendations of the committee, assuming that such recommendations were supported by adequate facts. (2) The committee agreed to operate as a cross-functional project team. (3) A schedule was adopted to maintain user interest and enthusiasm; decisions by the committee would be made by consensus. (4) It was recognized that leadership of the committee was an important variable in realizing success of the work underway.[10]

Determining Strategic Fit

Projects are essential to the survival and growth of organizations. Failure in the management of projects in an organization will impair the ability of the organization to accomplish its mission in an effective and efficient manner. Projects are a direct means of creating value for customers—both customers in the marketplace and "in-house" customers, who work together in creating value for the ultimate customer in the marketplace. The pathway to change is through the use of projects which support organizational strategies. Future strategies for organizations entail a portfolio of projects, some of which survive dur-

---

[9]R. D. Archibald, "Projects: Vehicles for Strategic Growth," *Project Management Journal,* September 1986, p. 32.

[10]Paraphrased from "Using a Cross-Functional Team at Ford to Select a Corporate PM System," *pmNETwork,* August 1990, pp. 35–59.

ing their emerging life cycle and create value for customers. Since projects play such a pivotal role in the future strategies of organizations, senior managers need to become actively involved in the efficiency and effectiveness with which the stream of projects is managed in the organization. Surveillance over these projects must be maintained by senior managers to provide insight into the probable promise or threat that the projects hold for future competition. In considering these projects, senior managers need to find answers to the following questions:

- Will there be a "customer" for the product or process coming out of the project work?
- Will the project results survive in a contest with the competition?
- Will the project results support a recognized need in the design and execution of organizational strategies?
- Can the organization handle the risk and uncertainty likely to be associated with the project?
- What is the probability of the project's being completed on time, within budget, and at the same time satisfying its technical performance objectives?
- Will the project results provide value to a customer?
- Will the project ultimately provide a satisfactory return on investment to the organization?
- Finally, the bottom-line question: Will the project results have a strategic fit in the design and execution of future products and processes?

As senior managers conduct a review of the projects under way in organizations, the above questions can serve to guide the review process. As such questions are asked and the appropriate answers are given during the review process, an important message will be sent throughout the organization: Projects are important in the design and execution of our organizational strategies!

The question of the strategic fit of a project is a key judgment challenge for senior executives. Who should make such decisions? Clearly those executives whose organizational products and services will be improved by the successful project outcome should be involved. Senior executives of the enterprise should act as a team in the evaluation of the stream of projects that should flow through the top of the enterprise for assessment and determination of future value. Participative decision making concerning the strategic fit of projects is highly desirable. For some senior executives this can be difficult, particularly if they have been the entrepreneur who conceptualized and put the company together. Such founding entrepreneurs tend to dominate the strategic decision making of the organization, reflecting their ability in having created the enterprise through their strategic vision in developing a sense of future needs of products and services.

But senior executives, too, can lose their sense of future vision for the enterprise. Or they can become fixated on favorite development projects that may not make any strategic sense to the organizational mission and goals. For example, in a large computer company the founder's dominance of key project decisions drove out people whose perceptions of a project's strategic worth were contrary to that of the CEO. A new-products development group was abruptly disbanded by the CEO, who had sharp differences of opinion with the group executive over several key projects. This group executive had disagreed with the CEO on a key decision involving continuing development of a computer mainframe project whose financial promise was faint—if potentially attainable at all.

The Vision

Projects and organizational strategies start with a vision. A "vision is the art of seeing things invisible," according to Jonathan Swift.

The corporate vision statement of Whirlpool Corporation is, "Whirlpool, in its chosen lines of business, will grow with new opportunities and be the leader in an ever-changing global market." Implicit in the statement are commitments to market orientation, leadership, customer satisfaction, and quality.

The CEO of Motorola, Inc., holds the vision of "...a corporation that will look gigantic but have the dynamics of little teams." Motorola calculates that its project teams produce an average of four new or improved products each day. Additional reasons for the success of this company are a nonunion work force and a macho culture uniquely suitable to its professional class of highly trained engineers. In addition, the company has a huge cash flow to support R&D, capital investment, and training.[11]

During the strategic-fit review of organizational projects, insight should be gained into which projects are entitled to continued assignment of resources and which are not. Senior managers need to decide; the project manager is an unlikely person to execute the decision. Most project managers are preoccupied with bringing the project to a successful finish, and they cannot be expected to clearly see the project in an objective manner of supporting the enterprise mission. There is a natural tendency for the project manager to see the termination of the project as a failure in the management of the project.

---

[11]G. Christian Hill and Ken Yamada, "Staying Power," *Wall Street Journal,* December 12, 1992.

Projects are sometimes continued beyond their value to the strategic direction of the organization. The selection of projects to support corporate strategies is important in developing future direction.

A Project Selection Framework

A project selection framework is shown in Table 4.1. In the leftmost column is a set of evaluation criteria. The body of the table shows how a proposed new program to begin manufacturing system components in Europe might be evaluated.

The "criteria weights" in the second column of the table reflect their relative importance and serve to permit the evaluation of complex project characteristics within a simple framework. A base weight of 20 is used here for the major criteria related to mission, objectives, strategy, and goals. Weights of 10 are applied to the other criteria.

Within each major category, the 20 "points" are judgmentally distributed to reflect the relative importance of subelements or some other characteristic of the criterion. For instance, the three stages of strategy and the four subgoals are weighted to ensure that earlier stages and goals are treated to be more important than later ones. This implicitly reflects the *time value of money* without requiring a more complex "present value" discounting calculation.

The first criterion in Table 4.1 is the "fit" with mission. The proposal is evaluated to be consistent with both the "product" and "market" elements of the mission and is thereby rated to be "very good," as shown by the 1.0 probability entries at the upper left.

In terms of "consistency with objectives," the proposal is rated to have a 0.2 (20 percent) chance of being "very good" in contributing to the ROI element of the objectives, a 60 percent chance of being "good," and a 20 percent chance of being only "fair," as indicated by the probabilities entered into the third row of the table. The proposed project is rated more poorly with respect to the "Dividends" and "Image" elements.

The proposal is also evaluated in terms of its expected contribution to each of the three stages of the strategy. In this case, the proposed project is believed to be one which would principally contribute to stage 2 of the strategy. (Note that only certain assessments may be made in this case, since the stages are mutually exclusive and exhaustive.)

The proposal is similarly evaluated with respect to the other criteria.

The overall evaluation is obtained as a weighted score that represents the sum of products of the likelihoods (probabilities) and the 8, 6, 4, 2, 0 arbitrary level weights that are displayed at the top of the table. For instance, the "consistency with objectives—ROI" expected level weight is calculated as:

$$0.2(8) + 0.6(6) + 0.2(4) = 6.0$$

This is then multiplied by the criterion weight of 10 to obtain a weighted

TABLE 4.1 A Project Selection Model

Program/project evaluation criteria		Criteria weights	Very good (8)	Good (6)	Fair (4)	Poor (2)	poor (0)	Very level score	Expected Weighted score
"Fit" with mission	Product	10	1.0					8.0	80
	Market	10	1.0					8.0	80
Consistency with objectives	ROI	10	0.2	0.6	0.2			6.0	60
	Dividends	5		0.2	0.6	0.2		4.0	20
	Image	5			0.8	0.2		3.6	18
Consistency with strategy	Stage 1	10					1.0	0	0
	Stage 2	7	1.0					8.0	56
	Stage 3	3					1.0	0	0
Contribution to goals	Goal A	8					1.0	0	0
	Goal B	6	0.8	0.2				7.6	45.6
	Goal C	4		0.8	0.2			5.6	22.4
	Goal D	2					1.0	0	0
Corporate *strength* base		10				0.8	0.2	1.6	16
Corporate *weakness* avoidance		10				0.2	0.8	0.4	4
Comparative advantage level		10	0.7	0.3				7.4	74
Internal consistency level		10	1.0					8.0	80
Risk level acceptability		10				0.7	0.3	1.4	14
Policy guideline consistency		10			1.0			4.0	40

Total score 610

score of 60. The weighted scores are then summed to obtain an overall evaluation of 610.[12]

Of course, this number in isolation is meaningless. However, when various projects are evaluated in terms of the same criteria, their overall scores provide a reasonable basis for developing the ranking shown on the right side of Table 4.1. Such a ranking can be the basis for resource allocation, since the top-ranked program is presumed to be the most worthy, the second-ranked is the next most worthy, etc.

It can readily be seen that such a project selection process will enhance the implementation of the choices made in the strategic planning phase of management.

The critical element of the evaluation approach is its use of criteria that ensure that projects will be integrated with the mission, objectives, strategy, and goals of the organization and will reflect critical bases of strategy, such as business strengths, weaknesses, comparative advantages, internal consistency, opportunities, and policies.

Projects and Organizational Management

Projects, goals, and objectives must fit together in a synergistic fashion in supporting the enterprise mission. Project success by itself may not contribute to enterprise success. Projects might, early in their life cycle, show promise of contributing to enterprise strategy. A project that continues to support that mission should be permitted to grow in its life cycle. If the project does not provide that support, then a strategic decision faces the senior managers: Can the project be reprogrammed, replanned, and redirected to maintain support of the enterprise mission, or should the project be abandoned?

Project managers cannot make such a strategic decision since they are likely preoccupied with bringing the project to a successful finish, and project termination is not their responsibility. Such managers may lack an overall perspective of the project's strategic support of the enterprise mission. Therefore, the decision of what to do about the project must remain with the general manager, who is the project "owner" and has residual responsibility and accountability for the project's role in the enterprise mission and usually puts up the money for the project.

Project success is very dependent upon an appropriate synergy with the enterprise's success. The management of the project and the management of the enterprise depend on a synergistic management approach—planning, organizing, evaluation, and control tied together through an appropriate project-enterprise leadership. This synergy is shown in Fig. 4.2.

---

[12]Adapted from D. I. Cleland and W. R. King, *Systems Analysis and Project Management,* 3d ed. (New York: McGraw-Hill, 1983), pp. 68–70.

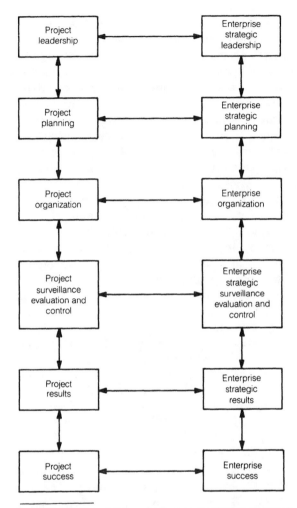

Source: David I. Cleland, "Measuring Success: The Owner's Viewpoint,"
(*Project Management Institute* Seminar/Symposium, Montreal, Canada,
September 1986): 6.

Figure 4.2   Project/strategic enterprise synergy.

Projects are designed, developed, and produced or constructed for a
customer. This customer or project owner may be an internal customer, such as a business unit manager who pays for product development by the enterprise central laboratory. An external customer might
be a utility that has contracted with an architectural and engineering
firm to design, engineer, and build an electricity generating plant.

Senior managers, who have the responsibility to sense and set the
vision for the enterprise, need a means of marshaling the resources of
the organization to seek fulfillment of that vision. By having an active

project management activity in the enterprise, an organizational design and a development strategy are available to assist senior managers in bringing about the changes and synergy to realize the organizational mission, objectives, and goals through a creative and innovative strategy. Leadership of a team of people who can bring the changes needed to the enterprise's posture is essential to the attainment of the enterprise's vision. As additional product and/or service and process projects are added to marshal the enterprise's resources, the strategic direction of the enterprise can be guided to the attainment of the vision. When projects are accepted as the building blocks in the design and execution of organizational purposes, a key strategy has been set in motion to keep the enterprise competitive. Such strategies are dependent on the quality of the leadership in the enterprise.

Compaq Computer Corporation CEO Eckhard Pfeiffer has provided the leadership in launching a long-term strategy initiative in that company. This planning effort was launched as soon as the immediate situation at the company was moving adequately toward correction. A comprehensive long-range strategy has been developed and put in place. The CEO has stated that the focus of the company is clearly on future strategy—a means to totally transform the company.

One of the more important strategic decisions made by the Compaq CEO was to launch development efforts into cut-rate personal computers (PCs). An independent business unit was organized into a project team to develop a low-price machine—a real Compaq.

Revised manufacturing strategies were developed to get costs down at plants in Houston, Singapore, and Scotland. The entire manufacturing process strategy was rethought. An entire system is now built on a single assembly line instead of making the motherboard in one building and the chassis in another. Testing of every subassembly was stopped in favor of testing a sample. All finished systems are still fully tested. Compaq leaned on suppliers to cut prices to bring down overall manufacturing costs.[13] Project planning contributed to the project planning strategy at Compaq.

Project Planning

Why is project planning so important? Simply because decisions made in the early phases of the project set the direction and force with which the project moves forward as well as the boundaries within which the work of the project team is carried out. As the project moves through its life cycle, the ability to influence the outcome of the project declines rapidly. After design of the project done early in the

---

[13] Catherine Arnst, et al., "Compaq," *Business Week,* November 2, 1992.

life cycle, the cost of producing the resulting product as well as the product quality has been largely determined. Senior managers tend to pay less attention during the early phases of the project than when the product development effort approaches the prototype or market-testing stage. By waiting until later in the life cycle of the project, their influence is limited in the sense that much of the cost of the product has been determined. Design has been completed, and the manufacturing or construction cost has been set early in the project. Senior managers need to become involved as early as possible, and they must be able to intelligently assess the likely market outcome of the product, its development cost, its manufacturing economy, how well it will meet the customers' quality expectations, and the probable strategic fit of the resulting product in the overall strategic management profile of the enterprise. In other words, when senior managers become involved early in the development cycle through regular and intelligent review, they can enjoy the benefits of leverage in the final outcome of the product and its likely acceptance in the marketplace. What happens early in the life cycle of the project essentially lays the basis for what is likely to happen in subsequent phases. Since a development project is taking an important step into the unknown—with the hope of creating something that did not previously exist—as much information as possible is needed to predict the possible and probable outcome. For senior managers to neglect the project early in its life cycle and leave the key decisions solely to the project team is the implicit assumption of a risk that is imprudent from the strategic management perspective of the enterprise.

Flexibility

The leading competitors in the world are moving toward a strategy of *flexibility*. Such strategy involves faster reading of the market. The use of concurrent engineering to commercialize products sooner, plus the use of flexible manufacturing systems to manufacture different products on the same line, switching from one product to another quickly, helps to keep costs down. Developing and using comprehensive just-in-time information systems for planning and control, gaining as much profit from short production runs as from long ones, and commercializing higher-quality products and services faster provide added flexibility.

Baxter Healthcare is testing a modular factory—an intravenous-solutions factory that can be shipped anywhere, set up in a week, and moved again anytime. At Kao Corporation, Japan's biggest soap and cosmetics company and the sixth largest in the world, an information system links everything: sales and shipping, production and purchasing, accounting, R&D, marketing, hundreds of shopkeepers' cash registers, and thousands of salespeople's handheld computers. The information is so complete that year-end financial statements can be turned out by noon of the first day of the new year. Kao can know if a new product will be successful within 2 weeks of launch through the melding of point-of-sale information from 216 retailers with a test-marketing operation called the Echo System, which uses focus groups and consumers' calls and letters to gauge customer response more quickly than market surveys can. At Fuji Electric, Japan's fourth largest maker of electrical machinery, a flexible manufacturing system using bar codes developed by a project team tells machines what to do. Before the flexible manufacturing system, Fuji filled orders in 3 days; now Fuji needs only 24 hours, using one-third as many workers and almost one-third less inventory, making about 8000 varieties—3 times more than before.[14]

Project planning and organizational renewal are linked through the development of organizational strategy. For example, Lawrence A. Bossidy, now CEO of Allied-Signal Company, upon joining the company established ambitious objectives including:

- An 8 percent annual revenue growth
- A total-immersion total-quality program
- A top-to-bottom change in human resources management

A statement of corporate vision and values listed these objectives, developed by the company's top twelve executives to include such things as being "one of the world's premier companies, distinctive and successful" and the values of satisfying customers, integrity, and teamwork. The vision helped to galvanize people. In addition, with these objectives as guidelines, Bossidy chopped $225 million from capital spending, reduced the annual dividend to $1 a share from $1.80, put eight small divisions up for sale, cut 6200 jobs, and combined ten data-processing centers into two.

The company formed *commodity teams*—cross-functional project teams of manufacturing, engineering, design, purchasing, and finance in such areas as castings, electronic gears, machine parts, and materials. Each team was responsible for picking the best suppliers in its specialty, with the chosen suppliers getting long-term national contracts. Suppliers were expected to bring down costs for themselves and for Allied-Signal.

---

[14]Thomas A. Stewart, "Brace for Japan's Hot New Strategy," *Fortune*, September 21, 1992, pp. 62–74.

Projects are usually paid for by the project owners, key members of project teams. The project owner has the residual responsibility and accountability for managing the project during its life cycle.

The Project Owner's Participation

Project owners cannot leave to others the responsibility for continuously measuring the success of the project, even experienced project management contractors and constructors. Foxhall stated:

> The owner must recognize that he is the key member of the project development team. Only he can select and organize the professional team, define his own needs, set his priorities and make final decisions. He cannot delegate these roles, so he must have a sustained presence in project management.[15]

The project owner clearly has responsibility for the efficiency and effectiveness of a contractor involved on the project. This requires a surveillance system to know what the contractor is doing and how well the contractor is performing. For example, one report noted:

> Another essential characteristic of a successful nuclear construction project is a project management approach that shows an understanding and appreciation of the complexities and difficulties of nuclear construction. Such an approach includes adequate financial and staffing support for the project, good planning and scheduling, and *close management oversight of the project.*[16]

In the nuclear power plan construction industry, project owners are taking a more proactive position in managing their projects. Project owners in the utility industry, driven by the need to better manage projects, have responded by building up personnel and developing improved management systems. Such involvement has enabled the owners to obtain better control over projects and reduce risk.[17]

Every project has (or should have) its owner: the agency or organization that carries the project on its budget and whose strategic plans include the project as an essential building block for future growth or

---

[15] William B. Foxhall, "Professional Construction Management and Project Administration," *Architectural Record,* March 1972, pp. 57–58.

[16] *Improving Quality and the Assurance of Quality in the Design and Construction of Nuclear Power Plants,* U.S. Nuclear Regulatory Commission, NUREG-1055, Washington, D.C., May 1984, pp. 2–17. (Emphasis added.)

[17] Theodore Barry & Associates, *A Survey of Organizational and Contractual Trends in Power Plant Construction,* Washington, D.C., March 1979.

survival. The project owner has the residual responsibility to approve and maintain oversight of the project during its life cycle. The project owner should be more than a corporation or a government agency. Rather the project owner should be identified by name, an individual recognized as the personal owner who assumes managerial oversight of the project as an element of future strategies.

Project owners can come from within the organization, such as

- A senior manager who budgets for a product or process development project

- A division profit-center manager who funds an R&D project to support a product improvement program

- A manufacturing manager who is converting a traditional factory to an automated, flexible manufacturing system

Outside project owners usually contract for the project work through architects, engineers, and constructors. The Department of Defense contracts for substantially all the work involved in designing, engineering, and manufacturing weapon systems. In the electric utility industry, many investor-owned utilities do not design and construct their own generating facilities, but hire architects, engineers, and constructors to perform most of the work. However, other utilities, such as Duke Power and Pacific Gas & Electric, perform a substantial portion of the design and construction for major projects in-house.

To put it simply, the project owner is the one who puts up the money to fund the project. On such a project funder rests the responsibility to see that those funds are used in a prudent and reasonable fashion. This requires adequate assessment of the project risk, project plans, and ongoing monitoring, evaluation, and control of the resources used on the project. Furthermore, an owner's decision to fund a project affects a variety of "stakeholders" who have, or believe they have, a stake in the project and its outcome. In some cases some of these stakeholders will seek legal redress if the project does not meet their particular expectations. Emerging case law establishes that project managers have the legal responsibility for the strategic management of projects.[18] These stakeholders and their predilections are discussed in Chapter 6.

Project owner's involvement on large construction contracts can range from total divestiture to total internal control of a project. One of the major growth areas of large international contractors such as

---

[18] For a more thorough analysis see Randall L. Speck, "The Buck Stops Here: The Owner's Legal and Practical Responsibility for Strategic Project Management," *Project Management Journal,* September 1988, pp. 45–52.

Fluor, Bechtel, and Parsons has been the implementation of large projects on behalf of an owner.[19] Blanchard suggests some broad generalities to define the responsibilities of the contractor, manager, and owner, as shown in Table 4.2.

Hansen describes several reasons for the success of a project for the construction of a facility for Republic Steel Corporation in Cleveland, Ohio:

- The intimate involvement of the owner with the planning and execution of the project

- A comprehensive feasibility study of the project during the strategic planning phase

- Ongoing project planning, coordination, and review

- The teamwork resulting from focusing on one clear-cut objective

- Commitment by the owner to support technical design decisions, project management objectives, and modern project management techniques[20]

Hansen's concluding comment charges project owners with a key responsibility: to make sure that the project will be managed by a solid team and that project management principles are known by all members of the project team.[21]

A landmark study of the design and construction of nuclear power plants found that deep involvement by utilities (owners) in cost, schedule, productivity, and quality considerations contributed to project success as much as close management oversight of the project and the project's contractors.[22]

Project success depends on a commitment by the owner to use contemporaneous project management theory and practice. Support of the enterprise mission comes about through the project owner's effective discharge of her or his strategic planning and management responsibility.

Successful project management depends on senior enterprise management for authority, strategic guidance, and support. Senior man-

---

[19]F. L. Blanchard, "Contracted Management—Clarifying the Roles of Owner and Manager," *Project Management Quarterly*, June 1983, pp. 41–46.

[20]Soren Hansen, "An Owner's Perception of Project Management," *1982 Proceedings*, Project Management Institute: III-J.1 to J.9.

[21]Ibid., III-J.9.

[22]*Improving Quality and the Assurance of Quality in the Design and Construction of Nuclear Power Plants*, Nuclear Regulatory Commission, Washington, May 1984, pp. 3–15.

TABLE 4.2   Contractor, Manager, and Owner Responsibilities

Contractor	
Engineering	1. Prepare detail design drawings.
	2. Prepare fabrication drawings for piping, structural steel, and concrete reinforcing.
	3. Prepare purchase specifications.
	4. Review vendor shop drawings.
	5. Prepare as-built drawings.
	6. Provide drawings and sketches as required for field crews.
Finance/ Procurement	1. Prepare progress invoices.
	2. Purchase materials and supplies.
	3. Maintain payrolls and records.
	4. Develop and submit changes as appropriate.
Construction	1. Plan and schedule plant and personnel.
	2. Supervise craft and labor crews.
	3. Operate and maintain construction equipment.
	4. Resolve labor disputes.
	5. Maintain clean and safe worksite.

Manager	
Engineering	1. Review contractor drawings for conformance to standards and job specifications.
	2. Interpret standards and specifications.
	3. Review vendor technical proposals for conformance to standards and specifications.
	4. Review and approve contractor quality assurance and quality control program.
	5. Inspect vendor supplied material.
Finance/ Procurement	1. Review and approve contractor progress payments.
	2. Review change requests. Prepare estimates and negotiate change settlements.
	3. Review and approve contractor and subcontractor financial qualifications.
	4. Prepare expenditure forecasts and other financial statements of job condition.
Construction	1. Inspect workmanship for conformance to drawings and specifications.
	2. Interpret specifications.
	3. Review contractor progress.
	4. Monitor contractor performance against contract requirements.

agers in turn depend on project managers for timely, cost-effective achievement of project results to support corporate strategy. Project management is a form of "strategic delegation" whereby senior managers delegate to project managers the authority and responsibility to do such things as building capital facilities, introducing new products, conducting research and development, and creating new marketing and production opportunities.

TABLE 4.2   (Continued)

	Owner
Engineering	1. Provide design basis and establish standards.
	2. Provide soil and other data.
	3. Resolve conflicts in interpretation of standards and specifications.
Finance/	1. Provide funds for the work.
Procurement	2. Identify any special material requirements or preferred equipment or vendors.
	3. Provide owner required insurance and indemnity.
	4. Approve changes.
Construction	1. Provide side and access.
	2. Obtain permits.
	3. Arrange utilities.

SOURCE: F. L. Blanchard, "Contracted Management—Clarifying the Roles of Owner and Manager," *Project Management Quarterly,* June 1983, pp. 42–43.

Project management also is a type of strategic management control. Senior managers can use project management as a way to ensure that key strategies are accomplished in an effective manner. A senior manager oversees the strategic direction of the enterprise by providing resources to accomplish the mission, objectives, goals, and strategies. By determining the success or failure of a project, senior management ensures that control systems are instituted to track strategic progress of the enterprise. As project managers make and execute key decisions, these key decisions should be reviewed by senior managers to determine if the decisions are consistent with corporate strategy. Senior enterprise managers commit a serious breach of responsibility and accountability for the management of the enterprise when they ignore or accept key project decisions without review. When adequate project evaluation is carried out to determine project success, senior managers get information on how effectively enterprise strategies are being implemented.

In order for the owner to do a credible job of measuring project success, several conditions must exist:

- An appropriate organizational design is in place which delineates the formal authority, responsibility, and accountability relationships among the enterprise corporate senior managers, project manager, functional manager, and work package managers.

- Adequate strategic and project planning has been carried out within the enterprise.

- Relevant and timely information is available that gives insight into the project status.

- Adequate management monitoring, evaluation, and control systems exist.

- Contemporary state-of-the-art management techniques are used in the management of the project.

- A supportive cultural ambience exists that facilitates the successful management of projects.

An important part of the strategic management of a project is to carry out such management in the context of a project management system.

Project Management System

Once the mission of the enterprise is established through the operation of a strategic planning system, planning can be extended to select and develop organizational objectives, goals, and strategies. Projects are planned for and implemented through a *project management system* composed of the following subsystems.[23]

The *facilitative organizational subsystem* is the organizational arrangement that is used to superimpose the project teams on the functional structure. The resulting "matrix" organization portrays the formal authority and responsibility patterns and the personal reporting relationships, with the goal of providing an organizational focal point for starting and completing specific projects. Two complementary organizational units tend to emerge in such an organizational context: the project team and the functional units.

The *project control subsystem* provides for the selection of performance standards for the project schedule, budget, and technical performance. The subsystem compares actual progress with planned progress, with the initiation of corrective action as required. The rationale for a control subsystem arises out of the need to monitor the various organizational units that are performing work on the project in order to deliver results on time and within budget.

The *project management information subsystem* contains the information essential to effective control of the projects. This subsystem may be informal in nature, consisting of periodic meetings with the project participants who report information on the status of their project work, or a formal information retrieval system that provides frequent printouts of what is going on. This subsystem provides the data to enable the project team members to make and implement decisions in the management of the project.

---

[23] David I. Cleland, "Defining a Project Management System," *Project Management Quarterly,* vol. 10, no. 4, 1977, pp. 37–40.

Techniques and methodology is not really a subsystem in the sense that the term is used here. This subsystem is merely a set of techniques and methodologies, such as PERT, CPM, PERT-Cost, and related scheduling techniques, as well as other management science techniques which can be used to evaluate the risk and uncertainty factors in making project decisions.

The *cultural ambience subsystem* is the subsystem in which project management is practiced in the organization. Much of the nature of the cultural ambience can be described in how the people—the social groups—feel about the way in which project management is being carried out in the organization. The emotional patterns of the social groups, their perceptions, attitudes, prejudices, assumptions, experiences, and values, all go to develop the organization's cultural ambience. This ambience influences how people act and react, how they think and feel, and what they say in the organization, all of which ultimately determines what is taken for socially acceptable behavior in the organization.

The *planning subsystem* recognizes that project control starts with project planning, since the project plan provides the standards against which control procedures and mechanisms are measured. Project planning starts with the development of a *work breakdown structure* which shows how the total project is broken down into its component parts. Project schedules and budgets are developed, technical performance goals are selected, and organizational authority and responsibility are established for members of the project team. Project planning also involves identifying the material resources needed to support the project during its life cycle.

The *human subsystem* involves just about everything associated with the human element. An understanding of the human subsystem requires some knowledge of sociology, psychology, anthropology, communications, semantics, decision theory, philosophy, leadership, and so on. Motivation is an important consideration in the management of the project team. Project management means working with people to accomplish project objectives and goals. Project managers must find ways of putting themselves into the human subsystem of the project so that the members of the project team trust and are loyal in supporting project purposes. The artful management style that project managers develop and encourage within the peer group in the project may very well determine the success or failure of the project. Leadership is the most important role played by the project manager.

Figure 4.3 depicts the project management system in the context of a public utility commission with all its subsystems. The utility owners responsible and accountable for the effective management of the project work through their boards of directors and senior manage-

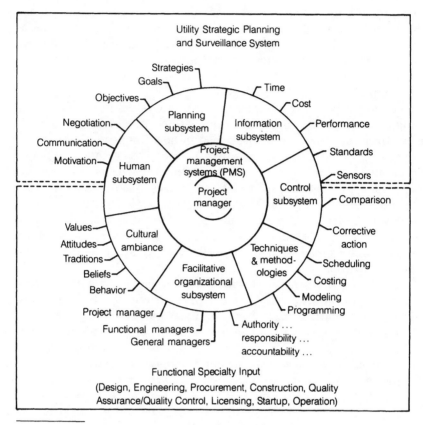

Utility Strategic Planning
and Surveillance System

Functional Specialty Input
(Design, Engineering, Procurement, Construction, Quality
Assurance/Quality Control, Licensing, Startup, Operation)

Source: Adapted from D.I. Cleland. "Defining A Project Management System." *Project Management Quarterly,* 1977, X, 4, p. 39.

Figure 4.3   The project management system.

ment with the project manager, functional managers, and functional specialists.

Two authors have suggested that three paths to market leadership can be realized by focusing on three *value* disciplines: (1) Operational excellence—providing customers with reliable products or services at competitive prices and delivered with minimal inconvenience; (2) customer intimacy—targeting markets precisely and then providing offerings that match these niches; and (3) product leadership—offering customers leading-edge products and services that constantly enhance the customer's use or application of the product.[24] Of these three value disciplines, product leadership is directly related to how

---

[24] Michael Toreacy and Fred Wiersema, "Customer Intimacy and Other Value Disciplines," *Harvard Business Review,* January-February 1993, pp. 84–93.

well the company uses a *project management system* to manage its product development activities through a project management philosophy.

Summary

Projects are key building blocks in the design and execution of strategies. The senior managers of the organization owning the project are responsible for approving and funding a project and for surveillance of a project during its life cycle. As a member of the project team, the owner should ensure that there is adequate planning for the project to include a suitable organizational design and the use of a project management system approach in the management of the project. A project management system provides a conceptual and practical model to use as a guide on how to manage the project through

- Substantive strategic planning
- A supportive culture
- Effective and efficient use of people
- Meaningful monitoring, evaluation, and control
- Contemporary techniques and methodologies
- Adequate functional specialty input

Projects must be strategically managed, always with an eye on the project's strategic fit with the organization's future. Project owners must be proactive in their selection and management of the project, regardless of whether the work is done by an in-house force or is subcontracted to outside designers, engineers, and manufacturers/constructors.

Organizational survival and growth in the competitive global marketplace depend on how well innovative ideas are captured and managed in delivering something of value in an organization's portfolio of products through the judicious management of organizational projects through their life cycles. To manage a project is to bring about the creation of something of value to customers out of someone's concept of doing something for the enterprise that has not been done before. The creation of something new by way of products through innovative organizational processes is key to coping with the inevitable change facing organizations today.

Discussion Questions

1. Discuss the importance of the strategic management of projects.

2. The chapter described one quantitative method for project selection. What are some other possible methods of project selection? What other factors can be included in the analysis?

3. Why is it important for general managers to take responsibility and accountability for the strategic fit of a project?

4. Discuss the importance of owner participation in measuring and controlling the success of a project.

5. What hinders senior management involvement in large organizational projects?

6. What kinds of questions need to be addressed in order to measure project success?

7. What contemporaneous state-of-the-art management techniques can be used to help control and measure project success?

8. Discuss the responsibilities of project owners with respect to strategic planning and management.

9. Discuss the importance of establishing policies that describe the organizational structure and the authority, responsibility, and accountability of managers within the structure.

10. List and define the various subsystems of the project management system.

User Checklist

1. Are the projects within your organization being managed from a strategic perspective? Why or why not?

2. What quantitative and qualitative methods does your organization use for project selection?

3. Does the top management of your organization accept the responsibility for determining the strategic fit of projects?

4. Does the top management of your organization accept the responsibility for monitoring the cost, time, and technical performance objectives of major projects?

5. How do the senior managers of your organization monitor the ongoing progress of major projects?

6. Do the key project managers use state-of-the-art management techniques to control the projects of the organization?

7. Are organizational projects being managed from a project management system perspective?

8. Does the top management of your organization accept the responsibility to develop and implement adequate strategic plans for the enterprise and for projects?

9. Are there adequate information systems available to support managers and professionals working on various organizational projects?

10. Does appropriate policy exist which defines the organizational structure and the fixing of authority, responsibility, and accountability of managers at each organizational level?

11. Does the top management of your organization foster an attitude that supports the management of projects?

5

The Board of Directors and Capital Projects[1]

"There is plenty of substantive evidence that '...too many corporate boards fail to do their jobs.'"

WALTER J. SALMON, "CRISIS PREVENTION: HOW TO
GEAR UP YOUR BOARD," *HARVARD BUSINESS REVIEW,*
JANUARY-FEBRUARY 1993, P. 68.

Boards of directors have been used in the business community for over 150 years. State general corporation laws require that all business corporations have boards, typically stipulating that the corporation "shall be managed by a board of at least three directors."

Once a project is funded and corporate resources are expanded to design, develop, and construct or manufacture the project, it becomes an important responsibility of the board to maintain surveillance over the efficiency and effectiveness with which corporate strategy is being implemented through the use of capital projects.

Surveillance

By maintaining surveillance over the status of major product and process projects within the enterprise, senior managers—to include

---

[1]This chapter is an extension of the paper "Capital Projects: The Role of the Board of Directors," presented at the PMI 1988 Annual Seminar/Symposium in San Francisco and published in the *1988 Proceedings,* September 1988, pp. 8–12. Appreciation is extended to Attorney Randall L. Speck, of Rogovin, Huge & Schiller, Washington, D.C., and Attorney Edward O'Neill, of the California Public Utilities Commission, for their helpful guidance in the preparation of this chapter.

members of the board of directors—can gain valuable insight into the effectiveness with which the enterprise is preparing for its future. There are, of course, limits to the number of projects that such managers can monitor; there are, however, certain projects whose outcomes can have major impact on the organization's future direction. Senior managers should review the adequacy of the planning for these projects and keep abreast of which projects are being executed to further corporate purposes. The projects in which the directors should be particularly interested include

- New-product and process development projects which have the promise of giving the company a competitive advantage in the marketplace. Projects which contain the possibilities of technological breakthroughs, or significant incremental improvements in products, and processes, should be of particular interest to the directors.

- Projects whose execution requires the commitment of substantial resources, such as the building of new facilities, or the development of major supporting organizational resources, such as restructuring or downsizing initiatives.

- Projects which are the outgrowth of a strategic alliance being negotiated for the sharing of resources, results, and rewards with another organizational entity. Research consortia, sharing of manufacturing facilities, and marketing facilities are some common examples.

- Other projects for supporting the strategic purposes of the firms such as major cost reduction initiatives; new major, corporatewide information systems; and investment opportunities.

When the directors accept the concept that projects are building blocks in the design and execution of organizational strategies, the directors gain the use of an important strategic management tool—the inventory of product and process projects under way in the enterprise. As the corporate directors sense competitive changes in the marketplace, or realize that new technological initiatives are coming forth from the research of competitors, or recognize any other major change in the enterprise's future, they need to ask a key question: What projects are under way in the company to meet—and exceed—these competitive threats coming out of the firm's environmental and competition system? If relevant product or process projects are not under way, then the firm's competitive position will be threatened, and projects to position the enterprise to meet these changes need to be undertaken in a forthright manner. If the directors become involved in regular and rigorous review of these important projects, an important message will be sent throughout the company: Projects are important to this company, for it is through projects that we are able to organize our resources to position ourselves for the uncertain future.[2]

Why have some boards overseeing capital projects not carried out their responsibilities? This chapter will attempt to answer this question by examining the role of the board of directors in respect to the strategic management of projects. To gain insight into why many boards seem to have been so ineffectual, the activities of several boards will be discussed. Then some constructive ideas will be offered about what the role, the information required, the actions, and the background of the board members should be.

Some Board Inadequacies

The problem of board inadequacies has been fairly widespread. Examples of where boards have not done their jobs well are easy to find in the business literature. Perhaps no other directors have so poorly served their owners as those in the banking industry.

The financial problems of thrifts continue to pose a threat to the financial health of the United States. The pace of losses continues to indicate that the government will continue to have trouble dealing with its huge liability in this area.

A recent survey of 2235 commercial bank CEOs reported in *Directors and Boards* found that "Boards of directors are surprisingly unimportant.... A solid majority of bank boards are *not* active contributors to the strategic success of their banks."[2] The passivity of the board at BankAmerica was noted during the difficult times that the bank went through.[3]

The Court of Appeals for the U.S. Ninth Circuit held that directors of a savings and loan could be sued for triple damages by a disappointed shareholder under the Racketeering Influenced and Corrupt Organizations (RICO) Act. The shareholder claimed that he was misled by the S&L's corporate reports, press releases, and offering circulars and that the directors should be held responsible. The court agreed. Under this ruling, directors can be individually responsible for "group-published information" about the company that could mislead or defraud shareholders. This principle has serious ramifications for corporate directors, who may be held account-

---

[2] David I. Cleland, "The Board of Directors and Projects," *pmNETwork,* January 1991, pp. 6–7.

[3] "BankAmerica Board: A Study in Inertia," *Los Angeles Times,* September 7, 1986, p. 2.

able for overly optimistic projections for a project's success or for failure to warn shareholders of impending problems.[4]

At General Motors, Roger Smith, CEO, kept the board of directors on a "very short leash" from 1981 to 1990. He withheld key financial data and budget allocation proposals until the day before meetings, and sometimes he distributed them minutes before the participants convened. The monthly meetings were carefully structured—Smith adjourned them promptly at 5 minutes before noon, leaving little time for discussions. Three of the fifteen members of the board owed Smith their jobs; another four had little or no business experience. By 1987, however, evidence of Roger Smith's mismanagement and GM's decline could not be ignored; when Smith tried to pack the board with three more insiders, the directors said no. After Stempel took office on August 1, 1990, several outside directors soon realized that they had made a mistake. Stempel, out of loyalty to old friends and old ways, was slow to make changes. He concentrated on the engineering and manufacturing of GM cars and trucks, an area in which he had made his name, but he seemed oblivious to organizational, cost, and marketing issues. Stempel's repeated admonitions for patience wore thin. Finally in the spring of 1992, the board revived its inactive executive committee and replaced Stempel with retired Procter & Gamble CEO John Smale as its head. A supplier who knows GM intimately said that "Stempel is a dynamite engineer, but he should never have made it to the top of the ladder. He was promoted past the point where he could do the company any good. Just fast-tracking to the next level doesn't help the company."[5]

The problems and strategic issues facing General Motors have been reported in detail in business periodicals. Out of the challenges facing GM have come a few lessons about the management of corporate America. Alex Taylor, writing in *Business Week,* has drawn up a few ideas about such lessons:

1. Corporate management cannot hide.

2. Directors can no longer take their responsibilities lightly.

3. Boards must move more decisively and in a more timely fashion.

4. Troubled companies are finding it advantageous to split the job of chair and CEO.

---

[4]James Leigland, "WPPSS: Some Basic Lessons for Public Enterprise Managers," *California Management Review,* Winter 1987, pp. 78–88.

[5]Alex Taylor, III, "What's Ahead for GM's New Team," *Fortune,* November 30, 1992, pp. 58–61.

5. The role of the board member is being redefined.[6]

In another industry, a court decision in 1985 sent tremors through the boardrooms. Ruling on a shareholder suit, the Delaware State Supreme Court found the board members of Trans Union Corporation personally liable for damages. The judges held that the directors were negligent when, in a 2-hour meeting dominated by the CEO, they agreed to sell the railcar leasing company to the Pritzker family's Marmon Group without first seeking independent counsel.[7]

On the Trans-Alaska Pipeline System (TAPS), the individual oil companies who owned the project formed an owner's committee to maintain oversight of the TAPS project. In addition, an owner's construction committee was established to administer the contract with Alyeska, the agent for the owners and their designated project manager. This committee, which was to act much in the manner of a board of directors, did not focus adequately on the strategic decision making on the TAPS project. Its members also improperly intervened in day-to-day operating decisions. A review of the record of this committee indicated little resolution of substantive strategic issues on the project, such as

1. The development of a master strategic plan for the project
2. Early integrated life-cycle project planning
3. Design and implementation of a project management information system
4. Development of an effective control system for the project
5. Design of a suitable organization[8]

Controversy continues to surround the management of the Trans-Alaska pipeline. Quality control inspectors for the consortium that oversees the pipeline have claimed that intimidation of inspectors has played a major role in how such inspectors did their jobs. Other inspectors found that their efforts to build a surveillance system that complied with the Alyeska Pipeline Service Company's own quality control manual met stiff resistance. Other accusations include the

---

[6] Paraphrased from Judith H. Dobrzynski, "A GM Postmortem: Lessons for Corporate America," *Business Week,* November 9, 1992, p. 87.

[7] Stratford P. Sherman, *Fortune,* July 18, 1988, pp. 58–67. © 1988, Time, Inc. All rights reserved.

[8] David I. Cleland, Prepared direct closing testimony, Trans-Alaska Pipeline System, Alaska Public Utilities Commission, Federal Energy Regulatory Commission, Washington, October 19, 1984.

reduction in the number of inspectors as well as the quality of the documentation available to them to do their jobs. Also, some of the inspectors were told to stop reporting quality problems via official channels because it was making the projects group "look bad."[9]

Too many corporate boards are overpopulated with members of management. Inside directors tend to be committed to the way things have always been done and to their own ideas. Outside directors often have insufficient information about the company, and in too many situations, they receive information concerning the matters scheduled for a board meeting only shortly before the board is convened. In practice, when the CEO encourages board members to meet with senior company managers on a regular basis, outside of the formal board meetings, this increases the likelihood that the outside directors will be able to have a fuller grasp of what is really going on in the company.

The nuclear industry is another striking example of the laxity of the directors. In the nuclear industry all too many utilities have boards that have neglected to exercise "reasonable and prudent" strategic management in their oversight of nuclear power plant projects. As a result, administrative courts have disallowed substantial costs from inclusion in the customer rate base for the utility. In many cases, a failure of the board to participate in key decisions has set the stage for the major difficulties later in the project's life cycle.

The clear responsibility and accountability of the board of directors can be demonstrated by reviewing a few key litigation conclusions drawn from the nuclear power industry.

- Cincinnati Gas & Electric Company reached a $14 million settlement in a shareholder suit that charged directors and officers with improper disclosure concerning a nuclear power plant.

- The Washington Public Power Supply System (WPPSS) defaulted on interest payments due on $2.5 billion in outstanding bonds in part because of the failure of its directors. Communication at the senior levels of the organization, including that of the board of directors, tended to be "informal, disorganized, and infrequent."

- On the Long Island Lighting Company Shoreham project, the public utility commission determined that "The company should be able to show that its directors...were attentive to the project's progress, and aggressively pursued cost containment measures

---

[9]Allanna Sullivan, "Alaska Pipeline Gets `Sham' Safety Checks, Former Workers Say," *Wall Street Journal,* August 4, 1992.

wherever there were reasonable opportunities to do so."[10] Noting the small proportion of board minutes devoted to addressing the Shoreham project, the commission remarked on the "lack of urgency in the board's approach to the project's large cost escalations." The commission also was concerned with the board's "lack of involvement" regarding the critical decision to replace the project's construction management firm. In addition, it found that "prudence dictated that the board carefully examine management's plan and its potential consequences."[11]

■ On another nuclear project in the state of Washington, the Washington Utilities and Transportation Commission determined that a number of ominous external occurrences should have caused the officers and directors of the Puget Sound Power and Light Company to call for an in-depth cost-effectiveness study, something they neglected to do.[12] In a separate opinion, one of the commissioners elaborated:

> It is clear the deficiency extends to the company's board of directors. Board minutes...provide no indication that Puget's board either was informed of the magnitude of the problem by management or on its own motion requested management to study the economic consequences of continued investment in the...plant.[13]

■ In a review of the role of the board of directors of the Diablo Canyon project, an expert witness testified that the board's decisions and actions were either limited or nonexistent in regard to several key decisions and actions. These included the approval of a strategic project plan and the decision that the company act as its own architect and its own engineering and construction manager. Furthermore, the board did not give proper attention to the choice of a basic organizational design for the project, nor to the implications of the discovery made during the construction of the plant that there was a major earthquake fault in close proximity to the plant. Nor did the directors make a full assessment of the flawed quality assurance and control procedures that led to major design deficiencies in the plant. The board also had too little to say about

---

[10]*Long Island Lighting Company,* 71 Pub. Util. Rep. 4th 262 (N.Y.P.S.C. 1985).

[11] Ibid. p. 273.

[12] *Washington Utilities & Transportation Commission (WUTC)* v. *Puget Sound Power & Light Co.,* 62 Pub. Util. Rep. 4th 557 (WUTC 1984).

[13] Ibid., p. 598.

the selection of a project manager and constructor in the final phases of the plant's construction.[14]

At key decision points in that project, the board of directors' role was little more than that of a passive onlooker. The failure of this board to insist upon thorough information and its inaction in the face of serious problems confronting the project were incautious, far from what one would expect a "reasonable and prudent board" to carry out.

In this same case it was found that from the very outset, the board's role as deficient in overseeing the selection of the plant site. The selection was not even considered by the board but was relegated to the chief executive officer's advisory committee, a top-level executive body whose authority was purely advisory. Although this committee evaluated the site for the nuclear plant, it was done during one of their regular meetings along with nineteen other agenda items, allowing only 5 minutes per item on average. Later, during the construction of the plant, an earthquake fault was found offshore, and it caused the Nuclear Regulatory Commission to order a redesign of the plant to bring the plant up to a higher earthquake design configuration. The redesign of the plant and the subsequent reconstruction increased the total cost of the plant by approximately $1.4 billion.

It is clear that the boards of the various nuclear projects mentioned above could have helped to reduce their project's problems or reduce the threats that faced their projects by careful, informed involvement in key project matters on a regular basis.

Exemplary Board Behavior

The inadequacies of those boards mentioned up to this point reflect a pattern of inactivity and of ignorance concerning the problems and threats that buffeted the projects. It is clear that the boards of the various projects, nuclear and otherwise, could have helped to reduce their problems and the associated threats that faced their projects by careful, informed involvement in key matters on a regular basis. This has been done on some nuclear plant projects. For example, the Pennsylvania Power and Light Company's board of directors played an active role on the Susquehanna nuclear plant project, as stated in a letter to the author:

> Our Board of Directors was kept abreast of project activities on a monthly basis. The project issued a monthly report to the Board prior to their

---

[14]David I. Cleland, Rebuttal testimony Diablo Canyon project, California Public Utilities Commission, Division of Ratepayer Advocate, Application Nos. 84-06-014 & 85-08-025, San Francisco, June 20, 1988.

meetings. The Project Director was then available at the Board meeting to discuss the report. In addition, for several of the critical construction years, the Board held an expanded meeting at the plant site annually. This permitted Board members to view progress firsthand and permitted additional nuclear topics to be included in the agenda.

The monthly reviews...also served as the regular, integrated review of the project by the project manager/project team. These reviews included senior management from our engineer/constructor...Senior representation from the reactor manufacturer was also present when appropriate. These meetings focused on performance and progress and highlighted issues significant to management. The reporting of progress and performance was an integrated team effort.

This plant earned high marks from the Nuclear Regulatory Commission in its latest Systematic Assessment of Licensee Performance (SALP). Susquehanna earned the highest rating possible in 9 of 11 categories and the second highest rating in the remaining two areas. This gave Susquehanna the second-highest average rating of all nuclear reactors in this country.[15]

There are other examples of good board review. On the $2.1 billion Milwaukee Water Pollution Abatement Program initiated in 1977, a comprehensive review of the status of the projects in that program is conducted on a monthly basis by the owner's senior managers. The program manager is present to explain the program's status and to answer any questions posed by these senior managers. The senior managers, in turn, keep the board of commissioners of the Milwaukee Metropolitan Sewerage District informed on a regular basis. This complex, high-visibility program, which has held the attention of many stakeholders during its life cycle, is on schedule and close to the original project budget estimates. The continued review by the senior managers and the commissioners is a major reason this project has been successful.

Some corporations have special meetings of the board to deal with major capital projects in the corporation's strategic plans. Besides providing more concentrated time for discussion on the projects, the social events of such meetings provide the opportunity for the directors to learn about the capability and knowledge of the senior corporate executives as well as something of the credentials of the other directors.

The Board's Responsibilities

Directors are the representatives of the owners of the corporation. Boards often move glacially, if at all, in designing and developing the

---

[15] PP&L Shareowners' Newsletter, July 1, 1988.

strategic management initiatives for the enterprise. Companies can become noncompetitive and dwindle, often without any intervention initiatives encouraged by the directors. Today increasingly impatient owners, representing such groups as government officials, shareholder activities, and institutional investors, are taking the lead in evaluating and changing the attitudes of investors.

The corporate governance system may be in place—the senior managers of the enterprise and the directors to provide the strategic direction for the enterprise. But these officials, failing to set and follow up on the strategic initiative of the enterprise, often set the game plan unknowingly for corporate decline, leading to failure. Leadership is a critical function for individual and collective roles in discharging the director's functions.[16]

Directors exercise a special kind of management surveillance. Although generally not concerned with short-term operational matters, directors should be alert to *any* problems and opportunities that are significant to the long-term performance of the company, such as profitability trends, competitive threats, increased costs, loss of future business opportunities, loss of market share, regulatory changes, and quality problems. Observation of any of these problems should alert the directors to the need for an investigation or audit of the company's strategies. Such an audit should determine whether the corporation's strategies have been designed to cope with these difficulties and what the possible and probable long-term impact of the current operations would be.

The directors should expect the corporation's senior managers to manage the organization's resources in a reasonable and prudent manner. Why should any less be expected of the directors themselves? Although their involvement in the corporate affairs is necessarily much broader, the directors need to determine to what extent the senior managers are executing their own responsibilities in the planning, organizing, and control of corporate resources. In other words, the directors are still managers in the truest sense of the word. As managers, they should be expected to perform as any other senior manager, differing only in degree. Because corporate resources are at stake, commissions or omissions at the corporate level are vastly more serious than at lower levels in the organization.

The directors are the "most senior" managers in the corporation; they should set an example for reasonable and prudent management on the part of the corporate senior managers who are concerned with the strategic planning and operational effectiveness and effi-

---

[16]Paraphrased from Myron Magnet, "Directors, Wake Up," *Fortune,* June 15, 1992, pp. 85–92.

ciency of the corporation. To accomplish this, the directors must demand high performance from the senior managers by ensuring that strategic planning and surveillance are carried out in the corporation, and that efficient and effective operational performance is realized.

Corporate strategy is clearly one key responsibility of the corporate board of directors. Strategy, according to Chandler, is "the determination of the basic long-term goals and objectives of an enterprise, and the adoption of courses of action and allocation of resources necessary for carrying out these goals."[17]

The New Governance

Directors are becoming more proactive in discharging their fiduciary responsibilities on the company's board of directors. At Westinghouse Electric, major losses caused key stakeholders to call for major reform in the way the corporation was being managed. One group of individual investors, the United Shareholders Association, filed four shareholder resolutions with Westinghouse, including one that asked the independent directors to evaluate the company's strategy and leadership. The strategy of the company to install a series of measures to entrench management has been questioned. The Westinghouse board of directors is perceived as being passive and doesn't even have a nominating committee. Both the United Shareholders and the New York City Teachers' Retirement System have asked for the creation of a nominating committee of outside directors.[18]

Many students of corporate governance are searching for the means to improve the board of director's management of the enterprise. The boardroom coup at General Motors and the working together of shareholders and management at Westinghouse Electric are heartening, for they show how large companies can be changed without hostile takeovers and without the pain that accompanies such takeovers. At Westinghouse, a series of reforms have been instituted: A board committee made up of outside directors exclusively will oversee director nominations and corporate governance matters. An independent compensation committee has been created with its own consultants. The board at Westinghouse has been further reformed so that all directors are elected annually; ensure full confidentiality in shareholder voting, and adopt a bylaw mandating that a majority of the board be made

[17]Alfred D. Chandler, Jr., *Strategy and Structure: Chapters in the History of the Industrial Enterprise,* (Cambridge, Mass.: MIT Press, 1962), p. 13.

[18]Judith H. Dobrzynski, Michael Schroeder, and Stephen Baker, "The Rebels Are Banging on Westinghouse's Boardroom Door," *Business Week,* November 16, 1992, p. 48.

up of independent, outside directors. Out of the lessons learned from the General Motors and Westinghouse experiences is a growing realization that the U.S. corporate governance process is now achieving a refreshing balance of power with shareholders playing meaningful oversight roles.[19]

The responsibility of the directors to see that a proper corporate strategy has been developed is addressed by Andrews, a notable authority on the role of directors. He states, "A responsible and effective board should require of its management a unique and durable corporate strategy, review it periodically for its validity, use it as the reference point for all other board decisions, and share with management the risks associated with its adoption."[20] Strategies include a delineation of corporate means to support capital projects. Although the board is not expected to work out corporate strategy, it is the board's duty to ensure that senior managers have a strategy for the company. Strategies include a delineation of corporate means to fund and support capital projects.

The Role of Projects

In 1968, a landmark study of the practices of senior management in leading industrial corporations noted the responsibilities of directors for project management. The study was conducted by Paul Holden and several members of the faculty at the Graduate School of Business at Stanford University. Their findings established that project management was an important factor in overall enterprise management. The study further found that the high-level committee (such as the board of directors) was widely used as a valuable organizational design to

1. Establish broad policies

2. Coordinate line and technical management

3. Render collective judgments on the evaluation of corporate undertakings

4. Conduct periodic review and monitoring of ongoing programs and projects[21]

---

[19] Paraphrased from John Pound, "Westinghouse Lights Boardroom Path," *Wall Street Journal,* December 11, 1992.

[20] Reprinted by permission of the *Harvard Business Review.* Excerpt from Kenneth R. Andrews, "Director's Responsibility for Corporate Strategy," *Harvard Business Review,* November-December 1980, p. 30. Copyright © 1980 by the President and Fellow's of Harvard College; all rights reserved.

[21] Paul E. Holden, et al., *Top Management* (New York: McGraw-Hill, 1968), pp. 6, 71–74, 108–109.

Major projects are key building blocks in the design and execution of corporate strategy. This is a fundamental principle all too often missed by key corporate managers and directors. Project management is not recognized for what it is: *a process for the creation of something that does not currently exist but is needed to support future corporate purposes.* When perceptive directors recognize the intertwining of projects and corporate strategies, project management takes on a new significance in the management of the corporation. Unfortunately, some directors have not recognized this fundamental principle.

Lack of plans for the corporation's future is an indication of board ineptitude. As Louden states, "The fact that many companies' plans for the future are either nonexistent or committed to paper only is another example of board ineptitude. The board and management cannot leave a company's future to chance; it must not only plan it, but then make it happen."[22]

Before the project starts, the board should take action to require that a project plan be developed and presented for its review. Why should a board concern itself with the plan for projects? Several principal reasons are suggested:

1. The board needs specific evidence that corporate managers have a planned process for managing projects.

2. The project plan provides a performance standard against which project progress can be evaluated as the directors carry out their strategic monitoring, evaluating, and control responsibilities.

3. If the project team, project manager, and responsible general managers know that the board will review the project plan, a clear message will reverberate through the organization: This project is important.

4. Knowing the project plan can help to give the board a reference point for other key corporate decisions which interface with the capital project such as recapitalization issues, product introduction plans, and support facilities.

5. The evaluation of the project plan and of management's adherence to it allows continual evaluation of key managers.

In some cases a committee of the board, such as the executive committee, is given the authority to act for the full board. Such a delegation without adequate monitoring by the outside directors can have a deleterious effect, particularly if the executive committee's deliberations are not reviewed or are accepted with only minimal questioning.

---

[22]J. Keith Louden, "The Board Audit," *Directors and Boards,* Winter 1977, p. 23.

Even with an active and component executive committee, the board should reserve for itself a regular review of capital projects. Such reviews should include discussions of the cost and schedule of the project and future strategies for the resolution of any problems known or anticipated on the project.

In their concern for the review of capital projects, the directors should not forget their responsibility to oversee the ways that the general and senior managers maintain surveillance over the projects. Senior managers are expected to demonstrate reasonable foresight in anticipating needs for state-of-the-art project management processes and techniques. The general manager of the owner of the project, working with other managers, establishes appropriate objectives, goals, and strategies; resource allocation plans; policies; procedures; performance standards; and information systems, to provide feedback in order to compare actual results with planned results. The corporate president has the responsibility to delegate authority and the accountability to appropriate senior managers to support both the corporate and the project purposes.

The existence of projects in organizations is one clear indication that the organization is changing and is attempting to meet changing future environments. This is a key point not to be missed by senior managers and directors.

The Organizational Design

An important part of corporate strategy is an appropriate organizational design for the implementation of strategy. Koontz states that "although the board need not be concerned with detailed company organization planning or changes, it should reserve to itself final approval of the *basic* company organizational pattern and major authority delegation.[23] The directors should ensure that an appropriate organizational design is in place for the project. The design should delineate the formal authority, responsibility, and accountability relationships among the senior managers, project manager, functional managers, and work package managers of the enterprise.

Russell D. Archibald, an expert witness evaluating a utility's nuclear plant project organization in a rate case litigation, found serious deficiencies in one utility's project organization and staffing. His findings were

- The absence of a true project manager
- Inadequate planning and control supporting staff

---

[23]Harold Koontz, *The Board of Directors and Effective Management* (New York: McGraw-Hill, 1967), p. 65.

- Lack of definition of responsibilities and inadequate policies and procedures for fulfilling assigned responsibilities[24]

These deficiencies were found to contribute to schedule delays and cost overruns on this project.

Capital projects can contribute to the success (or failure) of the organization. Capital projects must be reviewed on a regular basis by the board as a way of ascertaining the effectiveness with which progress is being made toward a successful future.

Project Reviews

Directors and senior managers who clearly recognize their responsibilities should feel the need to regularly review projects along with other major organizational activities. Why should the board concern itself with review of the capital projects? The board needs specific information that the projects are being designed and developed according to plan and in support of corporate strategies. By reviewing the projects on a regular basis, an important message is sent throughout the organization that projects are important to the survival and growth of the organization.

Then, too, knowing the status of the projects can give the board a reference point for the review of management actions and recommendations that are interdependent with the other projects and strategies in the organization's strategy. Directors will gain an appreciation of the underpinnings of strategy such as policies, resource commitments, and executive and professional development to support the company's strategies along with its capital projects. By having the directors insist that the company have a strategy and a management philosophy for capital project review, another mechanism is in place for facilitating the continuous evaluation of senior managers.

Some projects reach the point where their continuation does not make sense for the organization. Because of the vested interest that the project manager and the project team have in the project, they are in the least logical position to recommend termination of the project. But total reliance on the senior managers to do this evaluation is not sufficient because the board is the corporate conscience to make an independent evaluation of where the project stands within corporate strategy. Therefore, both senior managers and directors are the most appropriate decision makers to recommend termination of the project.

---

[24]Russell D. Archibald, testimony on project management, Diablo Canyon rate case, California Public Utilities Commission, San Francisco, Exhibit no. 11, 175, March 1987.

How is the project review best done? Here is a prescription to guide directors' surveillance of capital projects:

1. Accept a philosophy that projects are indeed basic building blocks in the design and execution of corporate strategies, requiring ongoing strategic management and surveillance.

2. Conduct a formal review of the strategic plan for the project to determine if appropriate technology is planned and if suitable management systems are in place to keep abreast of the project by all the principal managers.

3. Require special briefings on the project during key periods of the project's life cycle, such as finalization of design, commitment to construction or prototype manufacturing, design reviews, engineering completion, preliminary customer acceptance, or delivery of the first production unit.

4. Go out and "kick the tires." Use plant or construction site visits to observe firsthand what is really happening on the project.

5. Insist that the project manager (and the responsible general manager) appear before the board on a regular basis to give a status report on the project.

6. Question and question again any funding changes on the project to ascertain what caused the change and what the longer-term impact would be.

7. Carefully deliberate on what information the board needs to do its job on capital projects, and relate this information to the major decisions or actions that require board scrutiny.

8. If things on the project are not fitting together well, or if major questions and issues are emerging for which answers are not forthcoming, consider a performance audit of the project.

The foregoing list hints at overtones of interference with senior management responsibilities. Perhaps so. But as one reviews some of the major project failures of the recent past, a clear message comes through; most of these failures can be attributed to the failure of senior management *and* the board of directors to follow some of the basic "commonsense" prescriptions just outlined. What is the cost of not following these commonsense principles? Imprudent financial performance, delay of effective strategies, waste of corporate resources, and support of a corporate culture that condones poor quality in the management of corporate resources.

During the review of capital projects, with the project managers present to answer questions, the review should be structured to focus discussion and debate on the hard questions about the projects. Both the bad news and the good news of the project should get attention.

The board should be concerned about the schedule, cost, and technical status of the project, as well as an ongoing assessment of the strategic fit of the project. Does the project continue to occupy a building block in the design and execution of corporate strategies? If not, why not? If there is adverse information about the project, what significance does the information have for the directors in coping with their responsibilities?

One of the ways managements can keep their boards informed about coming projects, according to Maynard, is to encourage directors to visit company plants and offices.[25] The directors should visit the project site to have an extended project review and to inspect the construction or manufacturing activities. Maynard further recommends scheduling periodic presentations on subjects of special interest. According to him, subjects suitable for such treatment include "special reports on large capital projects."[26]

This discussion about the need for a regular review of the project implicitly assumes that performance standards exist which provide the basis for reaching a judgment of where the project stands. Experience has shown that such assumptions cannot always be made. If a comprehensive project plan and performance standard for the project do not exist, then monitoring, evaluation, and control of the project are difficult, if not impossible.

Something is added to the discipline of the project team simply because the project is reviewed by the board of directors. When the project team knows that a formal presentation on the project's status will be required by the board, the team will be motivated to do a better job of thinking through the problems and of being prepared with solutions, explanations, or rationales.

What do the directors need to know to adequately review the project? The key to satisfaction of this need is the quality of the information provided to the board.

Information for the Board

The *Corporate Director's Guidebook* makes the point that "the corporate director should be concerned with the establishment and maintenance of an effective reporting system."[27] A reporting system involving capital projects takes the form of a *project management information system* (PMIS), which contains the intelligence essential to the effec-

---

[25] H. B. Maynard, *Handbook of Business Administration* (New York: McGraw-Hill, 1970), pp. 3–20.

[26] Ibid.

[27]*Corporate Director's Guidebook,* The Business Lawyer, American Bar Association, January 1978, p. 14.

tive monitoring, evaluation, and control of the project. Corporate directors require such information to determine the efficiency and effectiveness with which corporate resources are being used on the project. Also, the directors need other corporate information relative to the enterprise's forward planning. This includes critical events and issues facing the enterprise that often might have a strong project context such as new products, facilities, and recapitalization strategies. The project's cost, schedule, and technical performance considerations are certainly worthy of a director's ongoing surveillance.

Juran and Louden, in a book published in 1966, addressed the information that the board requires to fulfill its obligation to exercise due diligence and to increase the knowledge which directors have about the company. Juran and Louden spoke of the "philosophy of completeness," regarding information as an essential part of the climate in which the board and management operate. They stated, "Under this philosophy the rule with respect to information for the board is: *Resolve all doubts in favor of completeness.*"

According to the authors, the practical result of the philosophy of completeness is the *advance information package* in widespread use in many companies. According to them,

> This package is sent to the directors in advance of each meeting to include the agenda which is a listing of the topics which are to be discussed at the meeting. It is not merely a table of contents; it serves also as a kind of notice of what is to come up at the meeting. (By strong implication, anything not on the agenda will be regarded as a surprise.) In some companies the agenda carries notations showing just what actions, if any, the board is being asked to take with respect to each item.[28]

Juran and Louden also recommended that the typical information package for board approval include not only the project proposals on expenditures and actions which are on the list of reserved board powers but also those actions which chart a new course.

Obviously, no board can expect to oversee a capital project without comprehensive, accurate, timely information at an appropriate level of detail. Thus an important starting point for an analysis of a board's performance on capital projects must be the information it requests and receives. If this information is deficient or misleading, the board cannot possibly monitor, evaluate, control, and direct the company's strategic efforts. In addition to adequate information regularly furnished to the board, a regular review of the status of the capital project is needed, with the project manager present to answer any ques-

---

[28] Reprinted by permission of the publisher from *The Corporate Director*, by J. M. Juran and J. Keith Louden, pp. 257–258 © 1966 AMACOM, a division of American Management Association, New York. All rights reserved.

tions and to provide visible evidence that the project is being adequately managed.

The reports furnished to the board on the project's status are important tools to help the directors do their job. At the minimum, such reports should contain summary information which helps the directors meet their responsibilities: the surveillance of the project's cost, schedule, technical performance objectives, and the probability of continued strategic fit in the enterprise. The project manager has the responsibility to see that the project's status report provides sufficient intelligence for the directors to reach a conclusion about where the project stands.

The typical board meets on a monthly basis. Prior to a meeting, the directors usually are provided with an agenda and appropriate supporting materials for review so that they are able to do their "homework."

The need for the directors to have time in advance for the study of the board's meeting agenda and proposals is clearly stipulated by Harold Koontz, a notable scholar on the operation of boards of directors, who states that the outside director should have time to do her or his homework. Therefore, an effective board operation dictates that advance copies of the agenda of the forthcoming meeting be provided as well as copies of proposals to be considered by the board, along with other appropriate documentation and background information.[29] Don't forget that the CEO controls what goes on the board agenda. Without an agenda and without adequate information on the proposals coming before the board, an outside director, however independent, is in a difficult position. An alert board, bolstered by adequate and timely information, will sense conditions in the project that justify a project audit.

For just those reasons mentioned above, one corporation currently in project-related litigation provides an example. The board members' effectiveness at the directors' meeting was limited because the agenda items and information for each meeting were generally not provided until just before the meeting. The result was that the directors' ability to ask discerning questions about this project during review was limited because of the inadequate time they had to do their homework.

Some important things to consider in the use of project-related information for the board include

1. Presenting important issues on the project to the directors before, and not after, corporate senior management has taken a firm position

---

[29] Harold Koontz, *The Board of Directors and Effective Management* (New York: McGraw-Hill, 1967), p. 159.

2. Making sure that the directors get any important information before the board meeting in order to make an informed judgment about the project

3. Not burying the project information in a stack of corporate information

4. Allowing the directors sufficient time to make a decision in which they have confidence

5. Making sure there is time at the board meetings for a full discussion of the project with the project manager present to answer questions

6. Using the board committees, such as the executive committee and the audit committee, to do detailed analyses and present their recommendations to the full board

The Performance Audit

If the information reported to the board and obtained during the project manager's status report reveals project inadequacies or problems, a performance audit may be in order. Independent performance audits on large projects can provide valuable insight for the board and other corporate managers. An independent performance audit on a project may be defined as an in-depth, process-involving analysis of a project's performance and outlook. The analysis should cover both the project and its management. The intent of a performance audit is to evaluate the success or failure of the project and its management. Project performance audits are best made at key points in the project's life cycle or when the project is being buffeted by important problems or changes whose effects may not be fully fathomed. Heyel has noted, "Regardless of intent, a failure to investigate independently may be deemed culpable ignorance and a breach of duty to stockholders.[30] While the full board may order the audit, a subcommittee of the board can make sure the audit is appropriately executed and followed up with the most efficient and productive remedial action.

Although project history is relevant, since past events provide a base from which the project moves forward, the performance audit should not be done to find fault or to debate over past disappointments. Rather it should use the past to develop a better understanding of how current and future performance on the project can be improved.

On one large water pollution abatement system project, an audit was conducted prior to initiation of detailed planning to turn the proj-

---

[30] Carl Heyel, *The Encyclopedia of Management,* 3d ed. (New York: Van Nostrand Reinhold Co., 1982), p. 222.

ect results over to the user. This audit disclosed several contract modification changes that were being unduly delayed and that could have
had an adverse influence on the operational availability of the system. By discovering the delay in these changes through the audit, the
project manager was unable to initiate remedial strategies to get the
project back on schedule and meet its operational date.

In the performance audit, an analysis of the management of the
project can be broken down into two parts: the quality of the processes by which the project is managed and the quality of the managers
and professionals that are working on the project. Because an important responsibility of the board is to evaluate the management capabilities of the senior officers, performance evaluation of major capital
projects gives excellent insight into how well the senior officers of the
company are positioning the enterprise for its future. An independent
performance audit appraises results so that the board and its subcom-
mittees can objectively evaluate the need for and extent of remedial
strategy and resources required. Failure to conduct an independent
performance audit on an ailing or failing project may very well be
considered culpable negligence and a breach of duty to the stockholders, leading to legal action.

Cultural Considerations

Over time considerable camaraderie develops among members of the
board of directors and the corporate managers. This camaraderie
makes it difficult for outside directors to remain objective regarding
corporate matters—and makes it unlikely that any director would
want to play the role of a spoiler by challenging the board's actions.
Yet there would be value in having a forum where consensus could be
developed regarding viewpoints and concerns of the outside directors.
One writer on the subject has suggested the appointment of a management advisory committee composed of outside directors only.
Through such a collective consensus the role of a spoiler could be
played without jeopardy of any individual outside directors. Most
public companies have an audit committee and a compensation committee. Having an advisory committee would be an extension of such
committees and would bring another fiduciary watchdog to the board
of directors' processes.[31]

Directors (and senior managers) influence the culture of the organization, and that culture in turn influences projects. Corporate culture
is reflected in the key values held by members of the organization.

---

[31]John L. Grant, "Shield Outside Directors from Inside Seduction," *Wall Street
Journal,* November 23, 1992.

Managerial and professional behavior is influenced by what the people perceive as the "corporate way of doing things." The value orientation, leadership style, and example set by senior managers greatly influence the behavior of the people.

A cultural unit such as a corporation has many subcultures: the departments, the work groups, and the project teams. Each helps to determine individual behavior. Culture influences managerial philosophy which in turn affects the organizational philosophy. The organizational culture is affected by the existence—or absence—of plans, policies, procedures, guidelines, rules, and basic values in the organization.

The attitudes expressed by senior managers can have a significant effect on the organization's culture. Communication by senior management can influence the outcome of the project. Davis has noted that senior managers' most important task is to foster a corporate environment that facilitates honest and frank disclosures in dealing with a budget-breaking project. He further notes that the senior executives' discouraging of cover-ups and recriminations depends on their management style.[32] A corporation that does not commit itself to comply with government regulations sends an important message throughout the organizational hierarchy. On the other hand, a senior corporate management that takes the lead in developing and promulgating policies that demand full cooperation and disclosure to government bodies will find such policies echoed and enforced throughout the company's organizational structure.

In the nuclear plant construction industry, the Nuclear Regulatory Commission found a direct correlation between the project's success and the utility's view of NRC requirements. More successful utilities tended to view NRC requirements as minimum levels of performance, not maximum, and the utilities strove to achieve increasingly higher, self-imposed goals. This attitude covered all aspects of the project, including quality and quality assurance.[33]

During a performance audit of a large project, it was found that the attitudes, values, beliefs, and behavior demonstrated by senior management of the organization were detrimental to the successful outcome of the project. In an assessment of the corporate culture of this project, it was found that senior management had condoned a culture which contributed to various problems on the project with significant injurious results, such as

---

[32] David Davis, "New Projects: Beware of False Economies," *Harvard Business Review*, March-April 1985, p. 97.

[33] Nuclear Regulatory Commission, NUREG-1055, *Improving Quality and Assurance of Quality in the Design and Construction of Nuclear Power Plants*, Washington, May 1984, pp. 2-1 to 2-6.

1. A lack of candor and openness in dealing with government agencies, particularly the Nuclear Regulatory Commission

2. Management leadership which encouraged the destruction of documents which might have negatively affected the company during customer rate litigation

3. A lack of commitment to adequate communications within the company concerning the status of the project

4. Not taking a conservative approach to unknown factors in the design and construction of the project

5. The general lack of leadership to solve problems on the project in a timely manner

6. Reliance on past management philosophies and practices and a failure to recognize the impact of new technology on both the design of the project and the use of contemporaneous project management practices

Protecting the Board

How does the board of directors protect itself from charges of imprudent and unreasonable management in regard to capital projects? To begin with, the directors must have an active involvement with capital projects. The board of directors' meetings should include project reviews, evidence of sound information, and timely action on all project matters. The project manager must be present at each major review to explain the status of the project. But it is not enough to have the review. It is important that the board provide a paper trail. This consists of written evidence that the board's approval or disapproval of a project is sound and is based on adequate information.

Aside from the importance to the corporation to have this history for its own deliberations, it is the way to avert or deflect capital project related lawsuits. The testimony of the company's senior managers alone cannot fully substantiate the existence of a review process; it must also rest on an official record. And that is what the minutes of the board's meeting become—the official record of the board's deliberations. This record accurately reports what was considered and what was done about matters on the project that might provoke controversy. The absence from the minutes of any notation about major capital projects and their review may be regarded by the courts as indicative that there was no plan or procedure for the overseeing of the projects.

The minutes constitute the official collective action of the board, and the key to the directors' liability is to be found in them. Although the minutes are not irrefutable proof, they do, according to Vagts, constitute "highly persuasive evidence." He goes on to say, "While it is possible to introduce eyewitness statements to refute what was recorded in the minutes, it is an uphill battle to contradict that formal record."[34]

Board actions

The best evidence of the reasonableness and prudence of board oversight is the record of any action taken by the board. As has been noted, on major capital projects one should expect to see clear evidence of timely and decisive action on the part of the directors and the board committees, to ensure that key problems are being handled effectively by senior and project managers and that precursors of potential future problems are identified and addressed. Any actions taken by the board should be documented in the board minutes not only to establish the legitimacy of the board's oversight of the capital project, but also to reinforce the corporate culture in terms of the care taken regarding capital projects.

What actions should the board take?

Another crucial question in evaluating a board's performance on capital projects is: What action did it take on the project? Once a project's funding has been approved, the directors should approve a strategic plan and a suitable organizational design for the project and should select a suitable site and a qualified architectural engineer/consturction manager (AE/CM). If the corporation elects to do its own AE/CM work, then assurance should be given that corporate resources are in place to do the job. Ongoing regular review of the project, including full understanding of any funding changes, is a must for the board. This review can be more effective if the project manager is present at the board meeting to answer questions and to clarify the project's status. Finally, if things do not look right on the project, an audit may be considered by the board.

Protecting the individual director

How can the individual director meet the standards of reasonableness and prudence in carrying out directorship duties? At the minimum, the director should be conscientious in attending all regular and special board meetings. She or he should insist on receiving the board meeting agenda and its supporting information in sufficient time to

---

[34] Reprinted from the *Harvard Business Review*. Excerpt from Detlev F. Vagts, "Why Directors Need to Keep Records," *Harvard Business Review*, November-December 1978, pp. 28–44. Copyright © 1978 by the President and Fellows of Harvard College; all rights reserved.

thoroughly study the decisions expected at the board meeting. If a director is not comfortable with the decisions made or desires more information about them, he or she should state the appropriate concerns with the request that they be reflected in the minutes. When directors wish to vote no on a decision, they should make sure that the no vote is recorded.

Board members should embrace the philosophy of serving in the best interests of the stockholders, rather than in the interests of the senior manager and the inside directors. Members should be careful about assuming senior management competence. In most instances where directors have gotten into trouble, it has been the result of either senior manager incompetence or the intemperate exercise of managerial responsibilities.

The directors themselves can develop ideas about how they may be reasonable and prudent by studying the management concepts and processes of successfully managed corporations.

Selection of Directors

Every corporation should have formalized criteria for the election of the directors, including the insider-outsider mix, occupational expertise, and length of tenure. Used as guidelines, such criteria can be varied to accommodate different requirements for the board. Considering the importance of project management to the corporation, the board should include individuals who have had experience in either the management of projects or the senior executive oversight of such projects. If the projects involve new technology, then at least some of the outside directors should have experience in that technology. Directors should be chosen who have experience in the industry or knowledge about the business the corporation pursues. In large integrated corporations, this is difficult, but by careful choice of the directors, a collective understanding of the corporation's business can be known. If the board does not have outside directors with such experience, then the board should request external assistance in the form of project performance audits and consultations to evaluate and question the project's status.

In the nuclear power plant industry, several projects experienced extraordinary cost and schedule overruns. These were caused in part by the lack of expertise in nuclear plant design, engineering, and construction on the part of the senior utility managers. It seems, however, that even a reasonable amount of common sense would have prompted the directors to question the status and the overall management of the project. It was not clear that such inquiry was made by the directors.

Summary

Because projects are essential to the survival and growth of organizations, failure in project management will have an impact on an organization's ability to accomplish its future purposes. The greater the use of projects in accomplishing organizational purposes, the more dependent the organization is on the effective and efficient strategic management of those projects.

The corporate owners look to the board of directors for proper conduct of the corporate business. The directors are therefore obliged to be guided by what is in the best interests of the owners. Two key questions that a "reasonable and prudent" board ought to be concerned about in meeting their fiduciary responsibilities for the management of capital projects are, "What do the board members need to know about the project? and What actions should the board take on the project?

Individual corporate directors can help themselves and in so doing help the company as well by asking the questions, "Do we really know the status of our key capital projects? and If not, why not? This requires preparation on the part of the directors. The effectiveness of any review of a project requires that the board members be adequately prepared to evaluate a project review and to evaluate the project information being presented.

Conscientious keeping of minutes to reflect the performance of directors' duties on capital projects is a must. At the minimum, the minutes should show what project deliberations and actions the board has taken. Although the minutes are not absolute proof, they constitute highly persuasive evidence, a record which is difficult to contradict.

In this litigious U.S. society, corporate boards charged with "unreasonable and imprudent" behavior increasingly face legal action. The concept of "ordinary prudence" is constantly being widened, and directors are cautioned to be sure that they have the proper information to take action on and maintain surveillance over capital projects.

Discussion Questions

1. What kind of evidence might indicate that a company's board of directors has been inadequate in its monitoring of major undertakings? Explain.

2. What actions and activities indicate that a company's board of directors has taken an active interest in major projects? Explain.

3. Briefly describe some of the major responsibilities of a board of directors with respect to project management.

4. "Projects are key building blocks in the design and execution of corporate strategy." Explain what is meant by this. What ramifica-

tions does this idea have with respect to the responsibilities of a corporate board of directors?

5. Cite and explain some of the reasons for the need for board interest in a project plan.

6. How can a board of directors ensure that the organization design will be effective for accomplishment of corporate strategies and projects?

7. What specific questions should be addressed by the board in project review meetings?

8. What kind of information about a project should be prepared for and presented to the board of directors? Explain.

9. What is the purpose of a performance audit? Under what circumstances might a board of directors consider such an audit? Why?

10. Discuss the effect of corporate culture on organizational performance. What role does the board of directors play in shaping corporate culture?

11. What steps can be taken to protect a board of directors from litigation and subsequent court actions? Explain.

12. Discuss the importance of proper board member selection for organizational effectiveness.

User Checklist

1. What evidence indicates the possibility of inadequate board-of-director attention to the projects within your organization? Does any evidence suggest that your organization's board of directors has been adequately involved in the corporation's major undertakings?

2. What responsibilities do you believe the board of directors should be taking but has not? Explain.

3. How do the major projects within your organization contribute to strategic plans and achievement of objectives and goals? What does this suggest about the need for board involvement?

4. Does your corporation's board of directors receive information about major project plans? What contributions do they make to these plans?

5. What attention has the board of directors of your organization given to the organizational design? What attention is needed?

6. Is the board involved in project review meetings? Why or why not?

7. What questions are addressed by the board of directors with

respect to project's progress? What questions should they be asking?

8. What kind of project status information is presented to the board of directors? Is information presented on a regular basis and in advance of meetings?

9. Under what circumstances might a project audit be needed on a major project that your organization is involved in?

10. What board actions have had an impact on the corporate culture of your organization? Explain.

11. Have any of your organization's projects undergone scrutiny in litigation? How could the company have been better prepared for such litigation?

12. Is your corporate board of directors staffed with knowledgeable, competent members? Why or why not?

6

Project Stakeholder Management[1]

"Smile at the claims of long descent."
LORD ALFRED TENNYSON, 1809–1892

Stakeholder management is an important part of the strategic management of organizations. There is abundant literature in the management field that establishes the need to analyze the enterprise's environment and its stakeholders as part of the strategic management of the enterprise. See, for example, F. J. Aquilar,[2] W. R. Dill,[3] H. Mintzberg,[4] and Weiner and Brown.[5] The concept and process of project stakeholder management will be presented in this chapter.

Political, economic, social, legal, technological, and competitive environments affect an enterprise's ability to survive and grow. Project managers need to identify and interact with key institutions and individuals in the project's systems environment. For example, see Radosevich and Taylor,[6] as well as Burnett and Youker.[7] An

---

[1]Portions of this chapter have been paraphrased from David I. Cleland, "Project Stakeholder Management," *Project Management Journal,* September 1986, pp. 36–43. Used by permission.

[2]F.J. Aquilar, *Scanning the Business Environment* (New York: Macmillan, 1967).

[3]W. R. Dill, "Environment as an Influence on Managerial Autonomy," *Administrative Science Quarterly,* March 1958, pp. 409–443.

[4]H. Mintzberg, *The Structure of Organizations* (New York: Prentice-Hall, 1979).

[5]E. Weiner and A. Brown, "Stakeholder Analysis for Effective Issues Management," *Planning Review,* May 1986, pp. 27–31.

[6]R. Radosevich and C. Taylor, *Management of the Project Environment* (Washington: Department of Agriculture, 1980).

[7]N. R. Burnett and R. Youker, EDI Training Materials, (Washington: International Bank for Reconstruction and Development, 1980).

important part of the management of the project's systems environment is an organized process for identifying and managing the probable stakeholders in that environment. This management process is necessary to determine how the probable stakeholders are likely to react to project decisions, what influence their reaction will carry, and how the stakeholders might interact with each other and with the project's managers and professionals to affect the chances for success or a proposed project strategy. Cleland and King,[8] Rothschild,[9] King and Cleland,[10] Freeman,[11] and Mendelow[12] have presented strategies for dealing with stakeholders in the corporate context.

The management of a project's "stakeholders" means that the project is explicitly described in terms of the individuals and institutions that share a stake or an interest in the project. Thus the project team members, subcontractors, suppliers, and customers invariably are relevant. The impact of project decisions on all of them must be considered in any rational approach to the management of a project. But management must also consider others who have an interest in the project and by definition are also stakeholders. These stakeholders are outside the authority of the project manager and often present serious management problems and challenges.

Organizational Stakeholders

Organizational stakeholders have been defined in the context of a business organization. Table 6.1 shows a model of generic organizational claimants (stakeholders) and their claims (stake) for a business organization. The model requires the key managers to develop an appropriate strategy to manage the organization through

- Identifying appropriate stakeholders
- Specifying the nature of the stakeholder's interest
- Measuring the stakeholder's interest

[8] D. I. Cleland and W. R. King, *Systems Analysis and Project Management,* 3d ed. (New York: McGraw-Hill, 1983).

[9] W. E. Rothschild, *Putting It All Together: A Guide to Strategic Thinking* (New York: AMACOM, 1976).

[10] W. R. King and D. I. Cleland, *Strategic Planning and Policy* (New York: Van Nostrand Reinhold, 1978).

[11] R. E. Freeman, *Strategic Management—A Stakeholder Approach* (Boston: Pitman, 1984).

[12] Aubrey Mendelow, "Stakeholder Analysis for Strategic Planning and Implementation," in *Strategic Planning and Management Handbook* (New York: Van Nostrand Reinhold, 1985).

TABLE 6.1   Organizational Claimants and Their Claims

Claimants	Claims
Stockholders	Participate in distribution of profits, additional stock offerings, assets on liquidation; vote of stock, inspection of company books, transfer of stock, election of board of directors, and such additional rights as established in the contract with the corporation.
Creditors	Participate in legal proportion of interest payments due and return of principal from the investment. Security of pledged assets; relative priority in event of liquidation. Participate in certain management and owner prerogatives if certain conditions exist within the company (such as default of interest payments)
Employees	Economic, social, and psychological satisfaction in the place of employment. Freedom from arbitrary and capricious behavior on the part of company officials. Share in fringe benefits, freedom to join union and participate in collective bargaining, individual freedom in offering up their services through an employment contract. Adequate working conditions.
Customers	Service provided the product; technical data to use the product; suitable warranties; spare parts to support the product during customer use; R&D leading to product improvement; facilitation of consumer credit.
Supplier	Continuing source of business; timely consummation of trade credit obligations; professional relationship in contracting for, purchasing, and receiving goods and services.
Governments	Taxes (income, property, etc.), fair competition, and adherence to the letter and intent of public policy dealing with the requirements of "fair and free" competition. Legal obligation for business people (and business organizations) to obey antitrust laws.
Union	Recognition as the negotiating agent for the employees. Opportunity to perpetuate the union as a participant in the business organization.
Competitors	Norms established by society and the industry for competitive conduct. Business statesmanship on the part of contemporaries.
Local communities	Place of productive and healthful employment in the local community. Participation of the company officials in community affairs, regular employment, fair play, local purchase of reasonable portion of the products of the local community, interest in and support of local government, support of cultural and charity projects.
The general public	Participation in and contribution to the government process of society as a whole; creative communications between government and business units designed for reciprocal understanding; bearing fair proportion of the burden of government and society. Fair price for products and advancement of the state of the art in the technology which the product line offers.

SOURCE: D. I. Cleland and W. R. King, *Systems Analysis and Project Management,* 3d ed. (New York: McGraw-Hill, 1983), p. 45.

- Predicting what each stakeholder's future behavior will be to satisfy her or his stake

- Evaluating the impact of stakeholder's behavior on the project team's latitude in managing the project

The value of using a model like Table 6.1 is to establish a point of departure for developing a model appropriate to a project. It is interesting to know that an environmental group may be concerned about the outcome of a project. But it is vital that the project team have a specific delineation of the various strategies that a stakeholder, such as an environmental group, intends to employ in satisfying that stakeholder's goals and objectives, along with a prediction of the future impact of that stakeholder's actions on the project's outcome. For example, a project manager who must make a recommendation concerning the design of a new plant must be aware of state and local land use, plant design, tax laws, and the area's likely pattern of growth. The project manager must be aware of the local political climate, availability of a skilled labor force, and public attitudes toward the location of the plant in the community. To put all aspects of the stakeholders together requires an understanding of how to apply the management process in dealing with project stakeholders.

Corporate executives are becoming more aware of the need to consider the needs of the stakeholders in their management of the company. For example, NCR, in support of its mission of "creating value for our stakeholders," believes it must first satisfy the legitimate expectations of every person with a stake in the company. NCR attempts to satisfy their stakeholders' expectations by promoting partnerships in which everyone is a winner. The company describes this commitment to its mission in the following way:

> We believe in building mutually beneficial and enduring relationships with all of our stakeholders, based on conducting business activities with integrity and respect.
>
> We take customer satisfaction personally; we are committed to providing superior value in our products and services on a continuing basis.
>
> We respect the individuality of each employee and foster an environment in which employees' creativity and productivity are encouraged, recognized, valued and rewarded.
>
> We think of our suppliers as partners who share our goal of achieving the highest quality standards and the most consistent level of service.
>
> We are committed to being caring and supportive corporate citizens within the worldwide communities in which we operate.
>
> We are dedicated [to] creating value for our stakeholders and financial communities by performing in a manner that will enhance the return on their investments.[13]

---

[13] Courtesy NCR Corporation.

Project Stakeholders

Each project has its own unique set of stakeholders. For example, on the O'Hare Development Program (ODP), a $1.6 billion, 10-year expansion program of Chicago's O'Hare International Airport, many different stakeholders were involved. Their involvement is described as follows:

> The City of Chicago is involved on a daily basis at levels from the Mayor's Office to purchasing. Many City departments and other City consultants provide guidance and significant contributions to the ODP. Additional government agencies involved include the Federal Aviation Administration, the Illinois Department of Transportation and the Illinois State Toll Highway Authority. Specialized Architect/Engineer design firms and contractors are selected by the City to execute each project within the Program. Each must be supplied with information, formatted to suit their particular needs and level of participation.[14]

A classic case of stakeholder involvement is found in the Milwaukee Water Pollution Abatement Program (WPAP). In this project, not unlike many others, stakeholders had a major impact on the success of the project. Groundwork was laid for stakeholder involvement in this program through the policy of the Environmental Protection Agency (EPA), which recognizes the need for the citizenry to be involved in the planning of major public works projects and requires a public involvement program on EPA grant-supported projects.

It was necessary to keep the public informed every step of the way on this huge and complex $2.2 billion project to renovate and upgrade the sewage system of Milwaukee and its suburbs. Legislative and judicial actions set the direction of the Water Pollution Abatement Program at Milwaukee. A tight timetable and the involvement of 27 separate municipalities, compounded by the need to undergo massive renovation of an existing sewerage system without disrupting service, added to the complexity of the project. CH2M Hill, an international firm of engineers, planners, economists, and scientists that had been in business for 43 years, and its consortium of principal associate consultants were selected to manage the Milwaukee WPAP. Stakeholders played key roles in the planning and outcome of this program. The care that was taken to listen carefully to stakeholders' concerns and the addressing of these concerns in the planning and execution of the WPAP were crucial to the successful outcome of the program. The program management team placed speakers on key local community platforms, gained editorial support from local media, and worked carefully to gain the endorsement of key stakeholders in the top polit-

---

[14]Paul B. Demkovich, "Goal Achievement through Program Control Systems on the O'Hare Development Program," *Project Management Institute Seminar/Symposium*, October 1987, p. 303.

ical business and public-interest organizations. Keeping a balance between the interests of the stakeholders and those of the program manager's corporate body was one of the most difficult strategies undertaken in the program. Recognition of the stakeholders' interests in the project and having capability on the project team to deal with these interests were considered one of the key factors to the success of this important project.[15]

Wideman establishes that good public relations (PR) are an essential part of successful project management. His recommendations for a project PR program would help to manage the project stakeholders by

- Maintaining adequate project communications that promote good understanding of the project by team members
- Keeping the various "publics" up to date on the progress and performance of the project
- Responding to any misleading information that might be circulating about the project.

Targets for the Wideman project PR program would include

- The project work force
- The project users
- Business and professional groups
- Business media
- The local community
- The community at large
- Special interest groups
- Elected representatives and government administrators
- The news media
- Labor groups
- Educators and school groups
- Taxpayers
- The industrial sector of the project[16]

Successful project management can be carried out only when the responsible managers take into account the potential influence of the project's stakeholders. An important part of the project planning is

---

[15] See Henry F. Padgham, "The Milwaukee Water Pollution Abatement Program: Its Stakeholder Management," *pmNETwork,* April 1991, pp. 6–18.

[16] R. Max Wideman, "Good Public Relations an Essential Part of Successful Project Management," PMI 1985 *Proceedings,* vol. 1: pp. 6–7.

the identification of all project stakeholders and their relevant stakes in the project. Stakeholder analysis during the planning of the project is particularly useful for the development of strategies to facilitate the "management" of the stakeholders during the life cycle of the project.

Project stakeholders include not only the obvious members of the project team but also those principles in the political, economic, social, legal, and technological environments in which the project exists. In some cases the stakeholders will be highly organized and motivated, such as some environmental groups have been in influencing the construction of nuclear power generation plants.

Project stakeholders can be large and powerful vested interests. The Hong Kong plan for the world's biggest construction project, which includes new port facilities, expressways, and a huge suspension bridge, is becoming a test of wills between London and Beijing over who determines the crown colony's future. Many U.S. firms are involved, such as Bechtel International and Morgan Stanley, which can share in the billions of dollars of work that could go to U.S. companies. The colonial government's plan for the airport is criticized by Hong Kong millionaire developer Gordon Y. S. Wu, who challenges the colonial government's plan as poorly conceived and too expensive. He has received Beijing's blessing for an alternative privately financed airport that could save billions of dollars. All in all, there are many "stakeholders" who are claiming their appropriate "stake" in this huge project. Without doubt, the project will not get underway until the key stakeholders see their interests adequately represented—a task that will probably take a long time to resolve.[17]

Because project stakeholder management assumes that success depends on taking into account the potential impact of project decisions on all stakeholders during the entire life of the project, the project team faces a major challenge. In addition to identifying and assessing the impact of project decisions on stakeholders who are subject to the authority of the management, the team must consider how achievement of the project's goals and objectives will affect, or be affected by, stakeholders outside their authority.

The former head of the Bonneville Power Administration in Portland, Oregon, describes the challenges and anxieties involved in making a commitment to public involvement over some company projects and the awesome challenge in making that commitment work. Peter Johnson has become a convert, stating that "...public involvement is a tool that today's managers...must understand."[18]

---

[17] Pete Engardio, "A Test of Wills in Hong Kong," *Business Week,* October 8, 1990, p. 56.

[18] Peter T. Johnson, "How I Turned a Critical Public into Useful Consultants," *Harvard Business Review,* January-February 1993, pp. 56–66.

Youker found in his experiences with the World Bank that in reviving the status of the implementation of its entire portfolio of projects, many of the most important problems of implementation lie in the general environment of the project and are beyond the direct control of the project manager.[19]

Project stakeholders, often called *intervenors* in the nuclear power plant construction industry, can have a marked influence on a project. At one nuclear power plant, numerous bomb threats over the life of the project lengthened construction schedules, shut down work on select areas, frustrated managers and professionals, and forced more intensive security provisions, including physical searches of people, equipment, and vehicles. Antinuclear blockades and demonstrations impacted productivity. In the fall of 1981, the Abalone Alliance, an antinuclear organization, attempted to blockade the plant. The plant had to pay for housing and feeding the plant operating crew, management staff, national guard troops, and law enforcement officers. Costs associated with such intervenor action, such as work and absenteeism because of the physical threats, could not be calculated.

Examples of Stakeholder Influence

Some recent project management experiences highlight the role of these stakeholders:

In the investigation of the management prudence on the Long Island Lighting Company (LILCO) Shoreham Project, Suffolk County, the New York State Consumer Protection Board, and the Long Island Citizens in Action (intervenors) argued that the project suffered from pervasive mismanagement throughout its history. The record, in the view of these intervenors, established that approximately $1.9 billion of Shoreham's cost was expended unnecessarily "as a result of LILCO's mismanagement, imprudence or gross inefficiency."[20]

One reason that the Supersonic Transport program failed in the United States was that the managers had a narrow view of the essential players and generally dismissed the key and novel role of the environmentalists until it was too late.[21]

---

[19] Robert Youker, *Managing the International Project Management Environment,* Management Planning and Control Systems, 5825 Rockmere Drive, Bethesda, MD 20816-2443.

[20] *Case 27563, Long Island Lighting Company-Shoreham Prudence Investigation,* State of New York Public Service Commission, Recommended Decision by Administrative Law Judges Wm. C. Levey and Thomas R. Matias, March 13, 1985, p. 57.

[21] Mel Horwitch, "The Convergence Factor for Successful Large-Scale Programs: The American Synfuels Experience as a Case in Point," in D. I. Cleland (ed.), *Matrix Management Systems Handbook* (New York: Van Nostrand Reinhold, 1984).

Some stakeholders can provide effective insight into strategic issues facing an industry. For example, in the nuclear power generation industry, the Advanced Reactor Development Subpanel of the Energy Research Advisory Board's Civilian Nuclear Power Panel submitted a report in January 1986 on the status of the advanced reactor development program in the United States. This comprehensive report reported on the three key areas of this program: problem justification and current realities, program redirection, and advanced reactor program recommendations. The recommendations of this report gave clear direction for future reactor development, leading to more economical and fuel-efficient reactors. Such recommendations help to develop future strategies for other stakeholders such as electric utilities and their suppliers, the Department of Energy, state public utility commissions, etc. More importantly, the proceedings of the Advanced Reactor Development Subpanel provide a forum for an exchange of viewpoints about nuclear power among stakeholders, some of whom may be viewed as adversaries by other stakeholders. For example, the Union of Concerned Scientists, a prominent antinuclear group that represents intervenors in proceedings before the Nuclear Regulatory Commission (NRC), has been critical of a "cozy relationship" between government regulatory officials and utility officials.[22]

State public utility commissions (PUCs) are key and formidable stakeholders in the design, engineering, construction, and operation of nuclear power generating plants. In the past few years, state PUCs have prevented the recovery of billions of dollars in generating plant construction costs. Some utilities have been penalized for imprudent spending on nuclear plants; others have been told that their plants were not needed. For example, the Pennsylvania State Public Utility Commission ruled that the Pennsylvania Power and Light Company's newly opened 945-MW $2 billion Susquehanna Unit 2 nuclear plant would provide too much generating capacity for the utility's customers. The utility was allowed to recover only taxes, depreciation, and other operating costs. The Missouri Public Service Commission recently disqualified Union Electric Company from charging ratepayers for $384 million of the $3 billion spent on the new Callaway nuclear plant in central Missouri. The commission cited high labor expenses, improper scheduling of engineering, and "inefficient, imprudent, unreasonable, or unexplained costs" during 4 years of delay.[23]

Diverse stakeholders, or intervenors, are taking active roles in rate-setting case hearings. For example, when the Union Electric Company

[22] *The Phoenix Gazette,* June 27, 1984, p. PV-12.

[23] William Glasgall, "The Utilities' Pleas Falling on Deaf Ears," *Business Week,* June 17, 1985, p. 113.

of St. Louis, Missouri, instituted proceedings for authority to file tariffs increasing rates for electric service, the following parties were granted permission to intervene in the proceedings:...25 cities, the state of Missouri, the Jefferson City school district, the Electric Ratepayers Protection Project, the Missouri Coalition for the Environment, the Missouri Public Interest Research Group, Laclede Gas Company, Missouri Limestone Producers, Dundee Cement Company, LP Gas Association, Missouri Retailers Association, the Metropolitan St. Louis Sewer District, and the industrial intervenors—American Can Company, Anheuser Busch, Inc., Chrysler Corporation, Ford Motor Company, General Motors Corporation, Mallinckrout, Inc., McDonnell Douglas Corporation, Monsanto Company, National Can Corporation, Nooter Corporation, PPG Industries, Inc., Pea Ridge Iron Ore Company, River Cement Company, St. Joe Minerals Corporation (Monsanto et al.).[24]

The Nuclear Regulatory Commission is a proactive stakeholder in the management of nuclear power plant projects. Its principal interest is the licensing of nuclear plants to ensure quality assurance, safeguards, inspection, and proper operation. Its influence in the industry is substantial. In addition to licensing individual plants, the NRC conducts studies in the design, engineering, and licensing of plants. In 1984 it published a landmark study of existing and alternative programs for improving quality and the assurance of quality in the design and construction of commercial nuclear power plants.[25]

Competitors are key stakeholders, particularly during the competitive phase before the architect and engineer, project manager, or constructor firm is selected during a source selection process. During this competitive phase, an in-depth analysis of competitors is essential to winning a contract. The business literature contains descriptions on how to access the competition.[26] A potential winning contract can become a loser if the competition is ignored.

Additional Examples of Successful Stakeholder Management

There are some excellent examples of successful stakeholder management:

---

[24] *Cases No. ER-85-160 and EO 85-17,* State of Missouri Public Service Commission, Jefferson City, March 29, 1985.

[25] W. Altman, T. Ankrum, and W. Brach, *Improving Quality and the Assurance of Quality in the Design and Construction of Nuclear Power Plants.* A Report to Congress (NUREG-1055), Office of Inspection and Enforcement, Nuclear Regulatory Commission, Washington, May 1984.

[26] Richard Eells and Peter Nehemkis, *Corporate Intelligence and Espionage* (New York: Macmillan, 1984).

- Care was taken during the design and construction of the Hackensack Meadowlands sports complex to develop cooperation among the groups concerned with environmental impact, transportation, development, and construction.

- On the James Bay Project special effort was made to stay sensitive to social, economic, and ecological pressures.[27]

- James Webb and his colleagues at NASA were adept at stakeholder management during the Apollo Program. NASA gained the support not only of the aerospace industry and related constituencies, but also of the educational community, the basic sciences, and the weather forecaster profession.[28]

- At the Niagara Mohawk Power Corporation in Syracuse, New York, plans for achieving public acceptance of the atom as a source of electric power began long before the company had any specific plans for constructing its own nuclear plant. Niagara Mohawk began to inform the public of progress in using the atom for electric power generation soon after the Atomic Energy Act was signed in 1954. A full-scale, successful public relations program was carried out before, and continued after, the initiation of the project.

- Florida Power & Light established a special office near the NRC headquarters to facilitate exchange of information during the licensing process for its plant.

- Senior management of Arizona Public Service established the following policy concerning the NRC:

    Don't treat NRC as an adversary; NRC is not here to bother us—they see many more plants than the licensee sees; inform NRC of what we (APS) are doing and keep everything up front; and nuclear safety is more important than schedule.

Project Stakeholder Management (PSM) Process

The principal justification for adopting a PSM perspective springs from the enormous influence that key external stakeholders can exert. Arguably, the extent to which the project achieves its goals and objectives is influenced by the strategies pursued by key stakeholders. Stakeholder management leading to stakeholder cooperation enhances project objective achievement, while stakeholder neglect hinders it.

---

[27] Peter G. Behr, "James Bay Design and Construction Management," *ASCE Engineering Issues, Journal of Professional Activities,* April 1978.

[28] E. Ginsburg, J. W. Kuhn, and J. Schnee, *Economic Impact of Large Public Programs: The Nash Experience* (Salt Lake City, Utah: Olympus Publishing, 1976).

In working with project managers to develop a project strategy which encompasses a PSM philosophy, the following basic premises can serve as guides for the development of a PSM progress:

- PSM is essential for ensuring success in managing projects.

- A formal approach is required for performing a PSM process. Multiyear projects are subject to so much change that informal means of PSM are inadequate. Reliance on informal or hit-or-miss methods for obtaining PSM information is ineffective for managing the issues that can come out of projects.

- PSM should provide the project team with adequate intelligence for the selection of realistic options in the management of project stakeholders.

- Information on project stakeholders can be gained from a variety of sources, some of which might superficially seem to be unprofitable.

PSM is designed to encourage the use of proactive project management for curtailing stakeholder activities that might adversely affect the project and for facilitating the project team's ability to take advantage of opportunities to encourage stakeholder support of project purposes. These objectives can be achieved only by integrating stakeholder perspectives into the project's formulation processes and developing a PSM strategy. The project manager is then in a better position to influence the actions of the stakeholders on project outcome.

Some objectives for PSM might be as follows:

- Ensure the availability of timely, credible, and comprehensive information of the capabilities and the options open to each stakeholder.

- Continue to identify the probable strategies of the stakeholders.

- Determine how key stakeholders' strategies might affect current project interests.

- Continuously monitor and provide comprehensive information about probable actions in the project-stakeholder environment that might have an impact on the interests of the project.

- Organize the collection, analysis, and dissemination of stakeholder information for the project team.

Failure to recognize or cooperate with adverse stakeholders may well hinder a successful project outcome. Indeed, strong and vociferous adverse stakeholders can force their particular interest on the project manager at any time, perhaps at the time least convenient to the project. PSM is thus a necessity to allow the project manager to set the timetable to maintain better control. A proactive PSM process is designed to help the project team develop the best possible strategies.

A Model of the PSM Process

The PSM process consists of executing the management functions of planning, organizing, motivation, directing, and controlling the resources used to cope with external stakeholders' strategies. These functions are interlocked and redundant; the emergence of new stakeholders might require the reinitiation of these functions at any time during the life cycle of the project. This management process is continuous, adaptable to new stakeholder threats and promises and to changing strategies of existing stakeholders. Putting the notion of stakeholder management on a project life-cycle basis emphasizes the need to be aware of stakeholder influence at all times.

The management process for the stakeholders consists of the phases depicted in Fig. 6.1 and discussed in this section.

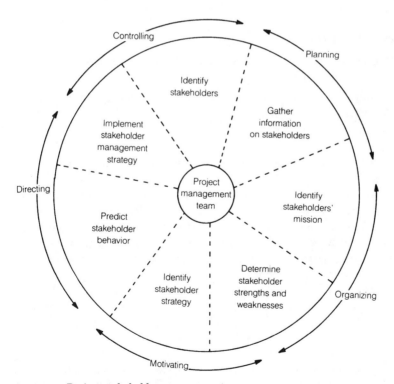

Figure 6.1   Project stakeholder management process.

Identification of stakeholders

The identification of stakeholders must go beyond the internal stakeholders. Internal stakeholders must, of course, be taken into account in the development of project strategies. Their influence is usually supportive of project strategies since internal stakeholders are an integral part of the project team. A prudent project manager would ensure that these internal stakeholders play an important and supportive role in the design and development of project strategies. Such a supportive role is usually forthcoming since the project manager has some degree of authority and influence over these individuals.

But external stakeholders may not be supportive. External stakeholders usually are not subject to the legal authority of the project manager; consequently, such stakeholders provide a formidable challenge to manage. A generic set of external stakeholders includes

- Prime contractor
- Subcontractors
- Competitors
- Suppliers
- Financial institutions
- Government agencies; commissions; judicial, legislative, and executive branches
- The general public represented through consumer, environmental, social, political, and other "intervenor" groups
- Affected local community

Figure 6.2 depicts a sample model of project stakeholders, both internal and external.

Freeman points out that historical analysis of an organization's interface with its environment is useful in identifying potential stakeholders.[29] The development of a list of the "strategic issues" that currently face and have faced the parent organization and industry over the past several years can be useful in identifying stakeholders who have been involved in these issues.[30]

Stakeholders whose stake in the project is sufficient for them to attempt to play an influential role affecting the outcome of the project should be identified and their significant actions and strategies ana-

---

[29]NUREG 1055, *Improving Quality and the Assurance of Quality in the Design and Construction of Nuclear Power Plants,* A Report to Congress, Division of Quality Assurance, Safeguards, and Inspection Programs, Office of Inspection and Enforcement, Nuclear Regulatory Commission, Washington, May 1984.

[30]Freeman, op cit.

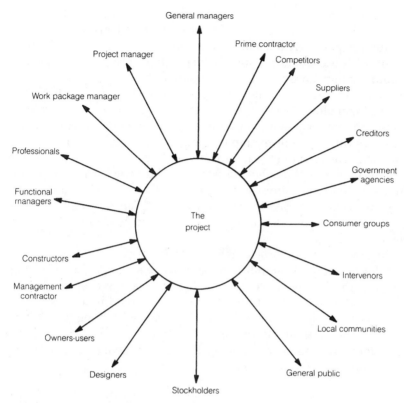

Figure 6.2 Project stakeholder network.

lyzed and cataloged. Several major issues regarding these stakeholders must be addressed by the project manager:

- Who are the most formidable stakeholders?
- What are their strengths and weaknesses?
- What are their strategy and the associated probabilities of their being able to successfully implement that strategy?
- What resources are at the stakeholders' disposal to implement their strategies?
- Do any of these factors give the stakeholder a distinctly favorable position in influencing the project outcome?

On megaprojects, the list of stakeholders can become impressive. The nuclear power industry is a case in point. Nuclear power is, from some viewpoints, an emotional issue aggravated by the accidents at Three Mile Island and Chernobyl. Before these accidents the public had a false sense of security; a continuing lack of education about radiation produced a fear of the unknown. Many stakeholders' mission, in whole or in part, is to reshape public and legislative opinion about nuclear power. A nuclear power plant project team needs to be aware of all these potential stakeholders; there are many. A partial list would include more than 50 stakeholders.

Although historical perspective can give insight into a project's probable stakeholders, the project team should be alerted to strategic issues in the competitive and environmental systems that can change the project's future.[31] For example, one key strategic issue facing the U.S. nuclear power industry is to foster public acceptance of nuclear power. Recognizing this, the industry has launched a major public relations campaign to improve its image. The U.S. Committee for Energy Awareness (CEA) launched a $20 million advertising campaign to facilitate public acceptance and understanding to foster agreement and support.[32]

The interaction of the project team can identify external stakeholders. By discussing and compiling a list of some strategic issues facing the project, the less obvious stakeholders can be discovered. Once a list of the stakeholders has been developed, it should become an integral part of the project plan and should be reviewed along with other elements of the plan during the project's life cycle to determine if the stakeholders' perceptions or views of the project have changed. To do so will require information about the stakeholders.

Gathering information

Gathering information about the project stakeholders is similar to collecting information on competitors.[33] To systematize the development of the stakeholder information means that questions such as the following need to be considered:

- What needs to be known about the stakeholder?
- Where and how can the information be obtained?
- Who will have responsibility for the gathering, analysis, and interpretation of the information?

---

[31] The Conference Board defines a strategic issue as "a condition or pressure, either internal or external...that will have a significant effect on the functioning of the organization or its future interests." See J. K. Brown, "This Business of Issues: Coping with the Company's Environments," *The Conference Board Report,* no. 758, 1979.

[32] *The Phoenix Gazette,* June 27, 1984, p. PV-12.

[33] The techniques described here are paraphrased in part from W. R. King and D. I. Cleland, *Strategic Planning and Policy,* (New York: Van Nostrand Reinhold, 1986), chap 11., pp. 246–270.

- How and to whom will the information be distributed?
- Who will use the information to make decisions?
- How can the information be protected from "leaking" or misuse?

Some of the information collected on the project's external stakeholders may include sensitive material. One cannot conclude that all such stakeholders will operate in an ethical fashion. Consequently, all information collected should be assumed to be sensitive until proved otherwise and protected accordingly. This suggests the need for a security system patterned after a company's business intelligence system. Some information should be available only on a need-to-know basis while some should be available to all interested parties.

The following precautions should be considered in planning for a PSM information system:

- One individual responsible for security
- Internal checks and balances
- Document classification and control such as periodic inventory, constant record of whereabouts, and prompt return
- Locked files and desks
- Supervised shredding or burning of documents no longer useful
- Confidential envelopes for internal transmission of confidential documents
- Strict security of offices containing sensitive information

Information on the stakeholders is available from a wide variety of sources.[34] In obtaining such information, the highest standards of ethical conduct should be followed. The potential sources of stakeholder information and the uses to which such information can be put are so numerous that it would not be practical to list all sources and uses here. The following sources are representative and can be augmented according to a particular project's needs:

- Project team members
- Key managers
- Business periodicals such as the *Wall Street Journal, Fortune, Business Week, Forbes,* and others
- Business reference services—*Moody's Industrial Manual, Value Line Investment Security,* etc.

---

[34] Ibid.

- Professional associations
- Customers/users
- Suppliers
- Trade associations
- Local press
- Trade press
- Annual corporate reports
- Articles and papers presented at professional meetings
- Public meetings
- Government sources[35]

Once the information has been collected, it must be analyzed and interpreted by the substantive experts. The project manager should draw on the company's professional personnel for help in doing this analysis. Once the analysis has been completed, the specific target of the stakeholder's mission can be determined.

Identification of mission

Once the stakeholders have been identified and information gathered about them, analyze the information to determine the nature of their mission or stake. This stake may be a key building block in the stakeholder's strategy. For example, the Nuclear Regulatory Commission manages the licensing of nuclear power plants to promote the safe and peaceful commercial use of the atom. A useful technique to better understand the nature of the external stakeholders' claim in the project is to categorize their stake as supportive or adverse to the project. It is in the best interest of the project manager to keep the supportive stakeholders well informed of the project's status. Deal carefully with the potentially adverse stakeholders. Information on these stakeholders should be handled on a need-to-know basis because if such information is available to adversarial stakeholders on the project, it can be used against the project. However, communication channels with these stakeholders should be kept open, for this is critical to getting the project point of view across. Adversarial stakeholders will find ways to get information on the project from other sources which can be erroneous or incomplete, giving the opportunity for misunderstanding and further adversarial behavior.

---

[35] Ibid.

Determining strengths and weaknesses

Once the stakeholders' mission is understood, then the stakeholders' strengths and weaknesses should be evaluated. An assessment of stakeholders' strengths and weaknesses is a prerequisite to understanding the success of their strategies. Such analysis is found in nearly all prescriptions for a strategic planning process.[36] This process consists of the development of a summary of the most important strengths on which the stakeholders base their strategy and the most significant weaknesses they will avoid in pursuing their interests on the project. Identifying five or six strengths and weaknesses of a stakeholder should provide a sufficient data base on which to make a judgment about the efficacy of a stakeholder's strategy.

An adversary stakeholder's strength may be based on such factors as

- The availability and effective use of resources
- Political alliances
- Public support
- Quality of strategies
- Dedication of members

Accordingly, an adversary stakeholder's weaknesses may emanate from

- Lack of political support
- Disorganization
- Lack of coherent strategy
- Uncommitted, scattered membership
- Unproductive use of resources

Once these factors have been developed, each proposed strategy for coping with the stakeholders can be tested by answering the following questions:

- Does this strategy adequately cope with a strength of the stakeholder?

  Does this strategy take advantage of an adversary stakeholder's weakness?

- What is the relative contribution of a particular stakeholder's strength in countering the project strategy?

---

[36]W. E. Rothschild, op. cit.

- Does the adversary stakeholder's weakness detract from the successful implementation of his or her strategy? If so, can the project manager develop a counter strategy that will benefit the project?

Identification of stakeholder strategy

For a proposed strategy to be successful, it should be built on a philosophy which recognizes the value of going through a specific strength-weakness analysis to develop project strategy. This can be done, however, only if there is a full understanding of the stakeholder's strategy.

A *stakeholder strategy* is a series of prescriptions that provide the means and set the general direction for accomplishing stakeholder goals, objectives, and mission. These prescriptions stipulate what resource allocations are required; why, when and where they will be required; and how they will be used. These resource allocations include plans for using resources, policies and procedures to be employed, and tactics used to accomplish the stakeholder's purposes.

Prediction of stakeholder behavior

Based on an understanding of external stakeholder strategy, the project team can proceed to predict stakeholder behavior in implementing strategy. How will the stakeholder use resources to affect the project? Will an intervenor stakeholder picket the construction site or attempt to use the courts to delay or stop the project? Will a petition be circulated to stop further construction? Will an attempt be made to influence future legislation? These are the kinds of questions, when properly asked and answered, that provide a basis for the project team to develop specific countervailing strategies to deal with adversary stakeholder influence.

In some cases, a stakeholder will provide help to another stakeholder. For example, a group of dedicated nuclear advocates formed an industry association to ensure the nuclear operating safety that the Nuclear Regulatory Commission could not provide. This association, the Institute of Nuclear Power Operations (INPO), is dedicated to improving the safety of nuclear plants. INPO sets safety standards and goals, evaluates plant safety, and provides troubleshooting assistance to its sponsors. INPO oversees the training of plant operators and supervisors. In its role as a stakeholder of nuclear power, INPO works closely with the Nuclear Regulatory Commission. If INPO finds areas for improvement in a utility's operation, it is the utility that alerts the Nuclear Regulatory Commission.[37]

---

[37] For more on the role of INPO see James Cook, "INPO's Race against Time," *Forbes,* February 24, 1986, pp. 54–55.

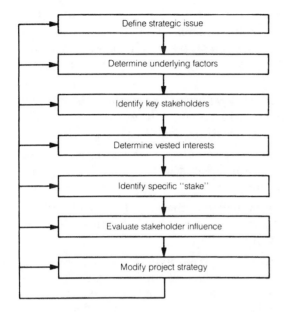

Figure 6.3 Stakeholder impact evaluation process.

To better predict stakeholder behavior, the project team should take the lead in analyzing the probable impact of the stakeholder on a project. A step-by-step approach for analyzing such impact on a project would consist of the following, depicted in Fig. 6.3, and described below:

First, identify and define each potential strategic issue in sufficient detail to ascertain its relevance for the project. Next determine the several key factors which underlie each issue and what forces have caused that issue to emerge. These forces usually can be categorized into political, social, economic, technological, competitive, or legal forces.

Then identify the key stakeholders that have, or might feel that they have, a vested interest in the project. Remember that several different stakeholders may share a vested interest in one strategic issue. Stakeholders usually perceive a vested interest in a strategic issue because of

- *Mission relevancy.* The issue is directly related to the mission of the group. For example, members of the Sierra Club see the potential adverse effect of a nuclear power plant project on the environment.

- *Economic interest.* The stakeholders have an economic interest in the strategic issue. A union would be vitally interested in the wage rates paid at a project construction site.

- *Legal right.* A stakeholder has a legal right in the issue, such as the Nuclear Regulatory Commission, which has the power to grant operating licenses for nuclear generating plants.

- *Political support.*   Stakeholders see the issue as one in which they feel the need to maintain a political constituency. A state legislator would be concerned about the transportation of toxic wastes from a power plant to a repository site within the state or the transportation of wastes across the state.

- *Health and safety.*   The issue is related to the personal health and safety of the group. Project construction site workers are vitally interested (or should be) in the working conditions at the site.

- *Lifestyle.*   The issue is related to the lifestyle or values enjoyed by the group. Sports groups are interested in the potential pollution of industrial waste in the forests and waterways.

- *Opportunism.*   The issue is one that the group can rally others around, with the goal of increasing the group's political power at the expense of the project.

- *Survival.*   The issue is linked to the reason for existence of a group of stakeholders. For example, members of the investment community see clearly the financial risks of nuclear plant construction today, considering the uncertainty in the licensing of a nuclear power plant.[38]

Once the stakeholders have been identified, clarify the specific stake held by each stakeholder, then judge how much influence the stakeholder might have on the project and its outcome. Table 6.2 summarizes such influences. This table should be developed by the members of the project team who are in the best position to identify the probable impact of a stakeholder's vested interest. By perusing the table a manager can get a summary picture of which stakeholders should be "managed" by the project team. Stakeholders whose interest scores high on the table should be studied carefully and their strategies and actions tracked to see what effect such actions might have on the project's outcome. Once the potential effect is determined, then the project strategy should be modified through resource reallocation, replanning, or reprogramming to accommodate or counter the stakeholder's actions through a stakeholder management strategy.

Project audit

An independent audit of the project conducted on a periodic basis will also help the project team to get the informed and intelligent answers they need on strategic issues and stakeholder interests. Both internal and external audits performed by third parties to analyze the proj-

---

[38] Paraphrased from Edith Weiner and Arnold Brown, "Stakeholder Analysis for Effective Issues Management," *Planning Review,* May 1986, pp. 27–31.

TABLE 6.2   Stakeholder Interests

Stakeholder Interest	Stakeholders										
	1	2	3	4	5	6	7	8	9	10	11
Mission Relevance											
Economic Interest											
Legal Right											
Political Support											
Health and Safety											
Life Style											
Opportunistic Competitive Survival											

Vested   Interest
      H - High
      L - Low
      M - Medium

ect's strengths, weaknesses, problems, and opportunities can shed light on how well the stakeholders are being managed. There is a symbiotic relationship between the project and its stakeholders. The project cannot exist without its stakeholders; conversely, the stakeholders rely to some extent on the project for their existence.

Implementing stakeholder management strategy

The final step depicted in Fig. 6.1 in managing the project stakeholders is to develop implementation strategies for dealing with them. An organizational policy which stipulates that stakeholders will be managed actively is an important first step of such implementation strategies. Once this important step has been taken, additional policies, action plans, procedures, and allocation of supporting resources can be made to make stakeholder management an ongoing activity. Once implementation strategies are operational, the project team has to

- Ensure that the key managers and professionals fully appreciate the potential impact that both supportive and adverse stakeholders can have on the project outcome.

- Manage the project review meetings so that stakeholder assessment is an integral part of determining the project status.

- Maintain contact with key external stakeholders to improve the chances of determining stakeholders' perception of the project and their probable strategies.

- Ensure an explicit evaluation of probable stakeholder response to major project decisions.

- Provide an ongoing, up-to-date status report on stakeholder status to key managers and professionals for use in developing and implementing project strategy.

- Provide a suitable security system to protect sensitive project information that might be used by adverse stakeholders to the detriment of the project.

Henry F. Padgham, former president and chairman of the Project Management Institute, who has managed many successful large projects, believes that "Project management today demands that we pay attention to all who have a stake in our projects."[39]

Summary

Project stakeholders have the means of influencing the project regardless of whether the project team likes it. Yet on those projects where a sincere effort was made to get the stakeholders involved in the project deliberations, a more effective decision-making process was created. The project's adversaries have something to offer, even if it is nothing more than a challenge for the project team to sharpen their review and knowledge on how the project is managed. By listening to the concerns of the project stakeholders and soliciting their advice on how to bring about a friendly reconciliation of differences of opinion and conflicting needs, everyone associated with the project learns. By getting the project stakeholders involved in the decision-making process of the project, the project team gains authority and a favorable image, leading to an enhanced legitimacy on the project decisions. Indeed, just filling the formal, legal requirements of involving the stakeholders is not enough. The project leader has to get them involved so that the stakeholders feel that their concerns and viewpoints are given equal time.

Project stakeholders on projects in the private sector are now as powerful as those in the public domain, such as a government agency where political pressures from stakeholders can cause debate, delay, and even cancellation of the project. Management of the stakeholders on public projects requires planning and attending many meetings, some initiated by the project manager and others, often adversarial, organized by the stakeholders. Identification of real and imagined problems, listening to concerns and suggestions, and responding as

---

[39] Henry F. Padgham, *pmNETwork*, April 1991, p. 18.

forthrightly as possible to questions and comments are all part of the project stakeholder management process.

Project team members need to be made aware of the importance of giving adequate attention to the concerns of all stakeholders and to receiving training and guidance on how to deal with the concerns of the stakeholders. Knowing how to follow the model suggested in this chapter is an important part of the training that is required. Teaching project team members how to organize a public meeting, how to organize and run such meetings, how to listen in an empathetic way, and how to sharpen their writing skills is an important part of the project team development activities. Telling the project team members—and telling them again—of the importance of respect, dignity, and trust and of the need to be open and forthright in dealing with the stakeholders is always very important. Realistically, however, in some circumstances the information regarding a project will have to be treated as confidential and will not be disclosed outside the organization without the express permission of senior managers. Every item of information that is confidential needs to be examined so as to truly ascertain the wisdom of disclosing or keeping that information confidential.

The specification of a project stakeholder management process helps to ensure the timely and credible information about the capabilities and options open to each stakeholder. Once these options have been identified, the project team is in a position to predict stakeholder behavior and how such behavior might affect the project's outcome. Then the project team can develop its own strategies to best manage the stakeholders.

Discussion Questions

1. What is meant by a *project stakeholder?*

2. Describe a project management situation from your work or school experience, and list the projected stakeholders.

3. Discuss the importance of keeping all project stakeholders informed on the issues relevant to them with respect to projects.

4. In the nuclear power plant described in the chapter, what could the project managers have done to prevent intervenors from disrupting the construction of the plant?

5. Why is it important for project leaders to develop a project stakeholder management (PSM) process? Discuss stakeholders' potential impact on the attainment of project objectives and goals.

6. List and discuss the objectives of PSM as described in the chapter.

7. List and describe the steps in the PSM process.

8. List some sources of information on project stakeholders.

9. What questions must management address to assess the potential impact of an adversarial stakeholder?

10. What factors indicated a vested interest by a stakeholder in a strategic issue of the project?

11. What additional steps must management take once stakeholders and their potential impacts have been identified?

12. What factors of organizational culture contribute to effective management of stakeholders?

User Checklist

1. Does your organization continually seek to identify project stakeholders? In what ways?

2. How does your organization manage the interrelationships among project stakeholders? Do any written policies exist that assist in the management of stakeholders?

3. In what ways does your organization seek to manage intervenors?

4. What stakeholder impacts are typical in your organization?

5. Describe a recent project in your organization that was successful in the management of stakeholders. What led to this success?

6. Describe your organizational philosophy and attitudes toward the PSM process.

7. Are there any formal ways that the project managers in your organization accept responsibility for the PSM process?

8. In what ways do project managers go beyond identification in assessing stakeholder impact?

9. What sources are used or can be used to gather information on the project stakeholders?

10. Do project managers attempt to predict stakeholder behavior? In what ways?

11. Are the project stakeholder issues addressed in project audits? What questions are asked or can be asked to help the project team identify and control strategic issues?

12. What proactive measures are taken to ensure continual management of stakeholders? How can the top managers of your organization support the PSM process?

7

Strategic Issues in Project Management[1]

"Every advantage...is judged in the light of final issue."

DEMOSTHENES, 384–322 B.C.

The concept of "strategic issues" has emerged as a way to identify and manage factors and forces that can significantly affect an organization's future strategies and tactics. The importance of strategic issues has therefore appeared in the literature primarily in the context of the strategic management of an organization. King has put forth the notion of *strategic issue management* as an integral element of the strategic management of organizations,[2] and Brown also has dealt with strategic issues in the management of organizations.[3]

This chapter will describe an approach to the assessment and management of strategic issues facing project teams as well as some strategic issues that have had an impact on contemporary projects. Project owners need to be aware of the possible and probable impacts of strategic issues. The project team leader has the primary responsibility to focus the owner's resources to deal with project strategic issues. This chapter will suggest three key aspects of strategic issue management: a need to be aware of strategic issues facing a project,

---

[1]David I. Cleland, "Strategic Issues in Project Management," *Project Management Journal,* March 1989.

[2]William R. King, "Strategic Issue Management," chap. 15, in W. R. King and D. I. Cleland (eds.), *Strategic Planning and Management Handbook* (New York: Van Nostrand Reinhold, 1986).

[3]J. K. Brown, "This Is Business of Issues: Coping with the Company's Environment," *The Conference Board Report,* no. 758, 1979.

an approach for the assessment of the strategic issues, and a technique for the management of strategic issues.

Sometimes the existence of strategic issues in an industry fosters the use of project management techniques in a fashion not previously used. For example, intense foreign competition in the U.S. automobile industry has prompted U.S. automobile manufacturers to develop innovations in the design of their cars. Cutting costs and cutting car design-development time are other key strategic issues facing U.S. producers. Their response to the need to reduce the time it takes to manufacture a car has, in part, been to use project management techniques in the form of an organizational alignment and a process of engineering manufacturing called *simultaneous engineering* or *use of product design teams.* In this approach, a project team is formed with representatives from design, engineering, manufacturing, marketing, finance, and suppliers working together to design the car, taking into consideration all the disciplines required to create the car. The result: shorter car model product-development cycles with consequent cost savings, improved quality, and a more competitive product in the world car market.

When the Japanese automaker Nissan considered building a plant in the United States, it recognized that a strategic issue facing that project was the adaptability of the local community and the workers to the Nissan culture. By carefully selecting their employees and using exchange trips to Japan, and by orientation sessions at the plant in Tennessee, the Japanese managers were able to resolve this strategic issue, resulting in a successful production facility characterized by model employee-management relations.

A. Jaafari discusses the strategic issues in the management of macroprojects in Australia by first looking at the typical pattern of managerial relationships that occur and must be administered in such macroprojects. These occur between

- Each participating owner and the joint venture or company acting as the collective body for owners (herein referred to as the *owner*)
- The owner and the government(s)
- The owner and the lenders
- The owner and purchasers of the end product(s)
- The owner and insurer/underwriters
- The owner and project manager or engineer-constructor
- The owner and constructors/suppliers, fabricators
- The owner and the designer[4]

---

[4]A. Jaafari, "Strategic Issues in Formulation and Management of Macroprojects in Australia," *International Journal of Project Management,* vol. 4, no. 2, May 1986.

These relationships emerge as the project stakeholders are identified and the nature of their stake is determined. Stakeholders are those persons or organizations that have, or claim to have, an interest or share in the project undertaking. Strategic issues can arise from many different stakeholder groups: customers, suppliers, the public, government, intervenors, and so forth.

In a project, a strategic issue is a condition of pressure, either internal or external, that will have a significant effect on one or more factors of the project, such as its financing, design, engineering, construction, and operation.[5] Some examples of the way that contemporary projects have faced strategic issues follow.

On the U.S. Supersonic Transport Program, the managers had too narrow a view of the essential players or stakeholders and generally dismissed the impact of the environment-related strategic issues surrounding the program until it was too late. Environmentalists, working through their political networks, succeeded in stopping the U.S. supersonic program.[6]

The life cycle of the Tennessee-Tombigbee Waterway provides insight into the negative role that strategic issues can play.[7] On this waterway project, strategic issues played a role in the consideration of funding for this project over many decades. Political considerations, lawsuits, environmental factors, and social factors delayed approval and construction of the project for extended periods. Although the actual construction of this waterway took almost 14 years, the waterway was 175 years in the making. As far back as 1810, the citizens of Knox County in Tennessee petitioned Congress to provide a waterway to Mobile Bay. Congress finally authorized the first federal study in 1974, but the project was delayed through 22 presidential administrations, 55 terms of Congress, eight major studies and restudies, and two major lawsuits. This waterway is one of the largest civil works projects ever designed and built by the Army Corps of Engineers. About 234 miles long, the project cost $2 billion and required more than 114 major contracts during its construction period.

In contrast to the handling of the Tennessee-Tombigbee Waterway, in the Midwest a Water Pollution Abatement Program costing approximately $2.5 million successfully faced challenging strategic issues at

[5]Definition derived from W. R. King and D. I. Cleland (eds.), *Strategic Planning and Management Handbook* (New York: Van Nostrand Reinhold, 1986), chaps. 1, 4, and 15.

[6]Mel Horwitch, *Clipped Wings: The American SST Conflict* (Cambridge, Mass.: The MIT Press, 1982).

[7]Paraphrased from General Kenneth McIntyre, *The Tennessee-Tombigbee Waterway,* Stone & Webster Engineering Corporation, Boston. Paper presented at the Larger Scale Programs Institute, Colloquium on Research Priorities for Large Scale Programs, Austin, Tex., March 1985. This project is also described in Chap. 1.

the outset and during the early years of the program. The development of a master plan for the project included the development of appropriate environment impact statements. This master plan could not be changed without court and Environmental Protection Agency (EPA) approval. Since the funding for the project included EPA federal grants, state grants, general obligation bonds, and tax district levies, the courts became involved in the planning and execution of the project. The Army Corps of Engineers reviewed all construction contract documents before bidding, reviewed all change orders to the construction contracts, reviewed completed construction, and audited contract administration procedures. All the work that received federal grant participation ultimately was audited by the EPA and Army Corps of Engineers, as well as state and local auditors. In addition, the General Accounting Office conducted periodic reviews of the project. All these stakeholder groups became involved in the legal and regulatory strategic issues that arose on this project. Successful management of this project included the management of not only the project team, but also the project stakeholders and the strategic issues that faced this project throughout its life cycle.

Strategic issues can emerge at any time during a project's life cycle. The following is an illustration of how costly it can be to ignore them. On a large nuclear power plant project, an offshore earthquake fault was discovered only a few miles from the plant site. This occurred midway through the project's life cycle. Although the discovery of this fault was obviously a significant strategic issue, there was little evidence that the senior managers of the owner organization demanded and received a "satisfactory accounting" or made any in-depth inquiry to determine its full ramifications. The potential strategic implications of the fault should have prompted the corporate board of directors to

1. Ask for an immediate, in-depth study of its possible and probable effects on the design of the plant.

2. Acknowledge the need to forthrightly resolve the effects of the earthquake fault on the seismic design of the plant.

3. Order a full-scale audit of the current status of the plant.

The project owner was not able to provide any evidence that the board of directors or the executive committee of the board considered the available options of

1. Withdrawing its license application or stopping work

2. Significantly reducing work at the site pending a full-scale investigation of the implications of the fault

3. Accelerating offshore investigations to speed resolution of any questions that might have been raised

There was no evidence that the board of directors considered any options other than that of continuing work, so that after the plant was completed, the board members were faced with the enormous costly problem of redesigning the plant so that it could function safely in spite of its poor location.[8] Public concern over the seismic-geologic potential safety of this plant was expressed through the organized efforts of several intervenor or stakeholder groups acting through the courts to require reassessment, or even cancellation, of the plant.

The successful completion of any substantial public works project is dependent upon the recognition and management of strategic issues surrounding the social, political, legal, and economic aspects of the project as well as the cost, schedule, and technical performance aspects. On these public works the project can expect to encounter strategic issues such as

- Land acquisition challenges

- Environmental impacts

- Political support or uncertainty

- Advocacy usually related to who conceives, champions, nurtures the project and provides ongoing maneuvering to keep the project alive and well—a task partially fulfilled by the project managers

- Intervenors ranging from such organizations as local newspapers to vested interested groups such as the Sierra Club

- Competitors who would like to see the project fail so they could pick up some of or all the action

An Application of the Concept of Strategic Issues: Nuclear Construction Industry

Strategic issues vary depending on the industry and the circumstances of a particular project. In the material that follows, the nuclear plant construction industry is used to illustrate the concept of strategic issues as applied to a select industry. This industry has been chosen because of the many strategic issues that have faced that industry—issues which relate to a particular project as well as to the many generic issues that confront project owners, managers, con-

---

[8] Paraphrased from testimony submitted by the author during litigation on the Diablo Canyon rate case, California Public Utilities Commission, Division of Ratepayer Advocates, Application nos. 84-06-014 and 85-08-025, June 1988.

structors, designers, regulators, investors, local communities, consumers, and other vested stakeholder groups.

A project that has as long a life cycle as a nuclear power generating plant will be affected by many issues (some of them linked) that are truly strategic in nature. For example, the typical strategic issues that a nuclear power plant project faces today include

- Licensability

- Passive safety

- Power costs

- Reliability of generating system

- Nuclear fuel reprocessing

- Waste management

- Capital investment

- Public perception

- Advocacy

- Environment

- Safeguards[9]

The U.S. nuclear power industry has had extraordinary challenges in the past years such as uncertain licensing procedures, project cost and schedule control problems, quality assurance disputes, intervenor actions, and other conditions which are strategic issues to be dealt with by a project team in managing a nuclear power plant project. A discussion of these issues follows.

Licensability

All U.S. nuclear plants, to be licensed, must meet federal codes and standards as well as the nuclear regulatory guides for the particular design. But many of these codes, standards, and guides are not applicable to a new concept and design that have not been licensed previously. The first-of-a-kind becomes precedent setting and will receive a commensurate amount of attention from the Nuclear Regulatory Commission (NRC) staff—so much so that joint groups will be set up with representation from the Department of Energy (DOE), NRC, and a bevy of consultant experts to answer the thousands of questions posed by the NRC staff and to draft appropriate

---

[9]These strategic issues were developed during the conduct of a research project by D. I. Cleland and D. F. Kocaoglu, *The Design of a Strategic Management System for Reactor Systems, Development and Technology,* Argonne, Ill.: Department of Energy with the assistance of A. N. Tardiff and C. E. Klotz of the Argonne National Laboratory.

revisions to the existing federal codes and regulations as well as to set up future guides for the new concept.

This strategic issue can take years to resolve when one includes the judicial, state, and local hearing processes that a nuclear plant must face. The lack of firm and predictable policy emanating from the NRC now adds to the risk and uncertainty involved in the management of this strategic issue. Such issues and uncertainties are reflected in the increased costs and schedules for the project. The challenge facing the NRC is forthright—remove the uncertainty of the current licensing process that exists today. The NRC that licenses the plant, and the state and local governments that conduct hearings to ascertain the proper allocation of costs for the utility's rate base, are key stakeholders in the project.

Passive safety

All the commercial reactors built and operated in the United States today require the activation, within a prescribed period, of an auxiliary shutdown system, either automatic or manual. At present, if one allows the reactor to operate without adding reactivity (a process similar to adding coal to a fire) and assuming that the cooling systems remain effective (the pumps operate, the valves open and close on cue, the heat exchangers transfer heat, etc.), the reactor should eventually bring the auxiliary system into operation. The difficulty comes when the auxiliary system cannot halt or lower the reactivity (like removing coal from the fire) and/or maintain the effectiveness of the cooling systems.

Passive safety, as it relates to a nuclear power plant, refers to the plant's ability to take advantage of inherent, natural characteristics to move itself into a safe condition without the need to activate an automatic auxiliary safety system or a set of predetermined operator procedures to do the same.

Passive safety is the dominant strategic issue facing the nuclear power generating industry today. This issue is both social (it would help overcome fear of nuclear power) and technical (design and operating considerations). The nuclear accidents at Three Mile Island and Chernobyl have intensified the search for a nuclear power plant that promises passive safety. Nuclear vendors and utility companies are the key stakeholders interested in passive safety. Indeed, all of us are stakeholders in wanting economical and safe power-generating capacity in the modern world.

Power costs

The components of power costs are capital costs, operations, and maintenance (O&M), and fuel costs. For a typical nuclear power plant, the capital cost component is 4 times the O&M cost, which is approximately equal to the fuel cost. Hence, it is evident that capital cost is the most significant component and is discussed in more detail below. One of the significant factors leading to the current hiatus in orders for new nuclear power plants is that these plants are extremely capital-intensive and have relatively low fuel costs. Coal- and oil-fired plants have a relatively low capital cost component while their fuel costs are extremely high.

Construction times for many recent U.S. nuclear plants have exceeded 10 years. The U.S. licensing and judicial procedures have accounted for much of the delay, but other factors, such as imprudent project management, also have taken their toll. Whatever the reasons, the delays have an extraordinary impact on the resultant capital investment in these plants even before they have produced 1 kWh of electricity. The interest paid on the capital to build the plant commonly is greater than 50 percent of the capital investment in the plant. As a result, there has been an inordinate increase in the capital cost component so that nuclear power has now lost its competitive power cost edge over its closest competitor, coal. Some of or all the following approaches might be pursued to alleviate this problem:

- Reform and remove uncertainties in the licensing process.
- Design the plants to be constructed faster on site.
- Build smaller plants.
- Supply turn-key plants with guarantees.
- Simplify the plants and reduce the amount of material used.
- Develop standard plant design.

Utilities, nuclear reactor manufacturers, architectural and engineering firms, plant constructors, and state regulatory commissions are the principal stakeholders concerned with the strategic issue of power costs.

Reliability of generating system

The reliability of a nuclear power plant must be extremely high, particularly in the safety systems and components. There are reliability differences from one model to another; i.e., one might have fewer moving parts, fewer systems, fewer components, and fewer things to go wrong.

Plants designed and constructed under stringent quality assurance controls will be more reliable than plants where the quality standards have been relaxed. Concepts that utilize more factory-built than on-site fabricated and assembled systems tend to be more reliable since quality assurance can be applied more easily at the factory. Gravity and natural circulation-dependent systems tend to be more reliable than forced-circulation systems. The importance of these and more reliable approaches to a nuclear power plant cannot be overemphasized, particularly in view of Three Mile Island, Chernobyl, and the resultant skeptical public attitude toward nuclear power. Utilities are the principal stakeholders here.

Nuclear fuel reprocessing

Commercial nuclear fuel reprocessing in the United States is virtually nonexistent. Instead, the U.S. government has agreed, for a price, to accept the spent fuel from U.S. reactors for long-term storage. Europe and Japan, however, have viable programs to recover for future use the nuclear fissionable fuel from spent fuel assemblies. Any concept, such as the breeder, which requires reprocessing technology must carry the burden of developing this technology as well as the nuclear proliferation stigma attached to it. Thus, any future nuclear plant in the United States may require the arrival of a liquid-metal reactor technology which provides for the use of reprocessed fuel. The time frame for such fuel reprocessing capability is circa 2040 by best current estimates. Utilities and reactor manufacturers are the principal stakeholders.

Waste management

Public reaction to shipments of nuclear waste is becoming increasingly severe. Hence, minimum waste streams and minimum movement of such wastes outside the plant boundaries are advisable. The waste disposal program conceived and managed by the U.S. government and the nuclear power industry to store radioactive fuel safely is being challenged under public pressure. Unreasonable management and cost overruns aside, one of the biggest issues for the nuclear power industry is what to do with the 1500 metric tons of lethal atomic waste that it produces each year. Utilities, states where storage sites are located, and the general public are vested stakeholders in this strategic issue.

Capital investment

Closely akin to the strategic issue of power costs are the financial exposure and risks that investors of nuclear power plants have experienced over the last several years. For example, the Pennsylvania State Public Utility Commission recently ruled that the Pennsylvania Power and Light Company's newly opened, 945-MW, $2 billion Susquehanna Unit 2 nuclear plant would provide too much generating capacity for the utility's customers. The utility was allowed to recover only taxes, depreciation, and other operating costs.

There have been awesome financial implications for all too many nuclear plants. One of the most sobering has been the experience of the Washington Public Power Supply System (WPPSS). WPPSS's default on interest payments due on $2.5 billion in outstanding bonds can be laid on the failure of WPPSS management. Management style in WPPSS did not keep pace with the growing size and complexity of the organization. Communication at senior levels of the organization, including the board of directors, tended to be "informal, disorganized, and infrequent."[10] To renew support of nuclear power in the financial communities, it is important that the current conditions change along the lines noted in the discussion of the power cost issue in this article. Investment institutions are the principal stakeholders as well as the state public utility groups that must rule on the acceptability of a capital investment cost into the utility's rate base.

Public perception

Table 7.1 demonstrates the strategic issue of public perception quite clearly. The experts rank nuclear power 20th in the list of high-risk items, whereas the other groups rank it first or close to first. Note that X-rays and nonnuclear electric power fall into the same pattern. When the United States converted from direct current to alternating current in the early 1920s, a similar negative public reaction resulted. Some extensive innovative technical, social, and managerial approaches must be developed and implemented to change perceptions.

Aggravated by the nuclear accidents at Three Mile Island and Chernobyl, the increasingly negative public perception of nuclear power and its associated risks has made this strategic issue more acute, and the need for government research programs more pressing.

Advocacy

Not many government interest research programs can proceed through the government bureaucracy without a strong advocate who can gain substantial support for the program. The base of support must be broad and must include, as is the case with the research in the Advanced Reactor Development Program, key individuals within the DOE, the White House, the Office of Management and Budget, Congress and its staff offices, the nuclear community (the stakeholders), the scientific community (National Science Foundation, National

---

[10]James Leigland, "WPPSS: Some Basic Lessons for Public Enterprise Managers," *California Management Review,* Winter 1987, pp. 78–88.

TABLE 7.1   Risk: A Matter of Perception. Four Groups Rank What's Dangerous and What's Not

	Experts	League of Women Voters	College students	Civic club members
Motor vehicles	1	2	5	3
Smoking	2	4	3	4
Alcoholic beverages	3	6	7	5
Handguns	4	3	2	1
Surgery	5	10	11	9
Motorcycles	6	5	6	2
X-rays	7	22	17	24
Pesticides	8	9	4	15
Electric power (nonnuclear)	9	18	19	19
Swimming	10	19	30	17
Contraceptives	11	20	9	22
General (private) aviation	12	7	15	11
Large construction	13	12	14	13
Food preservatives	14	25	12	28
Bicycles	15	16	24	14
Commercial aviation	16	17	16	18
Police work	17	8	8	7
Firefighting	18	11	10	6
Railroads	19	24	23	20
Nuclear power	20	1	1	8
Food coloring	21	26	20	30
Home appliances	22	29	27	27
Hunting	23	13	18	10
Prescription antibiotics	24	28	21	26
Vaccinations	25	30	29	29
Spray cans	26	14	13	23
High school and college football	27	23	26	21
Power mowers	28	27	28	25
Mountain climbing	29	15	22	12
Skiing	30	21	25	16

People were asked to "consider the risk of dying as a consequence of this activity or technology."

SOURCE: Decision Research, Eugene, Ore. (© *Washington Post,* May 21, 1986).

Academy of Sciences, certain universities), the financial community, and others. With such backing, the public generally supports the program. A single-effect advocate also can be an essential ingredient. Military aircraft and the aircraft carrier had Billy Mitchell; the nuclear submarine fleet had Hyman Rickover; the space program had

Werner von Braun—the list is long of successful efforts led by able champions. Thus, a reactor manufacturer who contemplates obtaining government funds to research advanced nuclear reactors should determine what advocacy existed for such research, both in the government and in the corporation.

Environment

From an environmental viewpoint, the nuclear advocates had essentially convinced the general public that nuclear power plants were environmentally benign—until the media convinced the public otherwise after the Three Mile Island incident. The Chernobyl incident reinforced the sense that nuclear power was a serious threat to the environment and to life itself. Certainly the environmental impact of the Chernobyl accident on its surrounding environment is as yet uncertain.

Reassuring the public that there will be no future Chernobyl-type accidents will be no easy task. Much work must be done to convince people that such an accident cannot occur in the United States. This certainly must be convincingly transmitted to the stakeholders who are the potential owners of nuclear power plants, the administration, Congress, and above all the general public itself. A most environmentally benign and inherently safe nuclear plant would go a long way to settling this issue. Unfortunately, such a plant may be decades away.

Safeguards

The objective of nuclear safeguards is to keep fissionable material out of unauthorized hands. A nuclear plant security system that does this better than another should have a competitive edge. For example, if throughout the fuel cycle of a particular plant, the plant configuration prevents the fissionable fuel from being deployed and used as source material for a weapon, then one could say that the plant is proliferation-proof.

Managing Project Strategic Issues

Project issues often are nebulous, defying management in the literal sense of the word. It is important that the project team identify the strategic issues the project faces and deal with them in terms of how they may affect the outcome of the project. In the assessment of the issues, some may be set aside as not having a significant impact on the project. These would not be reacted to, but would be monitored to see if any changes occur that could affect the project. Of course, some significant issues may not be subject to the influence of the project team.

The early identification of issues is important so that there can be an early decision on how issues are to be handled. An issue tends to go through a life cycle such as described in General Electric's approach to public issues, where phases of *conversion, contention, legislation,* and *regulation* are discussed.[11]

A useful technique to identify strategic issues facing a project is to keep a running tally of all issues that face the project and then take time to have the project team discuss these issues to see which ones are *operational* (short-term) and which are *strategic* (in the manner described in this book). Once the project team has been acquainted with the notion of strategic issues, each member should be encouraged to note any emerging issues for discussion and review at one of the regular project team meetings. During this meeting all issues should be reviewed, selecting those which appear to be strategic and assigning a member of the team to follow the issue and keep the project team aware of it and its implications on the project's future. More serious issues may require the appointment of an investigative subproject team who will report back to the full team. An example of how one project team's awareness of strategic issues early in the project's life cycle proved useful appears below.

A kickoff meeting of the project team and the senior managers from the owner's organization was held to get the project team organized and to start preliminary project planning. During this three-day meeting a tally was made of issues known to impact or have potential future impact on the project. Some issues were determined to be truly strategic, and the group decided to track them to determine their significance. If such a tally had not been done and if the preliminary discussions had not been carried out, it is highly probable that some of the more important issues might not have surfaced until the project was into its life cycle. By then an orderly and timely resolution of some of these issues would have been difficult, if not impossible. This suggests that an important part of any project review meeting is to discuss and update the current project issues to see which ones might be added. By the same process, those issues judged as no longer important could be put aside.

The project team requires a philosophy on how to manage strategic issues. A phased approach is suggested as portrayed in Fig. 7.1. These phases are discussed below.

Issue identification

Identifying some of the issues often can come about during the selection of the project to support the organizational strategy. During the selection process the following criteria can be addressed to determine if the project truly supports organizational strategy:

---

[11]J. K. Brown, op. cit.

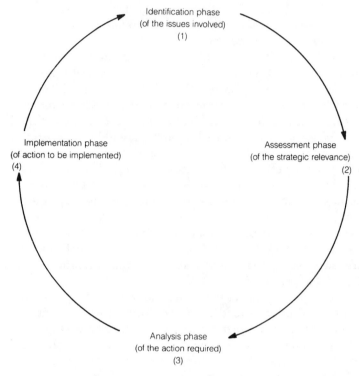

Figure 7.1   An approach for the management of project strategic issues

1. Does the project support a strength that the enterprise holds?
2. Does it avoid a dependence on something that is a weakness of the enterprise?
3. Does the project support an organizational need?
4. Is there a customer who is willing to pay for the project?
5. Can the project owner assume the risk that is involved in the project?
6. Are the resources and management skills available to bring the project to completion on time and within budget?[12]

As the decision makers seek the answers to these questions, there will be some strategic issues which emerge naturally. Other issues can be identified by the project team during its planning, evaluation, and control meetings.

---

[12]Paraphrased from D. I. Cleland and W. R. King, *Systems Analysis and Project Management,* 3d ed. (New York: McGraw-Hill, 1985), pp. 67–68. These questions are similar to those asked during the project selection process. See chap. 4, p. 84.

For example, during a customer review of a bid package for a new weapon system, an aerospace contractor's project proposal team discovered that the customer had serious doubts about the contractor's cost-estimating ability. This concern prompted the contractor to engage a consultant to conduct a survey of its customers to assess its image in two general areas: *product image* (price, quality, reliability, etc.) and *organizational image* (quality of personnel, responsiveness, integrity, etc.). Both structured and unstructured personnel interviews were conducted with key customer personnel. One significant outcome of this image survey was the perception by key customer personnel that the contractor's cost estimates were far too conservative, invariably resulting in excessive cost overruns. The contractor's key executives were shocked by the customer's perceptions of its cost performance credibility. This matter of credibility immediately became an urgent strategic issue within the contractor's organization. A task force was formed to investigate the issue and recommend a strategy on how to deal with it. In their deliberations the task force found that the contractors' cost performance was in fact quite credible, and that the perception held by the customer's key people was not valid. Consequently, the contractor mounted an advertising and indoctrination program to change the customer's viewpoint by working through the field marketing people and by visiting the customer's offices to present the actual facts on contractor cost performance. The result was a resolution of the strategic issue in the contractor's favor. Had the project proposal team not been alerted to this potential strategic issue, the contractor may well have continued to lose government contracts.

By maintaining close contact with the customer, an opportunity is provided to identify issues that can have an impact on the project. Another technique is to examine the stakeholders on the project to see if the nature of their claims suggests any strategic issues.[13] As each stakeholder group is reviewed, the following questions should be addressed:

1. What stake do the stakeholders have in the project?
2. How might the stake affect the outcome of the project?
3. What resources and influence do the stakeholders have to push the satisfaction of their stake?
4. Can the project live with the stakeholder's purposes and motivation?
5. Can the outcome of the stakeholder's claim on the project be predicted?

---

[13] D. I. Cleland, "Project Stakeholder Management," *Project Management Journal,* vol. 17, no. 4, September 1986, pp. 36–44.

6. What can the project team do about these claims?

Other techniques can be used such as the *nominal group technique*[14] or brainstorming to aid in the identification of issues.

Perhaps the best way to identify issues is to ensure that the project team is well organized, well managed, and well aware of the larger systems context (economic, political, social, technological, and competitive) of the project. If the team meets these conditions, there is a better likelihood that most of the important and relevant strategic issues will surface.

Assessment of an issue

The act of assessing an issue entails judging its importance in terms of its impact on the project. King has suggested four criteria for first assessing an issue as strategic and then moving to subsequent states of management of the issue:[15]

- Strategic relevance
- Actionability
- Criticality
- Urgency

The *strategic relevance* of an issue relates to whether it will have a long-term impact (more than one year) on the project. Most of the strategic issues mentioned earlier in this chapter could be considered to be strategically relevant, such as licensability, passive safety, power costs, etc. Strategic relevance addresses the question: Will this strategic issue influence the project strategy or the likely consequences of the strategies that are being followed on the project? If an issue is strategy-relevant, then the project manager has two basic courses of action: Try to live with the issue's impact, or do something about the issue.

But some strategic issues will be beyond the authority and resources of the project manager to resolve. In such situations a third course is open to the project manager: Elevate the issue to senior managers for their analysis and possible evaluation. Even though senior managers are aware of the issue, the project manager retains residual responsibility to see that the issue is "tracked" and given due attention.

---

[14]The process is explained in A. H. Van de Ven and H. L. Delbecq, "Nominal versus Interacting Group Processes for Committee Decision Making," *Academy of Management Journal,* vol. 14, no. 2, 1971.

[15]W. R. King, "Strategic Issue Management," in W. R. King and D. I. Cleland (eds.), *Strategic Planning and Management Handbook* (New York: Van Nostrand Reinhold, 1986, pp. 252–264.

The *actionability* of a project issue deals with the capability of the project term and the enterprise to do something about the issue. For example, the issue of licensability of a new nuclear power plant is critical to the decision of whether to fund such a plant. A company can help to resolve the licensability of nuclear power plants by participating with the industry's groups that are trying to influence the Nuclear Regulatory Commission either directly or through congressional persuasion to do something about the uncertainties related to licensing. Such participation would be useful in influencing the strategic issue as well as for keeping informed about the status of the issue. The related strategic issue of funding support for a power generating plant would be an issue that the enterprise would actively try to resolve by working with investment bankers in the financial community.

A project may face strategic issues about which little can be done. Keeping track of the issue and considering its potential impact on project decisions may be the only realistic action the team can take. Key project managers should always be aware that there are issues that may be beyond their influence.

The *criticality* of an issue is the determined impact that the issue can have on the project's outcome. The issue of growing congressional disenchantment with the U.S. Supersonic Transport Program arose from the concern of the environmentalists over the sonic boom problem. Proactive environmental groups along with the general public exerted political influence which contributed to the termination of that program. Project advocates recognized too late that the sonic boom controversy was the critical fulcrum for the environmentalists to use for their public and congressional support.

If a preliminary analysis of an issue indicates it is noncritical, then the issue should be monitored and periodically evaluated to see if its status has changed.

The *urgency* of an issue has to do with the time period in which something needs to be done. All else being equal, if an issue should be dealt with immediately, it must take precedence over other issues. Urgent issues emerging during the project planning should be considered as a "work package" in the management of the project. Someone should be designated as the issue work package manager to look after the issue, particularly during its urgency status.

The accident at the Three Mile Island nuclear plant and the subsequent uncertainties over plant design and licensing posed serious and urgent strategic issues for all nuclear plants in the design and construction phases of their life cycle. Although most project managers would have considered this an urgent issue, there were limits as to what could be done, except to track the issue and try to influence the NRC and other government agencies through the industry's societies and political contacts.

H. Ross Perot's controversial contract for a project with the U.S. Postal Service faced a strategic issue soon after the award was announced. The contract immediately drew fire because it was awarded without competitive bidding. The General Accounting Office began an investigation, followed by a U.S. Senate resolution requesting that the contract be put on hold pending further study. The General Services Administration's Board of Contract Appeals nullified the contract. It is not known if the lack of competitive bidding with the U.S. Postal Service was ever considered as a possible "strategic issue" by the Perot Systems Corporation team. But that is the way things have turned out. It has become an issue with considerable urgency affecting a major project for that corporation.

Analysis of action

Identification and assessment of an issue are not enough; the issue has to be managed so that its adverse effect on the project is minimized and its potential benefit is maximized. The issue work package manager is in charge of collecting information, tracking the project, and ensuring that the issue remains visible to the project team. That manager should also coordinate decisions made and implemented regarding the issue.

In the analysis of action required to deal with an issue, seeking answers to a series of questions like the following can be helpful:

1. What will be the probable effect of the issue in terms of impact on the project's schedule, cost, and technical performance and the owner's strategy?

2. Who are the principal stakeholders who have an interest in the project? What will be the impact on their probable strategy?

3. How influential are these stakeholders?

4. What strategy should the project team develop to deal with these issues?

5. What might be the real cost in relation to the apparent cost to the project owner, and will other projects being funded by the project owner be affected?

6. What specific action will be required, and what will it cost the project owner?

The action developed to deal with the issue may, at the minimum, consist of simply monitoring the issue and giving status reports to the project team. Some issues, however, may require a more aggressive approach. The issue work package manager may find it useful to think of the issue as having a life cycle, with such phases as conception, definition, production, operations, and termination, and to identify the key actions to be considered and accomplished during each phase. The manager should be specific and should stipulate what will be done, when it will be done, how to do it, where, and who will be in charge of implementing the action leading to resolution of the issue.

Implementation

However it is dealt with, the resolution of an issue or the mitigation of its effects requires that a *project plan of action* be developed and implemented. Indeed, the resolution of a strategic issue can be dealt with as a miniproject requiring the execution of the management functions—planning, organizing, direction, and control—and all these functions entail some degree of work breakdown analysis, scheduling, cost estimating, matrix responsibility, information systems, design of monitoring and control, and so on. What resources are to be used to resolve the issue and who should take the leadership role in resolving that issue are the crucial questions to be answered.

Summary

The successful management of a project requires an awareness and management of the strategic issues that face that project during its life cycle. Since a strategic issue is inseparable from a project, such an issue should be treated as a project work package with someone in charge who, working with the project team, develops a strategy for successfully coping with the strategic issue.

There are four basic steps to dealing with project strategic issues:

1. Issue identification
2. Assessment of the relevance of the issue
3. Analysis of action
4. Implementation of action

Discussion Questions

1. Define *strategic issue.*
2. Select a project management situation from your work or school experience, and list the strategic issues.
3. What methods might project managers employ to identify the strategic issues of a project?
4. What approaches can be used by project leaders to assess the impact of a strategic issue?

5. What management techniques can be used to address strategic issues?

6. Discuss the importance of consideration of public perception.

7. What roles do environmental issues play in projects such as power plants and other major construction projects?

8. List and define the elements of the phase approach to dealing with strategic issues.

9. In identifying the strategic issues of a project, management can ask questions pertaining to the project stakeholders. What kinds of questions should be asked?

10. What is meant by the *strategic relevance* of an issue?

11. How can management assess the criticality and urgency of a strategic issue?

12. How can managers ensure that project team members are aware of and understand the project strategic issues?

User Checklist

1. Do the project managers of your organization understand the concept of strategic issues? How do they manifest this understanding in managing projects?

2. Do any formal methods exist in your organization for strategic issue management? What are they? How are they used?

3. Do the project managers of your organization attempt to identify project interfaces that can seriously impact the outcome of a project? Explain.

4. Does top management use any postproject appraisals to help uncover strategic issue-related problems? Does management see the value in postproject appraisals?

5. Does the management of your organization recognize the importance of understanding public perception? In what ways do project managers control public perception?

6. Are there any outside advocates that can be or are effective in altering public opinion in favor of your organization's projects?

7. Do project managers assess the environmental impacts of projects? In what ways?

8. Could the phase approach to managing strategic issues be used effectively in your organization? How?

9. What kinds of questions does management ask in attempting to identify strategic issues? Are the right questions being asked?

10. Does management seek to identify the relevant issues for each project stakeholder?

11. Does management identify the strategic relevance of each issue and determine the actionability, criticality, and urgency? In what ways is this done? What other methods could be used?

12. Are project team members made aware of strategic issues? How? Do they then attempt to monitor these issues as they relate to their own work packages?

Organizational Design for Project Management

8

Organizing for Project Management

*"...to our worship of quantity and indiffer-
ence to quality, to our unthinking devotion to
organization, standardization..."*
DANIEL GREGORY MASON, 1873–1960

In this chapter we examine the project-driven organization, including its alternatives in coping with the use of cross-functional teams
characteristic of the *matrix* organization. The chapter will offer
some suggestions on how to deal with the matrix organization,
including a brief insight into the systems nature of such an organizational design.

The systems view of an organization emphasizes the interrelatedness of organizational forces and stresses an integrated totality
rather than a provincial view. A systems-oriented organization is a
dynamic, purposeful goal-seeking entity. A systems viewpoint is
based on the notion of the interdependency of subsystems. Barnard
stated, "The primary efforts of leaders need to be directed to the
maintenance and guidance of organizations as whole systems of activities."[1] Explicit in project management is the systems idea of the temporary organization, constantly changing, fluid, and varied. It is the
emergence of such temporary organizations that has modified the traditional concept of organizational design.

Here are a few examples of how deficiencies in the organizational
design affect project success (and failure):

---

[1]Chester I. Barnard, "The Nature of Leadership," *Organization and Management*
(Cambridge, Mass.: Harvard University Press, 1948), pp. 88–89.

- On the Shoreham Generating Plant project of the Long Island Lighting Company, the organizational arrangement left lines of authority and responsibility blurred and unclear from the start. The lack of adequate organization was a major deficiency that significantly prejudiced the utility's ability to manage the project. Over the life of the project, despite repeated complaints about role confusion and tangled lines of authority and unclear accountability, the senior managers of the utility failed to create an organizational framework that allowed its managers to direct and manage the construction of the plan efficiently.[2]

- An investigation of the Trans-Alaska Pipeline System (TAPS) project indicated that organizational structure significantly influenced project performance.[3]

- A Rand Corporation study of "new technology" process plant construction found that the most prominently mentioned management-related reason for increased costs was "diffused decision-making responsibility for a project."[4]

- The fatal launch of Challenger is an example of some difficulties that had their genesis in a faulty organizational design. NASA's leaders were preoccupied with raising money for NASA from Congress. The organizational components of NASA were supposed to work together, but the Marshall, Kennedy, and Johnson Space Centers behaved more like baronies, not communicating with each other or with the top of NASA. The flow of information up and down the NASA hierarchy was, according to *Fortune* magazine, as flawed as the now notorious O rings.[5] The Marshall Space Center had an ambiguous chain of command with a reporting relationship to the Johnson Space Center in Houston, but not under Johnson's management control. The Marshall Center also reports to the Office of Space Flight at NASA headquarters and in theory cooperates closely with the Kennedy Center in Florida. However, the anomalies in the organizational reporting relationships are further blurred by cultural factors which allowed jeal-

---

[2]Paraphrased from the Recommended Decision by Administrative Law Judges C. Levey and Thomas R. Matias, Case no. 27563, *Long Island Lighting Company-Shoreham Prudence Investigation,* State of New York Public Service Commission, March 13, 1985.

[3]T. F. Lenzner, *The Management, Planning and Construction of the Trans-Alaska Pipeline System* (Anchorage, Ala.: Pipeline Commission, 1977).

[4]Rand Corporation, *A Review of Cost Estimation in New Technologies: Implications for Energy Process Plants,* Santa Monica, Calif., July 1978.

[5]Michael Brody, "NASA's Challenge: Ending Isolation at the Top," *Fortune,* May 12, 1986.

ousy and rivalry to exist among Marshall, Johnson, and Kennedy Centers. Also, there was resistance to NASA headquarters' oversight of their operations.[6]

In response to the need to manage projects better, some companies have undergone organizational realignment. Prior to 1981, the project managers at Consolidate Edison Company Inc. resided in the construction department. These project managers were responsible for a large number of projects at all dollar levels and of various degrees of importance to the company's operation. Since the project managers were concerned with construction management duties, little time was available for effective project management.

The company corrected this weakness and formed a new project management department independent of the construction function. The new department reports to the senior vice president for construction, engineering, and environmental affairs. A specific set of objectives was established for the new department, a chief project manager was appointed to administer the day-to-day activities of the department, and project managers were held accountable by the senior vice president for their project goals. Project management was further strengthened by specific delineations of project authority and responsibility criteria, careful selection of project managers, and the development of policies and procedures for project evaluation and control.[7]

In some cases, a company will modify its organizational design to reduce the number of organizational levels in the corporate structure. At General Electric, the traditional organization headed by a general manager who had people under her or his command responsible for designing, manufacturing, and marketing a product is being changed. In GE's manufacturing business, functional work such as engineering and marketing is being centralized. A product manager is appointed who is responsible for coordinating all the functions involved in making and selling a product. Such individuals command a small staff and negotiate separately with specialists in design, engineering, production, marketing, and distribution. Operating in a *matrix* mode, these product managers represent one of the current shifts from top-down hierarchies to horizontal management as a means to reduce work force and the number of organizational levels in modern organizations.[8]

Project management has led the way in the formalization of the erosion and crossing of organizational boundaries. In today's competi-

---

[6] Ibid.

[7] William J. Bennett, "Project Management at Con Edison," *Project Management Institute Seminar/Symposium,* 1982.

[8] Peter Hultz, "How Managers Will Manage," *Fortune,* February 2, 1987, pp. 47–50.

tive world, the crossing of many boundaries—functional, geographic, organizational—is showing promise of becoming a way of life. Jack Welch, CEO of General Electric, says that "to create what we call 'boundaryless' companies, we no longer have the time to climb over barriers between functions like engineering and marketing, or between people—hourly, salaried, management, and the like. Geographic barriers must evaporate....We've got to simplify and delegate more—simply trust more. We need to drive self-confidence deep into the organization. We have...to convince our managers that their role is not to control people and stay on top of things, but rather to guide, energize, and excite."[9]

Surely project managers, who have had to survive in boundaryless organizational designs, are well equipped to provide leadership in reaching the boundaryless companies envisioned by Jack Welch.

The Project Organization

The term *project organization* is used to denote an interorganizational team pulled together for a specific purpose. Personnel are drawn from the organization's functional units to perform a specific task; the organization is temporary, built around the purpose to be accomplished, rather than on the basis of functional similarity, process, product, or other traditional bases. When such a team is assembled and superimposed on the existing structure, a matrix organization is formed. The matrix organization encompasses the complementary functional and project units. Figure 8.1 is a model of the matrix organization.

Before we examine the matrix organization, a brief review of other means of organizing is needed. Organizational theorists have developed various ways of dividing the organization into subunits to improve efficiency and to decentralize authority, responsibility, and accountability through a process of *departmentalization,* with the objective of arriving at an orderly arrangement of the interdependent parts of the organization. Departmentalization is integral to the delegation process. The most widely used system of departmentalization includes

- *Functional* departmentalization where the organizational units are based on distinct common specialties such as finance, engineering, and manufacturing

- *Product* departmentalization by organizing into distinct units responsible for a major product or product line

---

[9]Jack Welch, 1992 General Electric Annual Report.

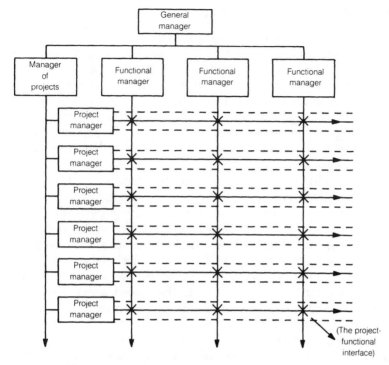

Figure 8.1   A basic project management matrix.

- *Customer* departmentalization where organizational units are designated around customer groups such as the Department of Defense

- *Territorial* departmentalization with people located in units based on geographic lines, e.g., western U.S. marketing zone

- *Process* departmentalization where the human and other resources are based on a flow of work such as an oil refinery

In the late 1950s and early 1960s, these traditional forms of organizing resources were proving inadequate to cope with the need to integrate the disparate organizational activities required of such ad hoc endeavors as a project. Experimentation with alternative, more flexible forms of organization was used to meet the demands of the evolving, dynamic "projects" business. The result was a blend of the functional structure and a designated focal point for managing a project within an enterprise. The *project-driven matrix organization* evolved as essentially a network of interactions between a project team and the traditional functional elements of an organization.

Various Forms of the Project Organization

A variety of project-driven organizational forms exists. At one extreme is the *pure project organization,* where the project manager is given full authority to run a project as if it were a one-product company; at the other extreme is the pure functional organizational department on a traditional basis, reflecting the traditional hierarchy. In the middle lies a variety of project-functional combinations of the matrix organization. Each of these forms has certain advantages and disadvantages; no one form is best for all projects, or even best for one project throughout its entire life cycle. The essence of project organization is flexibility. The project can be built around the organizational strategy; as the strategy changes, so must the focus of the organization.

Five different project organizational designs have been identified by researchers in the field: (1) the *functional,* where the project is divided and assigned to appropriate functional entities with the coordination of the project being carried out by functional and higher-level managers; (2) the *functional matrix,* where the project manager is vested with the authority to coordinate the project across the functions of the enterprise with the functional managers retaining authority and responsibility for their specialized areas of expertise; (3) the *balanced matrix,* where the project manager shares the authority and responsibility with the functional managers, and by joint effort the project and functional managers provide direction to the project and share in the decision process; (4) the *project matrix,* where a project manager oversees the project and has the authority and responsibility for completing the project and the functional managers assign the technical specialists needed to provide expertise for the team's work; and (5) the *project team,* where core personnel from the functional areas are assigned to the project on a full-time basis and the functional managers have no formal involvement.[10]

In one study of the significance of project management structure on the success of 546 development projects, it was found that projects relying on the functional organization or a functional matrix were less successful than those which used a balanced matrix, project matrix, or project team. The project matrix outperformed the balanced matrix in meeting schedule and outperformed the project team in controlling cost.

Basic definitions of the types of structures in this study were similar to the types described in earlier research by Larson and Gobeli:

---

[10]Erik W. Larson and David H. Gobeli, "Project Management Structures: Is There a Common Language? *Project Management Journal,* June 1985, pp. 40–44; and Jay R. Galbraith, "Matrix Organization Designs—How to Combine Functional and Project Forms," *Business Horizons,* February 1971, pp. 29–40.

- *Functional organization.* The project is divided up and assigned to relevant functional areas with coordination being carried out by functional and upper levels of management.

- *Functional matrix.* A person is designated to oversee the project across different functional areas.

- *Balanced matrix.* A person is assigned to oversee the project and interacts on an equal basis with functional managers.

- *Project matrix.* A manager is assigned to oversee the project and is responsible for completion of the project.

- *Project team.* A manager is put in charge of a core group of personnel from several functional areas who are assigned to the project on a full-time basis.[11]

Earlier in this chapter the term *matrix* was introduced. In the material that follows, a detailed examination of the matrix organizational design will be made. Before such examination is done, a brief review of the *pure* project organizational approach is needed to set the stage for the explanation of the matrix design.

In the pure approach, the project is truly like a minicompany. The project team is independent of major support from any major functional units or departments. Minor functional support—in such matters as industrial relations, payroll, and public relations—is provided by a functional element that takes care of the entire organization. The major advantage of the pure project organization is that it provides complete line authority over the project personnel; the project participants work directly for the project manager, with the chief executive (or some other general manager) in the main line of authority. One of the strongest disadvantages of this type of organization is that the cost is increased because of duplication of effort and facilities. In addition, since there would be no reservoir of specialists in a functional element, there might be a tendency to retain personnel on the project long after they were needed. A functional group is needed to look toward the future and work to improve the company's technical functional capability for new projects.

The matrix organization

A mixed project and functional structure, or matrix organization, is desirable for managing certain projects within desired cost, schedule,

---

[11]Erik W. Larson and David H. Gobeli, "Significance of Project Management Structure on Development Success," *IEEE Transactions on Engineering Management,* vol. 36, no. 2, May 1989, pp. 119–125.

and performance standards. The mixture can lie anywhere between the pure project and the pure functional extremes, the exact structure being determined by the particular project requirements.

Matrix is defined in the dictionary as "a situation or surrounding substance within which something originates, develops, or is contained." Horace Beck uses the term *matrix* in the context of folklore thus: "Folklore must be maintained in the matrix of the culture for some time before it can be accepted as genuine."[12]

The *matrix* organizational design emerged in the early 1960s as an alternative to the traditional means of organizing people serving on project teams. The matrix enjoyed popularity in the 1970s and early 1980s. Original concepts of the matrix organizational design emphasized the individual and collective roles of members of the project team. In some cases, companies went too far in trying to escalate the matrix organizational design throughout the breadth and length of the organization. Texas Instruments pulled back from the extensive matrix organizational design, citing it as one of the key reasons for the firm's economic decline.[13] Xerox Corporation reportedly abandoned the matrix form, claiming that it created a deterrent to product development.[14] Other signs of disenchantment with the matrix organizational design appeared. One of the more assertive was offered by Peters and Waterman in their book *In Search of Excellence,* in which they claim that the matrix was complicated and ultimately an unworkable structure which "...degenerates into anarchy and rapidly becomes bureaucratic and non-creative."[15]

The matrix has been described in considerable detail in the project management literature and in the research findings of this organizational design. Galbraith differentiated several forms of matrix, ranging from the functional organization to the pure project organization.[16] Most researchers and writers who explore the matrix organizational form agree that this organizational design is basically a middle ground between the traditional means of organizational design and an organizational form having the line authority and

---

[12] Warren Morris (ed.), *The American Heritage Dictionary of the English Language,* (Boston: Houghton Mifflin, 1976), p. 806.

[13] "An About Face in TI's Culture," *Business Week,* July 5, 1982, pp. 21–24.

[14] "How Xerox Speeds Up the Birth of New Products," *Business Week,* March 19, 1984, pp. 58–59.

[15] Tom Peters and Robert Waterman, *In Search of Excellence,* (New York: Harper and Row, 1982), p. 49.

[16] Jay Galbraith, "Matrix Organizational Design—How to Combine Functional and Project Forms," *Business Horizons,* February 1972, pp. 29–40.

responsibility to manage the project team as if it were an integral organizational unit.

Advocates of the matrix organizational design offer many reasons for its efficiency and flexibility in marshaling and using the resources to support a project. Critics are quick to point out that the matrix arrangement is cumbersome, costly, and difficult to understand. As mentioned earlier, Larson and Gobeli offer a description of the different forms of matrix design in terms of the relative influence of the project and functional managers, i.e., the *functional matrix, the balanced matrix, the project matrix, and the project team.* They also offer an insightful description of the advantages and disadvantages of the different matrix structures. They conclude that although the matrix has its disadvantages in terms of being cumbersome, chaotic, and anarchical, its popularity is not diminishing, but rather is the dominant mode for completing development projects.[17] Follow-on research by Larson and Gobeli leads them to conclude that different management structures can be applied at different phases of the project life cycle, and that there is no one best way to organize the project team except that the functional matrix and the functional organizational design for managing projects are less effective than a form that provides strong project leadership.[18]

Prescription of the expected formal individual and collective roles to be expected in the matrix organization is needed. Table 8.1 suggests a boilerplate model that can be used as a guide to such formal prescription. The use of the linear responsibility charting technique outlined in Chap. 9 is a productive way to develop these roles and—in that development—educate the people as to how they should operate in the matrix organization.

---

[17]Erik W. Larson and David H. Gobeli, "Matrix Management: Contradictions and Insights," *California Management Review,* Summer 1987, pp. 126–138.

[18]Erik W. Larson and David H. Gobeli, "Organizing for Product Development Projects," *Journal of Product Innovation Management,* vol. 5, 1988, pp. 180–190.

TABLE 8.1   The Project—Functional Interface

Project manager	Functional manager
■ What is to be done?	■ How will the task be done?
■ When will the task be done?	■ Where will the task be done?
■ Why will the task be done?	■ Who will do the task?
■ How much money is available to do the task?	■ How well has the functional input been integrated into the project?
■ How well has the total project been done?	

Matrix organizational designs emerged to deal with the enigma and perceived inconsistency of having two or more "bosses"—a reflection of the fascination that conventional wisdom held concerning the impropriety of violating Fayol's principle of "unity of command." In today's team-driven organizations, the authority-responsibility-accountability relationships are complex, ever-changing, and based as much on individual (or group) ability to influence other people as on the formal authority of a defined organizational position. Given these considerations, what is the general nature of the matrix organizational design? Several observations can be offered:

- A formal matrix organizational design should be described along the demarcation suggested in Table 8.1. This formal design should not be inflexible, but should be offered as a way in which the authority-responsibility-accountability patterns should normally operate.

- The ability to influence other people through the continued demonstration of one's knowledge, skills, and attitudes is the final determining factor in achieving successful integration of individual and collective roles in the matrix design. However, one could make much the same statement about a management position in any type of organization.

- The growing use of alternative forms of teams in contemporary organizations will continue to make the matrix organizational form more acceptable and more flexible and will provide for bringing a philosophy for bringing people together—regardless of their "home" organization—into a focus to accomplish organizational purposes.

- *Matrix,* then, is more a state of mind to encourage people to work together to create value for themselves and for the organization.

- As an organization works in the matrix context, the structural form of the matrix will tend to erode and become institutionalized into the overall manner in which people relate to each other in their individual and collective roles. In such organizations, matrix is described as "simply the way we do things around here," truly a key element in the organization's culture.

Focus of the matrix design

Managers should heed the advice given 20 years ago by one of the early writers in the then-emerging field of project management. Middleton offered the advice that neither the role of the project manager nor that of the functional manager should dominate in using project management. He further briefly described the general relative roles of these managers and charged top management with the responsibility for resolving the conflicts between them.[19] Middleton's advice is particularly appropriate to those managers who are considering the use of the matrix organization.

The matrix form of organization demands attention, for many managers do not have a clear, consistent concept of what it means. Although the matrix is used in a wide variety of different organizations, there is not a full understanding of its structure, processes, and impact on the parent organizational system. A matrix organization is a network of interfaces between a project team and the functional elements of an organization. As additional project teams are laid across an organization's functional structure, more interfaces come into existence. The authority, responsibility, and accountability patterns found in these interfaces are delineated in subsequent portions of this chapter.

In its most elemental form, a matrix organization looks like the model in Fig. 8.2, where the interface of the project and functional elements come about. The interface of these elements centers on the project work packages. The underlying concept of the work package is simply that of management by objectives and the decentralization of authority, responsibility, and accountability. Implementation of the project requires that the total job be broken down into components (hardware, software, and services) and then that these components be further broken down into assignable work packages. Each work package is basically a "bundle of skills" that an individual or individuals have to perform in the organization. A work package is

---

[19]C. J. Middleton, "How to Set Up a Project Organization," *Harvard Business Review,* April 1967, p. 82.

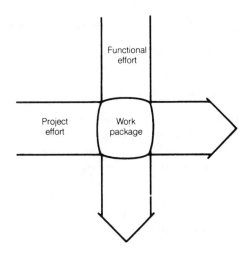

Figure 8.2 Interfaces of the project and functional effort around the project work package.

negotiated with, and assigned to, a specific manager or professional. The individual who accepts the work package agrees to specific objectives and goals which are measurable and to detailed task descriptions, specification, milestones, budget for the work package, etc. This work package manager or professional is then held fully responsible for the work package meeting its objective on time and within budget.

The underlying premise of the matrix organizational form is that project objectives can best be reached if the organization's resources can be directly oriented toward those objectives without regard to traditional organizational structures and constraints. The organization form of the matrix is used as a means to an end; it can be readily adapted to a changing environment. As the organizational need for new projects changes, the matrix structure tends to be fluid. Since organizations are organized around specific projects, the matrix is in a constant state of flux as projects are completed and resources are deployed to new or other current projects.

Importance of work packages

The key to the successful matrix organization is a careful definition of the *work breakdown structure* (WBS) for the project and the development of an organizational structure that most appropriately fits the WBS.[20] Within that WBS the work packages provide the focal point for the matrix organization. One large program, the Water Pollution Abatement Program[21] in Milwaukee, Wisconsin, consisted of five major project elements or work packages:

- Jones Island wastewater treatment plant rehabilitation and expansion
- South Shore wastewater treatment plant expansion
- Conveyance systems
- Solids disposal
- Hydraulics and controls

Organizationally, a project manager was assigned the authority and responsibility for accomplishing each major program work package and subsidiary work packages. Figure 8.3 depicts the strong matrix organization used in this program.

---

[20]The concept of the WBS and the work package are discussed in Chap. 11.

[21]The program was defined as the entire undertaking in this effort, a $2.2 billion effort that consisted of many projects.

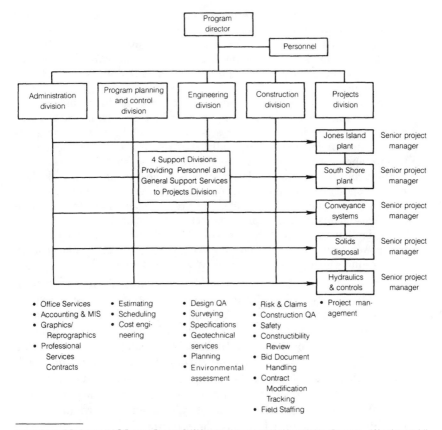

Source: Henry F. Padgham, III, VP/Program Director, CH2M Hill, Inc., Milwaukee, WI, "Matrix Within A Program— A New Approach," (Project Management Institute Seminar/Symposium, October, 1984): 161 – 165.

Figure 8.3 Matrix organization during the early program phases.

The Project-Functional Interface

Projects are essentially horizontal; the functional organization, as exemplified by the traditional organization chart, is vertical. The basic dichotomy found in matrix organizations centers around a project-functional interface reflected in Table 8.1. The syntax of the statements in that table is to provide a simple set of key words, as indicated by italics.

The "interface" described in [Table 8.1] is a very broad way of portraying the authority and responsibility relationships in the matrix organization which can be used as a point of departure to develop an understanding of the *web of relationships* found in the matrix organization.

The interface clearly describes how project managers accomplish project ends by the managing of relationships within the total organization.

There are few things which project managers can do alone. They must rely on the support and cooperation of other people within the organization. They must look to functional managers for specific support. Indeed, project managers *get things done by working through others* in the classic sense of the phrase, which is often used as a definition of successful management.

This managing of organizational relationships is three-dimensional. Upward, project managers must relate to their boss, who is either a general manager or a *manager of projects*. Horizontally, they relate to members of their project team. Diagonally, they relate to functional managers and to representatives of other organizations—e.g., the customers.

Managing these sets of relationships is a most demanding task. It is nearly impossible, if care has not been taken to describe the formal authority and responsibility relationships that are expected within the organization. This means making explicit the network of relationships that project managers have in each of the three dimensions. To whom do they have to relate? What are the key relationships? What is the work breakdown structure around which action is expected? Who works for whom?[22]

The matrix provides a sound basis for balancing the use of human resources and skills within the total organization as people are shifted from one project to another. A project can be viewed as a small business within a larger enterprise whose ultimate goal is to go out of business when the project is terminated. Hence as the enterprise has a stream of projects that is flowing through the organization, each project in a different phase of its life cycle, the opportunity exists for the general manager to balance human resources in the organization, applying these resources where necessary to keep the stream of projects flowing freely and effectively in the organization.

The key to making the matrix work effectively is to recognize the complementary roles that exist and to carefully delineate the relative authority, responsibility, and accountability for the people filling these roles.

A Controversial Design

The *matrix* organizational design and the *matrix* organizational concept have had problems and abuses. Part of the problem in the use of the matrix design has been characterized as caused by, or corrected through, a *weak* or *strong* matrix design. A *weak* matrix is one characterized by the following:

- A failure on the part of key participants to understand the basic principles and roles involved in the matrix

---

[22]David I. Cleland and William R. King, *Systems Analysis and Project Management,* 3d ed. (New York: McGraw-Hill, 1983), p. 351. Reproduced with permission.

- An inherent suspicion and distrust of any organizational design which departs from the management principle of *unity of command* in which one is expected to receive orders and direction from only one individual

- Functional managers who feel threatened by an apparent superiority of the project objectives and goals over those of the functional entity

- A failure on the part of senior management to see to it that some basic documentation is prepared to describe the formal and reciprocal roles of the key managers involved on the project: the project manager, functional managers, and work package managers

- A lack of appreciation on the part of the project manager and key staff to understand and respect the role of the functional professionals and their authorities and responsibilities in the management of the project

- Poor selection of project and functional managers

- The project manager who sees his or her role as simply a coordinator rather than as a manager in the truest sense of the word

- A project manager who fails to understand the many stakeholders on the project—even those outside of the parent organization—who have to be "managed" to fulfill the project ends

- Lack of trust, integrity, loyalty, and commitment on the part of the project team members

- Failure to develop and maintain the project team

- Putting the functional managers on report to senior managers rather than working out the conflict and challenges that are bound to occur in the management of the project

- Indecisiveness on the part of the project manager who would rather defer decisions to the senior managers than make as many decisions as possible on the project, referring only those that must be made by the senior executives

Conversely, a *strong* matrix exhibits these characteristics:

- Care has been taken by senior managers to define the individual and collective authority-responsibility roles of the project manager, functional managers, and work package managers.

- The project manager and the other key managers feel a strong sense of personal ownership and responsibility for their work and are willing to share ownership and responsibility, their resources, and the rewards to be followed from the successful projects.

- The project manager is given full authority and responsibility and is expected to exercise managerial prerogatives in managing the project so that it is completed on time and within budget and satisfies its technical performance objectives.

- The project manager knows how to delegate, demands excellent performance by the functional managers and the members of the project team, and is willing to accept full responsibility for the project.

- The project manager is prompt and judicious in resolving conflicts and disputes that will inevitably arise in the program.

- Project problems are taken to senior management as a last resort, but senior management is informed at all times of the status of the project.

- High performance and quality standards are expected from the functional entities participating on the project.

- The project team does not interfere in the prerogatives of the functional managers and does not permit the functional managers to interfere in the management of those portions of the program which lie within the jurisdiction of the project team.

- The project manager remains focused on the prudent and reasonable management of the project and appreciates that the project is basically a building block in the strategic management of the enterprise.

Clearly there are many more projects that are successful using the *strong* matrix than those using the *weak* matrix.

The *bottom line* is to select project managers and other key managers who will be dedicated to their jobs, understand them, seek unambiguous definition of their roles, and are willing to assume responsibility for the project. Such selection will help to ensure that a strong matrix emerges.

No One Best Organizational Design

The best organizational design to use in the management of projects is dependent on the particular circumstances of the project and its organizational and stakeholder environment. Tracey Kidder, in his Pulitzer Prize–winning book *Soul of a New Machine,* describes a product development effort at Data General on the Eagle Team in the development of a new standard in miniframe computers.[23] The book describes the massive effort carried out by a project team of specialists protected from organizational politics and interruptions, engaged

---

[23] Tracey Kidder, *Soul of a New Machine,* (Boston: Little, Brown, 1981).

in creating something that has not been done before. Peters and Waterman support the use of a project team like the one used in the *Soul of a New Machine.* Peters and Waterman are highly critical of the matrix organizational design.[24] Larson and Gobeli found in their research that the matrix is still the most popular approach to managing development projects.[25]

Global Project Organizations

As global competition intensifies, there will be more global projects and strategic alliances among companies and countries. Project managers will no longer be concerned solely with a "domestic" project— each domestic project has a good likelihood of becoming global in nature.[26] Each global project, like a domestic project, is unique, one of the key characteristics of projects. But global projects will be distinctive in that the project team, working across companies and countries, will encounter situations in which boundaries will cause new challenges in customs, cultures, and practices. The traditional matrix structure common to the project-functional interface will take on a global nature. Granted that the matrix structure in a domestic project is complex, in the global project this structure becomes even more complex. It is important that the formal role of the project manager be carefully delineated and that role and the roles of the team members be specific in terms of their authority, responsibility, and accountability. The chances of project success in the global project depend on many major forces and factors. If care is not taken at the outset of the project to clearly stipulate—to all the stakeholders' understanding—the managerial and leadership role of the project manager and the project team, the opportunity for a successful project is clearly diminished.

Organizational design arrangements for "managing" the customer need to be considered.

Project Customer Relationships

The interactions between a customer project office and industry agencies can be appreciated by reviewing Fig. 8.4. The interactions suggested by the figure are only a partial illustration of the number, size, and intensity of the project interrelationships. For example, on a

---

[24] Peters and Waterman, op. cit.

[25] Larson and Gobeli, "Matrix Management," op. cit.

[26] See David I. Cleland and Roland Gareis, *Global Project Management* (New York: McGraw-Hill, 1993), for a comprehensive review of the management of global projects.

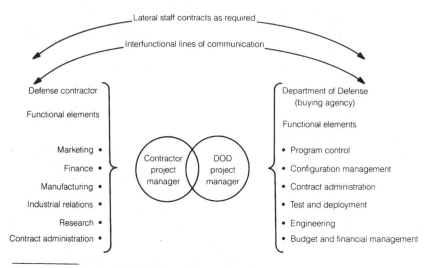

Source: Adapted from David I. Cleland, "Project Management—An Innovation in Management Thought and Theory," *Air University Review* (January–February 1965): 19.

Figure 8.4   Customer-project manager relationships.

major government project the project manager and office personnel interact with the highest levels of government and industry. Contractors doing business with these organizations tend to develop project offices which mirror the skills of the government project office. The relationship of the two organizations—the military department and the defense contractor—revolves around the two project managers, as illustrated. Although we use an example drawn from the defense industry, the same basic model could be used to describe any customer-project management situation.

Unifying the parts of the organizational components of the project and its stakeholders is a necessary activity of organizing the project. Unification is particularly important between the project prime contractor and the project owner. A prudent project owner will want to have a sound organizational design through which the owner's needs and the needs of the project contractor can be planned, understood, and met. This organizational design must reflect the reciprocal authority and responsibility tied to the work packages of the project—essentially providing answers to the specificity of individual and collective roles—and the level of involvement of each party in the management of the project.

Organizational Networking

A project manager is at the focal point of an interconnected network of alliances with members of the project team and with a varied set of people inside and outside the organization—in short, the stakeholders. A network is a set of reciprocal relationships that stabilizes the project work, giving it predictability and synergism. Networks stretch horizontally, vertically, and diagonally to the project's internal and external stakeholders. The strength and viability of these networks depend much on the ability of the project manager to build and maintain alliances with the many people who can help, hinder, or be indifferent to the needs of the project. These networks of relationships with all the project's stakeholders are a valuable asset that the project manager possesses in meeting the opportunities and problems of a project. The importance of networking in solving project problems is found in the example of the L-1011 wide-bodied plane project undertaken by the Lockheed Aircraft Company.

In the late 1960s, Lockheed Corporation began its project to build the L-1011 and in 1969 contracted with Rolls-Royce for the British aircraft engine company to design and manufacture the huge jet engine, the RB211, for the aircraft. In 1971 Rolls-Royce, with the job half completed and costs running far ahead of projections, nearly went under. To save the contract, Lockheed had to help Rolls-Royce secure renewed financial backing from the British government. The quest plunged Haughton, the Lockheed CEO, into negotiations with lateral contacts, all of them external to Lockheed. These included the British secretary of state for defense; the prime minister; a syndicate of Lockheed's 24 bankers that had to decide whether to save the L-1011 or put Lockheed into receivership; and the six U.S. airlines that had ordered L-1011s and were alarmed at the prospect of either not receiving their planes or being asked to agree to a higher price. The U.S. government also got involved through President Richard Nixon and Assistant Secretary of Defense David Packard.

After 6 months of innumerable meetings, Haughton put together an agreement acceptable to his corporation and all the lateral parties involved. The British government pledged to pay for all further costs of supplying the engine; Lockheed agreed to pay $180,000 more for each engine; the six customer airlines agreed to extend the corporation's line of credit, provided the U.S. government guaranteed repayment; and Congress narrowly approved a bill that guaranteed Lockheed's loans. Haughton is credited with accomplishing this feat "by tireless efforts, diplomatic skill, and the fact that he was trusted by all sides."[27] The networking carried out by the chairman of Lockheed was instrumental in saving this project and the two corporations involved. Indeed, during this period Chairman Daniel Haughton became the real project manager of the L-1011 project.

---

[27]John Newhouse, "The Sporting Game," *The New Yorker,* July 5, 1982.

A project manager must network with the project stakeholders for one compelling reason. The project manager depends on these stakeholders and cannot get the project finished without them. The project manager's ability to build and maintain these networks depends on the project manager's authority and how that authority is perceived by the project stakeholders. The project manager's reputation, alliances, position, favored standing, diplomacy, influence, communication skills, and persuasive skills all help to facilitate the building and maintenance of the network. The project network connects like tentacles with diverse project stakeholders, establishing relationships and quid pro quos designed to support the project needs.

The art of networking is one of the most unceasing challenges facing the project manager. Most of the project manager's daily activities deal with the ongoing discovery and creation of relationships directed toward supporting project needs. The project team members need freedom in pursuing their technical expertise, on one hand, and yet must be brought together and unified in supporting the project needs, on the other. A healthy and successful team is marked by healthy relationships. Without this relating leading to networking, the team weakens and may stumble along as a collection of individuals, but die as a team. Interacting, interfacing, and building networks in harmony with others, the team should become a unity of cooperative effort.

Most successful relationships in a project team are an ongoing process of trial and error, negotiations, resolution of conflict, authority, responsibility, evaluation, planning, execution, commitment, accountability, organizing, control, and communication—the elements are as complex as any scientific formula. Team members must approach these relationships as a creative challenge requiring concentration, innovation, and careful tending and cultivation. Networking requires an open mind, and courage and flexibility to compromise when the project team's well-being and the project's outcome are at stake. It demands that the team members seek maximum fulfillment of their technical expertise, yet tolerate disappointment when their technical position is reduced to preserve the overall synergy of the project. Such disappointment and even feelings of rejection require that the team members nourish the attitude that they will try again and again without any guarantee that future disappointments will not happen, that the project manager and the team members continuously work at the skills required for building and maintaining relationships necessary for effective networking.

The experts who are members of a project team can impair the team ambience by always insisting that they are right and by being afraid to reveal their most endearing qualities—the imperfections. Team members all too often see this as something they must do, lest they lose the respect of their contemporaries and their status. So strongly are team members affected by the need to hide their imperfections that they may even run the risk of destroying the valued relationships that make the team effective and a winner. Rigidly adhering to their rightness, the team members (including the project leader) stifle discussion and exasperate others on the team who grow weary of always hearing about "the world according to me." The project team all too often fails to see that nothing has been gained if the final result means being fearful of building relationships, of networking, and of confronting issues.

Summary

In this chapter we have presented some ideas about organizational design for project management. People could probably devise more varied organizational arrangements than there are companies or projects. Varied as these arrangements might be, they would all be based on the concept of pulling together technical and managerial talents into a team, to operate without limits of discipline or organizational lines in undertaking a project. The organization form that finally evolves out of the project requirements will undoubtedly be a compromise between pure project management and standard function alignment—some form of the matrix model.

Why use *matrix* organizational design? The principal reasons include the following:

- The dedicated project team is the most effective way of providing a focal point to pull together and integrate functional disciplines in the organization.

- The resources can be shared—an effective compromise to having each functional entity unilaterally control all its own resources.

- Centralized functions in the enterprise can be assembled and maintained to provide resources to the product and process development effort underway.

- Projects can be managed to include both technical and business considerations to support a need for product or process change in the enterprise.

- The authority and responsibility of the project manager and the functional managers can be adequately defined so that each knows and respects the other's territory.

Companies are becoming more *boundaryless,* using more horizontal organizational designs, linking traditional functions with project teams, and forming strategic alliances with customers, suppliers, and even competitors. As a result of the use of different organizational designs, new "boundaries" are being developed which are more psychological than organizational, boundaries which grow out of the new authority-responsibility-accountability networks that are developing—relationships that are developed to individuals networking in their different organizational roles rather than roles defined in a formal organizational structure. Relationships are created and abandoned at the right time as needed to keep innovation, productivity, quality, and organizational efficiency and effectiveness moving in the right direction and with the appropriate force.

In the matrix organization, formal lines of authority and responsibility must be set out clearly. These lines will be crisscrossing; fuzziness is bound to emerge even with the best of documentation to describe the organization.

The concept of networking is a way to expand the "organization" that the project manager uses in successfully completing the project.

Discussion Questions

1. Discuss the importance of an adequate organizational design in the management of a project.

2. For what reasons might an organization need to modify its organizational design?

3. Discuss the range of matrix organizational forms.

4. What factors contribute to the dynamic nature of a matrix organization?

5. Discuss the various forms of traditional departmentalization. In what situations would each of these forms be advantageous?

6. List and discuss the weaknesses of the pure functional organization. What kinds of failures could result from using this form of organizational design on a large project?

7. Discuss the advantages and disadvantages of the pure project organization. In what situations might this form be best?

8. Describe the matrix organizational form. What are its advantages and disadvantages?

9. What are some of the unnecessary characteristics of a successful matrix organization?

10. Discuss the advantages and disadvantages of the alternative forms of the matrix organization. In what situations would each work best?

11. Why is it important for project managers to develop networking skills?

12. What can top managers do to support the matrix organization?

User Checklist

1. Do the project managers in your organization understand the interrelatedness of organizational forces? Why or why not?

2. Does the current design of your organization leave lines of authority and responsibility clear? Why or why not?

3. Project organizations range from pure functional to pure project. Where does your organization's design fit? Is it appropriate?

4. Are the factors which contribute to a dynamic organization present within your organization? Why or why not?

5. How is your organization departmentalized? Is this the most efficient departmentalization possible? What design might improve organizational efficiency?

6. Does the management of your organization understand the advantages and disadvantages of the various organizational forms? How does it use this knowledge in designing organizational structure?

7. Are the work packages of each project carefully related to the organizational structure? Is the organizational design appropriate for managing the work breakdown structure?

8. Is the use of human resources and skills balanced within the total organization? Explain.

9. Is there an effective means for conflict resolution over organizational roles established within your organization? How are conflicts handled?

10. Is your current organizational design successful and effective? Why or why not? What criteria for success are lacking?

11. Has the management of your organization considered possible alternative forms for structuring the organization? What other forms might be effective?

12. Do the project managers within your organization understand the notion of networking? Are they effective at forming alliances with project stakeholders?

9

Project Organization Charting[1]

"And one man in his time plays many parts."
WILLIAM SHAKESPEARE, 1564–1616,
As You Like It

The organizational model that is commonly called the organizational chart is derided in the satirical literature and in the day-to-day discussions among organizational participants. However, organizational charts can be of great help in both the planning and implementation phases of project management.

The Traditional Organizational Chart

The traditional organizational chart is of the pyramidal variety; it represents or models the organization as it is supposed to exist at a given time. At best, such a chart is an oversimplification of the organization and its underlying concepts which may be used as an aid in grasping the concept of the organization.

Unfortunately, too often the policy documentation describing the role of a project manager will describe this manager's relationship with the functional organizations as a "dotted line" relationship, which can mean anything one wishes it to mean. In this respect, Davis and Lawrence note that for generations managers have lived with the fiction of dotted lines to describe secondary reporting rela-

---

[1] Some of the ideas in this chapter have been paraphrased from the articles by David I. Cleland and Wallace Munsey, "Who Works with Whom," *Harvard Business Review,* September-October 1967, and Dundar F. Kocaoglu and David I. Cleland, "A Participative Approach to the Development of Organizational Roles and Interactions," *Management Review,* October 1983, pp. 57–64.

tionship in the organization.[2] One suspects that managers use a dotted line on an organizational chart because at the time the chart was developed the relationship had not been completely defined. The use of a dotted-line technique in depicting authority and responsibility gives a manager a great deal of flexibility. The price of this flexibility is confusion and unclear understandings of reciprocal authority and responsibility.

Usefulness of the traditional chart

The organizational chart is a means of visualizing many of the abstract features of an organization. In summary, the organizational chart is useful in that

- It provides a general framework of the organization.
- It can be used to acquaint the employees and outsiders with the nature of the organizational structure.
- It can be used to identify how the people tie into the organization; it shows the skeleton of the organization, depicting the basic relationships and the groupings of positions and functions.
- It shows formal lines of authority and responsibility, and it outlines the hierarchy—who fills each formal position, who reports to whom, and so on.

Limitations of the traditional chart

The organizational chart is something like a photograph. It shows what the subjects look like, but tells little about how individuals function or relate to others in their environment. The organizational chart is limited in that

- It fails to show the nature and limits of the activities required to attain the objectives.
- It does not reflect the myriad reciprocal relationships between peers, associates, and many others with a common interest in some purpose.
- It is a static, formal portrayal of the organizational structure; most charts are out of date by the time they are published.
- It shows the relationships that are supposed to exist, but neglects the informal, dynamic relationships that are constantly at play in the environment.

---

[2]Stanley M. Davis and Paul R. Lawrence, "Problems of Matrix Organization," *Harvard Business Review,* May-June 1978, p. 142.

- It may confuse organizational position with status and prestige; it overemphasizes the vertical role of managers and causes parochialism—a result of the blocks and lines of the chart and the neat, orderly flow they imply.

A key part of the organizational design of an enterprise is the determination of the individual and collective roles of the people in the organization, as well as the development of a full understanding of these roles by the people as they carry out their responsibilities. The lack of clearly defined and understood roles can have disastrous results on the management of a project—or on the management of any organization. Role definition for the team members working within the organizational processes is critical. Active involvement and cooperation by the team members are sorely needed. People have a much greater propensity to become proactively involved when they have a clear understanding of their roles, of the roles of other members of the team, and of how the team members collectively carry out the work of the project.

Role definition within the project team is a key consideration in developing the team. When a new team is formed, or when new objectives and goals are developed for the team, or when any key circumstance about the team or its mission changes, such as additional responsibilities, then the definition and understanding of individual and collective roles become important. If the team is intended to be interactive and synergistic, role understanding is critical. Allocating authority and responsibility to the team is an important first step. But the team must understand the authority and responsibility associated with both individual and collective roles, must be committed to those roles, and must be proactive in developing the personal influence that gives added power to the execution of these roles.

How can the individual and collective roles of the project team be established, particularly as the team members work with the project stakeholders? Two organizational charts are needed: the traditional chart which portrays the general framework of the organization and the linear responsibility chart, which is useful to determine the specificity of individual and collective roles in the organization.

Linear Responsibility Charts

The *linear responsibility chart* (LRC) is an innovation in management theory that goes beyond the simple display of formal lines of communication, gradations or organizational level, departmentalization, and line-staff relationships. In addition to the simple display, the LRC reveals the work package position couplings in the organization. The LRC has been called the *linear organization chart,* the *responsibility*

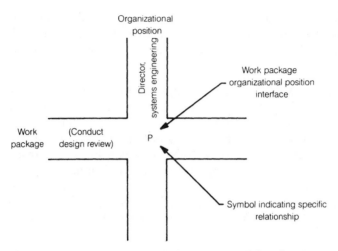

Figure 9.1   Essential structure of a linear responsibility chart.

interface matrix, the *matrix responsibility chart,* the *linear chart,* and the *functional chart.*

The LRC shows who participates, and to what degree, when an activity is performed or a decision made. It shows the extent or type of authority exercised by each position in performing an activity in which two or more positions have overlapping involvement. It clarifies the authority relationships that arise when people share common work.

Figure 9.1 shows the basic structure of an LRC, in terms of an organizational position and a work package, in this case "conduct design review." The symbol P indicates that the director of systems engineering has the primary responsibility for conducting the system design review.

Work packages

The work elements of the hierarchical levels of the work breakdown structure are called *work packages.* They are used to identify and control work flows in the organization, and they have the following characteristics:

- A work package represents a discrete unit of work at the appropriate level of the organization where work is assigned.

- Each work package is clearly distinguished from all other work packages.

- The primary responsibility of completing the work package on schedule and within budget can always be assigned to an organizational unit, and never to more than one unit.

- A work package can be integrated with other work packages at the same level of the work breakdown structure to support the work packages at a higher level of the hierarchy.

Work packages are level-dependent and become increasingly more general at each higher level and increasingly more specific at each lower level.

Work package/organizational position interfaces

The organizational positions and the responsibilities assigned to them in carrying out the work package requirements constitute the basis for the LRC. It is developed by specifically identifying responsibilities on each of the work packages. The responsibilities are defined at the work package–organizational position interfaces, by using symbols or letters to depict relationships. Some symbols are in Fig. 9.2 and defined below:

A   *Approval.* Approves the work package.

P   *Primary responsibility.* The prime authority and responsibility for accomplishment of work package.

R   *Review.* Reviews output of the work package. For example, the legal department reviews a proposal bid package submitted by the proposal manager.

N   *Notification.* Notified of the output of the work package. As a result of this notification, the individual makes a judgment as to whether any action should be taken.

O   *Output.* Receives the output of the work package and integrates it into the work being accomplished. For example, the contract administrator receives a copy of the engineering change orders so that the effects of changes on the terms and conditions of a project contract can be determined.

I   *Input.* Provides input to the work package. For example, a bid/no bid decision on a contract cannot be made by a company unless inputs are received from the manufacturing manager, financial manager, contract administrator, marketing manager, and the manager of the profit center organization.

W   *Work is done.* Accomplishes the actual labor of the work package. This legend is used when the work is done by a position other than where the primary responsibility resides.

I*   *Initiation.* Initiates the work package. For example, new product development is the responsibility of the R&D manager, but the process generally is initiated with a request either from the profit center manager or from the marketing manager.

If W, A, R, and I* are not separately identified, then P is assumed to include them.

Work packages	Contract admin.	Mfg. manager	Financial manager	Profit ctr. division manager	R&D manager	Marketing manager	Mgmt. council	Comments
Setting corporate objectives	I,O	I,O	I,O	I,O	I,O	I,O	P	
Developing corporate maintenance agreements	P	N	I,N	I,A		I,N		
Negotiating customer contracts	I,R	I,N	R	P				A
New product development	I,O	I	I*,O	P	I*,R			
Developing bid strategies	I,O	I,O		I,O		P		
Preparing the annual budget	I,O	I,O	P	I,O	I,O	I,O		A
Developing master schedule for operators	N	P	N	I,N	I,N			
Establishing standard costs		W	P	I,O				

Legend:
- *P*   *Primary responsibility*—The prime authority and responsibility for accomplishment of work package
- *R*   *Review*—Reviews output of work package.
- *N*   *Notification*—Is notified of output of work package.
- *A*   *Approval*—Approves work package.
- *O*   *Output*—Receives output of work package.
- *I**   *Invitation*—Work package initiated by.
- *I*   *Input*—Provides input to work package.
- *W*   *Work is done*—Accomplishes actual labor of work package.
  - P includes W
  - P includes A
  - P includes I*
  - A includes R
  - Unless otherwise specified

SOURCE: Dundar F. Kocaoglu and David I. Cleland, "The RIM Process...A Participative Approach to the Development of Organizational Roles and Interactions." Reprinted by permission of publisher from *Management Review,* October 1983, American Management Association, New York. All rights reserved.: 61

Figure 9.2 Sample linear responsibility chart (LRC).

In Fig. 9.2 a sample LRC is shown for a project-driven organization. Each column of the LRC describes how a certain organizational position operates in the company. In a similar way, the rows contain information about how certain jobs are accomplished and who does what for whom in carrying out the work package requirements.

Taken as a whole, the LRC is a blueprint of the activity and information flows that take place in the organizational interfaces in a company.

The authority-responsibility patterns and the organizational interdependencies can be read directly from the chart. Once the LRC is developed, it can be sorted for each organizational position, first with all the Ps, then with Is, Os, and so on. When managers look at the sorted work packages related to their organizational units, they immediately see a listing of the activities for which they have direct responsibility and those for which they support the other units in the organization. Basically, the LRC is a delineation of *what* they do for each work package. If they look at the LRCs horizontally, they see *whom* they interact with and *how* the LRC identifies their contact points in the organization, and the nature of contacts they are to maintain.

The LRC is a valuable tool as a succinct description of organizational interfaces. It conveys more information than several pages of job descriptions and policy documents by delineating the authority-responsibility relationships and specifying the accountability of each organizational position. However, by far the most important aspect of LRC is the process by which the people in the organization prepare it. If the LRC is developed in an autocratic fashion, it simply becomes a document portraying the organizational relationships. But if it is prepared through a participative process, the final output becomes secondary to the impacts of the process itself. The open communications, broad discussions, resolution of conflicts, and achievement of consensus through participation provide a solid basis for organizational development and managerial harmony. By the time the LRC is developed in this way, the organization goes through such an "education" that the chart becomes secondary.

A Project Management LRC

The LRC can be very useful for project managers to use to understand their authority relationships with their project team members. For a simple project, these relationships may be easy to depict; for more complex projects, a series of descending charts from the macrolevel of the project to successively lower levels may be necessary.

Figure 9.3 shows an LRC for project-functional management relationships within a matrix organization. Slightly different symbols are used in this example. The development of such a chart, combined with the discussions that usually accompany such a development, can help greatly to facilitate an understanding of project management and how it will affect the day-to-day lives and activities of the team members.

Developing the LRC

The development of the project LRC is inherently a group activity—getting together with the key people who have a vested interest in the

Activity	General Manager	Manager of Projects	Project Manager	Functional Manager
Establish department policies & objectives	1	3	3	3
Integration of projects	2	1	3	3
Project direction	4	2	1	3
Project charter	6	2	1	5
Project planning	4	2	1	3
Project—functional conflict resolution	1	3	3	3
Functional planning	2	4	3	1
Functional direction	2	4	5	1
Project budget	4	6	1	3
Project WBS	4	6	1	3
Project control	4	2	1	3
Functional control	2	4	3	1
Overhead management	2	4	3	1
Strategic programs	6	3	4	1

Code

1: Actual responsibility
2: General supervision
3: Must be consulted
4: May be consulted
5: Must be notified
6. Approval authority

Figure 9.3   Linear responsibility chart of project management relationships.

work to be done. The following plan for the development of an LRC has proved useful:

1. Distribute copies of the current traditional organizational chart and position descriptions of the key people.
2. Develop and distribute blank copies of the LRC.
3. At the first opportunity, get the people together to discuss:
   a. The advantages and shortcomings of the traditional organization chart
   b. The concept of a project work breakdown structure (WBS) and the resulting work packages
   c. The nature of the linear responsibility chart, how it developed, and how it is used
   d. A simple way of establishing a code to show the work package–organizational position relationship (getting a meeting of the minds on this code is very important because individuals who believe the code to be either too fine or too coarse will find it difficult to accept)
   e. The makeup of the actual work breakdown structure with accompanying work packages
   f. The fitting of the symbols into the proper relationship in the LRC

4. Encourage an intensive dialogue during the actual making of the LRC. In such a meeting, people will tend to be protective of their organizational "territory." The LRC by its nature requires a commitment to support and share the allocation of organizational resources applied to work packages. This commitment requires the ability to communicate and decide. This process takes time, but when the LRC is completed, the people are much more knowledgeable about what is expected of them.[3]

Much of the success of project management depends on how effectively people work together to accomplish project objectives and gain personal satisfaction. The development of a project LRC can greatly contribute to achieving this.

Summary

Many problems in project organizations can be traced to an important oversight: No one took the time to clarify roles of the project team. Who does what? Who works for whom? As a result of this failure to clarify roles, much psychological and social energy is tied up trying to seize more power or territory in the organization or to rationalize not getting a job done. Conflicts that are not confronted in the project team are played out in indirect and destructive ways. In the typical project there are challenges in developing a cultural ambience supportive of interpersonal confidence, trust, loyalty, and commitment. Territorial imperatives often drive a person to think only in terms of an individual role and to neglect how that role interfaces with other roles in the organization or the project. Not much is accomplished on a project team if the individual members do not work together.

The LRC chart and its associated process afford each individual an opportunity to discuss her or his role as well as the roles of the key people with whom the individual works: supervisors, subordinates, and members of the project team. Those discussions are carried out in the context of authority, responsibility, and accountability. As these relative roles are discussed, appropriate questions of "territory" emerge. Some of these questions can be resolved at the LRC meeting; the more difficult ones are identified for future resolution. Throughout the LRC process, the project manager should be aware that the discussions about relative roles will "unclothe" the organization. Overlaps and gaps between authority and responsibility are laid out for all to see. Conflict, much of which may have remained hidden,

---

[3]David I. Cleland and Dundar F. Kocaoglu, *Engineering Management* (New York: McGraw-Hill, 1981), pp. 47–50.

tends to come out into the open. Things that have fallen through the cracks start surfacing. The net result of the process is a better understanding of organizational roles and an agreement on who works for whom and under what circumstances.

A combination of the traditional and the LRC charts provides the team both an overview and a specific prescription of the relative individual and collective roles each person performs. Authority, responsibility, and accountability therefore are defined in specific terms which facilitate a role understanding by all the members of the team.

Discussion Questions

1. What are some of the advantages of the traditional organizational chart? What are its limitations?

2. How can traditional organizational charts be made more useful?

3. Define the linear responsibility chart in terms of its structure.

4. What are work packages? How can they be developed?

5. Define each of the symbols which are used to describe the responsibilities at the work package–organizational position interface.

6. For what purposes can an LRC be used?

7. Discuss the importance of using nonambiguous charting symbols to clarify roles.

8. List the steps involved in the development of the LRC.

9. Why is it important for this development to be a group activity?

10. Discuss the limitations of the LRC.

11. Describe the team building inherent in the development of the LRC.

12. Describe a simple project management situation from your work or school experience, and develop a linear responsibility chart for that situation.

User Checklist

1. Does your organization keep an updated traditional organizational chart? What is the usefulness of this chart to the organization?

2. Do the managers in your organization understand the limitations of the traditional chart for managing projects? How do they address these limitations?

3. What alternatives to traditional organizational charting are used by your organization in order to clarify roles? Explain.

4. Does your organization use any form of linear responsibility charting? Why or why not?

5. Are the responsibilities and roles of project team members clear to the project manager and other managers? Are they clear to the team members themselves?

6. What does the management of your organization do to make roles clear? How are role conflicts handled?

7. How do alternatives to traditional organizational charts assist in the communication process on projects within your organization?

8. Do the project managers of your organization understand the concept of a work package? How are work packages developed?

9. What charting symbols or other indicators are used by your organization to define the responsibilities at the work package–organizational position interfaces? Are these indicators nonambiguous?

10. How do project managers within your organization develop the LRC or other organizational charting? Is the development a group activity? Why or why not?

11. How is team building accomplished on large projects? Could the development of an LRC be useful?

12. Are discussions held between the project managers, team members, and other project stakeholders to clarify authority, responsibility, and accountability? Why or why not? How can these discussions contribute to the success of the project?

10

Project Authority[1]

*"But man, proud man, drest in a little brief
authority."*
WILLIAM SHAKESPEARE, 1564–1616,
Measure for Measure

In the previous chapter we described several organizational design
alternatives for managing projects. These descriptions dealt with the
structural alignment of the matrix organization. In this chapter we
will broaden the concepts of authority, responsibility, and accountability.

Authority is essential to any group or project team effort. The legal
authority that is exercised by an individual comes from the organizational position occupied by the individual. Such authority is granted
or delegated from a higher authority level in the organization. The
ultimate source of authority in organizations can be traced to the
owners of the organization. In a business organization, the shareholders elect the board of directors of a company. These directors have the
authority given to them by the corporate charter and bylaws to manage the corporation on behalf of the shareholders. The authority of
the board of directors is broad, is of a fiduciary nature, and is the
starting point for the delegation and redelegation of authority within
the organizational structure. The board of director's authority role in
project management is to study and approve key strategy proposals,
particularly those risky projects which involve a substantial portion
of corporate resources, and to maintain surveillance of the project
during its life cycle.

---

[1]Some of the ideas in this chapter have been paraphrased from David I. Cleland,
"Understanding Project Authority," *Business Horizons,* Spring 1967.

Project managers face a unique authority challenge in the management of their projects. Usually project managers have only a few people working directly for them—their small administrative staff. Yet the project manager has to practice a subtle form of delegation in letting others—the functional specialists—become the experts and provide the technical input to the project team.

Sometimes the authority of the project manager is very explicit. For example, at Honda the project team that developed new vehicles has engineers, designers, financial analysts, marketing experts, and manufacturing people all report to a single project leader who had "line" authority over them and their work. Chrysler, in contrast, was divided by functional disciplines, as departments with their own functional agendas competed. The result? The Chrysler system took longer, cost more, and sometimes led to compromises such as in quality.[2]

A project manager has to watch someone else provide the technical input in which the project manager may have experience and expertise. The project manager must be patient when someone accomplishes a task less proficiently than the project manger might be able to. The project manager must shift from the role of specialist to generalist—a leader in the management functions of planning, organizing, motivating, and control. This takes the project manager away from the technical aspect of the project, allowing the project team members to be the experts in the technical work they represent.

Defining Authority[3]

Authority is a conceptual framework and, at the same time, an enigma in the study of organizations. The authority patterns in an organization, most commentators agree, serve as both a motivating and a tempering influence. This agreement, however, does not extend to the emphasis that the different commentators place on a given authority concept. Early theories of management regarded authority more or less as a gravitational force that flowed from the top down. Recent theories view authority more as a force which is to be accepted voluntarily and which acts both vertically and horizontally.

Although authority is one of the keys to the management process, the term is not always used in the same way. Authority is usually

---

[2]Bradley A. Stertz, "Detroit's New Strategy to Beat Back Japanese Is to Copy Their Ideas," *Wall Street Journal,* October 1, 1992.

[3]Portions of this material have been taken from David I. Cleland and William R. King, *Systems Analysis and Project Management,* 3d ed. (New York: McGraw-Hill, 1983), chap. 12.

defined as a legal or rightful power to command or act. As applied to the manager, authority is the power to command others to act or not to act. The manager's authority provides the cohesive force for any group. In the traditional theory of management, authority is a right granted from a superior to a subordinate.

There are two types of project authority. One, *de jure* project authority, is the legal or rightful power to command or act in the management of a project. Inherent in this authority is the legal right to commit or withdraw resources supporting the project. The legal authority of a project manager usually is contained in some form of documentation; such documentation of necessity must contain, in addition, the complementary roles of other managers (e.g., functional managers, work package managers, general managers) associated with the project.

Having legal authority is a start. However, to be a successful manager, an individual must develop capabilities in the *de facto* aspects of authority.

The second type of authority, *de facto* project authority, is that influence brought to the management of a project by reason of a particular person's knowledge, expertise, interpersonal skills, or personal effectiveness. De facto project authority may be exercised by any of the project clientele, managers, or team members.

The importance of interpersonal skills and communication abilities to the project manager is keynoted in a study done in 1988 by a consulting firm. In more than 100 interviews with clients of design firms, the responses were emphatic that technical competence is not sufficient in managing a complex project. Project managers who have political savvy and the ability to communicate are important. It was found during these interviews that when something went wrong on a project, seven times out of ten the cause was a breakdown in communication, not a breakdown in technology. In additional experiences in conducting employee attitude surveys by this consulting firm, it was found that the most salient link to overall job satisfaction and low turnover is communication within the firm. In this firm's experience with clients, interview data, and attitude survey data the firm managers identified five types of communication skills essential to successful project management: interpersonal communication, presentation and public speaking, conflict management, negotiation, and writing.[4]

In another study it was found that project managers and project personnel believe that expertise and reputation were the most helpful sources of influence in the management of technical projects. It was

---

[4]John Simonds and Margaret Winch, "Human Side of Project Management," *pmNETwork*, February 1991, pp. 23–31.

further determined that technical expertise and organizational expertise are two sources of influence that are available to project managers. Expert power comes to the project manager through background and experience, technical achievement, participation in past projects, and longevity.[5]

Ford and McLaughlin in their research remind us that classical management theory holds that parity of authority and responsibility should exist. In project management there may not be such parity across the various stages of the life cycle. They note that few empirical data have been collected to test the hypothesis that parity does not exist and that this lack of parity is the cause of many management problems. In their research report collected from 462 information system managers, the data indicated that in the majority of cases parity did not exist.[6]

A major part of de facto authority is the ability of the project manager to influence others whose cooperation and support are needed to provide timely resources to support the project. Part of the ability to influence is the competence to work effectively with project team members, functional managers, general managers, and project stakeholders. A project manager must have some technical skill in the technology embodied in the project, not only to participate in the rendering of technical judgments but also to gain the respect of team members who have in-depth technical knowledge and skills. Interpersonal skills provide power to the project manager in influencing the many professionals and managers with whom the project manager works. Developing and maintaining a successful track record that gets people to work with the project manager are, in themselves, a form of power in influencing. The ability to influence is directly related to how others perceive one's expertise. Another source of power is to pay attention to and recognize the performance of other people who work with you, such as team members, managers, and stakeholders. In other words, acknowledge the performance of other people as you would like to have your own good performance recognized. This recognition can take many forms, such as letters of appreciation, phone calls to thank the person, a public thanks in a meeting, comments to a person's manager, a citation in the person's personnel file, stopping by the person's desk to say, "Thanks for your help," a personal note of thanks, some token of appreciation such as a lunch, a book, flowers,

---

[5]Christopher G. Worley and Charles J. Teplitz, "The Use of 'Expert' Power as an Emerging Influence Style within Successful U.S. Matrix Organizations," *Project Manual Journal,* March 1993, pp. 31–34.

[6]Robert C. Ford and Frank S. McLaughlin, "Using Project Teams to Create MIS Products: A Life Cycle Analysis," *Project Management Journal,* March 1993, pp. 43–47.

or pen-and-pencil set. Sometimes praising a person's work to members of the peer group works well—inevitably that praise will be reported to the person.

Matrix implications

The *matrix* organizational design to support the management of projects has been given much attention in the project management literature. Whatever controversy and disenchantment that the matrix design has caused, it cannot be forgotten that the different alternative uses of the matrix that have been tried have been a search for how authority and responsibility could be shared by those organizational entities cooperating in bringing about a focal point to manage the sharing of resources to support organizational projects. Most "failures" in the use of matrix have been caused by one or more of the following relative authority-responsibility factors:

1. Failure to define the specificity of authority and responsibility of the project and functional people relative to the work packages for which each is solely and jointly responsible.

2. Negative attitudes on the part of project, functional, and general managers and team members who support a sharing of authority and responsibility over the resources to be used to support organizational projects.

3. Lack of familiarity with the theoretical construction of the matrix and the context in which that organizational design is applied.

4. Failure on the part of senior managers to bring about the development of some basic documentation in the organization that prescribes the *formal* and relative authority of managers and team members associated with a project team.

5. Failure to do adequate project team development to include how the team will operate in a cultural ambience of the enterprise where project resources, results, and rewards are shared.

6. Existence of an organizational culture that believes and reinforces the traditional "command and control" notions of authority and responsibility being primarily *vertical* in their flow downward through the organizational hierarchy.

7. Failure on the part of organizational leaders to recognize that the traditional organizational model in the vertical flow of authority and responsibility is rapidly being eroded by the increasing use of computer and communication technology, the increasing pace of change, and the success which alternative organizational designs are enjoying such as found in the use of self-directed teams, quali-

ty teams, task forces, and the growing use of participative management to include employee empowerment.

8. Failure to modify the traditional pyramid to a design that has fewer levels, with more options for personal movement and flexibility among and within organizational levels. This modification includes the reduction in the number of middle managers and the changes in their roles from one of approval and control to problem solving and facilitation of the means for people to work together to accomplish organizational ends.

9. And finally the failures of managers to promote synergy and unity within and between organizational levels and with outside stakeholders so that resources, results, and rewards can be shared. This type of promotion requires true teamwork, discussion, cooperation of all organizational members, education, and the opening and maintenance of many lines of communication.

When project management is introduced in an organization, it is essential that these authority roles be understood and accepted by general managers, project managers, and functional managers. This understanding can be facilitated if all the managers concerned jointly participate in the development and publication of a policy document containing a description of the intended authority and responsibility relationships characterized by Fig. 10.1.

A significant measure of the authority of project managers springs from their function and the style with which they perform it. Project managers' authority is neither all de jure (having special legal foundations) nor all de facto (actual influence exercised and accepted in the environment). Rather, their authority is a combination of de jure and de facto elements in the total project environment. Taken in this context, the authority of project managers has no organizational or functional constraints, but rather diffuses from their office throughout and beyond the organization, seeking out the things and the project stakeholders it wishes and needs to influence and control.

The power to reward

Not only do teams change the culture and the modus operandi of the organization, but also they change the manner in which organizational rewards are provided to people. As people serve on teams and rotate from team to team, performance evaluations are more difficult. In most organizations the team does not yet assume a major part in appraising team performance.[7] Of the organizations surveyed by

---

[7] Richard S. Wellins, William C. Byam, and Jeanne M. Wilson, *Empowered Teams,* (San Francisco: Jossey Bass, 1991), p. 3.

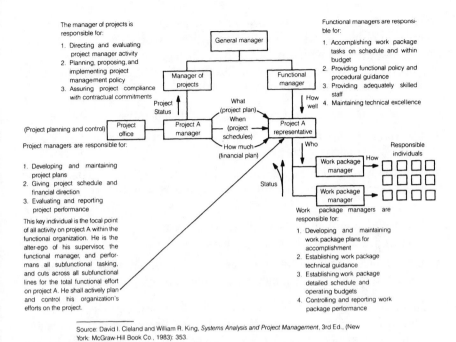

The manager of projects is responsible for:

1. Directing and evaluating project manager activity
2. Planning, proposing, and implementing project management policy
3. Assuring project compliance with contractual commitments

(Project planning and control)

Project managers are responsible for:

1. Developing and maintaining project plans
2. Giving project schedule and financial direction
3. Evaluating and reporting project performance

This key individual is the focal point of all activity on project A within the functional organization. He is the alter-ego of his supervisor, the functional manager, and performans all subfunctional tasking, and cuts across all subfunctional lines for the total functional effort on project A. He shall actively plan and control his organization's efforts on the project.

Functional managers are responsible for:

1. Accomplishing work package tasks on schedule and within budget
2. Providing functional policy and procedural guidance
3. Providing adequately skilled staff
4. Maintaining technical excellence

Work package managers are responsible for:

1. Developing and maintaining work package plans for accomplishment
2. Establishing work package technical guidance
3. Establishing work package detailed schedule and operating budgets
4. Controlling and reporting work package performance

Source: David I. Cleland and William R. King, *Systems Analysis and Project Management*, 3rd Ed., (New York: McGraw-Hill Book Co., 1983): 353.

Figure 10.1   Project-functional organizational interface.

Development Dimensions International, the Association for Quality and Participation, and *Industry Week,* 46 percent indicated that leaders outside the team handle appraisals, 17 percent said that the responsibility is shared, and 37 percent responded that the team takes the lead in appraising performance.[8] On the basis of these surveys, team performance appraisal is changing—teams are accepting such appraisal responsibility—and at the same time management is moving slowly in relinquishing appraisal prerogatives.

In the project-driven organization, people—and teams—have considerable mobility. It becomes a challenge to keep abreast of where people are on teams. Cypress Conductor, a San Jose, California, maker of specialty computer chips, developed a computer system that tracks its 1500 employees as they crisscross functions, teams, and projects.[9]

Reverse delegation

The effectiveness with which project managers exercise authority depends to a large degree on their legal position as well as on their per-

---

[8] Ibid.

[9] Brian Dumaine, "The Bureaucracy Busters," *Fortune,* June 17, 1991, pp. 36–50.

sonal capabilities. But there are ways in which project managers can operate to enhance their basic authority. One way is to guard against *reverse delegation,* which occurs when the person to whom authority has been delegated gives authority back to the delegator. This reverse delegation usually happens under the following conditions:

- The team member wants to avoid risky decisions.

- The team member does not feel that the functional manager is adequately supporting the project.

- The team member lacks confidence, wants to avoid criticism, or feels that the necessary information and resources are lacking to do the job.

- The team member feels that the project manager wants to keep involved in the details of the project.

- The project manager has not been explicit in establishing what is expected of the team member in supporting the project.

Effective delegation is a necessary but not sufficient condition to ensure an effective organizational design to support the project. Organizing a project means many things, one of which is the establishment and maintenance of meaningful authority, responsibility, and accountability relationships among the project team members and other people having a vested interest in the project. Without an adequate, committed process of delegation, there is no effective organization and things can easily "fall through the cracks" in the project.

Documenting project authority

Project managers should have broad authority over all elements of their projects. Although a considerable amount of their authority depends on their personal abilities, they can strengthen their position by publishing documentation to establish their modus operandi and their legal authority. At a minimum, the documentation (expressed in a policy manual, policy letters, and standard operating procedures) should delineate the project manager's role and prerogatives in regard to

1. The project manager's focal position in the project activities
2. The need for a defined authority-responsibility relationship among the project manager, functional managers, work package managers, and general managers
3. The need for influence to cut across functional and organizational lines to achieve unanimity of the project objectives

4. Active participation in major management and technical decisions to complete the project

5. Collaborating (with the personnel office and the functional supervisors) in staffing the project

6. Control over the allocation and expenditure of funds, and active participation in major budgeting and scheduling deliberations

7. Selection of subcontractors to support the project and the negotiation of contracts

8. Rights in resolving conflicts that jeopardize the project goals

9. Having a voice in maintaining the integrity of the project team during the complete life of the project

10. Establishing project plans through the coordinated efforts of the organizations involved in the project

11. Providing an information system for the project with sufficient data for the control of the project within allowable cost, schedule, and technical parameters

12. Providing leadership in the preparation of operational requirements, specifications, justifications, and the bid package

13. Maintaining prime customer liaison and contact on project matters

14. Promoting technological and managerial improvements throughout the life of the project

15. Establishing a project organization (a matrix organization) for the duration of the project

16. Participation in the merit evaluation of key project personnel assigned to the project

17. Allocating and controlling the use of the funds on the project

18. Managing the cost, schedule, and technical performance parameters of the project[10]

The publication of suitable policy media describing the project manager's modus operandi and legal authority will do much to strengthen his or her position in the client environment. In practice, we find many types of de jure authority documentation. A sample of a project/program management charter appears in Table 10.1.

As in the example, care should be taken to delineate the legal posi-

---

[10]David I. Cleland and William R. King, *Systems Analysis and Project Management,* 3d ed. (New York: McGraw-Hill, 1983), pp. 337–338. Reprinted with permission.

TABLE 10.1   Typical Charter of Program Project Manager (Matrix Organization)

Position title: Program Manager

Authority

The program manager has the delegated authority from general management to direct all program activities. He or she represents the company in contacts with the customer and all internal and external negotiations. Project personnel have the typical dual-reporting relationship: to functional management for technical performance and to the program manager for contractual performance in accordance with specifications, schedules, and budgets. The program manager approves all project personnel assignments and influences their salary and promotional status via formal performance reports to their functional managers. Travel and customer contact activities must be coordinated and approved by the program manager.

Any conflict with functional management or company policy shall be resolved by the general manager or his or her staff.

Responsibility

The program manager's responsibilities are to the general manager for overall program direction according to established business objectives and contractual requirements regarding technical specifications, schedules, and budgets.

More specifically, the program manager is responsible for (1) establishing and maintaining the program plan, (2) establishing the program organization, (3) managing and controlling the program, and (4) communicating the program status.

1. *Establishing and maintaining the program plan.* Prior to authorizing the work, the program manager develops the program plan in concert with all key members of the program team. This includes master schedules, budgets, performance specifications, statements of work, work breakdown structures, and task and work authorizations. All of these documents must be negotiated and agreed upon with both the customer and the performing organizations before they become management tools for controlling the program. The program manager is further responsible for updating and maintaining the plan during the life cycle of the program, including the issuance of work authorizations and budgets for each work package in accordance with the master plan.

2. *Establishing the program organization.* In accordance with company policy, the program manager establishes the necessary program organization by defining the type of each functional group needed, including their charters, specific roles, and authority relationships.

3. *Managing the program.* The program manager is responsible for the effective management and control of the program according to established customer requirements and business objectives. He or she directs the coordination and integration of the various disciplines for all program phases through the functional organizations and subcontractors. He or she monitors and controls the work in progress according to the program plan. Potential deficiencies regarding the quality of work, specifications, cost, or schedule must be assessed immediately. It is the responsibility of the program manager to rectify any performance deficiencies.

4. *Communicating the program status.* The program manager is responsible for building and maintaining the necessary communication channels among project team members to the customer community and to the firm's management. The type and extent of management tools employed for facilitating communications must be carefully chosen by the program manager. They include status meetings, design reviews, periodic program reviews, schedules, budgets, data banks, progress reports, and team colocation.

SOURCE: Harold Kerzner and Hans J. Thamhain, *Project Management Operating Guidelines* (New York: Van Nostrand Reinhold, 1986), p. 68.

tion of the project manager. This constitutes an obvious source of power in the project environment. While this gives project managers the right to exercise that power, the significance of authority under the project-functional interface cannot be understated. While project managers may have the final, unilateral right to order affairs in the project, it would be foolhardy for them to substitute their views without fully considering the "crystallization of thinking" of the other stakeholders in their project. Project managers rarely hope to gain and build alliances in their environments by arbitrarily overruling the team members who contribute to a project. They may not have the control for such arbitrary action. Even if they did, they should be most judicious in using authority in such a manner so that the culture in which the project team is operating is not adversely affected.

Authority operates in the context of responsibility and accountability. These concepts are presented in the following material.

What Is Responsibility?

Responsibility, a corollary of authority, is a state, quality, or fact of being responsible. A responsible person is one who is legally and ethically answerable for the care or welfare of people and organizations. A person who is responsible is expected to act without specific guidance or being told to do so by a superior authority. To be responsible is to be able to make rational decisions on one's own, to be trusted to make such decisions, and to be held liable for one's decisions. Archibald, a noted author in the field of project management, notes the following concerning the project manger's responsibility:

> If the project manager's responsibilities are divided among several persons (such as one man for engineering, another for scheduling, a third for cost, a fourth for contract administration, etc.) such division is the most common cause of projects not achieving their objectives. Unless one person integrates the efforts of the project engineer, the project contract administrator, and so on, it is not possible to evaluate the project effectively to identify current or future problems and initiate corrective action in time to assure that the project objectives will be met.
>
> The project manager cannot actually perform all the planning, controlling and evaluation activities needed, any more than he can perform all the technical specialty activities required. Project management support services must be provided to him, and he must direct and control these support activities. The hazard is that the support activities may exist, but in the absence of an assigned project manager, they are not properly used.[11]

---

[11] R. D. Archibald, *Managing High-Technology Programs and Projects* (New York: Wiley, 1976), p. 39.

Some companies are very explicit about their project manager's responsibilities. For example, within the Fluor Corporation, a major engineering/construction company, project managers have "...total responsibility for the execution of the project from its earliest stages right through to completion.[12]

What Is Accountability?

Accountability is the state of assuming liability for something of value, whether through a contract or because of one's position of responsibility. A professional is held accountable for excellence in the quality of the service rendered to the organization. Project managers have dual accountability: They are held answerable for their own performances and for the performance of people who comprise the project team. One of the basic characteristics of managers is that they are held accountable for the effectiveness and efficiency of the people who report to them.

Authority, responsibility, and accountability can rest with a single person or with a group of people. An example of pluralism in this sense is found in the use of a plural executive at the top-management level of organizations such as a management council or the board of directors. The plural executive serves as an integrator of top-management decision making and implementation. The increasing complexity and size of many large organizations have created managerial responsibilities beyond the capabilities of one individual. The plural executive that has been created by organizations usually acts in an advisory capacity to the chief executive by providing stewardship for the strategic management of the company. The specific authority of such plural executives depends on the character establishing such a body. Authority, responsibility, and accountability within the matrix context are the cohesive forces which hold the organization together and make possible the attainment of the organization's cost schedule and technical performance objectives. Figure 10.2 is one way of portraying these forces. The existence of cost, schedule, and technical performance objectives in this figure means that the degree of completeness of authority, responsibility, and accountability at each level in the model can influence any of or all the parameters.

Summary

In this chapter we addressed the de jure and de facto elements of authority. A project manager can never be granted all the authority

---

[12] Robert M. Duke, "Project Management at Fluor Utah Company, Inc.," *Project Management Quarterly,* vol. 8, no. 3, September 1977.

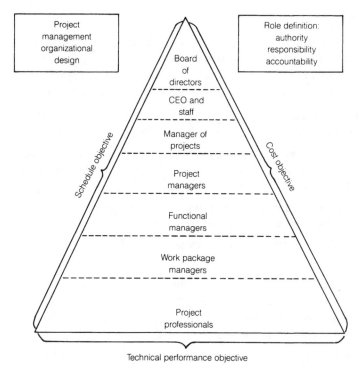

Figure 10.2   Project management organizational design.

necessary to discharge his or her project management responsibilities. That manager must develop de facto sources and uses of authority through the development of knowledge, skills, expertise, personality, interpersonal skills, ability to build and maintain alliances, and so forth.

Projects can fail because of authority, responsibility, and accountability ambiguities. Documentation of the project manager's and other key managers' authority in the project is a must. Criteria for the delineation of the legal authority of such managers were provided in the text of this chapter.

The last measure of authority is the individual's ability to influence all the people who have some interest in the project and, in so doing, to deliver the project on time, within budget, satisfying both the project objectives as well as the strategic objectives of the project owner.

The linear responsibility charting process described in Chap. 9 is an excellent tool to use in getting down to the specifics of authority in project management. Once an LRC is completed, the project team will have a better understanding of their individual and collective authority, responsibility, and accountability.

Discussion Questions

1. Describe a project management situation from your work or school experience. What role did project authority play in the management of the project? Did authority ambiguities exist?

2. Discuss the importance of clear definitions of project authority.

3. Define authority. Discuss the changing view of traditional authority. Discuss the difference between de jure and de facto authority.

4. In adapting to the position of project manager, a specialist must develop the ability to use her or his authority to delegate. How can a manager shift from the role of specialist to generalist?

5. In what situations might the managers of an organization find it necessary to redefine authority relationships?

6. What difficulties do project managers often face in exercising project authority?

7. Discuss the project-functional interface. How can clear lines of authority help in managing this interface?

8. What is meant by reverse delegation? Under what conditions might it be present? How can it be avoided?

9. Discuss the importance of negotiation between project and functional managers.

10. What is the purpose of documenting project authority?

11. What is the difference between authority, responsibility, and accountability?

12. What role does power play in project management? List and discuss some power sources.

User Checklist

1. Think about the various projects within your organization. How is project authority managed? Are there authority ambiguities?

2. Do you feel that the authority of the project managers in your organization is clearly defined? Why or why not?

3. How do the specialists within your organization adapt to the roles of a generalist in project management?

4. Do the managers of your organization understand the need for definition of authority relationships? Explain.

5. Do the managers of your organization use both de jure and de facto authority? How?

6. Is the project-functional interface effectively managed within your organization? Why or why not? How can clearer lines of authority assist in this management?

7. How is project authority granted within your organization?

8. What barriers to delegation exist on the projects within your organization? How can these barriers be better managed?

9. Do the project and functional managers of your organization negotiate to achieve trade-offs among project objectives? Explain.

10. Is project authority documented? How?

11. Do the project managers of your organization understand and manage the difference between authority, responsibility, and accountability? Explain.

12. What power tactics are used by managers in your organization? Is their use productive or destructive toward achievement of organizational and project goals?

11

Project Planning

"Amid a multitude of projects, no plan is devised."

PUBLILIUS SYRUS, CIRCA 42 B.C.

Project planning is an important part of the "deciding" aspect of the project team's job—thinking about the project's future in relationship to its present in such a way that organizational resources can be allocated in a manner which best suits the project's purposes. More explicitly, project planning is the process of thinking through and making explicit the project's objectives, goals, and strategies necessary to bring the project through its life cycle to a successful termination when the project's product or service takes its rightful place in the execution of project owner strategies. This chapter will offer an overview of the project planning function.

Project planning is a rational determination of how to initiate, sustain, and terminate a project. Two authors define the basic concepts of project planning as developing the plan in the required level of detail with accompanying milestones and the use of available tools for preparing and monitoring the plan.[1] Project planning and control are interrelated. Levine has presented a useful flowchart model, Fig. 11.1, to show this interrelationship.

Project planning has played a key role in the outcome of successful nuclear power plant projects in an industry where many projects have had grave difficulties. For example, at the Erie Nuclear Power Plant project, an overall plan was prepared at the project beginning. This plan provided the basis for controlling and coordinating the

---

[1]Harold J. McNeil and Kenneth O. Hartley, "Project Planning and Performance," *Project Management Journal,* March 1986, p. 36.

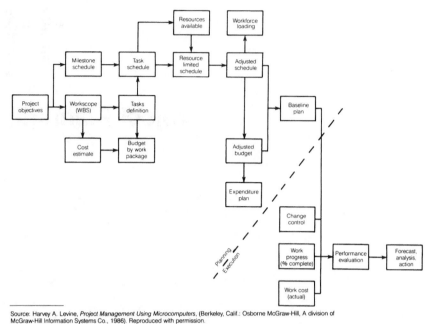

Source: Harvey A. Levine, *Project Management Using Microcomputers*, (Berkeley, Calif.: Osborne McGraw-Hill, A division of McGraw-Hill Information Systems Co., 1986). Reproduced with permission.

Figure 11.1   A flowchart of typical planning and control functions.

activities of the participating parties.[2] At Florida Power and Light's St. Lucie Unit 2 plant, adequate project planning contributed to project success by calling for the appointment of a project management organization in the early stages of the project, an early total project schedule, and the planning, scheduling, and implementation of an effective start-up program.[3]

Planning Realities

The planning ethos of the 1970s, rooted in the extrapolation of history, has been discredited by the "bends" in the trends exemplified by the oil crises and the political and social upheavals of the late 1980s and early 1990s, and it is giving way to a new approach to strategic planning. This new approach is based on a *visionary* view of the future gained by a growing awareness of the possibility of long-term

[2] Barry M. Miller and Charles D. Williams, "Management Action through Effective Project Controls: A Case Study of a Nuclear Power Plant Project," *1978 Proceedings of the Project Management Institute,* Los Angeles, October 1978, vol. 2, pp. G.1 to G.5.

[3] Paraphrased from W. B. Derrickson, "St. Lucie Unit 2—A Nuclear Plant Built on Schedule," *1983 Proceedings of the Project Management Institute,* Houston, October 1983, vol. 5, pp. E.1 to E.14.

strategic alliance building, the sharing of risk in exploiting new technologies and processes leading to earlier commercialization, and continuous improvement of product and process development and implementation in maintaining a competitive edge.

Planning is the most challenging activity of a leader or manager. Planning starts with the development of a *vision—the ability to see something that is invisible to others.* People in general find that it is more comfortable to do than to plan. All too often people equate activity with progress—and taking time to think through a plan of action for the future is not considered active management or leadership. Planning involves thinking through the possibilities and the probabilities of the future—and then developing a strategy for how the organizational resources will be positioned to take advantage of future competitive conditions.

Planning is a responsibility of the project leader. Finding ways to get the full-hearted cooperation of team members will facilitate the planning process and improve the chances of the development of a plan of action to which members of the project team are committed.

Planning for the use of resources precedes the monitoring, evaluation, and control of resources. Insufficient front-end planning, unrealistic project plans, and failing to estimate the degree of complexities and the objectives of the project will lead to reduced accomplishment of project objectives. When planning is done by an active, participating project team, the interactions and communications among the team members help to develop the team, give the team members greater ease in dealing with each other, and are a guide for the future use of organizational resources.

A Conceptual Model of Planning

Project planning must be preceded by comprehensive organizational strategic planning, since projects are integral elements of organizational strategies. A conceptual model depicting the strategic context of organizational planning which includes both strategic planning and strategic implementation appears in Fig. 11.2.[4] These elements are discussed in this section.

The Vision

Planning starts with a *vision.* A manager who has intelligent foresight, unusual competence in discernment or perception, is said to

---

[4]Adapted in part from David I. Cleland and William R. King, *Systems Analysis and Project Management,* 3d ed. (New York: McGraw-Hill, 1983), p. 63.

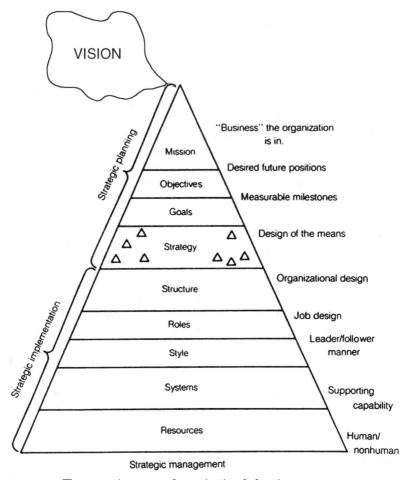

Figure 11.2 The strategic context of organizational planning.

have vision. A vision is a mental image produced by the imagination. Jonathon Swift described vision as "...the art of seeing things invisible to others." A vision and planning are intertwined. For example, Orin E. Smith, president and CEO of Engelhard Corporation, describes the strategic direction of the company in terms of a *vision* which is to be a world-class competitor. He notes:

> That's our vision, our aim, and our commitment. I intend to do whatever has to be done to make Engelhard a world-class competitor—and to keep it that way....We know where we're going. Beyond that, we know how to get there. We have the programs in place to do just that. First, a total quality management process we call "Exceptional Quality" or "EQ."

World-class competitors don't just believe in quality, they *live* quality. They demand it of their management, their employees and their suppliers.[5]

The strategy to accomplish EQ in Engelhard Corporation is to reexamine every step of how products are delivered to customers, fostering complete breakthroughs in the redesign of manufacturing and business processes and the development of more complete and focused long-term strategies for the company's businesses. The main thrust of the company's growth plan is catalysts, particularly environmental catalysts. Further strategies include a rigorous vigilance about costs and through EQ an attempt to overtake competitors and qualify as the supplier of choice. A people-oriented strategy includes unlocking the power of the individual to make a difference.[6]

How important is it to have a vision? One study that benchmarked extraordinary business teams provides compelling evidence on the importance of direction for the teams. Team members stated that the most important factor for high performance was a *clear and elevating vision*. Team members felt the vision was worthwhile.[7]

An effective vision has several key elements: The phrase describing the vision is short and concise and can be easily memorized. The phrase reflects a repeatable basic theme or shared value growing out of a discussion and testing of the vision. And the phrase is meaningful and important to every member of the organization. When the vision statement is believed and frequently talked about by people it takes on a life of its own and becomes important to everyone.

Organizational Mission

The apex of the model in Fig. 11.2 is the organization's *mission*—the culminating strategic point of all organizational activity and the most general strategic choice that must be made by the organization's managers. The organization's mission answers the basic question, What business are we in? One project-oriented firm defined its mission thus: "We are in the business of designing, developing, and installing energy management systems and services for the domestic, nonresidential market."

Boeing Company, which uses project management widely, in its 1991 annual report describes the mission of the company as "...to be the

---

[5]"Postmeeting report, *Annual Meeting of Shareholders,* May 7, 1992.

[6]Ibid.

[7]Carl Larson and Frank LaFasto, *What Must Go Right / What Can Go Wrong* (Newbury Park, Calif.: Sage, 1989).

number one aerospace company in the world, and among the premier industrial firms, as measured by quality, profitability, and growth."

Organizational objectives

The ongoing end purposes that must be achieved in the long term are *organizational objectives,* stated in quantitative or qualitative terms. Objectives are organizational performance criteria to be achieved and measured in the utilization of organizational resources. A computer company defines one of its objectives as leading the state of the art of technology in its product lines.

Another company defines one of its objectives in these terms: "To achieve a compounded earnings growth rate of 15 percent and a 20 percent return on capital by being the leader in providing scientists and educators worldwide with laboratory products and service systems created through technology, integrity, and a commitment to excellence."

At Wal-Mart, the largest and highest-profit retailer in the world, there is a relentless focus on satisfying customer needs. The company's objectives in this regard are simple to define but difficult to execute: Provide customers with quality goods, and make the goods available when and where customers want them. Supporting these objectives is a reputation for absolute trustworthiness.

Organizational goals

An *organizational goal* is a milestone, such as a performance goal of 15 percent return on investment by a specific date. Goals are the basic component for measuring progress in attaining objectives in an organization. Completion of a project's cost, schedule, and technical performance objectives means that an organizational goal has been completed, such as the construction of a production facility. One company's goal was stated thus: "We intend by the end of 1987 to complete the construction of a new manufacturing facility which will complete the transition begun in 1983 from a predominantly R&D services company to an industrial manufacturer." Table 11.1 presents a classification of an organizational mission, objectives, and goals.

Organizational strategies

An *organizational strategy* is the design of the means, through the use of resources, to accomplish end purposes. Strategies are also action plans for setting the direction for the coordinated use of resources through the employment of programs, projects, policies, procedures, and organizational design and establishment of performance standards. The equilateral triangles in the strategy tier in Fig. 11.2 depict projects which have cost, schedule, and technical performance parameters.

TABLE 11.1 Taxonomy of Strategic Elements

Mission	Objective	Goal
■ A broad, enduring intent that an organizational entity pursues.	■ The target and critical results that must be achieved in the long term in an enterprise to contribute directly to the accomplishment of the enterprise's mission.	■ A specific time-sensitive milestone to be accomplished in using organizational resources.
■ An assignment changed to an organizational entity for the providing of products/services.	■ Performance criteria to be achieved and measured in the utilization of organizational resources.	■ The attainment of a goal signifies that progress has been made toward attaining organizational objectives and mission.
■ The overall strategic purpose toward which all organizational resources are directed and committed.	■ The desired future destination of the organizational entity stated in quantitative or qualitative terms.	■ Includes performance goals (e.g., 15% ROI by a specific date) and qualitative goals (product, development, project/program completion).
■ The "business" the organization is in.	■ Performance results (financial, productivity, market share, etc.) and qualitative results (image, personnel development, research) are included.	■ The basic component for measuring progress in attaining desired end results in an organization.
■ What the organizational entity is and what it intends to become. ■ The symbol around which all organizational effort is focused. ■ Supported directly by objectives.	■ Objectives are supported directly by goals.	■ Thus successful completion of a project means that an organization's goal has been achieved.

An important factor about projects bears repeating: Projects are building blocks in the design and execution of organizational strategies.

Organizational Structure

An organizational structure is the alignment of the human resources and functions of the organization. Organizational structures are undergoing significant change. Work is being reorganized; the decline of the traditional authoritarian hierarchies is a key change that is gaining favor. Teams, many of which are voluntary relationships, are arising as a basic organizational means to get things done. Continued downsizing of organizations, the reduction in the need for conventional managerial jobs, and the growing quantity of ambitious people with career expectations competing for a diminishing number of positions are other forces of change in the management of contemporary organizations. More than ever, people will have to take more responsibility for their own careers, including a commitment to a lifetime of learning. The old career paths no longer exist; organizations are streamlining their operations as never before. Employees will be rewarded for knowledge and adaptability; specialization will play a less important role, and generalism will grow in importance. The most employable people will be those who can move easily from one specialization to another and who are able to integrate diverse disciplines and perspectives.

Teamwork will continue to replace the traditional hierarchy as the dominant form of organizational design. People at all levels in organizations are sharing more power than ever before.

The ability to develop organizational values will be critical to successful leadership. The new workplace will be ferociously Darwinian, both for organizations and for the individuals. "Softer" management issues will become all-important. Although people will have greater empowerment and shared responsibility, the stress on individuals will be greater, and people will have a greater chance of burnout.[8]

Globalization is causing some of the significant changes in organizational structures. ABB, the global electrical equipment giant, is bigger than Westinghouse Electric Corporation and can compare to General Electric Company. ABB is truly an international enterprise without a national identity.

A *master matrix* gives everyone two bosses: a country manager and a business sector manager. The country managers run traditional, national companies with local boards of directors. About 100 such managers exist. Global business managers are organized into eight segments: transportation, process automation and engineering, environmental devices, financial services, electrical equipment, and three electric power businesses—generation, transmission, and distribution. The two bosses in the ABB matrix are not always equal. One advantage of this matrix system is that it makes it easier for business managers to use technology from other countries. Company execu-

---

[8]Stratford Sherman, "A Brave New Darwinian Workplace," *Fortune,* January 25, 1993, pp. 50–56.

tives say the value of the matrix system extends beyond the swapping of technology and products. For example, if one factory is performing poorly, solutions can be determined and then discussed and worked out across borders.[9]

Organizational roles

Organizational roles are the individual and collective parts played by the members of the organization. Organizational roles bring life to the structure of the enterprise. The material presented earlier on linear responsibility charts bears mentioning again regarding roles.

Manager and follower style

The *manager and follower style* is the manner in which knowledge, skills, and attitudes are expressed by the people who support the organized effort.

Part of the reason for the comeback of Goodyear Tire & Rubber Company has been the new management style brought forth by Stanley Gault, CEO of Goodyear and former CEO of Rubbermaid Company. Factory workers are required to take courses in business education. A closed-circuit television has been installed in many plants to keep workers informed of competitive developments such as earnings and stock prices. Output per worker-hour climbed 51 percent between 1985 and 1991. People at corporate headquarters at Goodyear say that Gault's presence "permeates" the headquarters—he is perceived as seldom giving orders, but everyone knows what he wants done. Gault runs the company on the basis of trust. The company's quarterly results are reported at meetings held in the headquarters auditorium, to which about 800 people are invited, and questions are taken from the floor. Every meeting is videotaped, and the tapes are distributed to the company's 88 plants around the world. Gault also is present to chair bimonthly meetings at which employees demonstrate improvements they have made and receive awards. Gault has also stepped up product development through the use of project teams, introducing twelve new tires this year.[10]

At Siemens Company in Germany, the management style is tailored to Germany's consensus-style corporate culture. At Siemens a new generation of executives is moving into power; for these executives a rigid hierarchy is out and an entrepreneurial drive is in. The

[9]Carla Rapoport, "A Tough Swede Invades the U.S.," *Fortune,* June 29, 1992, pp. 76–79.

[10]Peter Nulty, "The Bounce Is Back at Goodyear," *Fortune,* September 7, 1992, pp. 70–72.

company has been broken up into smaller units that are headed up by entrepreneurial managers.

At Siemens it has been a tough job to get the civil-service mentality culture to change. Thousands of middle-level managers refuse to take personal initiative and undermine others who do so. These managers were so used to taking and executing orders that they found it difficult to take initiatives on their own.[11]

Systems

Systems include the hardware and software systems that support the organizational activities, such as accounting, information, marketing, production, design, and so forth.

Technology embodied in organizational systems changes the way that organizational resources are utilized. For example, at Kao Corporation, Japan's biggest soap and cosmetics company and the sixth largest in the world, an information system developed through project management processes links everything: sales and shipping, production and purchasing, accounting, research and development, marketing, hundreds of shopkeepers' cash registers, and thousands of salesperson's hand-held computers. The information is so complete that year-end financial statements can be turned out by noon of the first day of the new year. Kao people can know if a new product will be successful within two weeks of launch through the melding of point-of-sale information from 216 retailers with a test marketing operation called the Echo System, which uses focus groups and consumers' calls and letters to gauge customer response faster than market surveys can.[12]

The use of personal computers has changed the way organizations work. Desktop computing power has empowered employees, provided them with increased information, and employees are able to do more things than was ever possible before computers became available. The hierarchy of the organization tends to flatten, process management becomes easier, and many of the things that managers and supervisors used to do (such as providing information needed for employees to do their work) become available to employees. Fewer managers and supervisors are needed. E-Mail is giving employees improved communication capabilities to facilitate the transmission of the intelligence needed to do a job, in particular when the doing of

---

[11] Gail E. Schares et al., "The New Generation at Siemens," *Business Week,* March 9, 1992.

[12] Thomas A. Stewart, "Brace for Japan's Hot New Strategy," *Fortune,* September 21, 1992, pp. 62–74.

that job requires ongoing and extensive interface with other organizational units and other project teams. Enhanced information capability, utilized through the computer, leads to improved concurrency in both the doing of the work and the management and supervision of the work. Continued improvement in information and computer technology will continue to alter both *how* and *where* people work. People can be part of a project team or other organizational unit without physically being there. Remote information exchanges and telecommunications are enhancing the ability of a person with a computer and a modem to be part of any organization wherever located. As computers, information, and telecommunication technologies are improved, there should be less need for employees to travel to customers, suppliers, and other organizational units.

An added benefit of such technologies will be an expanded work force to include disabled employees and those who have difficulty getting to and from work each day. The advent of state-of-the-art technologies provides an additional bonding needed to hold the project teams and other self-managed teams and business processes together. A feature report, "The New Computer Revolution" in the June 14, 1993 issue of *Fortune* magazine, "holds lessons for every manager." According to *Fortune,* the future course of this revolution will transform the way all businesses work. Project managers—and aspiring project managers—should read this article.

Organizational resources

Organizational resources are the human and nonhuman resources which are available to the organization to fulfill its mission, objectives, and goals.

Project Planning Model

Project planning begins within the framework of strategic planning in the organization. For example, the strategic planning phase at a steel corporation led to the approval of a comprehensive facility feasibility study for the location and configuration of the steel plant. As a result of this feasibility study, which evaluated seven alternative sites, the plant location was fixed at Cleveland, Ohio. During the planning for this facility, several options were considered, ranging from turn-key contract to construction management consultant to the owner acting as its own general contractor with subcontractors and/or in-house personnel. These options were considered in detail before final project planning was carried out with approval estimates and milestone schedules.

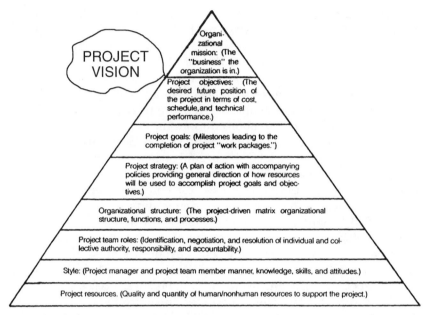

Figure 11.3 Strategic context of planning for the project.

The strategic context of organizational planning depicted in Fig. 11.2 can be transposed into a project-related model as portrayed in Fig. 11.3. Taken together, the elements of Fig. 11.3 comprise the key considerations involved in developing a project planning process.

The Project Planning Process

Projects often extend for many years into the future. Thus, a project plan for such projects becomes both operational (short-term) and strategic (long-term). It follows that the project planning process requires both operational and strategic thinking. Creativity, innovation, and the ability to "think prospectively" form the basis for the project planning process. The real value of such a process is a framework of things to consider for a project's life cycle. A project planner's philosophy encompasses characteristics such as

- The need to search out objective data that provide the basis for project planning decision making
- The value of questioning assumptions, databases, and emerging project strategies to test their validity and relevance
- An ongoing obsession with where the project should go and how it is going to get there

- A demonstrated ability to view project opportunities in the largest possible context and to constantly seek an understanding of how everything fits together during the project's life cycle

- A faith that, given ample opportunity, a *bisociation* will occur: the fitting together of separate events or forces on the project.[13]

Individuals making key project planning decisions today will have a long-term strategic impact on the organization. Generally, the strategic roles of key individuals involved in project planning are as follows:

- The *board of directors* reviews and approves (or redirects for further study) key project plans and maintains surveillance over the implementation of the plans.

- *Senior management* directs the design, development, and implementation of a strategic planning system and a project planning philosophy and process for the corporation.

- *Functional managers* are responsible for the integration of state-of-the-art functional technology into the project plans.

- The *project manager* is responsible for integrating and coordinating the project planning activity.

- The *work package manager* is responsible for providing input to the project plans.

- *Professionals* participate as required in contributing to the project planning processes.

Thus project planning is the "business" of many individuals in the organization.

By involving these individuals in the roles as described, key people are afforded the opportunity to participate in project planning. Of course, such participation will require relevant knowledge, skill, and insight into both the theory and practice of project planning. By maximizing the participation of key individuals in project planning, the overall value of the project plan should be improved. One large project-driven organization recognized the value of project planning like this:

> During the early 1960s, after hundreds of projects had been completed, it became apparent that many projects successfully achieved their basic project objectives, while some failed to achieve budget, schedule and performance objectives originally established.

---

[13]Arthur Koestler, *The Act of Creation* (London: Hutchinson & Co., 1964). He explains creativeness as the result of bisociation, of putting together unconnected facts or ideas to form a single new idea.

The history of many of these projects was carefully reviewed to identify conditions and events common to successful projects, vis-à-vis those conditions and events that occurred frequently on less successful projects. A common identifiable element on most successful projects was the quality and depth of early planning by the project management group. Execution of the plan, bolstered by strong project management control over identifiable phases of the project, was another major reason why the project was successful.[14]

Project planning may be considered a form of information development and communications. As the project team develops the project plan, the project team should learn more about the project goals, strategies, and team member roles. The project objectives then can be decided in terms of cost, schedule, and technical performance. Satisfaction of project goals is accomplished through the completion of the project work packages. The project strategy is a plan of action with accompanying policies, procedures, and resource allocation schemes, providing general direction of how the organizational effort will be used to accomplish project goals and project objectives.

Project Planning Considerations

All too often when people think of project planning, they perceive the use of only techniques and concepts such as PERT, CPM, or networking. These techniques will not be discussed in any detail in this book. Instead the footnote references can serve as useful guidelines in using PERT, CPM, and networking.[15] These techniques are important to use in the development of a project schedule; however, project planning includes a much wider scope of activity. Such concerns as objective and goal setting, cost estimating and budgeting, technology strategies scheduling, resource usage estimating, and specification of deliverables are key concerns. Project planning also involves a delineation of the organizational design to support the project as well as the information system and the control system which are used to model, evaluate, and reallocate resources as required during the execution of the project plan.

Project planning deals with the determination of what activities and what resources have to be utilized to ensure that the project is

---

[14]Robert K. Duke, H. Frederick Wohlsen, and Douglas R. Mitchell, "Project Management at Fluor Utah, Inc.," *Project Management Quarterly,* vol. 3, no. 3, September 1977, p. 33.

[15]Joseph J. Moder, "Network Techniques in Project Management," in D. I. Cleland and W. R. King (eds.), *Project Management Handbook,* 1st ed. (New York: Van Nostrand Reinhold, 1983), chap. 16, 303–309; and James J. O'Brien, *CPM in Construction Management,* 3d ed. (New York: McGraw-Hill, 1984).

adequately executed. Authority, responsibility, and accountability have to be planned so that members of the project team know what their specific roles are and how they relate to other members of the project team who are involved in executing work package activity. When is activity due? and What is the time duration of each activity? are key questions. What human and nonhuman resources are needed to execute each activity on the project? What are the estimated costs, and how are the budget and financial plans to be established to support the cost considerations of the budget?

One of the changes under way in contemporary organizations is more people involved in and carrying out the management functions.

Participative planning has been used effectively by AT&T. Participation is obtained through the use of workshops that include the entire project team and even customers in joint planning sessions. A planning process facilitator helps to guide the activities and to keep the project planning moving forward. The purpose of the workshops is to have the participants agree on high-level project plans, schedules, and project monitoring and evaluation strategies. Held at the beginning of a project, the workshops achieve the benefits of early planning, including overcoming planning problems and getting the team members involved early in the planning, which leads to more commitment and dedication to their role on the project. In addition, team members are given an early exposure to their individual and collective roles in the project and an opportunity to identify any interpersonal anxieties that might hinder team development and operation at a later date. These start-up workshops have been successful in producing planning deliverables, developing planning skills, and building team interaction and cohesiveness.[16]

Project planning and control techniques are many and varied. For example, in one survey, project planning techniques included

1. Work breakdown structure
2. Network
   a. Arrow scheme
   b. Node scheme
   c. Precedence Diagrams
3. Bar chart
   a. With precedence
   b. Without precedence
4. Critical path method (CPM)
5. PERT—statistics

[16]Dan Ono and Russell D. Archibald, "Project Start-up Workshops: Gateway to Project Success," *Proceedings of the 1988 Project Management Institute Seminar/Symposium,* San Francisco, September 17–21, 1988, pp. 500–554.

6. GERT simulation
7. Time/Cost analysis
8. Resource leveling
9. Computer assistance
10. Linear responsibility chart (LRC)[17]

The project manager is responsible for initiating action to bring about the development of a plan. In discharging the project leadership role, the project leader has the final responsibility for ensuring that "the right things are done" about the project plan. The complexities of doing the details of the project—doing things right—rests with the specialists who are members of the project plan. Planning becomes a method for coordinating and synchronizing the forthcoming project activities. Project planning should be undertaken after the project has been positioned in the overall strategy for the enterprise; then the detailed planning can be carried out.

Since planning involves thinking through the probabilities and possibilities of the project's future, a detailed cookbook recipe for planning cannot be provided. However, certain key work packages and planning tools have to be addressed in the development of the project plan of action. These planning work packages are described in the next section.

Work Breakdown Structure[18]

The most basic consideration in project planning is the *work breakdown structure* (WBS). The WBS divides the overall project into work elements that represent singular work units, assigned either with the organization or to an outside agency such as a vendor.

The WBS process is carried out in the following manner: Each project must be subdivided into tasks that can be assigned and accomplished by some organizational unit or individual. These tasks are then performed by specialized functional organizational components. The *map* of the project represents the collection of these units and shows the project manager many organizational and subsystem interfaces to manage.

The underlying philosophy of the work breakdown structure is to break down the project into *work packages* that are assignable and for which accountability can be expected. Each work package is a perfor-

---

[17]Khaled A. Bubushait, "A Survey of the Practices of Project Management Techniques in Different Industries," *Project Management Institute Seminar/Symposium,* Montreal, Canada, September 1986, p. 132.

[18]Paraphrased from D. I. Cleland and W. R. King, *Systems Analysis and Project Management,* 3d ed. (New York: McGraw-Hill, 1983), pp. 255–258.

mance-control element; it is negotiated and assigned to a specific organizational manager, usually called a *work package manager*. The work package manager is responsible for a specific objective (which should be measurable), detailed task descriptions, specifications, scheduled task milestones, and a time-phased budget in dollars and work force. Each work package manager is held responsible by both the project and the functional managers for the completion of the work package in terms of objectives, schedules, and costs.

The process of developing the WBS is to establish a scheme for dividing the project into major groups, then divide the major groups into tasks, subdivide the tasks into subtasks, and so forth. Projects are planned, organized, and controlled around the lowest level of the WBS. The organization of the WBS should follow some orderly identification scheme; each WBS element is given a distinct identifier. With an aircraft, for example, the WBS might look like this:

1.0 Aircraft
   1.1 Final Assembly
   1.2 Fuselage
   1.3 Tail
   1.4 Wing
   1.5 Engines

A graphic representation of the WBS can facilitate its understanding. Using numerical listings with deeper indentation for successively lower levels can aid in communications and in developing understanding of the total project and its integral subsystems, sub-subsystems, etc. For instance:

1.0 . . . .
  1.1 . . . .
    1.1.1 . . . .
      1.1.1.1 . . . .
      1.1.1.2 . . . .
      1.1.1.3 . . . .
    1.1.2 . . . .
    Etc.

Work packages follow from a WBS analysis on the project. When the WBS analysis is completed and the work packages are identified, a WBS comes into existence. A WBS can be represented by a pyramid similar to that used for describing the traditional organizational structure.

In the context of a project, the WBS and the resulting work packages provide a model of the products (hardware, software, services, and other elements) that completely define the project. Such a model enables project engineers, project managers, functional managers, and general managers to think of the totality of all products and services comprising the project as well as its component subsystems. The model is the focus around which the project is managed. More particularly, the development of a WBS provides the means for

1. Summarizing all products and services comprising the project, including support and other tasks

2. Displaying the interrelationships of the work packages to each other, to the total project, and to other engineering activities in the organization

3. Establishing the authority-responsibility matrix organization

4. Estimating project cost

5. Performing risk analysis

6. Scheduling work packages

7. Developing information for managing the project

8. Providing a basis for controlling the application of resources on the project

9. Providing reference points for getting people committed to support the project

Work packages are the goals to be accomplished on the project. There are certain criteria that should be applied to the project goals:

- Are the goals clear?
- Are they specific?
- Are they time-based?
- Are they measurable?
- Can they be communicated easily to the project team?
- Can they be clearly assigned to the work package managers/professionals?

The WBS provides a natural framework or skeleton for identifying the work elements of the project: hardware, software, documentation, and miscellaneous work to be accomplished to bring the project to completion. The WBS provides an identifier and a management thread to manage myriad aspects of the project. In some projects unique work packages are found. For example, in some global projects a cultural planning work package is included in the work breakdown structure. From this work package successful cultural training and orientation can be carried out.

Project Schedules

A key output of project planning is the *project master schedule,* along with supporting schedules, which is a graphic time representation of all necessary project-related activities. The project schedule establishes the time parameters of the project and helps the managers to effectively coordinate and facilitate the efforts of the entire project team during the life of the project. A schedule becomes an effective part of the project control system. For a project schedule to be effective, it must be

- Understandable by the project team
- Capable of identifying and highlighting critical work packages and tasks
- Updated, modified as necessary, and flexible in its application
- Substantially detailed to provide a basis for committing, monitoring, and evaluating the use of project resources.
- Based upon credible time estimates that conform to available resources
- Compatible with other organizational plans that share common resources

Several steps are required to develop the project master schedule. These steps should be undertaken in the proper sequence.

1. Define the project objectives, goals, and overall strategies.
2. Develop the project work breakdown schedule with associated work packages.
3. Sequence the project work packages and tasks.
4. Estimate the time and cost elements.
5. Review the master schedule with project time constraints.
6. Reconcile the schedule with organizational resource constraints.
7. Review the schedule for its consistency with project costs with technical performance objectives.
8. Senior managers approve the schedule.

Scheduling Techniques

Several scheduling techniques are useful in dealing with the timing aspect of the project resources.

Project planning bar charts

A technique for simple project planning and scheduling is based on the *bar chart*. This chart consists of a scale divided into units of time (e.g., days, weeks, or months) across the top and a listing of the project work packages or elements down the left-hand side. Bars or lines are used to indicate the schedule and status of each work package in relation to the time scale.

Figure 11.4 is an example of a project planning bar chart for the development of an electronic device. The work packages of the project are listed on the left-hand side, and the units of time in workdays are shown at the top. The light horizontal lines indicate the schedule for the project elements, with the specific tasks or operations written above the schedule line. Work accomplished is indicated by a heavy line below the schedule line.[19] The large V on the time scale at the top of the chart marks the time to which progress has been posted. Progress is posted at regular intervals. The sys-

---

[19] Project planning charts often use open bars (hence the name *bar charts*), with the ends indicating the start and completion times. Accomplished work is indicated by filling in the bar.

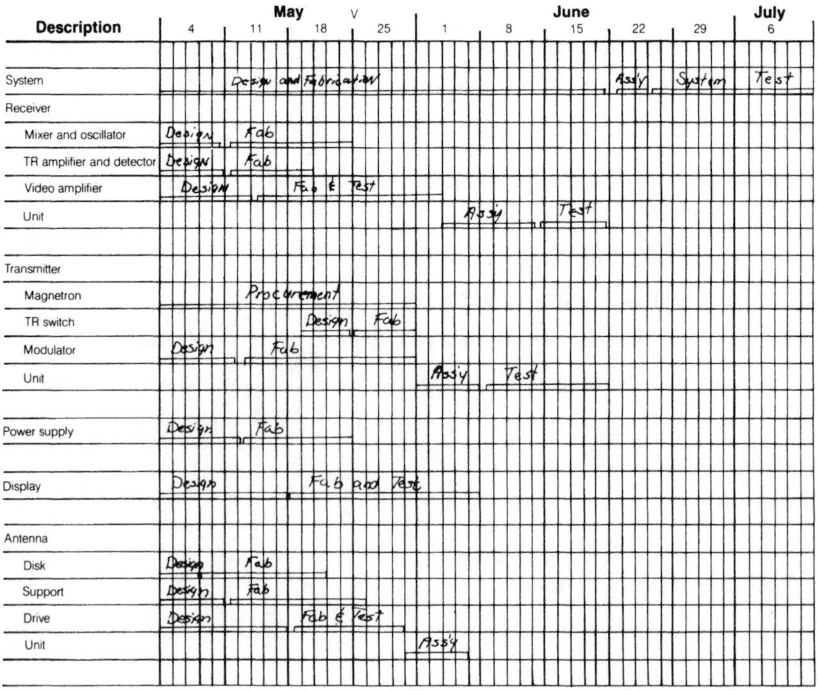

Figure 11.4 Project planning chart.

tem line in Fig. 11.4 indicates that the project as a whole is 6 days behind schedule. At the last posting, the receiver video amplifier was the farthest behind schedule. The display and antenna units were ahead of schedule.

Bar graphs are easy to develop and understand, and by showing the scheduled start and finish of the work packages they provide a simple picture of where the project stands. A variation of the bar chart is the *milestone chart* which replaces the bar with lines and triangles to indicate project status. A bar chart does not show work package interdependence and time-resource trade-offs. Network techniques used on larger projects help to plan, track, and control complex projects effectively.

Network Techniques

Network techniques best known as PERT and CPM came about in the 1950s. The network diagram of PERT/CPM technologies provides a more powerful measurement of time and work package relationships than either the bar chart or the milestone chart. The network diagram, basic to PERT/CPM techniques, provides a more dynamic interrelated picture of the events and activities and interrelationships relative to the project. The main value of the network technique is its ability to track time and cost considerations of the project. While PERT and CPM are excellent systems for keeping track of all activities on a large project, the planning value of network technique is considered to be as important as the control of the project work packages during the project execution.[20]

Project Life-Cycle Planning

The project life cycle is a key consideration in project planning. Once the appropriate work packages for each phase of the project's life cycle have been depicted, a substantial start has been made toward the development of the project plan. Figure 11.5 shows an example of how the work packages are to be accomplished by project phase. This model is also shown in Fig. 2.2 in a slightly different context.

Project Planning Elements

There are a few fundamental components in the project planning process. These elements include the outputs from the techniques and

[20] For a summary of network techniques see Hans J. Thamhain, *Engineering Program Management* (New York: Wiley, 1984), pp. 109–140.

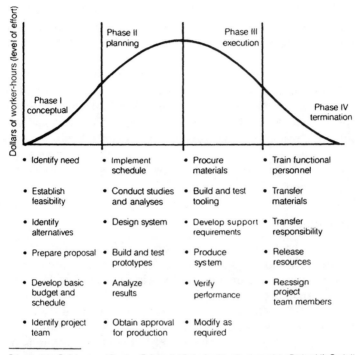

Phase II
planning

Phase III
execution

Phase I
conceptual

Phase IV
termination

Dollars of worker-hours (level of effort)

• Identify need	• Implement schedule	• Procure materials	• Train functional personnel
• Establish feasibility	• Conduct studies and analyses	• Build and test tooling	• Transfer materials
• Identify alternatives	• Design system	• Develop support requirements	• Transfer responsibility
• Prepare proposal	• Build and test prototypes	• Produce system	• Release resources
• Develop basic budget and schedule	• Analyze results	• Verify performance	• Reassign project team members
• Identify project team	• Obtain approval for production	• Modify as required	

Source: John R. Adams and Stephen E. Barndt, "Behavioral Implications of the Project Life Cycle,"
Project Management Handbook, D.I. Cleland and W.R. King (eds.). 2d ed. (New York: Van Nostrand
Reinhold Co., © 1988): 206 – 230. All rights reserved.

Figure 11.5   Tasks accomplished by project phase.

processes previously discussed as well as these elements discussed in
the material that follows.

Statement of work

A *statement of work* describes the actual work that is going to be performed on the project, which when combined with the specifications
usually forms the basis for a contractual agreement on the project.
As a derivative of the WBS, the statement of work (sometimes called
scope of work) describes what is going to be accomplished, a description of the tasks, the deliverable end products that will be produced,
such as hardware, software, tests, documentation, training, etc., as
well as references to specifications, directives, or standards. The
statement of work also includes input required from other tasks
involving the project and a key element of the customer's request for
a proposal.

Project specification

Specifications are the descriptions of the technical content of the project. These specifications must be compatible with the WBS and describe the various characteristics of the various subsystems in the project product or service which might include an overall system specification, hardware, software, test specifications, and logistics support.

Cost estimate

The cost estimate, which is used to keep up with the actual and projected cost of the project, usually has several levels, coordinated with the work breakdown system. One purpose of the cost estimate is to produce timely reports on the actual project cost versus the estimated cost for the project and the project work packages. The cost estimate also can be used to produce a detailed monthly cost breakdown for each element of the project. An element of the cost system is a report which provides weekly actual cost with estimated cost as well as comparing actual worker-hours with target worker-hours in manufacturing or construction.

The *cost account* usually is considered the basic level at which project performance is measured and reported. This account represents a specific work package identified by the WBS, usually tracked by information on a daily or weekly time card which ties in with the organizational cost accounting system.

Financial plan

Assuming the project budget, work package budget, and budgets for the appropriate cost accounts have been developed, financial planning involves the development of action plans for obtaining and managing the organizational funds to support the project through the use of the work authorization process.

The project manager usually authorizes the expenditure of resources on the project for work to be accomplished within the organization as well as on work subcontracted to vendors. The work authorization process is an orderly way to delegate authority to expend resources for the project. The work authorization document usually includes

1. The responsible individual and/or organization
2. A work package WBS
3. A schedule
4. Cost estimate and funding citation

5. A statement of work

Usually the work authorization document is in a one-sheet format that is considered a written contract between the project manager and the performing organization and/or person.

Functional plan

Each functional manager should prepare a functional operational plan that establishes the nature and timing of functional resources necessary to support the project plan. For example, the accounting/financial organization that supports the project manager should establish a plan for how the project budget can be monitored. Such a plan would be an information system for monitoring actual project costs and comparing them with budgeted costs.

Plan format

The organization and arrangement of the project plan depend on the nature of the project. The bare essentials of a project plan include

- A summary of the project that states briefly what is to be done and the methods and techniques to be used. It lists the deliverable end products in such a way that when they are produced, they can be identified easily and compared with the plan.

- A list of tangible and discrete goals, identified in such a way that there can be no ambiguity about whether a goal has been achieved.

- A WBS that is detailed enough to provide meaningful identification of all tasks associated with job numbers, plus all higher-level groupings such as work units or work packages.

- A strategy outlining how organizational resources will be used to accomplish project objectives and goals.

- An activity network that shows the sequence of elements of the project and how they are related (which can be done in parallel, which can start only when another is finished, etc.).

- Separate budgets and schedules for all the elements of the project for which some individual is responsible.

- An interface plan that shows how the project relates to the rest of the world, most particularly to the customer.

- An indication of the review process—who reviews the project, when, and for what purpose.

- A list of key project personnel and their assignments in relation to the WBS.

Project management manual

An important part of project planning is the development of organizational policies and procedures that support the project plan. Many organizations use a project management manual which tells all project participants what they have to do and how they have to do it. Bitner has suggested the contents for a representative project procedure manual.[21]

Project planning work packages

Even the task of planning a project should be broken down into work packages. Here is a general guide to these work packages:

- *Establish the strategic fit of the project.*   Ensure that the project is truly a building block in the design and execution of organizational strategies and provides the project owner with an operational capability not currently existing or improves an existing capability. Identify strategic issues likely to affect the project.

- *Develop the project technical performance objective.*   Describe the project deliverable end product(s) that satisfies a customer's needs in terms of capability, capacity, quality, quantity, reliability, and efficiency, etc.

- *Describe the project through the development of the project WBS.* Develop a product-oriented family tree division of hardware, software, services, and other tasks to organize, define, and graphically display the product to be produced, as well as the work to be accomplished to achieve the specified product.

- *Identify and make provisions for the assignment of the functional work packages.*   Decide which work packages will be done in-house, obtain the commitment of the responsible functional work managers, and plan for the allocation of appropriate funds through the organizational work authorization system.

- *Identify project work packages that will be subcontracted.*   Develop procurement specifications and other desired contractual terms for the delivery of the goods and services to be provided by outside vendors.

- *Develop the master and work package schedules.*   Use the appropriate scheduling techniques to determine the time dimension of the project through a collaborative effort of the project team.

---

[21] L. M. Bitner, "Project Management: Theory versus Application," *Project Management Journal,* June 1985, p. 67.

- *Develop the logic networks and relationships of the project work packages.* Determine how the project parts can fit together in a logical relationship.

- *Identify the strategic issues that the project is likely to face.* Develop a strategy for how to deal with these issues.

- *Estimate the project costs.* Determine what it will cost to design, develop, and manufacture (construct) the project, including an assessment of the probability of staying within the estimated costs.

- *Perform risk analysis.* Establish the degree or probability of suffering a setback in the project's schedule, cost, or technical performance parameters.

- *Develop the project budgets, funding plans, and other resource plans.* Establish how the project funds should be utilized, and develop the necessary information to monitor and control the use of funds on the project.

- *Ensure the development of organizational cost accounting system interfaces.* Since the project management information system is tied in closely with cost accounting, establish the appropriate interfaces with that function.

- *Select the organizational design.* Provide the basis for getting the project team organized, including delineations of authority, responsibility, and accountability. At a minimum, establish the legal authority of the organizational board of directors, senior management, project and functional managers, as well as the work package managers and project professionals. Use the LRC process to determine individual and collective roles on the project team.

- *Provide for the project management information system.* An information system is essential to monitor, evaluate, and control the use of resources on the project. Accordingly, develop such a system as part of the project plan.

- *Assess the organizational cultural ambience.* Project management works best where a supportive culture exists. Project documentation, management style, training, attitudes, all work together to make up the culture in which project management is found. Determine what project management training would be required. What cultural fine-tuning is required?

- *Develop project control concepts, processes, and techniques.* How will the project's status be judged through a review process? On what basis? How often? By whom? How? Ask and answer these questions prospectively during the planning phase.

- *Develop the project team.* Establish a strategy for creating and maintaining effective project team operations.

- *Integrate contemporaneous state-of-the-art project management philosophies, concepts, and techniques.* The art and science of project management continue to evolve. Take care to keep project management approaches up to date.

- *Design project administration policies, procedures, and methodologies.* Administrative considerations often are overlooked. Take care of them during early project planning, and do not leave them to chance.

- *Plan for the nature and timing of the project audits.* Determine the type of audit best suited to get an independent evaluation of where the project stands at critical junctures.

- *Determine who the project stakeholders are and plan for the management of these stakeholders.* Think through how these stakeholders might change through the life cycle of the project.

Management realities

Flawless planning, final fixed strategies, and simple organizational designs are an illusion today. Plans are "living documents" that change as competitive and environmental systems change. Communications and coordination take on added significance. Teams rather than fixed organizational structures are the order of the day. Integration becomes supreme as organizational processes are crossed as needed, and when needed, to pull together synchronized and quality efforts to produce customer value. For many managers who grew up in a "command and control" culture, the new paradigm of "consensus and consent" management is disquieting—some are never able to adapt to the new way of getting things done. Managers have become the servants of those they choose to rule. The new world is concerned with flexibility—in strategies, markets, projects resources, and people. In the past we managed as if the optimization of the parts of the organization—research, manufacturing, engineering, marketing, product development, and so forth—would lead to the optimization of the whole of the organization. It does not happen, and it has never happened. Today we optimize the integration of the organizational processes by using project teams as focal points to pull together the human and nonhuman resources needed to do the job. The major breakthroughs in improving organizational efficiency and effectiveness have come about because of the management of the organizational *processes* rather than the functional entities of the organization. The management of the organizational processes through a self-directed team has finally captured the essence of the interdependencies of the organizational functions.

Summary

A project plan is like a map. It is intended to guide people on the project team. Even an imperfect project plan is useful because it can serve as a pretext to start doing something on the project. What project managers often forget is that it is the action around a project plan that explains the plan's success, and not the plan itself. The world of project management is ambiguous unless the project manager is able to direct activity and produce something based on a plan of action.

Project management failures often come about because the project team members did not believe in, nor did they plan for, nor were they prepared to deal with simultaneous successes and failures, escalation of effects, and positive and negative feedbacks that occur in complex projects. If the project team members under the leadership of the project manager cannot sense the synergism of the project, they are not in the position to do anything about it. The principal way to gain control of a complex project is to simplify that project through the medium of a plan. The best way to simplify a complex project is to disconnect its parts so the parts do not get out of control and have adverse effects on each other and on the project itself. The first step in simplifying a project is to develop a scope of work and a WBS for that project and to start to build the project plan.

The project's objectives, goals, and strategies are the most important considerations in shaping the project's future and in allocating resources to support that future. The objectives and goals define the purpose of the project. The development of the project strategy deals with how policies, procedures, action plans, contingency plans, organizational design, team development and control processes, etc., all pull together to attain the project purposes.

Discussion Questions

1. What are some of the basic concepts involved in project planning? How can a complete project plan contribute to project success?

2. Define each of the key elements of organization planning as depicted in Fig. 11.2.

3. Discuss the relationship of project planning to strategic planning. Why is this relationship important?

4. List and discuss some of the traditional and modern planning practices.

5. Nearly all project stakeholders have some role in the project planning process. How are each of the key people afforded the opportunity to participate in project planning?

6. Describe a simple project management situation from your work or school experience. Develop a work breakdown structure for the situation.

7. What are some of the characteristics of an effective project schedule? Describe some of the scheduling techniques used in project management.

8. What are the relationships between the statement of work, project specification, cost estimate, financial plan, functional plan, and implementation plan? How are each developed and used?

9. List the essential elements of the project plan format.

10. What is the purpose of the project management manual? How does it support the project plan?

11. Discuss the nature of the relationship between effective planning and effective control. What are some of the elements of each?

12. Discuss the importance of scheduling project audits.

User Checklist

1. Are the key elements of organizational planning—mission, objectives, goals, strategies, and so forth—evident in your organization? Is project planning integrated into strategic planning? Explain.

2. Which of the project planning practices are used by your organization? How?

3. What role do each of the project stakeholders on projects within your organization play in the project planning process?

4. Do the project managers in your organization understand the concept of a work breakdown structure? Are work breakdown structures developed for every project? Why or why not?

5. How are project schedules developed? What scheduling techniques are used? Are these techniques effective? What other techniques might be more effective for project planning in your organization?

6. Is the project life cycle understood by the project managers in your organization? How is this concept integrated into the project planning process?

7. Which of the additional project planning elements—statement of work, project specification, cost estimate, financial plan, functional plan—are used by your organization? Which are not? Explain.

8. Are organizational policies and procedures developed to support the project plan? Would the development of a project management manual increase the effectiveness of the project planning process in your organization?

9. Do managers consider the strategic fit of projects to ensure that the project is truly a building block in executing organizational strategies? Explain.

10. Consider the project planning work packages. How do these work packages fit in your project planning?

11. How are the work packages assigned on major projects? Does management consider subcontracting work packages? Are logic networks and relationships developed for the work packages?

12. Does the organization perform risk analysis to assess the probability of setbacks in project schedules? Is the cultural ambience of the organization supportive of projects?

12

Project Management Information System (PMIS)

"Knowledge is of two kinds: We know a subject ourselves, or we know where we can find information about it."
SAMUEL JOHNSON, 1709–1784

In Chap. 4, the subsystems involved in a project management system are described. One of these subsystems, the project management information system (PMIS), contains the intelligence essential to the effective planning, organization, directing, and control of the project. The basics of a PMIS are covered in this chapter. All too often projects are characterized by too many data and not enough relevant information on where the project stands relative to its schedule, cost, and technical performance objectives as well as the project's strategic fit in the parent organization's strategies.

Information is essential to the design and execution of decisions allocating resources in the management of a project. Decisions coming out of the planning organization, direction, and control of the project must be based on timely and relevant information. Motivation of the project team and the discharge of leadership responsibilities by all managers associated with the project require information by which intelligent decisions can be made and executed.

Information is required for the operation of any enterprise. In organizations, the making and implementation of decisions depend on the character of the information available to the decision makers. Information flow is a critical consideration in the speed and effectiveness with which the efficient and effective use of resources is carried out in meeting the purposes of the enterprise.

Organizations of all sizes need information to design, produce, market, and provide after-sales support to the products and services that are offered to the customers. In large organizations the flow of information can be incomplete and sequential, often not getting to the people who need the information for their work in time to make the best decisions. Information can be found "lying around" in organizations waiting for someone who has the authority to make a decision. The best of information loses its value if it is not provided to the people who need it on a timely basis.

Sometimes the initiation of a project for the development of an information system for one element of the enterprise results in the broadening of information usage. For example, at 3M during the development of a Computer Integrated Manufacturing (CIM) approach for the company, a total integration of all the information technology for one of the company's plants was initiated. The name given to this effort became *integrated manufacturing systems* (IMSs). Tying the administrative systems into their CIM structures provided for broadening the notion of concurrency further in the management systems of the organization.[1]

Informal Information

Information systems for organizations include the *formal* information that is required to portray the organization's posture, strategies, and performance. In a broad sense, information also includes *informal* information which includes talk coming out of the informal, unofficial organization. This informal information can provide project managers with insight into how people really feel about the project. The perceptions that people have can be more important than the facts, and can influence their thoughts and actions. Knowing how the informal organization perceives what is going on can give managers an excellent insight into the effectiveness with which the project team is performing. An astute project manager will find ways to tie into the informal information channels, and in so doing will gain insight into how current strategies are being perceived by the team members and other stakeholders and how such strategies might best be changed to keep the project moving in the right direction.

---

[1] Tom Waldoch, "From CIM to IMS Spelled Success at 3M," *Industrial Engineering,* February 1990, pp. 31–35.

Information Failures

Not all projects are managed by using a relevant and reliable information system. For example, on the Shoreham project, the administrative law judges found that the Long Island Lighting Company (LILCO) nuclear power plant's

> measurement and reporting systems continually and repeatedly failed to accurately depict cost and schedule status at Shoreham. Lilco managers were unable to use Lilco's measurement systems to gain an accurate picture of what was happening on site and complained that Lilco's reporting systems were confused and cluttered.[2]

The judges left no doubt as to the overall responsibility of the LILCO board of directors for the Shoreham project:

> We conclude that the limited information presented to the Board was inadequate for it to determine project status on the reasonableness of key management decision or to provide requisite guidance and direction to Lilco management.[3]

Inadequate information systems on the Trans-Alaskan Pipeline System (TAPS) project contributed to the lack of adequate controls. Crandall testified:

> [T]here is little question that the control of TAPS required an adequate and well designed formal control environment to provide control information for senior managers. The volume of data to be processed indicated the need for computers in at least parts of this control environment.... Thus, had cost controls been in place in early 1974, at the very start of the project, they would have allowed management to minimize costs while still attaining realistic schedule goals...Thus, it is my opinion that if prudent cost controls, as part of a comprehensive control environment, had been installed at the start of construction, they would have helped assure completion of the project on or even before the schedule date.[4]

Describing PMIS

There are many descriptions of a PMIS. For example, in Fig. 12.1 Tuman presents a model of an information system in the context of information and control. In describing this model he states:

---

[2] Recommended Decision by Administrative Law Judges Wm. C. Levey and Thomas R. Matias on *Case 27563, Long Island Lighting Company—Shoreham Prudence Investigation,* State of New York Public Service Commission, March 11, 1985.

[3] Ibid.

[4] Keith C. Crandall, *Prepared Direct Rebuttal Testimony,* Alaska Public Utilities Commission, Trans-Alaska Pipeline System, Federal Energy Regulatory Commission, Washington, January 10, 1984, pp. 8–9.

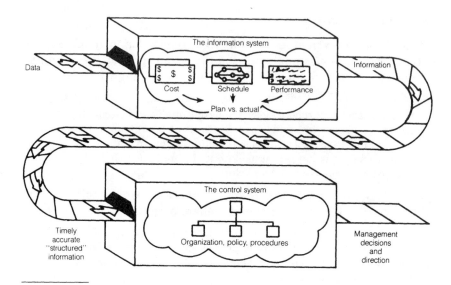

Source: John Tuman, Jr., "Development and Implementation of Effective Project Management Information and Control Systems," in David I. Cleland, and William R. King (eds.), *Project Management Handbook* (New York: Van Nostrand Reinhold Co., 1983): 499.

Figure 12.1   Information and control systems.

With this brief view of the "system" we can define the project management information and control system as the people, policies, procedures, and systems (computerized and manual) which provide the means for planning, scheduling, budgeting, organizing, directing, and controlling the cost, schedule, and performance accomplishment of a project. Implicit in this definition is the idea that *people plan and control projects,* and *systems serve people by producing information.* The design and implementation of the procedures and methodologies which integrate people and systems into a unified whole is both an art and a science. Some of the more pragmatic aspects of these procedures and methodologies are considered...[5]

The objective of an information system is to provide the basis to plan, to monitor, to do integrated project evaluation, and to show the interrelationships among cost, schedule, and technical performance for the entire project and for the strategic direction of the organization. In addition, information should provide a prospective view, to identify project problems before they occur, so they can be avoided or their results minimized.

---

[5]John Tuman, Jr., "Development and Implementation of Effective Project Management Information and Control Systems," in D. I. Cleland and W. R. King (eds.), *Project Management Handbook* (New York: Van Nostrand Reinhold, 1983), p. 500.

Information is required for the project team to continuously monitor, evaluate, and control the resources used on the project. Also, higher management must be kept informed of the status of the project to satisfy its strategic responsibility. There will be times when the project status will require the active involvement of senior management and/or the project owner. Thus, when project status is reported to higher-level management, the report should contain the key data stating the problem; the circumstances surrounding the problem; the cause; the potential impact on project cost, schedule, and other pertinent areas; a recommendation for the action to be taken; the expected outcome of the action; and what assistance is sought from senior management.

Several additional methods can be used to keep abreast of the project status, assuming that an effective project management information system is in place. An easy and important method is to go down and "kick the tires," to observe what is going on in the project. Informal discussions with project team members during these visits can also provide insight into the status of the project. Analysis and interpretation of formal written and oral reports are useful, as are graphic displays of information. An essential way of keeping informed is to have formal project evaluation and control meetings.

Some companies find the project evaluation and control process so important that they have set up a project "war room" to facilitate the review process. A "war room" or information center has significant implications for improving project management. At Martin Marietta Aerospace Company, an information center provides information as well as information services such as analysis of user information requirements, specialized assistance, technology support, education, and training. As a clearinghouse for information, the facility provides database searches as well as assisting users in deciding what products and services to use.[6]

Sharing Information

It is becoming more common for project information to be shared with the project stakeholders. When the project management information system provides information to stakeholders, the conditions for getting the stakeholders working together are facilitated. When project problems, successes, failures, challenges, and other issues are brought to the attention of the project stakeholders, there will likely be closer

[6]Mark D. Matthews, "Information Centers: Increasing Planning Effectiveness," *Project Management Institute Seminar / Symposium,* Milwaukee, Wis., October 1987, p. 110.

identification of the people with the project. If the stakeholders sense that the project manager is withholding information, there is the risk that stakeholders will perceive that the project manager does not trust them, since the information is not being shared. The sharing of information can promote trust, empathy, and more mature relationships among project stakeholders. Then, too, as the project stakeholders review information on the project, such as the problems that the project faces, they may have suggestions that can contribute to the solution of the problem.

Sharing of project information is one of the more important dimensions of keeping the team members working together cohesively and concurrently in the utilization of the project resources. Such sharing also facilitates the building of networks with the stakeholders through continuous interpersonal contact and dialogue. By using technology and a willingness to communicate, information systems can be designed for the project team that help everyone do a better job of making and implementing decisions in the utilization of project resources.

Every project manager has to ask key questions about the quality and quantity of information available to manage the project:

- What information do I need to do my job as project manager?

- What information must I share with the project stakeholders to keep them informed on the status of the project?

- What information do I need about other projects in the organization that interface with my project?

- What information do I require about the enterprise that provides me with insight into how the project fits into the overall strategy of the organization?

- What information do I require to coordinate my project's activities with other initiatives in the organization?

- What is the cost of my not having adequate information about my project—and about how that project interfaces with other projects in the overall organizational strategy of the enterprise?

- What information about the project *do I not need* to do my project management job? Remember, too, that I can be overloaded with untimely and irrelevant information.

Information Value

Project information provides the intelligence for managing the project. Information must be processed so that decisions can be made and executed. In the project planning role, information provides the basis for generating project action plans, schedules, network diagrams, projections, and other elements of planning. Information is essential to promote understanding; establish project objectives, goals, and strategies; develop mechanisms for controls; communicate status; forecast future performance and resources; recognize changes; and reinforce project strategies. The project planning function establishes a structure and a methodology for managing the information resources which encompass defining, structuring, and organizing project information, anticipating its flow, reviewing information quality, controlling its use and source, and providing a focal point for the project's information policies.[7]

Information is a valuable resource to be developed, refined, and managed by the project principals: project managers, functional managers, work package managers, project professionals, and the project owner. Project information is as much an essential resource as people, materials, and equipment. Information is also a key tool which facilitates—indeed, is essential to—the project management process. Information is needed to prepare and use the project plans, develop and use budgets, create and use schedules, and lead the project team to a successful conclusion of the project. Information, then, becomes both a key resource to the project stakeholders and a tool for all concerned to do their job. Information is important, but its role is limited. As Gilbreath states:

> It does not take the place of management skill, planning, project controls, experience, well directed intentions, or other project essentials. It will not shore up inherent inadequacies in organizations, approaches, or individuals.[8]

Gilbreath differentiates data and information. He states:

> A common misconception is that data equals information. Nothing could be further from the truth. Data is merely the raw material of information. It means virtually nothing without refinement. By refinement we mean the structuring of data into meaningful elements, the analysis of its content and the comparisons we make among data and preexisting standards, such as C, S, and T baselines. Only then does data become transformed into information. Data has no value unless it is transformed into structured, meaningful, and pertinent information, and information

---

[7] M. D. Matthews, "Networking and Information Management: Its Use by the Project Planning Function," *Information and Management,* vol. 10, no. 1, January 1986, pp. 1–9.

[8] R. D. Gilbreath, *Winning at Project Management—What Works, What Fails and Why* (New York: Wiley, 1986), p. 147.

has no value unless it leads to needed management action or precludes unnecessary action.[9]

Information has no real value except as it is used effectively in the management of the project. It does not automatically lead to an effective management process. Information does not ensure success, but lack of information can contribute to project failure.

Information is perishable. The management of a project requires planning, organizing, and controlling of resources on a moving target as the project evolves through its life cycle. Information on a project at a particular point in that life cycle can change quickly as new project problems and opportunities develop.

Gilbreath believes that information does not add to the project's value unless it has a structure at various levels through the company and the project organization in varying levels of detail. Properly structured project management information summarizes data concerning the project. It is passed up through the organizational hierarchy and is traceable downward to the source of information. Information helps the project team to understand where they have been, where they are, and where the project seems to be headed. Information also must be comparable to project plans and standards. Finally, Gilbreath believes that information must be pertinent to the project team's perspective, focused on their objectives and processes, consistent with what is going on, and targeted to evaluation of risk on the project.[10]

Information provides the basis for managing the project when the project manager is physically separated from the project. In other words, the information system is a substitute for the project manager being in all places at all times where the work is being carried out on the project. The farther away the project manager and the project owner are from the project, the more these key decision makers must rely on information to tell them what is going on. While direct observation and participation might be the best information concerning what is going on in the project, this is an impossibility on large complex projects. The more distant the project manager is from the project, the more important information becomes on performance standards as well as monitoring and control against these standards.

An important purpose served by a project management information system is that if it is properly organized and implemented, people who are "coasting" on their work packages can be identified immediately.

---

[9] Ibid., pp. 146–147.

[10] Ibid., p. 148.

Technological innovations in the development and use of information broaden the geographical considerations involved in designing and using information systems.

Companies today are separating their operations and putting thousands of miles between those operations. Warehouses are being built in Ohio because of its heartland location; data-processing offices are being set up where skilled farm-belt workers are available. Behind this decentralization is the growing sophistication of telecommunications. Facsimile machines, cellular phones, and sophisticated toll-free telephone arrangements have reduced the disadvantage of distance. Computer and telecommunication technologies developed in the past several years, such as electronic mail and facsimile transmissions, make the move to remote decentralized locations possible by facilitating instantaneous communications between distant posts. Moving people by airlines is becoming less of a requirement; spending endless hours in the air to be able to sit down and communicate with someone several thousand miles away is becoming less important.[11]

Telecommunications is one of the industries that is growing rapidly throughout the global community. The $600 billion per year global telecommunications industry is changing from a cartel of monopolies and entrenched suppliers to a global free-for-all. Corporate customers want global telephone networks; the companies that build them want global profits. Developed countries are trying to encourage competition, while developing countries see the clear need for improved communications to attract business investments. Some of the developing countries are demanding stringent conditions. For example, the Indonesian government put out project proposals for bids for 350,000 telephone lines of digital switching capacity. The government will not consider a bid unless it could offer a 25-year grace period before any payment became due. These conditions are beyond the capability of any corporation, especially for the financial considerations of a project of this magnitude.[12]

One aircraft manufacturer believes that air travel for business purposes will become less important as more sophisticated communications devices and techniques become available. This company believes that the people on business travel from one location to another carry within themselves a "bundle of information" that will be transferred to other person(s) at the end of the journey. Once the information is

---

[11] Brent Bowers, "Technology Allows Small Concerns to Exploit Distances," *Wall Street Journal,* October 28, 1991.

[12] Andrew Kupfer, "Ma Bell and Seven Babies Go Global," *Fortune,* November 4, 1991, pp. 118–128.

transferred, the traveler gets on the returning airplane and returns to the home office. Through modern telecommunications the bundle of information can be transmitted quickly without air travel for humans.

Problems with a PMIS

There are real challenges in developing a PMIS. These problems must be avoided or overcome if an adequate PMIS is to be developed. Gilbreath cites the uses and abuses of information. He opines that misuse of information is common, often sophisticated, and limited only by our imaginations.[13] He delineates the acceptable uses and common misuses of information. When correctly used, information helps to

1. Promote understanding (the project "cube")
2. Target controls (by quantifying risks, testing proposed controls, and initiating corrective action)
3. Dispel project phantoms (artificial failure factors)
4. Allow project transactions (such as progress payments)
5. Communicate status
6. Predict the future
7. Satisfy outside inquiries
8. Enhance resource usage (efficiencies)
9. Validate plans
10. Comprehend change
11. Sharpen and reinforce perspectives
12. Test expectations
13. Recognize failure

Information is often misused, in order to

1. Deceive or confuse
2. Postpone action
3. Create errors in the "information department"
4. Justify errors
5. Slow or divert processes
6. Support the status quo

---

[13] Gilbreath, op. cit., p. 152.

7. Mask failure (or dress it up)[14]

Does information ensure project success? Obviously not. Does a sophisticated computer-based information system ensure success? Obviously not. Many major projects that have failed employed computer-based information systems. Often information, lack of information, or inadequate information is blamed for the failure of managers to develop and use appropriate information systems.

Information lacks pertinence in the context of a project management system when the information cannot be used to ascertain past, present, or expected future status of the project. When the information lacks comparability to predetermined project management standards, its value is quickly lost. If the information does not provide the basis for analyzing the effectiveness with which the project resources are being used, it lacks usefulness. Information systems that do not reveal project problems immediately lose their value. Yet on many projects, bad news existed at the work package or lower level, and this bad news did not find its way through the project information system where it could be used appropriately on a timely basis by the project decision makers. Bad news simply does not flow uphill in organizations.

Gilbreath believes that management reports are only as good as the information they contain that promotes analysis and evaluation of the project. The best reports, according to Gilbreath, manage to

1. Isolate significant variances and identify the reasons they occurred

2. Emphasize the quantitative and specific rather than the subjective and general

3. Describe specific cost, schedule, and technology (C, S, and T) impacts on other project elements (other contracts, areas, trades, schedules, organizations, plans)

4. Indicate effects on project baselines (what revisions are needed, when, why)

5. Describe specific corrective actions taken and planned

6. Assign responsibility for action and give expected dates for improvement

7. Reference corrective action plans in previous reports (what happened?)[15]

---

[14] Ibid., pp. 152–153.

[15] Ibid., p. 160.

PMIS Software

Computer-based information systems to use in managing projects have become valuable for project managers. In earlier years project managers could use a computing capability through a substantial infracture. Today the personal computer has led to a flood of project management software packages. Archibald separates computer-based software for project management into three categories—scheduling, cost and resource control, and cost/schedule/integration and reporting.[16] The following references provide excellent insight into the uses to which project management software can be put.

Levine focuses on the planning, scheduling, tracking, and control of projects by using microcomputers.[17] This book includes an introduction to project management, the characteristics of project management software, and case histories of the use of project management software. A perusal of Levine's book will prepare project managers to make informed decisions about the best project management software available for a project's particular needs. Davis and Martin have evaluated project management software for the personal computer, including some guidelines for software selection.[18] Gilbreath offers advice on how to consider the use of project management software by noting that we need to understand our information needs and how we intend to organize and use the information. He notes that software failures often occur because the software does not match needs, organization, and intended uses. He concludes that poorly planned or performed projects are not helped by software.[19]

A good information system provides key input to the project decision makers. Projects that get into trouble often are found to lack information, or they have too much and the wrong kind of information. A good project management information system adds value to the data available on the project, and when those data are properly organized and structured, the project management team has a valuable resource to use.

---

[16]Russell D. Archibald, *Managing High Technology Programs and Projects* (New York: Wiley, 1976), pp. 204–210.

[17]Harvey Levine, *Project Management Using Microcomputers* (New York: Osborne McGraw-Hill, 1986).

[18]Edward N. Davis and Russell D. Martin, "Project Management Software for the Personal Computer: An Evaluation," *Project Management Journal,* December 1985, pp. V100–V106.

[19]Gilbreath, op. cit., p. 160.

Organizational Experiences

We can gain insight into theory and practice of project management information systems by reviewing the experiences of an organization that has designed and developed its own system. Johnston describes the experiences at the Sandia National Laboratories, Albuquerque, in PMIS methodology for research and development construction projects. A process is described which was followed at the laboratory to achieve a successful management information system to solve a problem where the key managers were entangled in myriad and complex data with convoluted software, but lacked management information to facilitate the decision-making process. Sandia National Laboratories initiated a three-step process to bring order out of the "existing chaos of the MIS." This process entailed

1. Assessing and analyzing the status of the current database and corresponding computer programs; i.e., where are we now?

2. Establishing a clear definition of expected results; i.e., where do we want to go?

3. Determining a logical progression to bridge between the two; i.e., how do we get there from here?[20]

The "Where are we now?" assessment included the following litany of the problems:

Failure in overall planning

- Lack of integrated overall plan.
- Data sets added at random without regard for interface.
- Parochial interests in each area so that no integration responsibility was established.
- Losing sight of purpose of establishing separate MIS—or never stating purpose.

Failure to define user requirements

- No definition of what a given piece of data would be used for or statement of need for that piece of data.
- No definition of summary reports generated as summaries roll up from detailed data.
- Lack of user-oriented report formats.

---

[20] Dawn M. Johnston, "Establishing a Successful Management Information System for Project Management," *Project Management Institute 1985 Proceedings*, vol. 1, pp. 1–2.

Failure to design for efficient implementation

- Levels of detail added without determination of source for the detail or time or resources involved to obtain data.
- Reinventing the wheel—repetition of data available from company system.
- No established boundaries—no analysis of need for certain information versus cost of obtaining that information.
- Lack of system support and training by the hardware/software vendor had caused an excessively long learning curve.
- Complex software design consumed an inordinate amount of time to debug.
- Lack of logic definition for relationships between data or data sets.

Failure to implement effectively

- Dollar value of an item would appear as a different amount on different report formats at the same time.
- Inability to retrieve relatively simple information on one report because of complex threading of database configuration.
- Inadequate edits of data input to use for checkpoints.[21]

In determining where the laboratory staff wanted to go in developing their information system, they addressed questions such as

1. What objective will the system serve?
2. What type of information should be provided?
3. What complicated information needs exist?
4. What are the independent and interdependent information needs?
5. How are different information facets integrated, and what is the relative importance of the different types of information systems?
6. What are the information process and turnaround requirements?

By getting answers to these questions the laboratory managers were able to establish the parameters for the information systems requirement.

An integrated multidisciplinary team analyzed the information system requirement. When the information system was finally designed, the team took the following steps to implement it:

---

[21] Ibid., pp. 3–4.

1. Survey the data elements.

   a. Analyze each data element in each data set by asking the following questions:

   - What is the need for this data element?
   - Does it belong in this data set?
   - Is it identified in the right sequence?
   - Should any data elements be eliminated?
   - Should any data elements be added?

   b. List all data elements that the team identified for elimination; list new elements to be added.

   c. Identify which data set each element belongs in.

2. Design the database.

   a. Draw the portion of the database that represents each major area, showing the relationships between data elements.

   b. Prepare the preliminary design of database configuration through integration of team designs.

   c. Hold joint meeting of teams to discuss and critique new design; determine any changes needed to accommodate integration of data sets in relationship to each other.

   d. Iterate required changes and finalize new database configuration.

3. Develop the software.

   a. Design end-result reports for users.

   b. Identify interim reports needed by users and programmers, and identify all computer programs that need to be written.

   c. Determine priority order of programming effort.

   d. Establish schedule for completion of programs, including time for review and iteration.[22]

In retrospect, the people who managed the development of that information system at Sandia National Laboratories concluded that the most difficult task in the process was hammering out acceptable compromises among the information clients who had different information requirements. The use of the team approach facilitated an integrated database framework which served everyone.

---

[22]Ibid., p. 7.

Planning for the PMIS

Planning for the PMIS is part of the total planning process for a project. Accordingly, the development of an information system for a project should reflect the work breakdown structure of that project; i.e., the total scope of work should be divided into a hierarchy of increasingly detailed, identifiable work tasks. There should be a similar hierarchy for all scheduling and cost code systems. Three elements should be interrelated throughout the cost and scheduling information system for the project: an identified work package, its associated cost code and schedule, and the organization responsible for the work.

In the planning context of a PMIS, a number of factors are essential to the establishment of an information system. The parent organization of the project should have in place the following:

1. An information clearinghouse function, particularly in the design and execution of projects to support corporate strategy

2. An established organizational design with supporting policies, procedures, techniques, and methodologies to manage the organizational information bases

3. Appropriate people who can work at the interfaces between information technology and the project needs

By forcing a systematic delineation of project work packages, the project work activities, and the integrated information components, the program manager can analyze the best way to translate the information to a format that produces useful information. Within an information center, the project information networks are a medium for organizing the structure and continuity of information over the life of the project. These networks provide an integrated perspective of the project work packages and their interrelationships. The networks provide methodology to identify work packages, information requirements and sources, information flows, and decision parameters.[23]

A project plan may be considered to be an information system which provides a time-phased array of work packages, appropriately sequenced to the WBS with resource estimates, to accomplish the project plan's scope of work within an appropriate time frame. This baseline project plan eases monitoring and analysis by showing the information needed to measure against the proper control points. As the project is worked and the actual status data become available, the

---

[23] Paraphrased from M. D. Matthews, "Networking and Information Management: Its Use by the Project Planning Function," *Information Management,* vol. 10, no. 2, January 1986, pp. 1–9.

project plan and the networks are updated to provide for the tracking and monitoring process.

Principles of PMIS

In the design, development, and operation of a project management information system, a few principles can be applied:

- Information is needed to manage the project—to plan for, organize, evaluate, and control the use of resources on the project.
- The quality of management of the project is related to the quality of the information on the project.
- Work package managers, the project manager, functional managers, general managers, senior managers and the other project stakeholders need information on the project to discharge their responsibilities on the project.
- The project WBS establishes the common denominator for information for management of the project.
- The information requirements for top-level managers fashion the requirement for information for other managers in the project.
- Information is needed to manage the project during its life cycle as well as during the pre-initiation and postinitiation phases of the project.
- Information is the medium to integrate and synchronize the varied systems in a project.
- Information to manage a project comes from a wide variety of sources—including formal reports, informal sources, observation, project review meetings, questioning—aided by formal evaluation and analysis as well as intuition as to what the information says about the status of the project.
- Information provides the basis for informed decision making by the project stakeholders.
- Information systems must reflect the user's management needs for making and executing decisions in the management of the project resources.
- The PMIS should interface with larger organizational information systems so that the status of the project as a building block in the design and execution of organizational strategies is easily discerned.
- Unless care is taken, a project can suffer from an overabundance of data and a dearth of relevant information.

■ The PMIS should be prospective and capable of providing intelligence on both the current and probable status of the project.

In addition the PMIS should do the following:

■ Be adaptable to differing customer requirements.

■ Be consistent with organizational and project policies, procedures, and guidelines.

■ Minimize the chances of managers being surprised by project developments.

■ Provide essential information on the cost-time-performance parameters of a project and on the interrelationships of these parameters, as well as the strategic fit of the project.

■ Provide information in standardized form to enhance its usefulness to all managers.

■ Be decision-oriented, in that information reported should be focused toward the decisions required of the managers.

■ Be exception-oriented, in that it focuses the manager's attention on those critical areas requiring attention rather than simply reporting on all areas and requiring the managers to devote attention to each.

■ Be a collaborative effort between users and analysts.

■ Be done by a multidisciplinary team who views the design, development, and implementation of the information system as a project itself, amenable to project management approaches.

Summary

Basically a project management information system is a communication device. Information systems provide the basis to define the project requirements and elements in a standardized way to communicate these requirements and elements to the project team and to the project owner as a basis for evaluating and measuring performance and directing and reprogramming the effort required to realize the project purposes.

Project managers in all types of organizations will find that they are working in increasingly complex and interdependent environments. In these environments, technological, social, economic, political, competitive, and legal concerns will have an impact on the outcome of projects. These outcomes have been described in terms of project stakeholders described in Chap. 6. In these environments project managers will deal with a broad range of issues, requirements, and strategies involving decisions which entrain complex forces well beyond what has happened in the past. Under such circumstances the project manager will be considered the source of knowledge and information about every aspect of the project. The project management information system will be increasingly important in the overall management of projects.

Discussion Questions

1. What is the importance of the information subsystem to the project management system (PMS)? What is the relationship of this subsystem to the other subsystems of the PMS?

2. What is the difference between data and information?

3. List and discuss some of the essential elements of a project management information system (PMIS). What is the purpose of a PMIS?

4. What gives information value? How can information be used as a resource and tool for project stakeholders?

5. What are some of the challenges in developing a PMIS?

6. Discuss some of the uses and misuses of information.

7. Describe a project management situation from your work or school experience. How was information managed? Was it an effective tool in project control?

8. PMIS software can be essential to managing projects. What characteristics of software must project managers assess in order to determine appropriateness?

9. Discuss the essential factors in the establishment of an information system.

10. What is the relationship between an information system and the work breakdown structure? How can this relationship be managed in order to produce useful information relevant to each work package?

11. List and discuss some of the principles of PMIS.

12. What is meant by the "exception-oriented" nature of a PMIS? Why is this characteristic important?

User Checklist

1. Does your organization have an effective PMIS for each of its projects? Explain.

2. Do project team members understand the difference between data and information? Do the measurement and reporting systems which they use generate data or information? Explain.

3. Describe the flow of information of projects within your organization. What information is effectively communicated? What information is often lacking?

4. Does the information system used on projects within your organization contain all the essential elements of a PMIS as described in the chapter? Why or why not?

5. Think about some of the recent projects completed by your organization. Was information effectively managed? Did the information system contribute to the success of the project?

6. Do the project managers in your organization understand the purpose of a PMIS? Explain.

7. Do the project managers in your organization understand the value of information? Is information used effectively as a tool in controlling projects?

8. What problems has your organization had with its information systems? How can these problems be managed on future projects?

9. Are there any misuses of information within your organization? Explain.

10. What PMIS software is used by your organization? How? Is the software appropriate? What other alternatives exist?

11. Have the managers of your organization taken the time to assess the effectiveness of the information systems within your organization? Explain.

12. Is the work breakdown structure of a project integrated into the PMIS? How?

13

Project Control

"I claim not to have controlled events, but confess plainly that events have controlled me."

ABRAHAM LINCOLN, 1809–1865

The final management function carried out by the project team is control, which is discussed in this chapter. *Control* is the process of monitoring, evaluating, and comparing planned results with actual results to determine the status of the project cost, schedule, and technical performance objectives. Control is also the constraining of resources through corrective action to conform to a project plan of action. The management function of control may be visualized as distinct steps in a control cycle model, as portrayed in Fig. 13.1. Monitoring and control are universal activities indispensable to effective and efficient operation of the control cycle.

Control is a fact-finding and remedial action process to facilitate meeting the project objectives and goals; its primary purpose is not to

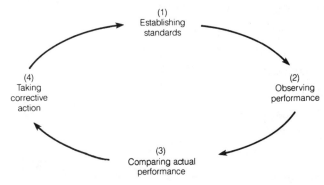

Figure 13.1 The control system.

determine what has happened (although this is important information), but rather to predict what may happen in the future if present conditions continue and if there are no changes in the management of the project. This enables the project manager to manage the project in compliance with the plan. The basis of effective project monitoring, evaluation, and control is an explicit statement of the project objectives, goals, and strategies which provide performance standards against which project progress can be evaluated. In the material that follows, more information will be given about each of the steps in the control cycle.

Steps in the Control Cycle

There are several distinct steps in the control cycle, depicted in Fig. 13.1. These steps in one sense are independent. In another, they are interdependent in the execution of project control. We'll consider performance standards first.

Performance standards

Project performance standards are based on the project plan, including at minimum the expectations for the project, established in the project objectives, goals, and strategies, relative to project cost, schedule, technical specifications, and strategic fit. Some key standards in project control include the following:

- Scope of work
- Project specification
- Work breakdown structure
- Work packages
- Core estimates and budgets
- Master and supporting schedules
- Financial forecasts and funding plans
- Quality
- Project owner satisfaction (strategic fit)
- Project team satisfaction
- Senior management satisfaction
- Stakeholder satisfaction
- Reliability
- Physical quantities of work

- Vendor/contractor performance
- Project management
- Innovation
- Resource utilization
- Productivity

A project should be evaluated by using several additional key standards:

- Effectiveness and efficiency in the use of the enterprise resources supporting the project. Were the right resources used in the most productive fashion to support the project?
- Expected technical performance quality of the product or service resulting from the project. Does the project promise to provide value to the customers?
- Development cycle time. Is the project being developed in sufficient time to meet or preempt competition?
- Strategic fit in organizational purposes. Does the resulting product or service complement existing products and services being provided in the marketplace?

It is important to recognize that performance standards are derivatives of project planning, as well as organizational planning, keynoting again the basic (but often forgotten) principle that proper planning facilitates proper control.

Performance observation

Project performance must be sensed—and that is where performance observation comes into play. *Performance observation* is the receipt of sufficient information about the project to make an intelligent comparison of planned and actual performance. Information on project performance can come from many sources, both formal and informal. Formal sources include reports, briefings, participation in review meetings, letters, memoranda, and audit reports. Informal sources include casual conversations, observations, and listening to the inevitable rumors and gossip that go on within the project team and in other parts of the organization. Talking and listening to the project stakeholders can be a useful source of information on the project's status. Informal meetings for lunch or coffee breaks can help to provide the total information "system" the project manager needs to have to know fully what is going on. Both formal and informal information sources are needed to keep up with the project's status. Feedback during performance observation consists of relevant data on the result of the project management process and provides the basis for making a judgment on performance through doing comparative analysis.

Comparing planned and actual performance

Comparing planned and actual performance based on the desired project standards gives the opportunity to get answers to two key questions about the project:

- How is the project doing?
- If there are deviations from the project plan, what caused these deviations?

Assessment of the project's status is an ongoing responsibility of the project team and the senior managers. Information obtained by performance observation is compared with the performance standards laid down in the project plan and when analyzed, forms the basis for reaching a judgment about the project's status and whether corrective action is required.

Corrective action

Corrective action can take the form of replanning, reprogramming, reallocating resources, or changing the way the project is managed and organized. The corrective actions that are available to the project manager center on the cost, schedule, and technical performance parameters of the project. The project owner may have finalized one or more of these parameters. Correcting a problem with one of the parameters of the project may have reverberations on one or both of the other parameters. Such potential reverberations should be considered by the project team when the alternatives for corrective action are being studied.

Monitoring and evaluation

Monitoring and evaluation are integral to control, as depicted in Table 13.1, and are key companions of the control function. *Monitoring* means to keep track of and to check systematically all project activities. This enables the *evaluation,* an examination and appraisal of how things are going on the project. As a direct link between planning and control, the monitoring and evaluating functions provide the intelligence for the members of the project team to make informed decisions about the project performance. Monitoring should be designed so that it addresses every level of management requiring information about

TABLE 13.1 Key Project Control Questions

---

1. Where is the project with respect to schedule, cost, technical performance, objectives, and goals?
2. Where are the project work packages with respect to schedule, cost, technical performance, objectives, and goals?
3. What is going right on the project?
4. What is going wrong?
5. What problems are emerging?
6. What opportunities are emerging?
7. Does the project continue to have a strategic fit with the enterprise mission?
8. Is there anything that should be done that is not being done?
9. Are the project stakeholders comfortable with the results of the project?
10. How is the project customer image—is the customer happy with the way things are going?
11. Has an independent project evaluation been conducted?
12. Is the project being managed on a total "project management systems" basis?
13. Is the project team an effective organization?
14. Does the project take advantage of the strength that the enterprise possesses?
15. Does the project avoid a dependence on the weakness of the firm?
16. Is the project making money for the company?

---

project performance and reflects the work breakdown structure of the project. Each level of management should receive the information it needs to make decisions about the project. In addition, monitoring should be consistent with the logic of the planning, organizing, directing, and motivating systems on the project.

Monitoring means to make sure sufficient intelligence is gained on the status of the project that an accurate and timely evaluation can be conducted of the project. Several issues have to be addressed by the project team in considering their monitoring and evaluation responsibilities:

- What to monitor and evaluate
- What monitoring tools to use
- When to monitor and evaluate
- Who should monitor and evaluate
- Where should the monitoring and evaluation be carried out

All activities of the project and its stakeholder environment should be monitored and evaluated, of course, done on an exception basis through the delegated responsibilities of the project team. A framework for doing the evaluation can consist of a series of key questions about the project which must be answered on an ongoing basis. If the project team can ask questions and get timely, credible answers, then the chances of knowing the project's true status are enhanced considerably.

Questions of this type can be used during regularly scheduled project review meetings to motivate discussions among the project team members and to encourage them to think retrospectively as well as prospectively about the project. Such thinking will prompt the team members to evaluate the project. Project review meetings should be held regularly by the project owner, senior managers of the project organization, the project team, the work package managers, and the project professionals.

A key question in reviewing any project is the degree of success that the project management team has had in the development of an integrated project management system for the project. Project evaluation, to be effective, must look both at the efficacy of the parts of the project (the subsystems) and at the project totality, expressed in such factors as attainment of the project's technical performance objective, completion schedules, and final cost. Monitoring and evaluation of the project require that the project team look inward to the project and the sponsoring organization as well as outward to the stakeholders and the general "system" environment in which the project is found.

The avoidance of cost and schedule overruns should be one of the key outcomes of any project control system. These are examples of how projects were able to stay within budget or exceed budget:

- The $630 million upper atmosphere research satellite is one of two large U.S. space projects that was kept on cost and schedule in part because the project team combined political savvy with technological conservatism to guard the project from controversy and keep it moving in the right direction. To cut costs and improve reliability, the spacecraft was designed by using technology that had been used before, such as plug-in modules for propulsion, communications, and navigation. By keeping a low profile the project proceeded without controversy. In addition, much of the success of this project can be attributed to a good plan, which is always an important factor in controlling the use of resources on a project and in determining the success of a project.[1]

- Another project, the Earth Observing System (EOS), an environmental satellite project, is now, by some estimates, $13 billion above its original cost projections and 5 years behind schedule. Its managers overestimated their political support and underestimated the technical challenge of the project. This project became mired in controversy from the start; the space agency proposed to build six of the largest, most complex satellites ever conceived for EOS

---

[1] Bob Davis, "A NASA Satellite Project Accomplishes Incredible Feat: Staying within Budget," *Wall Street Journal,* September 9, 1991.

and to back them up with one of the world's most sophisticated computer systems. The project was taking so much money that lawmakers and scientists feared it would take away funds from other projects considered to be more worthy. Although the White House and Congress approved the start of the project last year, now both have backed off as the project's riskiness became apparent.[2]

Management Functions Evaluation

You can use management-related activities to address representative key questions to evaluate the project. Assuming that a project management functions viewpoint is used as a baseline for evaluating a project, what should be measured?

Answers to these questions can give insight into how well the project is doing.

Project planning

1. Are the original objectives and goals realistic?
2. Is the plan for the availability of project resources adequate?
3. Are the original project schedule and budget realistic?
4. Is the plan for the organization of the project resources adequate?
5. Are there adequate project control systems?
6. Is there an information system for the project?
7. Were key project stakeholders brought into project planning?
8. Was facility planning adequate?
9. Was planning completed before the project was initiated?
10. Were potential users involved early in the planning process?
11. Was there adequate planning for the use of such management tools as project control networks (CPM/PERT), project or study selection techniques, information systems, etc.?

Project organization

1. How effective is the current organizational structure in meeting the project objective?
2. Does the project manager have adequate authority?
3. Is the organization of the project office staff suitable?
4. Have the interfaces in the matrix organization been adequately defined?

---

[2]Ibid.

5. Do key project stakeholders understand the organization of the project office?

6. Have key roles been defined in the project?

Program management process

1. Does the project manager adequately control project funds?

2. Are the project team personnel innovative and creative by suggesting project management improvements?

3. Does the project manager maintain adequate management of the project team?

4. Do the project team people get together on a regular basis to see how things are going?

5. Does the project office have an efficient method for handling engineering change requests?

6. Does the project staff seek the advice of stakeholders on matters of mutual concern?

7. Have the project review meetings been useful?

Project accomplishments

1. To what extent have the original project goals been achieved?

2. How valuable are the technical achievements?

3. How useful are the organizational and/or management achievements?

4. Are the project results useful in accomplishing organizational objectives?

5. Are the results being implemented?

6. Are the users being notified properly?

7. Is the customer happy with the project results to date?

Effective project control can be carried out only if there is adequate information about the project that can be used for monitoring and control.

Project information

The project team requires a project control system that provides key information on the status of the project. It needs several key systems to provide such information:

- An equipment, labor, and material information system that provides the basis for the effective and efficient utilization of the work force on the project. These cost factors are usually the largest contributors to the overall project cost; their status should be known to the project team and the owner.

- A cost control system so that the project team can determine whether the costs are in line with the project plan and to help understand deviations that may occur.

- A schedule control system to identify schedule problems so that cost-effective tradeoffs can be carried out as needed.

- A budget/financial planning/commitment approval system so that the data on the commitment, expenses, and cash flow of the project can be collected and analyzed and appropriate remedial action taken.

- A work authorization system that provides for the allocation of project funds to the functional organizations and outside vendors.

- A method of using the collective judgment of team members to judge the progress being made to satisfy the project's technical performance objective. To reach this judgment, the progress of the individual work packages must be assessed along with the progress on the integration of all work packages. This judgment can best be made by the project team in a group session by reviewing and assessing all the information the team has assembled and then reaching an informed judgment of where the project stands, for example, on project costs.

When to Monitor and Evaluate

When should you monitor and evaluate the project? The answer to this question is simple and straightforward. Monitor and evaluate the project during its entire life cycle.

For example, the James Bay Project had management controls which tied together all the project efforts from conceptual design through contract closeouts. Furthermore, the engineering department of the James Bay Energy Corporation (the project management organization for the James Bay Project) conducted quarterly board of consultants meetings to review engineering designs.[3]

Project evaluation is a process that extends throughout the project life cycle through to a "postmortem" that assesses the capability of the project to support organizational strategy in terms of a useful product or service which supports the organizational mission. There are four major types of project evaluation:

---

[3] Peter G. Behr, "James Bay Design and Construction Management," *Proceedings of the American Society of Civil Engineers,* vol. 104, no. E12, April 1978, p. 146.

1. *Preproject evaluation*—for the selection of a project to determine if it fits the objectives and overall strategy of the organization or enterprise.

2. *Ongoing project evaluation*—for measuring the status of a project during its life cycle.

3. *Project completion evaluation*—for an immediate assessment of success upon project completion.

4. *Postproject evaluation*—for a down-the-road assessment of project success after the dust and confusion have settled.

Planning for Monitoring and Evaluation

Clearly, part of project planning should include the development of a strategy on how the project will be evaluated during its life cycle. This planning is just as important as the planning for any other aspect of the project. In approaching the development of project evaluation strategy, there are several key requirements: the inclusion of an evaluation policy and the process; the commitment of all key managers involved in the project to an evaluation strategy for evaluation methodologies; and the use of both inside and independent evaluators who have the professional credentials to do a credible job of the evaluation process.

Not only does a periodic evaluation of the project as a normal and expected responsibility of the project team make good sense, but also evaluations on a periodic basis to examine the rationale and mandate for the project provide benefits. Such evaluations show that the principal managers have a concern for the degree to which the project objectives and goals are being achieved and the identification of any shortcomings in the management of the project. By having the principal managers insist on periodic and special evaluations, an important message is sent throughout the organization. A project owner who has contracted for the engineering, design, and development of the project's product would be foolhardy not to insist on regular and special evaluations of the project's progress. Indeed, a prudent project owner would actively participate in such evaluations.

Who Monitors and Evaluates?

The principal responsibility for project monitoring and evaluation rests with the project team and the project owner. The manager who has "general management" or "project owner" jurisdiction also shares in the residual responsibility for keeping informed on what is happening on the project. Where is the monitoring and evaluation carried out? Simply put, as close as possible to the action on the project; at the individual professional's level where the work is being done as well as at

- The work package level
- The functional manager's level
- The project team level
- The general manager level·
- The project owner's level

Each successive level's monitoring and evaluation would be more integrated, dealing with the project's total schedule, cost, and technical performance objectives. Finally, the project's strategic fit in supporting the owner's mission would be evaluated.

Project Audits

An important part of project evaluation can be done through the conduct of a project audit. Project audits provide the opportunity to have an independent appraisal of where the project stands and the efficiency and effectiveness with which the project is being managed. Periodic audits have to be planned. An audit should have as its purposes

- Determining what is going right, and why
- Determining what is going wrong, and why
- Identifying forces and factors that have prevented or may prevent achievement of cost, schedule, and technical performance goals
- Evaluating the efficacy of existing project management strategy, including organizational support, policies, procedures, practices, techniques, guidelines, action plans, funding patterns, and human and nonhuman resource utilization
- Providing for an exchange of ideas, information, problems, solutions, and strategies with the project team members.

A project audit should cover key functions, depending on the nature of the project, in both the technical and nontechnical areas, such as

- Engineering
- Manufacturing
- Finance and accounting
- Contracts
- Purchasing

- Marketing

- Human resources

- Organization and management

- Quality

- Reliability

- Test and deployment

- Logistics

- Construction

How often should an audit be conducted, given that a thorough audit takes time and money? Generally, audits should be carried out at key points in the life cycle of a project, and at times in those phases of the life cycle that represent go/no go trigger points, such as preliminary design, final design, first prototype, commitment to production, first use, warranty, and maintenance and service contracts.

An unplanned audit may be called for during the project life cycle if there is a sense by the principal managers that the project is in trouble or is heading for trouble. If there is uncertainty concerning the project's status, or if there has been a change in the strategic direction of the organization, an audit of the project may be in order. When a new project manager takes over a project, she or he should order an audit, both to become familiar with an unbiased view of the project and to come up to speed with the key issues and problems that are facing the project.

Pinto and Slevin have developed a *project implementation profile* (PIP) to use in making periodic assessments of the current status of or key factors concerning a project throughout its implementation process. Ten critical success factors for project success can be measured:

- Project mission

- Top management support

- Project schedule/plan

- Client consultation

- Personnel

- Technical tasks

- Client acceptance

- Monitoring and feedback

- Communication

- Troubleshooting

An added benefit of the PIP is to enable the project team to develop an overall picture of the current status of the project.[4]

Postproject Reviews

Much can be learned about the efficiency and effectiveness with which projects are managed in the organization through a *postproject review* (PPR). Postproject reviews are gaining more favor in the management of projects. In the nuclear power plant industry, such reviews have become commonplace to determine which project costs have been incurred reasonably, so the public utility commission can decide which costs can be passed on to the consumers of the nuclear plant's electricity. Other industries are conducting PPRs in the capital budgeting process. One view of this process is depicted in Fig. 13.2.

PPRs take a large view to examine the rationale for the project in the first place. The PPR also examines the strategic fit of the project into the overall organizational strategy. PPRs offer insight into the success or failure of a particular project as well as a composite of lessons learned from a review of all the projects in the organization's portfolio or capital projects. At British Petroleum, PPRs have become an integral part of the corporate planning and control process. British Petroleum has learned valuable lessons on each capital project, and general principles about project management have emerged over the 10 years that British Petroleum has been conducting such reviews. These principles are as follows:

1. Determine costs accurately.

2. Anticipate and minimize risk.

3. Evaluate contractors more thoroughly.

4. Improve project management.[5]

If the project plan contains a specific strategy for the conduct of PPRs, there will be subtle benefits through the discipline and team effort needed to do an adequate review. If the project team members know that the success (or failure) of the project will be evaluated at the project's completion, they should be motivated to do a better job of managing the project during its life cycle. These attitudes will permeate the culture of the organization and improve decision making in

---

[4]Jeffrey K. Pinto and Dennis P. Slevin, "Project Implementation Profile," XICOM, Incorporated, Tuxedo, N.Y., copyright 1992.

[5]Frank R. Gulliver, "Post-Project Appraisals Pay," Harvard Business Review, March-April 1987, pp. 128–132.

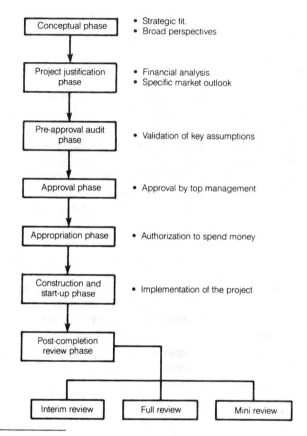

Source: Surendra S. Singhvi, "Post-Completion Review for Capital Projects," *May Planning Review* (1986): 37.

Figure 13.2   PPRs in the capital budgeting process.

the planning process for new projects to support the organizational strategies. This should result in better capital investment decisions and improve the organization's competitive chances.

Configuration Management and Control[6]

Most people recognize the need to plan and control budgets, schedules, and even performance specifications for a system that is under development. However, in complex projects, the elements that must be controlled are much more varied and detailed than is generally understood.

---

[6]Paraphrased from David I. Cleland and William R. King, *Systems Analysis and Project Management,* 3d ed. (New York: McGraw-Hill, 1983), pp. 376–377.

Configuration control (or engineering change management) represents one such level of specificity. In the development of complex projects, changes in the configuration of hardware and software reverberate through the system, causing problems with budgets, schedules, etc. Thus, such changes must be directly addressed and controlled. It is inadequate to attempt to effect control solely at a higher level.

Configuration management is the discipline which integrates the technical and administrative actions of identifying the functional and physical characteristics of a system (or product) during its life cycle. It is directly related to the project technical performance objective. Configuration management provides for controlling changes to these characteristics and provides information on the status of engineering or contract change actions.

The essence of configuration management comprises three major areas of effort: configuration identification, configuration status accounting, and configuration control.

Configuration identification

Configuration identification is the process of establishing and describing an initial system baseline. This baseline is described in technical documentation (proposal terms, specifications, drawings, etc.). The identification function provides for a systematic determination of all the technical documentation needed to describe the functional and physical characteristics of items designated for configuration management. Configuration identification also ensures that these documents are current, approved, and available for use by the time needed.

The concept of a baseline system requires that the total system requirements and the requirements for each item of the system be defined and documented at designated points in the evolution of the system. An evolutionary life cycle of the system from paper study to inventory items is prepared to plan for development and production status and to permit changes in the scope of the system.

There must be a recognized and documented initial statement of requirements. Once stated, any change in the system's requirements must be documented so that the current status may be fairly judged for performance requirements. A baseline is established when it is necessary to define a formal departure point for control of future changes in performance and design. Configuration at any later time is defined by a baseline model, plus all subsequent changes that have been incorporated. This baseline model provides a point of departure to manage future engineering and/or contract changes.

Configuration status accounting

Configuration status accounting is the process of recording and documenting changes to an approved baseline to maintain a continuous record of the status of individual items that make up the system. Configuration status accounting also shows what actions are required and what engineering changes are complete. Status accounting will identify all items of the initially approved configuration, then continually track authorized changes to the baseline.

Configuration control

Configuration control is the process of maintaining the baseline identification and regulating all changes to that baseline. Configuration control prevents unnecessary or marginal changes while expediting the approval and implementation of those changes which are necessary or which offer significant benefits to the system. Necessary or beneficial changes are typically those that correct inefficiencies, satisfy a change in operation or logistics support requirements, effect substantial life-cycle cost savings, or prevent or eliminate slippage in approved scheduling.

A configuration control board is a joint agency of the project clientele to act on all proposed changes. The configuration control board recommends final decisions on engineering changes and installs good engineering-change discipline in the system. This board can provide a single-point authority for coordinating and approving engineering-change proposals.

There are two basic potential costs of a contract change such as an engineering change. The first is the direct cost of the change itself, expressed in performing the substantive work of the change, e.g., redesign, engineering, and construction/manufacturing. The second is related indirectly to the change order, or the "ripple effect," e.g., additional supervision, consequential damages, decrease in productivity during the implementation of the substantive work, and so on.

Summary

This chapter suggests a strategy for managing control, including the monitoring and evaluation that must pervade control. To control a project means to get things working in accordance with the plan.

Serving on a project team is challenging; it can be damaging to the ego and emotions. When a project goes astray, everyone looks for someone to blame for the problems. Projects have a heavy organizational burden because they demand that people build and maintain lateral and horizontal relationships as project assignments come and go. To build trust and commitment among the team members, a project manager has to develop a personal meaning among the team members for the project objectives and goals, and then work with them in evaluating how effectively the team has produced project results. Models, systems, computers, or project planning and control processes and techniques do not control. People control. Thus there is the important personal side of control to consider.

The outcome of a project is dependent on people—those professionals and managers who have a responsibility to make the project happen. Thus, project control is control through people evaluation, an assessment of the quality of managerial and professional performance which can be measured by project results—delivering the project on time and budget.

Discussion Questions

1. List and briefly define the elements of the project control cycle. Why is control an important project management function?

2. What performance standards must be set in order to control a project? How can these standards be observed throughout the life of the project?

3. In what ways is corrective action carried out? What are some of the potential impacts of these corrective actions?

4. Discuss the personal nature of control. How can managers foster an environment that supports the control system?

5. Monitoring and evaluating are integral to control. Discuss what is meant by each. How do they relate? What kinds of questions must project team members ask in order to continually monitor and evaluate the project?

6. Discuss the importance of monitoring and evaluating with respect to all project stakeholders.

7. What project information is necessary for project control? Discuss the importance of the PMIS with respect to project control.

8. Outline a sequence of steps that would enable the project manager to monitor and evaluate project costs.

9. When should the project be monitored and evaluated? Discuss the ability to influence cost over the project life cycle.

10. Who should be responsible for monitoring and evaluating projects? Where should monitoring and evaluating take place?

11. What is required in a project audit? What purposes do project audits serve?

12. List and discuss some of the factors that lead to success of a project (with respect to project control).

User Checklist

1. Do the project managers in your organization understand the project control cycle? Explain.

2. Do project managers establish appropriate performance standards based on the project plan so that the control cycle can be effectively carried out? What performance standards are overlooked?

3. How is project performance observed in your organization? What comparisons are made to standards? What corrective actions are taken?

4. Is the cultural ambience of your organization supportive of the control systems? Why or why not?

5. What questions do project managers ask in order to monitor and evaluate project performance? Do managers consider the requirements of all project stakeholders in monitoring and evaluating project performance? Explain.

6. Is the PMIS within your organization effective at providing the necessary information for project control? How could the PMIS be improved?

7. How are project costs monitored? Is the system effective? What monitoring tools are used?

8. Are monitoring and evaluating done at the appropriate points in the project life cycle? Do project managers take advantage of the early opportunities to influence cost? Explain.

9. Are project monitoring and evaluating a part of the early project plans? Do evaluation policies and procedures exist? Are key managers committed to the evaluation strategy? Explain.

10. Are project audits performed on projects within your organization? Who is responsible for project audits? Are the audits effective? Why or why not?

11. What types of postproject reviews are carried out by your organization? How do these reviews contribute to the success of other ongoing projects?

12. What factors (with respect to project control) have contributed to the success of projects within your organization? Explain.

14

Project Termination

*"If you can look into the seeds of time, and say
which grain will grow and which will not."*
WILLIAM SHAKESPEARE, 1564–1516
Macbeth, Act I, line 58

Projects usually are terminated for two basic reasons: project success or project failure. Senior managers who "own" the project, and who see the project as a building block in the design and execution of organizational strategy, must create a cultural ambience that encourages projects to be successful, but also allows a project to fail if it has lost its strategic fit in the organization's plans for the future. Considerations in the termination of a project are dealt with in this chapter.

Project success means that the project has met its cost, schedule, and technical performance objectives and has been integrated into the customer's organization to contribute to the customer's mission. A successful project means that the organization has been successful in positioning itself for the future; a specific strategy has been designed and implemented.

Project failure means that the project has failed to meet its cost, schedule, and technical performance objectives, or it does not fit in the organization's future. Failure is thus a relative factor.

Project termination comes about for several reasons:

1. The project results (a product or service) have been delivered to the customer. If appropriate, service and maintenance contracts can be negotiated and consummated.

2. The project has overrun its cost and schedule objectives and/or is failing to make satisfactory progress toward attaining its technical performance objectives.

3. The project owner's strategy has changed such that the project no longer has a strategic fit in the owner organization's future.

4. The project's champion has been lost, thereby putting the continued application of resources on the project in doubt.

5. Environmental changes have emerged which adversely influence the project's future.

6. Advances in the state of the art hoped for in the project (such as in research and development) have not been realized, and therefore further funding is not forthcoming.

7. The project's priority is not high enough to survive in competition with higher-priority projects.

Of course, the lines of demarcation between the projects falling into these situations are not always clear. These situations merely provide a framework for approaching inevitable project termination questions.

Why Terminate?

Most projects do not have a sharp beginning. As the project enters its life cycle and as true costs, time, and performance parameters of the project become better known, senior management at some point must consider the inevitable decision of whether to discontinue the project. Project termination should not be viewed as a failure but rather as a strategic decision implemented when a project does not or may not support the organizational strategies. Adams and Dirlan note that large firms that are known for their leadership role in successful innovations are also the ones that have undertaken a large proportion of unsuccessful projects.[1] The organization that does not make the often difficult, yet necessary, decision to terminate a project at the appropriate time can incur significant costs.

Buell suggests a number of factors to consider before terminating a project.[2] The termination decision usually does not come up at any specific instant, but rather develops slowly during the life cycle of the project, arising out of the intelligence gained about the project during the project review. Unfortunately, terminating a project often is perceived as a result of someone's failure. Humans, not wishing to admit failure, often take less than an objective view of a project termination.

---

[1] W. Adams and J. B. Dirlan, "Big Steal, Invention and Innovation," *Quarterly Journal of Economics*, vol. 80, May 1966, pp. 167–189.

[2] C. D. Buell, "When to Terminate a Research and Development Project," *Research Management*, vol. 10, July 1967, pp. 275–284.

Still, there is a need during each review of the project to evaluate whether that project continues to be strategic or whether the project should be terminated.

Types of Project Termination

Spirer addresses project termination as consisting of two broad types: first, a natural termination when the project goals have been met and, second, an unnatural termination when some project constraints have been violated, performance is inadequate, or the project goals are no longer relevant to some overall needs. Emotional issues include

- Fear of no future work
- Loss of interest in task remaining
- Loss of project-driven motivation
- Loss of team identity
- Selection of personnel to be reassigned
- Reassignment methodology
- Division of interest

The natural termination of a project is concerned with

- Identification of remaining deliverable end products
- Certification needs
- Identification of outstanding commitments
- Control of charges to the project
- Screening of uncompleted tasks not needed
- Closure of work orders and work packages
- Identification of physical facilities assigned to the project
- Identification of project personnel
- Accumulation and structuring of project historical data
- Disposing of project material
- Agreement with client on remaining deliverable end products
- Obtaining needed certifications
- Agreement with suppliers on outstanding commitments
- Communicating closures
- Closing down physical facilities

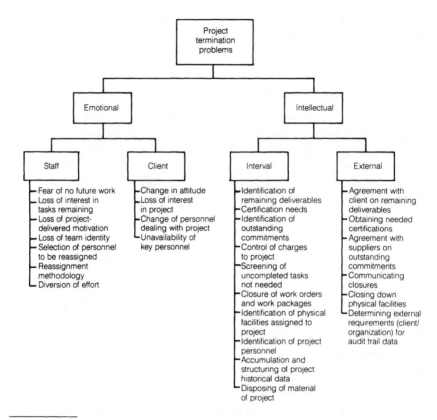

Source: Herbert F. Spirer, "Phasing Out the Project," in David I. Cleland and W.R. King (eds.), *Project Management Handbook*, (New York: Van Nostrand Reinhold Co., 1983): 248.

Figure 14.1   Work breakdown structure for problems of project termination.

- Determining external requirements for audit trail data.[3]

Spirer suggests the use of diagrams, and checklists as analytical tools for the management of project termination.[4] In addition, Spirer suggests a work breakdown structure for the problems of project termination, as shown in Fig. 14.1.

Strategic Implications

When the project is overrunning its costs and schedule, then termination should be considered. When termination is being considered, the

---

[3] Herbert F. Spirer, "Phasing Out the Project," in D. I. Cleland and W. R. King (eds.), *Project Management Handbook* (New York: Van Nostrand Reinhold, 1983), pp. 254–255.

[4] Ibid., pp. 256–260.

project should be evaluated from its strategic context: Does the project continue to have a strategic fit in the design and execution of organizational strategies? By asking and seeking complete and candid answers to the following questions, insight into the project's strategic context can be gained:

- Does the project continue to fit in the strategic plans of the organization?
- Does the project continue to complement a strength of the organization?
- Correspondingly, does the project avoid a dependence on a weakness of the organization?
- Is the project still consistent with the strategy of the sponsoring organization?
- Will the project continue to help that organization achieve its objectives?
- Will that completion of the project help that organization to accomplish its goals?
- If the project results are put into an operating mode, will these results provide a competitive advantage to the sponsoring organization?
- Is the project consistent with other projects and programs that are related to the strategic goals, objectives, and mission of the sponsoring organization?
- Can the project owner continue to assume the financial and other risks associated with the project?
- Does the project continue to represent a specific step along the way to the accomplishment of the project owner's objectives and mission?
- Does the project continue to be directly related to established strategies?
- Does the project team believe that the project continues to have a strategic fit in the design and execution of organizational strategies? If not, why not?

These questions are similar to those addressed in the selection of projects to support a company's strategy, discussed in Chap. 4.

The crucial element of the evaluation of a project during its life cycle is whether the project should be permitted to continue maturing in its life cycle, or whether it should be terminated in an orderly fashion. All too often a regularly scheduled project review considers only the status of the project as if that project were standing alone.

A project should be reviewed on a regular basis to determine its status on time, cost, and technical performance factors, as well as how that project stands in regards to the organizational strategies that it supports. A bottom-line question is to ask how well that project can be integrated with the mission, objectives, and strategies of the organization, as well as how it fits into the market strengths, weaknesses, comparative advantage, internal consistency, and key policies of the organization.

Major reviews of the project always should consider the alternative of project termination. Such considerations and analysis will be received with mixed emotions by the project owner and the project team. Experienced project management people can think of times when a project should have been canceled. The Lockheed L1011 project and the Washington Public Power Supply System debacle (often referred to as WHOOPS) are striking examples of projects that might better have been terminated when early difficulties were encountered. In the nuclear power plant construction industry, there are plants that have had awesome difficulties and, after many years of effort with billions of dollars invested, have not become operational. Even some that have been completed have not had their operating license approved.

Continuing the "Losers"

Why are some projects continued even though the project may be supporting a dying cause? The L1011 Tri-star Jet Program of Lockheed was known to be unlikely to earn a profit. For more than a decade it accumulated enormous losses. Since the program was Lockheed's reentry into commercial aviation, it became a symbol which broadened Lockheed's image beyond simply being a defense contractor.[5]

Staw and Ross suggest that there are several factors that encourage decision makers such as project managers and project owners to become locked into continuing strategies that cause the organization to lose: the project itself, managers' motivations, social pressures, and organizational pushes and pulls.[6]

Within the project itself, short-term problems are not likely to discourage the continuation of the project because such problems are usually looked on as necessary costs or investments for achieving the project's purposes. Project managers easily can view each setback as a temporary situation that can be corrected with more time and money.

---

[5] Barry M. Staw and Jerry Ross, "Knowing When to Pull The Plug," *Harvard Business Review*, March-April 1987, p. 71.

[6] Ibid.

A project's termination costs also may impede withdrawal. Managers sometimes don't fully fathom closing costs and salvage value when making the initial decisions to start the project. New projects are supposed to succeed rather than fail. Psychological factors influence the way the manager gathers information about the project and interprets and acts on that information. Managers often are rewarded for coping with short-run problems, "staying the course," and persevering to success. People often fail to recognize when a project is beyond hope. We have an uncanny ability to see only what is in accord with our beliefs and commitments. If a manager is convinced that a project will produce results, there is a predisposition to slant original estimates of costs and other data. Sometimes when managers recognize that a project is in real difficulties, they may choose to invest more resources in the project rather than accept failure.

Social pressures include the managers' unwillingness to expose their shortcomings and mistakes to others. If the project's success is tied to a perceived loss of power or loss of a job, then hanging on even in the face of grave difficulties makes sense to the decision maker. When an individual becomes identified with a project, he or she tends to defend the venture despite mounting losses and doubts about its feasibility. Then, too, managers are expected to "weather the storm" —like Churchill and Iacocca—and hang tough until they are successful. We see managers who are persistent as a sign of leadership; withdrawal as a sign of weakness. Given these perceptions, why would we expect managers to back off from a losing project?

Organizational pushes and pulls include the inertia that impedes withdrawal from losing projects. Sometimes it's just easier not to rock the boat. Organizational politics sometimes prevents a project termination. A project that supports a long-standing organizational strategy or company identity is not easily terminated even in the face of declining sales or profitability.

For example, the Deep Tunnel project in Chicago, designed to be a major addition to the city's sewer system, has absorbed millions of dollars and won't deliver any benefits until the entire system is completed. The expected date of completion continues to recede into the future; the cost for the work to be finished grows exponentially. Probably no one would have supported the project if the true costs had been known at the outset, yet once it is started, no one argues to kill the project. Project managers viewed each setback as a temporary situation correctable over time with more resources; more committed resources were perceived as investments toward a large payoff. The money spent was irretrievable; the pipe laid in the ground has no value unless the project is completed. It would cost a lot of money to take the pipe out of the ground. The decision makers were trapped in a course of action which virtually ensured that the project would not be terminated even if it were to cost less to do so.

Why do people get hooked into supporting a project far beyond the point where the project should have been terminated? Staw and Ross comment on the difference between an objective evaluation of the project's possible and probable future success and how this objectivity can be clouded by those people who manage the project and become emotionally attached to seeing that it is successful no matter what the odds—or the evidence—suggests.[7]

Projects are supposed to succeed, not fail. Yet a project that is a recognized failure can be a benefit to the organization. A company that cuts its losses by terminating a failing project has made an important and timely strategic decision—a decision that should be approached with as much discipline and analysis as the decision to launch the project. Project termination should not be considered as a failure, but rather as a necessary key decision in the design and execution of organizational strategies. Project termination is an integral part of the divestment phase of the project—to stop work on the project and transfer the results to the owner organization for use in the owner's ongoing business—in other words, institutionalization.

Orderly termination, for whatever reason, is a strategic management responsibility of senior managers. Termination is an option to be considered when one or more of the following conditions exist:

- There are serious cost and schedule overruns.

- Technical performance is compromised, or technical risks are too great.

- The project does not have a strategic fit in the sponsoring organization's future.

- The customer's strategy has changed.

- Competition has made or threatens to make the project results obsolete.

- The purposes for which the project was originally established have changed.

Projects in Trouble

When a project is experiencing serious cost and schedule overruns, termination may be a real issue, particularly from the strategic management perspective of the corporation. At such times, an outside audit should be conducted by either outsiders within the owner orga-

---

[7]Ibid., p. 68.

nization or an outside agency such as a consulting firm. Such audits can give insight into the reasons for the cost and schedule overruns and help to determine whether the project has become a termination candidate. At such times, senior managers' most important task is to create a cultural ambience that incorporates honest and frank disclosure.

If the project continues to play a vital role in the design and execution of organizational strategies and if it has sustained cost and schedule overruns, an important step must be taken to reevaluate the project as comprehensively as possible. Such an engineering review will enable senior managers to determine where the basic responsibility for cost and schedule overruns lay. If the review determines that the responsibility lies in an inadequate initial design, then engineering and redesign leading to a recosting and rescheduling of the project make good sense. During such a redesign, the doubtful or not fully understood parts of the project should be analyzed. The project team may not be able to terminate a project simply because that project team may have an understandably subjective review of the project. An audit should be conducted by an independent team, one that is not involved in the project. Such a team's effort could go beyond the audit and on into a full design review, recosting, and development of remedial strategy to get the project back on track. Senior managers who own the project also must be aware that a cultural ambience that encourages projects to succeed must also allow projects to fail if those projects fill no strategic role.[8]

Davis suggests several questions that should be asked when a project overrun threatens:

1. Does the project involve pioneer technology?
2. Is it a new project, and what experience has the project manager had in implementing this sort before?
3. Is it a bigger project than the company has handled before?
4. Was the costing done on the project before the design was completed?

If the answers to any of the three questions on the project's newness are yes, Davis opines that it is probable that you have a serious overrun. If the fourth question is answered in the affirmative, then it is likely that you have a serious overrun arising from incorrect estimates.[9]

---

[8] Paraphrased from David Davis, "New Projects: Beware of False Economies," *Harvard Business Review* (March-April 1985), pp. 95–101.

[9] Ibid., pp. 96–97.

Termination Strategies

If a project is to be terminated, some senior managers will replace the project manager with an individual who is skilled at closing out projects. Such a termination project manager would be wise to conduct an immediate review of the status of the work packages, along with the funding, schedule, and technical performance parameters. Several other things must be done:

- Ensure that all project deliverable end products have been provided to the project owner and that all project functional work is finished, along with any closeout of records.

- Review the status of all contracts to ensure that requirements have been met or provisions made if such requirements have not been duly satisfied.

- Work with the project team in developing and distributing a closeout plan that provides guidance for an orderly termination of all elements of the project.

- Maintain an ongoing surveillance of the closeout activities, including the closeout of all records and the disposition of materials.

- Notify relevant stakeholders of the termination.

- Ensure that all financial matters on the project have been satisfactorily terminated.

- Assist members of the project team to find other work in the organization.

- Prepare the project history, particularly a "lessons learned" report, so that future teams in the organization can benefit from the experiences of the project.

- Conduct a postcompletion audit of the project to identify strengths and weaknesses in the management of the project, what impact mistakes have had, how such mistakes can be avoided in future projects, and how that organization was affected, positively or negatively, by the project.

Evaluation of Termination Possibilities

Termination is always an option on every project. A strategy for management to use in dealing adequately with the ever-present termination issue should include these steps:

- Review the project and its strategic context on a regular, disciplined basis.

- Recognize the psychological and social forces that motivate one to "stay the course."

- Recognize that there is a prevailing belief and cultural force that encourage the commitment of more resources to solve current difficulties and ensure that success is "just around the corner."

- Define, with senior management participation, what constitutes both success and failure on the project. This definition is needed at the start of the project and should be reinforced at major review points during the project life cycle.

- Listen carefully to the concerns of others about the project. What are the project stakeholders saying? Are they saying that project termination is a good strategy?

- Evaluate the real ability of the project team to listen to and hear bad news. Does such news carry important information about the project's health, continuation, or termination?

- Ask whether the managers "bet too much of the farm" on the project where a termination would "break the bank," resulting in a perception of both organizational and personal failures.

- Determine if the project manager feels that a lot of people will have their futures adversely affected if the project is terminated.

- Step back and evaluate the project from an outsider's perspective. Use of an internal task force or audit team can help in getting such an outsider's viewpoint.

- Encourage project team members always to provide accurate information, even if that information contains messages that are not palatable and might suggest that project termination is an alternative worthy of full consideration.

- Consider replacing key members of the project team with new people who can bring a perspective less influenced by the project and past events. Consider replacement of the project manager.

- Build an organizational culture which supports the philosophy that projects are experimental, temporary uses of resources to support organizational strategies which require constant surveillance to guard against a project becoming an institution in the organization.

Termination Procedures

It is beyond the scope of this book to provide detailed termination procedures. Two books provide excellent guidance in this respect.

Archibald suggests some comprehensive checklists as aids in planning and controlling the work necessary to terminate a project. He concludes that there are benefits of using such checklists to do the following:

- Clearly indicate the closeout functions and responsibilities, reducing ambiguity and uncertainty.
- Reduce overlooking of important factors.
- Permit closeout progress to be monitored.
- Aid project team members with little or no experience in closing out a project.
- Inform other project team members about the activities of others during the closeout phase.[10]

Kerzner and Thamhain suggest a sample listing of typical activities in six areas to consider in managing the affairs of project closeout and transfer:

1. Documentation
2. Contract administration
3. Financial management
4. Program management
5. Marketing
6. Final management review[11]

Posttermination Activities

When projects are terminated, frequently certain posttermination activities are necessary to the project. Continuing service, maintenance, and logistic support may be an opportunity for future work. In some industries the follow-up service and maintenance contract work can be more profitable than the work of completing the project itself.

Audits can be a postcompletion activity. It is essential that the project managers ensure that adequate records are retained to support any postaudit activity that is initiated.

---

[10] Russell D. Archibald, *Managing High-Technology Programs and Projects* (New York: Wiley, 1976), p. 264.

[11] Paraphrased from Harold Kerzner and Hans J. Thamhain, *Project Management Operating Guidelines* (New York: Van Nostrand Reinhold, 1986), pp. 454–455.

British Petroleum (BP) conducts a *postproject appraisal* (PPA) of its major projects. British Petroleum's PPA strategies were also discussed in the *control* context in Chap. 13. Since the inception of PPAs in 1977, the company has appraised more than 80 of its project investments worldwide, including onshore and offshore construction projects, acquisitions, divestments, project cancellations, research projects, diversification plans, and shipping activities. The appraisals are done to improve company performance. Some characteristics of British Petroleum's postappraisal are as follows:

- Members of the appraisal team must have at least 15 years of broad-based experience with BP and have no affiliation with the projects they appraise.

- Project periods are examined from their conception usually until after they have become operational.

- Project records are reviewed, and all people involved in the project are interviewed. During the interviews, evaluators attempt to understand the psychology of the project members and the managers.

- Final appraisal reports are submitted to senior managers. Managers starting similar projects can review the reports.

- Four main lessons have been taught to BP management from their postproject appraisals: Determine costs accurately, anticipate and minimize risk, use a formal method to evaluate contractor selection and performance, and improve project management by setting up a "projects department" that helps project managers to develop and use project management techniques.[12]

As projects continue to be recognized as building blocks in the design and execution of organizational strategies, termination of those projects that do not further the purposes of the organization becomes important. Earlier in this book the point was made that senior managers can maintain surveillance over the stream of product and process projects as a way to determine if future strategies are evolving adequately. Of course, the principal purpose of such surveillance is to determine the schedule, cost, and technical performance promises of the department. Equally important is to view the stream of projects to determine which ones have a strategic fit with the enterprise's future purposes; also equally important is to identify those projects that should be eliminated if they are not consistent with the enterprise's evolving strategies.

---

[12] Frank R. Gulliver, "Post-Project Appraisals Pay," *Harvard Business Review*, March-April 1987, pp. 128–132.

In any project termination, it has to be clear what the project accomplished or did not accomplish. The project termination may be viewed differently by the customer, the contracting organization, the project manager, and the project team members. None of the stakeholders have the same stake in project completion and termination. The project termination manager must understand that. This requires that the project manager offer inducements of some sort to those stakeholders for whom termination is not seen as desirable. Clearly communicated project objectives and goals at the outset of the project, reinforced during the project's life cycle, can help to facilitate a harmony of viewpoints among the project stakeholders, particularly during termination time.

Summary

All projects eventually are terminated because of either success or failure. Projects that are successful join the operational strategy of the project owner's organization and support the business that organization is in. When a project is terminated for failing to accomplish its cost, schedule, or technical performance objectives, it usually is troublesome, requiring the reallocation of resources.

Most people associated with a project are disposed to make it succeed, even beyond a point of unwise cost increases or schedule delays. All too often project managers will ask for more time and more resources to make the project succeed, even beyond prudent justification.

Managers concerned with a project should approach major reviews of the project with the option of project termination open. There should be limits established beyond which continued expenditure of resources on the project just doesn't make strategic sense.

Discussion Questions

1. Discuss various situations in which projects may fail that indicate the need for project termination. How can managers recognize these situations?

2. List and discuss quantitative and qualitative factors that should be assessed when you consider project termination.

3. What are some of the emotional issues involved in project termination?

4. Describe some of the project manager's tasks with respect to project termination.

5. The strategic fit is an important aspect of major projects. What questions can managers ask in order to evaluate strategic fit?

6. Why are some projects continued even when failure is obvious? What role do psychological factors play?

7. What steps can managers take in order to comprehensively reevaluate an ongoing project so as to address the termination question?

8. Discuss some of the termination strategies described in the chapter.

9. Discuss the importance of an outsider's perspective on ongoing projects.

10. What are some of the steps involved in the termination procedure?

11. What posttermination activities are important? Why is generation of "lessons learned" important?

12. Customer acceptance is an important part of project termination. What can management do to ensure that the customer is satisfied with project results?

User Checklist

1. Does the cultural ambience of your organization encourage project success and also allow for failure? Describe some examples to explain your answer.

2. Are any of the ongoing projects within your organization in a situation that indicates project termination? Are these projects being terminated? Why or why not?

3. Do the managers of your organization usually recognize the need for project termination? Who has responsibility for eliminating those projects which have no further value for the organization?

4. What qualitative and quantitative factors are assessed by the project managers of your organization in order to make a termination decision?

5. How are the emotional issues of project termination addressed in your organization? Are project team members usually satisfied with termination decisions? Why or why not?

6. What tasks are performed by project managers in your organization during project termination?

7. Do the project leaders periodically assess the strategic fit of projects? What questions are posed?

8. Are projects in your organization which seem destined to fail often continued beyond where they should have been terminated?

Explain.

9. Do the necessary information and control systems exist to enable project managers to make a termination decision? Explain.

10. What termination strategies are used by project managers in your organization? How?

11. Do termination procedures exist for projects in your organization? What steps are involved?

12. Do project managers compile a list of lessons learned after the completion of a project? What other posttermination activities are done?

15

A Project Manager's Guide to Contracting[1]

"The first thing we do, let's kill all the lawyers."
                WILLIAM SHAKESPEARE, 1564–1616
                        King Henry VI

Although project managers are not normally trained in law, their day-to-day job activities require them to make decisions and take actions that can have significant legal impact on them and their companies. Some companies have established contract procedures for both negotiation and the administration of contracts. They routinely inform and train the managers of projects that may involve contracts about the details of these contracting policies. More commonly, however, project managers are handed a completed contract and are expected to proceed with little or no guidance until problems arise. The results can be extremely costly, time consuming, and embarrassing to the project manager and the company. Forward-thinking companies are finding it profitable to involve their project managers in the negotiation phase of a contract, particularly where performance to the letter of the contract constitutes the total project effort.

Project managers may direct a project for an eternal customer or conduct an internal project for their own employer. They may be involved in one or more contracting efforts and may select contractors to accomplish activities, groups of activities, or work packages, i.e., to

---

[1]This chapter was prepared by Dr. MaryAnne F. Nixon, assistant professor of business law in the School of Business, Western Carolina University, Cullowhee, North Carolina. Dr. Nixon is an attorney who consults and conducts seminars on the legal aspects of project management and teaches in the Master of Project Management degree program at Western Carolina University.

perform some subset or portion of the project. In any of these cases, project managers must assume the role of contract manager and ensure that contractors meet their obligations on time and on schedule and perform the work to the documented specifications. Thus project manager are likely to be involved in the contracting process in one way or another. Although they are not lawyers, project managers must certainly recognize the legal aspects of their own activities and be sufficiently aware of the implications to demand and obtain legal assistance where necessary.

How, then, can project managers best protect themselves and their companies in these activities? The key involves the methods used to limit the company's liability incurred through breach of warranties made either during negotiations or in the actual contract; through breach of clauses in the contract document included to address specific areas of liability; or through negligent acts or omissions in the administration of the contract.

This chapter presents several methods project managers can use to protect themselves and their companies during the negotiation of contracts and the conduct of projects. To perform effectively as contract managers, project managers must understand three key aspects of the contracting process: the basic negotiation of the contract, the clauses included in the contract to limit liability and share risk, and the implementation of the contract in a nonnegligent manner. Beyond that, project managers must understand the limits of their own knowledge and be prepared to obtain assistance from legal counsel when the situation demands more detailed knowledge of the law.

The Negotiation Process

Negotiation is a process in which parties with differing interests reach an acceptable agreement through a process of communication and compromise. According to Roger Fisher and William Ury in their book *Getting to Yes, Negotiating Agreement without Giving In,*[2] there is a straightforward, no-nonsense strategy for firmly pursuing your own interests while still getting along with those whose interests conflict with yours. This proven method of negotiation consists of four principles.

The first point is that it is important to separate the people from the problems, realizing that the "other side" is also represented by people who get angry, frustrated, fearful, hostile, and offended when they fail to interpret through their own personal points of view what

---

[2] Roger Fisher and William Ury, *Getting to Yes, Negotiating Agreement without Giving In,* (Boston: Houghton Mifflin, 1981).

has been said as it was intended. Conversely, the "other side" frequently involves people who do not mean what you understood them to say. The misunderstandings may reinforce existing prejudices and fuel an endless cycle of actions and reactions until a solution becomes impossible. The process of negotiation is doomed when we fail to deal with the other negotiator as a person subject to human reactions.

Fisher and Ury's advice in this area is to separate the substance of the negotiation from the relationship between the parties involved and to deal directly with the "people" problems which may exist. They suggest putting yourself in the other persons' position to see the situation from their point of view and to recognize and understand their emotions as well as your own. Successful negotiators will refrain from deducing the intentions of the other parties from the perspective of their own fears. Negotiators will not blame other parties for their own problems, but will discuss both sets of perceptions with the other parties. This will involve both sides in active communication. The successful negotiator will give credit for the good advice and ideas of others and will frame the final proposal so that it is consistent with their values. In this way the final proposal is more equitable for both sides.

The second point in successful negotiation is to focus on the common interests in the process rather than the opposing positions of the parties. The basic conflict in a negotiation normally lies in the goals of the parties being represented, and these goals usually can be reasonably well reconciled so that both parties "win." The difficulty in accomplishing this is that negotiators frequently become committed to specific positions and defend those positions without examining other ways of achieving the overriding goals or objectives. The difference is between strategic and tactical thinking. The tactical negotiator will defend the detailed position. The strategic negotiator will look for other positions that may aid both parties in achieving their goals. Behind the conflicting surface interests of the two parties can often be found common areas which can be identified and used to maximize the goal accomplishment of both parties. Strategic negotiators acknowledge the interests of the other party as a legitimate part of the problem, and they are flexible yet present well-defined ideas as solutions. They are firm in dealing with the problem yet open and supportive to the human being on the other side. This approach improves the relationship between the parties and increases the likelihood of reaching an acceptable agreement. Both parties attempt to attack the problem—not each other.

The third point Fisher and Ury make concerning successful negotiation is to generate a number of creative options prior to beginning negotiation. It is difficult at best to be creative under the pressure of the negotiation process and in the presence of the other party. At the negotiating table several options to advance shared interests can be presented, and the preferences of the other party can be solicited. The most preferable option can then be adjusted until an acceptable solution can be reached.

The fourth point is to insist that results be based on some objective criteria. Fisher and Ury point out that no matter how well you understand the interests, or how ingeniously you invent ways of reconciling those interests, conflict will continue. The best way to resolve this conflict is to base the solution on an objective standard other than the will of the two parties involved. That standard could be the market value, replacement cost, industry practice, allocation of risk based on investment, or a long-term cost/benefit analysis.

These four points combined are termed *principled negotiation,* a concept which involves developing an agreement based on the merits of the contract, as opposed to which party "wins" or "loses." It requires much practice and skill to become a successful "principled negotiator," but such an approach can be of inestimable value to the company and the project manager. This kind of relationship, and the mutual respect and satisfaction of both parties, frequently leads to add-on contracts and a continuing, profitable relationship between satisfied clients and contractors.

The Contract

During the negotiation of the contract as a whole, separate clauses must be understood and incorporated into the final document to limit the legal liability of the project manager and the company. The manager can assist in avoiding liability by understanding and using warranties, indemnification, liquidated damage clauses, and other clauses which limit liability.

Warranties

The concept of a warranty is based on the seller's written or verbal assurance to the buyer that the goods will meet certain standards. This warranty imposes a duty on the seller, who can be held liable by the buyer if this duty is breached. The buyer can either sue to recover damages or rescind or cancel the agreement. Two types of warranties are made when the seller enters an agreement with the buyer. *Expressed* warranties are promises actually spoken or written in the agreement, while *implied* warranties are promises that the Uniform Commercial Code automatically includes in a transaction, regardless of whether they are written into the contract. For example, the implied warranty of merchantability says that goods or products must be reasonably fit for the ordinary purpose(s) for which they are used.

This means that the quality must be comparable to the quality of goods which would pass without objection in the trade, and that the product will perform safely according to the general standards of the industry. The second warranty implied in a transaction is that of fitness for a particular purpose. This warranty arises when any seller knows the particular purpose for which the buyer will use the goods and the buyer relies on the seller's expertise in selecting suitable goods for that purpose. When express warranties overlap the implied warranties, conspicuously written express warranties will displace all inconsistencies in the implied warranties with exception of the warranty of fitness for a particular purpose.

Project managers can protect themselves against breech of expressed and implied warranties by being cautious in making statements regarding performance or design. The same caution and precision must be included in the wording of the contract. A good contract will contain a warranty which states a definite beginning and ending for the period during which the promises are to be upheld. It will state a specific remedy of repair or replacement and describe the costs which will be paid by each party if specific circumstances or problems occur. Most importantly, the warranty will specifically state the exact coverage, specifying whether it deals with the design, the manufacturing, or the operation of the product, or possibly some combination of the three. Remember, it can be as important to state what a warranty does not cover as it is to state what it does.

Lawsuits against contract managers are becoming alarmingly commonplace. The traditional standard applied to an individual's performance was based on negligence, i.e., performing with a reasonable standard of care. Thus, in order for negligence to be proved, it would need to be demonstrated that the manager failed to perform in accordance with the duty (as a reasonable manager would) defined in the contract. This failure would have to be established in court by expert testimony. Even though the end result of the contracted service failed to meet client expectations, the manager might not have performed the service negligently. Thus, there might be no basis for a claim.

Heretofore, professionals in the majority of jurisdictions have not been held to the higher standards of strict liability usually reserved for those involved in the production of goods. However, in some states, cases have made inroads into the strict liability area on the theory that design professionals deal in an exact science, that exact results can and should be expected, and that a detailed professional report, design, or plan is "manufactured" in the sense that it is created and sold as a means from which a final product can be produced. As a result, these products should be governed by the same standards as those referred to in the production of goods. In *Tamarac Development Co. v. Delamater, Freund & Assoc.*, 234 Kan. 618, 675 P2d 361 at 365, an architectural/engineering firm was held liable under a breach of implied warranty for failure to supervise and check the accuracy of the grading contractor's work for conformance with the specified planned elevations. The original suit was brought on negligence charges, but was barred because of the statute of limitations. The plaintiff then brought suit and was successful in a breach of implied warranty action, which has a longer limitation period!

The contract negotiator should be aware that inserting warranty language into contracts for performance of services can have the effect of raising the standard of duty. If services are warranted, they are guaranteed over and above the common-law duty to perform in a nonnegligent manner. Thus, if clauses are worded to require performance "to the highest standard of care," the contractor is in effect agreeing to increase his or her liability exposure.

Indemnification

Indemnification is the act of making reimbursement to a person for a loss already incurred by that person. There are two general types of indemnification: common-law and contractual. The common-law concept of indemnification can best be understood by an example of a factual situation: A contractor is under contract to complete a project for an owner on the owner's property. Someone—a worker, a trespasser, or even an innocent bystander—is injured on the worksite. Since the owner has a high duty to any persons on her or his property, the injured person may sue the owner to recover expenses and even exact punitive damages. Under common-law indemnification, the owner is entitled to recover any amount paid to the injured party from the contractor, provided that the owner did not contribute to the injury. If the owner contributed to the injury, the owner has no right to recover monies from the contractor.

Because of the harsh results to the owner for any contribution to the injury, two things have happened. First, distinctions have been drawn between active and passive negligence on the part of the owner. *Active negligence* is defined as the owner's actions which directly caused an injury. *Passive negligence* is identified as the owner's failure to act to prevent an injury. By virtue of these distinctions, owners have generally been allowed to recover judgments against them from the contractor if they are passively negligent, but not if they are actively negligent. Second, many states have adopted comparative negligence concepts which allocate financial responsibility on the basis of percentage of contribution to the injury. Because of these two concepts, owners wishing to limit their liability seek various contractual provisions in which contractors performing work agree to indemnify and hold the owners harmless against all claims, losses, and damages arising out of the work performed. Similarly, contractors seek to obtain agreements from owners to protect themselves against claims by third parties.

Most states have statutes which limit the use of contracts to relieve parties of responsibility for the consequences of their own negligence. On the other hand, most states will enforce indemnity agreements by which the company agrees to indemnify the owner. Traditional indemnity requires the party seeking reimbursement through such clauses to actually incur a loss before seeking reimbursement. In order to require the indemnifying party to undertake the defense of a claim from the outset, most contracts use the "hold harmless" language: "The owner shall be held harmless in all cases of injury arising from the operations of the contractor."

Indemnity provisions vary considerably from contract to contract as to the extent of the liability transferred. Some provisions may be so severe in their results that their legality hinges on whether they are contrary to public policy. These provisions can be categorized into three main classifications:

1. The broad form, the most severe of the three, obligates the indemnitor to indemnify and hold harmless the indemnitee against all loss arising out of the performance of the contract even if the indemnitee is solely responsible for the occurrence of the loss.

2. The intermediate form holds the indemnitor responsible for all claims or suits arising out of the contract except those arising out of the sole negligence of the indemnitee.

3. The limited form, one party agrees to indemnify the other only for the claims arising out of the indemnitor's negligence.

In situations where both parties are jointly negligent, both are generally held liable. Under this type of clause, the parties are basically reconfirming their liabilities under common law.

Protection can be built into the indemnity provision for the contractor by adding a cap to the amount indemnified, limiting it to the same amount provided in the limitation of liability provisions. (See "Liquidated Damages" below.) Additional protection for the contractor can be added by specifically wording the provision to indemnify third-party damages only. Without this language, indemnity obligations can be interpreted to hold the contractor liable for damages suffered by the owner. In negotiating these clauses, the approach of using reason and fair play should be taken with the other party. Consider the level of involvement or investment in the project, and allocate the level of risk accordingly. In negotiating third-party claims, the contractor should avoid responsibility for those claims resulting from actions of someone over whom the contractor has no control.

It is important to remember that the indemnity provision survives the completion of the contract. This is especially important in cases of claims by an injured employee who files suit against the employer, who in turn sues under the indemnification clause of a contract. While insurance will usually cover this type of claim, the high cost of premiums and the dollar deductibles may render this protection prohibitively expensive for many contractors.

Liquidated damages

Frequently, parties to a contract wish to transfer liability for delays in completion of the scope of work, including missing deadlines for the delivery of equipment and materials or failure to complete the project or any part thereof. If the contractor assumes liability for late completion or delivery, damages will be assessed in accordance with the terms of the contract. The damages specified are usually in terms of a specific amount of money to be paid for each day the work is late. Liability under these clauses can be limited in different ways depending on the circumstances surrounding the project. Keep in mind that excessively high amounts may be found to be punitive and thus deleted from the contract by a court of law.

A well-negotiated liquidated-damages clause will adequately protect the contractor if liability is defined within reasonable limits. The most common method is to negotiate a cap on the amount of damages to be paid. In general, the amount of damages should be justified in some way by the amount of loss incurred by the owner as a result of the late delivery or completion. This clause can also be structured to provide an incentive bonus for the contractor who completes the project prior to the designated date. Again, the bonus must be reasonably determined with a cap on the amount to be received in lieu of other compensation, and the amount of the bonus and the cap should be justified by the amount of savings and benefits accruing to the owner as a result of the early delivery or completion.

Other limitations of liability

Limitation-of-liability clauses in contracts are usually the result of company policy and are applied in all contract situations. Company policy will usually require the signature of an executive if liability is open-ended or if a limitation is over a set amount. Care must be taken, however, that the clause is tailored to fit the circumstances of the individual contract. Reliance on standard clauses lifted from the policy manual frequently leads to limitations which can be considered unreasonable in a court of law. If the limitation is found to be unreasonable, the company may be left open to a broad-scale liability, rather than to the limited scope initially intended.

One method of limiting a company's liability is to include a *force majeure* provision in the contract. This common contract clause is used to protect the parties in the event that part of the contract cannot be performed because of an unforeseeable event outside the control of either party or which could not be avoided by using due care. The key to the enforceability of this type of clause is the unforeseeability of the event causing the loss or damage. Work to be performed by unionized work teams involved in the renegotiation of wages or working conditions can foreseeably be delayed by strikes, work slowdown, or walkouts. Under these circumstances, the resulting damages could not be deemed unforeseeable, and damages would be assessed against the party in the best position to avoid or plan for the loss.[3]

A broad *force majeure* provision should also be included in providing for subcontractor delays. If total liability for subcontractor delays cannot be included in the *force majeure* provision, the contractor's liability for these delays should be dealt with elsewhere in the contract. This is frequently accomplished by structuring the contract so that damages are passed on to the subcontractors in amounts proportionate to the subcontractor's contribution to the overall task.

If the contract calls for performance or acceptance criteria prior to completion of the project, the contractor should contribute to the determination of the criteria. The contractor would also want to be involved in structuring the criteria and timelines for completion and client acceptance. When the performance criteria for a particular product do not fall within the normal use of the product being manufactured, acceptance criteria become one means of sharing the risk between the client and the contractor. Under such nonstandard conditions, it is imperative that the conditions be carefully defined and in consonance with the contractor's understanding of the appropriate use of the product being provided.

Another method for controlling liability involves the careful definition of scheduled deadlines or milestones for each phase of the scope of the work. The contractor should carefully review all scheduled deadlines to ensure they are reasonable given the contractor's capacity to perform. Ideally, the contractor will have proposed the major deadlines and milestones in the negotiation process. Such schedules should include a reasonable safety margin for dealing with potential problems in delivery.

When these limitation-of-liability clauses are negotiated, the other party to the contract will be more receptive if the clause is introduced at the outset of the negotiation rather than added as company boiler-

---

[3] Roger S. Mertz, "How Can I Limit My Monetary Liability by Contract Clauses?" *Avoiding Liability in Architecture: Design and Construction* (New York: Wiley, 1986), p. 279.

plate terminology at the conclusion of negotiations. From the outset of negotiations, the project manager must understand the reasons behind company policy and the terminology used in the limitation-of-liability clauses. The client's concerns with the clauses must also be addressed.[4] The project manager must understand both the policies and the terminology to be able to simultaneously address the needs of the client and protect the company's interests.

The most successful strategy is to negotiate a cap on the amount of liability, with the company prepared to accept a commercially reasonable amount of liability based on the circumstances existing at the time the negotiation is taking place. These circumstances include the cost of the contract, the scope of general insurance coverage obtainable (considering the often high deductible), the nature of the work, and the resources of the client. A reasonable level of liability will reduce the likelihood that the clause will later be dismissed as an exculpatory provision (wording which unreasonably relieves the contractor of an obligation for the safety or quality of the product), or considered to be a penalty to the contractor rather than a commercially acceptable allocation of risk. Either of these findings by the court would render the clause unenforceable. The wise negotiator will therefore carefully define the limitation-of-liability clause rather than hope that the courts will find a standard clause enforceable.

The breadth or brevity of the clause being used should also be closely scrutinized, since any ambiguities will be construed against the drafter of the clause. The clause which is too short or which has been reduced to "plain English" may increase the risk of ambiguity. If the limitation-of-liability clause is too general, it may be construed to cover only one type of legal obligation but not others. It is important to limit liability on all possible legal theories under which a claim may be made. Project managers should understand that liability lies in active and passive negligence principles as well as in the more commonly recognized breach of contract, tort, and indemnification.

Contract Administration

Contract administration includes the responsibility for supervising the work to be done under the terms of the contract, preparing and processing the changes that inevitably will be made, providing interpretation (with legal assistance if required) of contract language, and approving invoices as the work is being performed. Project managers need to be aware that in performing any of these responsibilities, conduct which could be deemed less than reasonable under the circum-

---

[4] Ibid., p. 281.

stances could give rise to charges of negligence against the manager, the company, or the employees by any other party involved in the contract. Such behavior could also lead to allegations of breach of contract. Usual company policy calls for executive-level personnel to have overall responsibility for establishing company contracting policy and ensuring that it is maintained consistently throughout all levels of administration. The negotiation, administration, and control of all client contracts must be in accordance with this established company policy. To this end, it is frequently the project manager who must establish or implement the appropriate control mechanisms to ensure that the company's most current contracting and compensation policies are being executed.

Several important elements of contract administration must be understood by the project manager. Prior to issuing a contract, it is the project manager's responsibility to ensure that all required signatures, comments, and approvals have been secured or documented. No work should be performed before the final contract is issued or, pending the contract, a formal letter of authorization to begin work has been received. This letter must specify precisely the work to be accomplished pending the contract as well as the obligation the company is willing to accept for completion of this work. The letter should also specify that the terms and conditions of the standard company contract expressly govern any work performed.

Another contract administration responsibility is maintenance of the contract files. As simple as this may sound to the uninitiated, the process of documenting the actions of the company and the contractor can become very complex. Careful documentation can also be critical to the company if legal problems arise later. "Maintaining the files" includes carefully referencing all communications concerning the project with the proper accounting, project, and/or job number. It also includes keeping copies of the contract itself and all contract-related documentation, especially all changes, addenda, or supplements to the original contract, and ensuring they are properly cross-referenced. The project manager should make it a habit to record daily events in a permanent and orderly manner. This information is usually recorded on company forms which request information about problems that have occurred, the dates on which management was informed of the problem, and the steps taken to generate a solution. Additional documentation in a contract file generally includes the request for proposal, memoranda of any verbal communications concerning the contract, all internal review and approval documents, subcontractor status report sheets, verification of employee hours and overtime, quality assurance documentation, materials price and delivery verification, and records of timely and accurate billing and invoicing. Additionally, the project manager must ensure that the cumulative services and billing for those company services do not exceed the approved scope and budget for the client.

Of particular note are changes that occur during the conduct of the contract. It is common practice in industry for contractors to "buy in" to a job: i.e., to bid well below expected costs, knowing they can "get well" by pricing later changes when the company is "locked in" to their services. A clearly understood and well-documented change control process is absolutely critical to the successful completion of the contract. The clear documentation of all changes, the price of changes involved, and the authorization to proceed must be included in the contract files, since this is a prime area for future litigation.

Summary

Successful project managers must be able to understand the key techniques used to allocate risks to the parties involved in a project. Contract clauses are used to protect a company but can also be a critical source of liability. As contract administrator or contract manager, project managers who have an understanding of practical contract management issues will be able to recognize the importance of carefully documenting the performance of the activities which they supervise. Project managers should be able to identify the principal bases of liability exposure in the contracts they are likely to encounter. They should know to get legal help when the complexity of the issue has exceeded their level of knowledge or responsibility. Most importantly, project managers must recognize the value of formal legal assistance in creating contracts that will avoid costly and lengthy legal settlements which are at best disruptive to them and their employers.

Discussion Questions

1. Why is it important for project managers to understand contract administration? What knowledge should they possess with respect to contract administration?

2. Discuss the four negotiation principles which were described in the chapter. What other management principles apply to the negotiation process?

3. Can knowledge of organizational and human behavior assist in the negotiation process? How?

4. Define the difference between express and implied warranties. Give some examples to explain your definitions.

5. What is your personal view of the responsibility of contract managers and professionals for negligence involving products and services?

6. What are the two types of indemnification? Explain the differences between them.

7. What methods can project managers and contract administrators use to protect against unusually high liability exposure?

8. Discuss the various methods for limitation of liability. Which of these should be applied (at a minimum)? Explain.

9. What clauses in contracts must project managers be particularly aware of? Why?

10. Describe several approaches for organizing the contract administration responsibilities within a project. Which of these would be most beneficial? Explain.

11. What are some of the responsibilities of contract administration personnel?

12. Discuss the trade-offs between negotiating a clear-cut, practical contract versus one which does not leave the owner or contractor "locked in."

User Checklist

1. Do the project managers in your organization possess enough knowledge about contract administration to effectively manage the negotiating and contracting processes? Explain.

2. Do contract negotiators in your organization follow the four principles of negotiation? How might they apply these principles better?

3. What training has been provided to the project managers in your organization so that they may better manage contracting procedures? What additional training is needed?

4. What express or implied warranties apply to the products or services provided by your organization? Explain.

5. In what situations might professionals or managers in your organization be held responsible for negligence? How might these situations be avoided?

6. What types of indemnity provisions are used in the contracts that your organization is involved in? Are they effective? Explain.

7. What recent suits have been brought against your company with respect to contract violations? How could these have been avoided?

8. What methods does your organization use to limit liability? Are these effective? Explain.

9. What contractual clauses have become important to maintaining the contracts that your organization is involved in? Why?

10. How are contract administration duties handled on projects within your organization? Is the organizational design effective for carrying out contract duties?

11. What roles and responsibilities are assigned to contract management personnel? Are these carried out efficiently?

12. Are the contracts that your organization is involved in usually clear-cut, or do they leave room for changes? What are the advantages and disadvantages of this approach?

Interpersonal Dynamics in the Management of Projects

16

Project Leadership

*"To be a leader of men one must turn one's
back on men."*

HAVELOCK ELLIS, 1859–1839

The concept of leadership is surely as old as the concept of organized activity. Organizations have been led with varying degrees of effectiveness by people called "leaders" since the development of organized societies. Leadership in the political, social, military, legal, economic, and technological environments has been celebrated and studied throughout history. Today these studies continue to try to understand what both separates and harmonizes leaders and followers.

Our view of a project leader is that individual who leads a project team during the project life cycle and accomplishes the project objective on time and within budget. In this chapter the concept of project leadership will be presented. But before discussing project leadership, we will present some ideas about the general nature of leadership.

What Is Leadership?

There are many definitions of leadership. Fiedler cites nearly a dozen different definitions with varying connotations and degrees of emphasis on elements. He defines a leader as "the individual in the group given the task of directing and coordinating tasks in relevant group activities or who, in the absence of a designated leader, carries the primary responsibility for performing these functions in the group."[1] Peter Drucker opines that effective leadership is based pri-

---

[1]Fred E. Fiedler, *A Theory of Leadership Effectiveness* (New York: McGraw Hill, 1967), p. 8.

marily on being consistent.[2] Arthur Jago defines leadership as both a process and a property. He states that leadership is the use of noncoercive influence to direct the activities of the members of an organized group toward the accomplishment of group objectives. He considers leadership in the context of a set of qualities or characteristics attributed to those who are perceived to successfully employ such influence.[3]

Jago notes that leadership is not only an attribute but also what the person does. Under this definition, then, anyone on a project team may take on a leadership role.

In his research Professor Hans J. Thamhain has identified that project management requires skills in three primary areas of abilities—leadership/interpersonal, technical, and administrative. He goes further and offers some suggestions for developing project management skills needed for effective project management performance.[4]

The subject of leadership has received much attention, yet we do not have a universally accepted definition of the term. James McGregor Burns' recent book, *Leadership,* cites one study with 130 definitions of the term.[5] Another book notes over 5000 research studies and monographs on the subject. The editor of a handbook concludes that there are no common factors, traits, or processes that identify the qualities of effective leadership.[6] Most books tend to equate leadership with a "hero person." Others view leadership as characterized by personal characteristics such as charisma, intelligence, energy, style, commitment, and so on. Other theorists view leadership as depending on anything from task conditions to subordinate expectations.[7]

Literally thousands of studies have explored leadership traits. Some of the traits relate to physical factors, some to abilities, many to personality, others to social characteristics. Of all the traits that have

---

[2]Peter Drucker, "Leadership: More Doing than Dash," *Wall Street Journal,* January 6, 1989.

[3]Arthur Jago, "Leadership: Perspectives in Theory and Research," *Management Science,* vol. 28, no. 3, March 1982. Copyright © 1982 by the Institute of Management Sciences.

[4]See Hans J. Thamhain, "Developing Project Management Skills," *Project Management Journal,* September 1991, pp. 39–44.

[5]J. M. Burns, *Leadership* (New York: Harper & Row, 1978), p. 2.

[6]B. M. Bass, *Stogdill's Handbook of Leadership: A Survey of the Theory and Research,* rev. ed. (New York: Free Press, 1981).

[7]Louis B. Barnes and Mark P. Kriger, "The Hidden Side of Organizational Leadership," *Sloan Management Review,* Fall 1986.

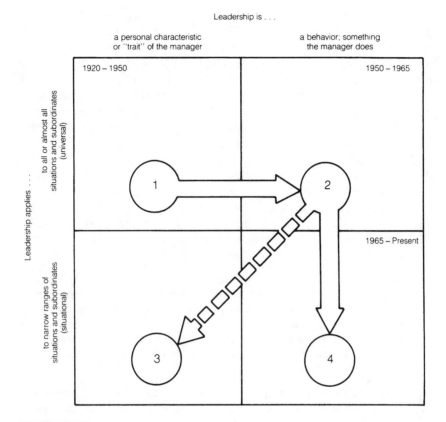

Leadership is . . .

Figure 16.1   Development of mainstream leadership theory.

been described, there appears to be most support for the roles of activity, intelligence, knowledge, dominance, and self-confidence.

Studies of Leadership

As Fig. 16.1 shows, early work on leadership searched for a single set of traits characterizing effective leaders. This emphasis dominated the research from its beginning until the 1950s. In the 1950s and 1960s, research moved from isolating leader characteristics toward a search for a universally effective leadership style. More recent research has changed to attempts to identify and match characteristics of situations and subordinates with characteristics and behaviors of managers.

Some leadership research has been devoted to studying the effects of autocratic and democratic approaches, with much time being spent on the issue of who should make the decisions—the leader or the followers. Another aspect of research into leadership has been the distinction between a "task" orientation and a "relations" orientation. Still another area of effort has been the study of the leader in "initiating structure" for followers, yet at the same time being considerate of them. Along with this has been increasing attention to the ability to promote change in individuals, groups, and organizations. This promotion of change and this dealing with the resistance to change have put emphasis on democratic, participative, relations-oriented, considerate leadership.[8]

Other views of leadership have taken a new direction, looking not only to the individual's traits but also to the behavior of the leader and those people who are being led. McGregor summarizes some of the generalizations from recent research on leadership, which portray "leadership as a relationship." According to McGregor:

> There are at least four major variables now known to be involved in leadership: (1) the characteristics of the leader; (2) the attitudes, needs, and other personal characteristics of the followers; (3) characteristics of the organization, such as its purpose, its structure, the nature of the tasks to be performed; and (4) the social, economic, and political milieu. The personal characteristics required for effective performance as a leader vary, depending on the other factors.

McGregor's viewpoint is important because "it means that leadership is not a property of the individual, but a complex relationship among these variables."[9]

Other approaches have explained leadership as a type of behavior, e.g., dictatorial, autocratic, democratic, and laissez-faire. The operating styles of these types of leaders consist of getting work done through fear (the dictator), centralizing decision making in the leader (the autocrat), decentralizing decision making (democratic leadership), and allowing the group to establish its own goals and make its own decisions (laissez-faire leadership).

Still other approaches deal with leadership as specific to the particular situation in which it occurs. Therefore, leaders have to be cognizant of the groups of people (superiors, subordinates, peers, etc.) to which they are related as well as the organizational structure, resources, goals, time variables, etc. This suggests the real complexities of trying

---

[8] Bernard Bass, "Leadership: Good, Better, Best," *Organizational Dynamics,* Winter 1985, pp. 26–49.

[9] Douglas McGregor, *The Human Side of Enterprise* (New York: McGraw-Hill, 1960), pp. 179–189.

to understand what leadership is all about. A basic conclusion can be drawn: Successful leaders must be adaptive and flexible—always aware of the needs and motivations of those whom they try to lead. Lenders must be aware of how they perform as leaders and how their behavior affects the performance of those on whom they depend. As leaders try to change the behavior of their people, a change in their behavior also may be needed.

Research into the matter of leadership continues, since we really know little of what it is and why it works sometimes and fails at other times. Project managers who strive to improve their leadership abilities should read in the area. The references at the end of the chapter can be helpful in this regard.

Leadership Style

An important part of leadership is the "style" with which the leader carries out the role. Much has been written about leadership style. Also, the characteristics of successful leaders have been examined in detail. What follows is just a sample of the abundant views on the subject.

John E. Welch, Jr., CEO of General Electric Company and a superb leader, will no longer tolerate autocratic, tyrannical managers in leadership positions. In a letter to shareholders, CEO Welch discussed management techniques and goals. According to him, GE "cannot afford management styles that suppress and intimidate" subordinates. Welch has categorized managers into several types:

1. A leader who delivers on commitments—financial or otherwise—and shares the values of the company has onward-and-upward prospects.

2. A leader who does not meet commitments but shares the company values will get a second chance, preferably in a different environment.

3. A leader who doesn't meet commitments and doesn't share values is soon gone from the company.

4. The fourth type is the most difficult to deal with. This individual delivers on commitments, makes all the numbers, but doesn't share the values. This individual is typically the one who forces performance out of people rather than inspires it—the autocrat, the big shot, the tyrant.

In today's environment, where it is necessary to have good ideas from every person in the organization, those people whose management styles suppress and intimidate are not needed. GE proclaims high priorities for focusing on customers, resisting bureaucracy, cutting across boundaries, thinking globally, demonstrating enormous energy, and being able to energize and invigorate others.

GE has sent many managers to observe highly successful Wal-Mart Stores, Inc., where the leadership factors of speed, the bias for action, and utter customer fixation have helped drive this high-discount store to success.[10]

Leadership style is in general of two types: *People-centered,* described as democratic, permissive, consensus-seeking, participative, follower-oriented, and considerate; and *task-centered,* described as structured, task-dominated, restrictive, directive, autocratic, and socially distant. Task-oriented leadership style usually is associated with productivity but may depress follower satisfaction, whereas people-centered leadership tends to enhance group cohesiveness but not consistently increase productivity.

Leaders, except for the likes of Napoleon, Alexander, or Ghengis Khan, whatever their style, all have their "superiors" to whom they must subordinate their wishes, or both they and their organization will probably fail. Managers (and leaders) who are successful in being promoted up through the organizational hierarchy have demonstrated an ability to lead their followers and to follow their superior leader. Emotionally and intellectually, a leader is wed to the conviction that an organizational unit cannot accomplish its mission without some degree of obedience at every level in the hierarchy. A leader needs obedience and discipline from followers and thus accords it to superiors. To demand obedience from one's followers but to withhold it from higher authority would constitute an inconsistency that would jeopardize the fundamental discipline of authority-responsibility-accountability which holds an organization together.

We have all seen or heard of mavericks who "march to a different drummer" and cannot function in a hierarchical organization and strike out on their own. Upon leaving and starting a new "business," these mavericks usually end up creating some form of a leader-follower organizational structure.

Effective leadership, then, is usually preceded by effective followership. A successful project leader doubtlessly has performed successfully as a follower. This success provided the basis for that individual's opportunity to become a successful leader. Followers provide the opportunity and legitimacy to the leadership role. In the changing, complex world of project management, we believe that tomorrow's project managers cannot successfully emerge without having learned the skills and developed the attitudes of followership.

---

[10]James C. Hyatt and Amal Kumar Naj, "GE Is No Place for Autocrats, Welch Decrees," *Wall Street Journal,* March 3, 1992.

The following examples can help to emphasize the differences of leadership style depending on both the leader and the circumstances.

Peter Ueberoth, "project manager" for the 1984 Olympics, is described as having a management style which ensures that he is in control at all times. His ego and inner toughness helped him to promote and successfully conclude a project with a global objective. His abilities in cultivating the stakeholders were instrumental in raising the money required for the Olympics. Ueberoth believes that a leader's role is to inspire people to greater efforts. He believes that authority is 20 percent given and 80 percent taken. If someone faltered on his project, he made a change and put someone in who could handle the job.[11]

Jimmy Treybig, chief executive officer of Tandem Computers, was somewhat of a legend in Silicon Valley. His management of Tandem was in a "laid back" style. The company had eleven vice presidents, but no organizational charts, no timeclocks, and no regular meetings with subordinates. He delivered motivational speeches in tents erected in the company parking lots. His Friday afternoon beer parties, which were unstructured communications carried out by people from different departments, became something of a legend. He used to manage through inspiration, believed that all employees would do the right thing if they appreciated the company's goal and their place in the organization. Treybig's grip on the company began to slip. His free, one-of-the-boys management style forced him to adopt a new approach. Management by inspiration was over—management by perspiration was in. Suddenly there was a fundamental change. Every part of the company was exposed to incredible scrutiny. There were new weekly staff meetings and quarterly staff reviews along with detailed assessment of goals. Treybig had become authoritative. He had cut expenses and increased productivity to increase revenues. Indeed, Treybig was now acting like a boss.[12]

Leadership style should not necessarily be consistent in all activities. On the contrary, project leaders should be as flexible as possible, gearing their leadership style to the specific situation and the individuals involved, that is, within the key elements of any leadership situation—the leader, the led, and the situation. Figure 16.2 shows a continuum of leadership behavior with the basic ingredient being the degree of authority used by a manager versus the amount of freedom left for subordinates. Autocratic, democratic, and laissez-faire leader-

---

[11] Paraphrased from "Master of the Games," *Time,* January 7, 1985.

[12] Brian O'Reilly, "How Jimmy Treybig Turned Tough," *Fortune,* May 25, 1987, pp. 102–103.

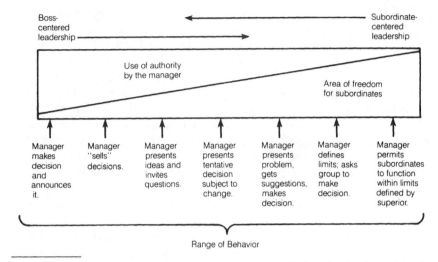

Figure 16.2   Continuum of leadership behavior.

ship styles can be identified across this continuum from boss-centered leadership to subordinate-centered leadership.

It is difficult to generalize about the characteristics of leaders. They come in all shapes, colors, and sexes. Some are brilliant, some are dull, some are articulate, some can write, some are proactive, and others are laid back. However, a few characteristics are found in leaders who have proven track records:

- They have their act together; their personal ambition drives them to succeed and the organization they are leading to succeed.

- They are visible to their people; they are not "absentee landlords." There is no doubt in anyone's mind that they are in charge and on top of everything.

- They are available to their people to listen, debate, and gather the necessary facts; and at the same time they are ready to say, "Let's do it."

- They are decisive and in the long-run make the decisions that turn out to be right. They know when to stop inputting information and recommendations into a decision and say, "OK, go do it."

- They see the best in the people with whom they work, not the worst. The leaders see winners and praise and develop these winners for higher levels of performance.

- They are simplistic and avoid making things complex. Good leaders make things simple, coming at people from different approaches until people are convinced, or people convince them that this or that is the way to do things.

- They are fair and patient, and usually they have a sense of humor that tides them and their people over the rough spots that come to any enterprise. Humility is a mark found in good leaders who recognize that they are leaders only because the followers have allowed them to remain in a leadership role.

- They work hard at leadership, at providing the people with the resources needed to do the job, and follow up to see if people are doing those jobs.

Project Leadership

What's the difference between leadership and management? Management is usually considered to be a more broadly based activity including functions other than leading. According to Davis:

> Leadership is a part of management, but not all of it. A manager is required to plan and organize, for example, but all we ask of the leader is that he gets others to follow....Leadership is the ability to persuade others to seek defined objectives enthusiastically. It is the human factor which binds a group together and motivates it toward goals. Management activities such as planning, organizing, and decision making are dormant cocoons until the leader triggers the power of motivation in people and guides them toward goals.[13]

The factor that empowers the project team and ultimately determines which projects fail or succeed is the leadership brought to bear on the project at all levels in the enterprise. When a project is undertaken in the implementation of an enterprise strategy, the key to making that project happen is the quality of leadership.

Project managers must not only manage but also lead. Project leadership should be appropriate to the project situation because leadership is a continuous, flexible process. There are no consistent characteristics of leadership to point to and flatly state: "That's what makes a leader." Decisiveness is often cited as a desirable leadership characteristic, yet if a leader makes a wrong decision, the organization can suffer. Each management situation, the people involved, the times, the characteristics of the followers, the urgency of the decision, and so on, all influence both the leaders and the followers.

---

[13] Keith Davis, *Human Relations at Work,* 3d ed. (New York: McGraw-Hill, 1967), pp. 96–97.

Project leadership is an interpersonal and strategic process which seeks to influence the project stakeholders to work toward closure of the project purposes. Project leadership takes place through interaction, not in isolation.

Project managers, like most managers in modern organizations, are both leaders and followers, operating in a culture where both formal and informal networking relationships proliferate. In such relationships networking goes beyond the project manager's formal authority, often leading to the use of influence over peers and superiors to affect the outcome of the project.

A project manager's leadership position encompasses three fundamental roles: the *interpersonal role,* which includes figurehead, leadership in liaison functions; an *informational role,* which entails disseminating information and acting as a spokesperson; and a *decision maker* in which the project manager acts as entrepreneur, resource allocator, and negotiator.[14]

Project leaders are the people who do the right thing; project managers are people who do things right. Bennis recognizes that both roles are important in management, but they differ profoundly. There are, according to Bennis, people in senior positions in organizations doing the wrong thing well. Part of the fault for having people do the wrong thing may well lie with our schools of management, where we teach people to be good management technicians but we fail to train people for leadership.[15]

Bennis goes further to identify the competencies found in people who exhibit effective leadership in their proven track records:

- Management of attention
- Management of meaning
- Management of trust
- Management of self

We will take these competencies and adapt them to the art of project leadership.

Management of attention

An apparent trait in most successful leaders is their ability to draw others to follow them toward a purpose. Often this purpose takes an early form of a dream or a vision. Because of the leaders' extraordi-

---

[14]These fundamental roles are described in Henry Mintzberg, "The Manager's Job: Folklore and Fact," *Harvard Business Review,* July-August 1985, pp. 54–56.

[15]Paraphrased from Warren Bennis, "Good Managers and Good Leaders," *Across the Board,* October 1984, p. 8.

nary commitment to their dreams, they communicate a commitment which attracts people to them. People enroll in the leaders' visions. A project manager who is effective usually knows what he or she wants to be done on the project and reflects this in a project plan.

The first leadership competency is a set of intentions, a vision, or a direction in the sense of the project objective, goals, and strategies. A project manager who has developed a project plan has taken an important step in becoming a project leader. The project leader's role is not merely to state the project objective, goals, and strategies, but to create a meaning for the project that team members can rally around. No matter how grand the project objective, the effective project leader must use a word, a model, or a slogan to make the vision clear to others. The project leader's goal is to go beyond a mere clarification or explanation, to the creation of what the project objective means in satisfying a customer or owner. The project manager integrates customer facts, concepts, and needs, and project team capabilities, into a meaning of the project for the project team and the stakeholders. At times the leader's most important task may be to communicate the project's objective to key stakeholders whose viewpoint could be supportive of, contrary to, or indifferent to the project objective.

Management of meaning

An important responsibility of senior managers as leaders is to communicate the meaning of the project results within the strategic fit of the corporate mission. When the project team members can sense that the project is a building block in the design and execution of enterprise strategies, an important step has been made toward giving the project meaning.

To make the meaning of the project apparent to the members of the enterprise, key enterprise managers must work at communicating the vision of the project through meetings and conversations.

Management of trust

Trust is an assured reliance on the character, ability, strength, or truth of someone or something. A project leader is someone in whom confidence is placed. An ambience of trust is essential to all organizations; the main determinants of trust are reliability and commitment. Reliability deals with the maintenance of a stable project management approach and a project culture which sets and expects high performance standards. Commitment means that the project team members, and the senior managers responsible for supporting the team, are pledged to making the project results happen. Team members want to follow a team leader they can count on, even if they disagree with the leader's viewpoint. A project leader who shifts positions frequently stands to lose the confidence and commitment of the people. One cannot emphasize enough the significance of constancy and focus in the management of a project.

Management of self

The first challenge most of us face is to manage ourselves. If we have knowledge and skills and are sufficiently motivated, then we stand a good chance of deploying the knowledge and skills effectively. Management of self is critical. Without it we can do more harm in a management position than good. Bennis notes:

> Like incompetent doctors, incompetent managers can make life worse, make people sicker and less vital...Some managers give themselves heart attacks and nervous breakdowns; still worse many are "carriers," causing their employees to be ill.[16]

Management of self means that you are not acquainted with the concept of failure. It means that a project leader and the team members can make mistakes, but they get those mistakes out of the way as soon as possible, learn as a result of them, and move ahead.

Project leadership can be recognized by outsiders and felt by the project team. Project leadership gives power and significance to the project effort. As noted by Bennis in organizations with effective leaders, four themes are evident:

> *People feel significant.* Everyone feels that he or she makes a difference to the success of the organization. The difference may be small—prompt delivery of potato chips to a mom-and-pop grocery store or development of a tiny but essential part for an airplane. But where they are empowered, people feel that what they do has meaning and significance.
>
> *Learning and competence matter.* Leaders value learning and mastery, and so do people who work for leaders. Leaders make it clear that there is no failure, only mistakes that give us feedback and tell us what to do next.
>
> *People are part of a community.* Where there is leadership, there is a team, a family, a unity. Even people who do not especially like one another feel the sense of community. When Neil Armstrong talks about the Apollo explorations, he describes how a team carried out an almost unimaginably complex set of interdependent tasks. Until there were female astronauts, the men referred to this feeling as "brotherhood." I suggest they rename it "family."
>
> *Work is exciting.* Where there are leaders, work is stimulating, challenging, fascinating, and fun. An essential ingredient in organizational

---

[16] Ibid., p. 10.

leadership is pulling rather than pushing people toward a goal. A "pull" style of influence attracts and energizes people to enroll in an exciting vision of the future. It motivates through identification, rather than through rewards and punishments. Leaders articulate and embody the ideals toward which the organization strives.[17]

In any discussion of project leadership, it is essential to recognize the types of challenges found in running a project—figuring out what to do and how to manage the creation of something that currently does not exist despite uncertainty, diversity, and an enormous number of problems and challenges; and getting a management job done through a diverse set of people despite having little direct control over most of them.

During a project manager's first months on the job, a lot of time is spent establishing where the project is and what plans should be established to get the project moving. In addition to setting plans, effective project leaders usually allocate significant time and effort to begin developing a network of cooperative relationships with the people they feel are needed to bring the project to a favorable outcome. This networking takes up considerable time as cooperative relationships with and among the stakeholders are developed. Project leaders can use a wide variety of face-to-face methods with the stakeholders, such as

- Doing favors for them in expectation of reciprocity

- Stressing the project manager's formal role

- Encouraging and convincing the stakeholders' identification with them

- Nurturing their professional reputation with others

- Maneuvering to make stakeholders feel they are dependent on the project manager for resources to use in their organizational elements

Project leaders can call on peers, corporate staff people, or professionals anywhere in the organization, when necessary, to support the project. Excellent project leaders ask, encourage, cajole, praise, reward, demand, manipulate, use politics, and generally work hard at motivating others through effective interpersonal skills in gaining and holding support for the project.

What should senior managers do to develop leadership capabilities in their project managers? Putting someone in the job because that person is a "good manager" can be risky. Unless the project is easy to

---

[17] Ibid., p. 11.

learn, it can be difficult for an individual to learn fast enough to develop a sound leadership approach; it would also be difficult to build a project stakeholder network quickly enough to effectively manage the project. The best approach would probably be to "grow" your own project managers. These are some of the things that senior executives can do:

- Identify the emerging young professionals who show a potential for leadership and management and put them in charge of one of the many small projects usually found in an organization. This would test the potential mettle of the professionals, expose them to the unstructured, ambiguous ambience of a project, and provide some experience in networking.

- Send the neophyte to a formal training course to open some vistas, but it is highly doubtful that leadership can be learned in a classroom environment. Too often these courses deal with overly simplistic people relationships or suggest some tools such as time management, quantitative methodology, behavioral science, or "how to run meetings" courses, which give little insight into the realities of leading a dynamic project. Nevertheless some formal course work would probably be useful. An alternative would be to encourage the leader-to-be to begin and continue a professional reading program on leadership. By reading several good books on leadership, at least some questions can emerge in the reader's mind as to what knowledge, skills, and attitudes are usually found in effective leaders.

- One of the best things that senior management can do is to maintain ongoing surveillance of the project, evaluating performance, coaching the project leader when required, and ensuring that contemporaneous project management techniques are being used. Indeed, senior managers can set an example of outstanding management, including the integration of the project in the design and execution of enterprise strategies.

Leadership Competencies

The project manager's success as a leader is dependent on a set of personal capabilities. *The project manager should understand the technology involved in the project.* The word *technology* is used in the sense of a method followed to achieve a practical purpose. Under this broad definition, any of the means used to provide useful products and services have a "technology" content. Engineering, science, computers, manufacturing, and after-sales service have obvious elements of technology. Government, educational, military, and ecclesiastical organizations employ elements of technology in meeting their mission and objectives. The technology involved in an engineering school is different from the technology of a school of business. Projects developed within these organizations would require a project manager who had an understanding and mastery of different technologies. A project to develop a new computer would require a different understanding of that technology than the development of a new airplane.

How much depth of understanding should the project manager have in the technology related to the project? There is a risk factor to be considered. If the project manager spends too much time keeping up with the technological details, the managerial aspects of the project could be neglected. A rule of thumb is suggested: The project manager should have enough understanding of the technology of the project to ask the right questions and know if correct answers are being given. If there are detailed or in-depth questions to be asked—and answered—then the project manager should seek the guidance of the appropriate member(s) of the project team. In some cases technological issues may be so important to the project that a task force of experts should be appointed to study the issues and make appropriate recommendations to the project manager.

Another key capability of the successful project manager is to have that blend of interpersonal skills to build the project team, to work with the team and other project stakeholders so that there is a culture of loyalty, commitment, respect, dedication, and trust. The ability to work with and through people—and in so doing win their support—is crucial to the success of the project. As discussed earlier, the project manager must depend on many people from different parts of the project to support the project and to work diligently to give quality results on the work packages for which they are responsible. The ability to function as a *leader* within the context of an acceptable and admired interpersonal style is important. All of us tend to do better when we work with a manager or leader whom we respect, who treats us with respect and dignity, and who is a pleasant person to work with. Also remember, the single greatest cause for failure of managers is their lack of interpersonal skills, a fact that has been demonstrated many times, not only in practice but also in research.

An understanding of the management process is another critical skill required of the project manager. This means that the project manager must know the fundamentals of the management functions of planning, organizing, motivation, direction, and control. The fundamentals that the project manager must know, as well as the project team members, include the fundamentals outlined in this book. People who become project managers and who come from one of the technologies of the project have a particular challenge here. For example, a successful engineer who is appointed to a project manager position will usually have a strong tendency to try to keep fully abreast of engineering considerations in the project. She or he will probably tend to pay more attention to the engineering aspects of the project because that is the portion most easily understood. All that attention to engineering considerations means that less time is available for oversight of the other project work packages—and less time is available to truly perform in a managerial and leadership position on the project.

The ability to see the systems context and strategic context of the project is another characteristic of the skillful project manager. This means that the project is viewed as a set of subsystems or interrelated elements. These interrelated elements operate so that actions taken on one of the elements may produce a change in any of the other elements within the total project system. For example, the model of a project management system given in Chap. 4 carries this important message: The systems framework of managing a project implies that consideration be given to myriad relationships which have both formal and informal implications. A partial or parochial approach to the management of the project will set the stage for difficulties or at best the chance that efficiency and effectiveness will be reduced. In the systems view, the project manager should consider the probable impact of forces outside the project on the project's outcome. In Chap. 6 the idea of project stakeholders is introduced, and the advice was given that the potential impact of stakeholder actions on the project should be one of the considerations in the planning for and execution of decisions on the project. Also, each project is part of a larger system. These larger systems include the political system, the economic system, the technological system, the legal system, the social system, and the competitive system. Within these larger systems there are always forces that can help, or hinder, or even defeat project purposes. A project manager who takes the systems approach in viewing these systems has improved chances for identifying forces outside the project that could influence the project and its outcome.

The project manager needs to know how to make and implement decisions within the systems context of the project. Making a decision requires the management of such fundamentals as

- Defining the decision problem
- Developing the databases required to evaluate the decision
- Considering the alternative ways of using the resources to accomplish the project purposes
- Undertaking an explicit assessment of the risk and cost factors to be considered
- Selecting the appropriate alternative

- Developing an implementation strategy for the selected alternative
- Implementing the decision

The making of decisions is much more complex than is implied in the above fundamentals. However, if these fundamentals are used as a philosophical guide to the making and execution of decisions, the probability of having more timely and successful decisions is enhanced.

Of course the key characteristic of the successful project manager is the ability to produce results—the delivery of the project's technical performance results on time, within budget, and so that a contribution is made to the strategic purpose of the enterprise.

Most of the literature on project management offers additional characteristics—and at times a seemingly endless list—that successful project managers should possess. These characteristics usually include but are not limited to the following:

- Ability to plan and organize the project resources
- Ability to identify and solve problems
- Team-building skills
- Ability to see the big picture
- Financial acumen
- Ability to communicate and resolve conflict
- Negotiation skills
- Creativity and innovation skills

The characteristics of successful project managers are not much different from those of any manager—*except* that project managers must be able to put their *knowledge, skills, and attitudes* to work in the distinctive culture of the management of an ad hoc project. Keep in mind that the project manager manages *the processes* involved in the project work packages arising out of the appropriate functional entities and disciplines supporting the project. As an integrator-generalist, the project manager provides a focus and synergy for the totality of the project work packages—the embodiment of the work packages of the project into an entity that supports organizational strategic purposes. Indeed, the project manager is the *general manager* of the project as far as the enterprise is concerned.

An experienced viewpoint

At a meeting of experienced senior project managers in a large "systems" company chaired by the author, nine of the participants were asked to write down a phrase, word, or sentence describing the characteristics of good project leaders whom they had encountered in their careers. Another eight of these project managers were asked to describe the characteristics of poor project leaders they had known in their careers. The responses of these project managers are shown in Table 16.1. The contrast between good and poor project leaders is evident. You, the reader, should ask yourself how you would describe your own leadership style—and whether you fall under the good or poor leadership column.

Summary

Perhaps more than in any other organizational form, leadership skills are essential in the management of a project. A project by its very nature involves a team composed of diverse people with varied disciplinary backgrounds. The ability to successfully manage a project team, to motivate the people, and to create a cultural and organizational design which is conducive to innovation requires solid leadership knowledge and skills. Project managers have to deal with project team members and other stakeholders over whom they usually have little or no formal authority. As the project is being managed, the project managers have to cross interorganizational and stakeholder lines to gain support and resources to support the project. Even with little formal authority, project managers also have to manage conflict within the project. It is the amalgamation of the technical, organizational, managerial, and social factors that ultimately determines the success of the project.

Lack of leadership may be easier to recognize by team members than by the project leaders themselves. Leaders who surround themselves with people who tend to be mirror images of the leader operate in a "closed system," reinforcing the team's—and the leader's—parochial vision, and oblivious to the lack of leadership effectiveness. When the organization fails, too often it comes as a surprise to the leader, who continued to think that everything was on the right track and the support of the followers was ensured.

Project leaders, like all leaders, depend on their followers, peers, friends, or spouses at critical times. Once the leader recognizes this dependency, then the leader is well advised to build strong networks and alliances with those followers. In the management of a project team, such networking and alliances become critical, for they are the principal means of influencing the team members.

A project leader leads the project team and other principal stakeholders through formal and informal transformation of decision elements into decisive actions in pursuit of agreed objectives and goals. This process entails an interactive complex of project strategy formulation and implementation. It takes time. It is challenging. And stakeholder roles shift during the life cycle of the project.

TABLE 16.1   Good and Poor Project Leaders

Good project leader	Poor project leader
Positive attitude; recognition; knowledgeable supervisor.	Uses authority-position title to direct people—does not try to understand or solve. Does not listen effectively—ignores or rejects input not politically acceptable. Changes scope or direction at will while blaming others for doing the wrong things.
Interest in personal aspects of employees (family situations, etc.); anticipates concerns (problems) before they become evident. Excellent role model; decisive.	
Clearly communicates a vision of what is to be accomplished, who challenges and motivates. Key is that manager gives measurable parameters by which to chart progress. A "results-oriented" manager.	Does not ask for help; does not set an example for the followers; does not know the technical aspects of the process.
Can see a vision of the future for the business, communicates it to the people involved in the business, and allows the personnel involved to make contributions toward the goals. Exhibits trust, support, and willingness to take blame and suffer disappointment, yet still trust and support.	Lets the managers run the business in an undisciplined manner. Does not stay on top of the problems when they arise. Cares only about the bottom line. Does not commend, only criticizes.
	Does not translate the vision (if there is one)—does not explain why. Pays little attention to implementation—"That's just this month's buzzword."
Helps subordinates set a direction for work and allows them to grow toward that goal. Is a mentor, not a master. Knows where everyone is going and why everyone wants to get there—and is able to convince others to follow.	Does not listen to other ideas. Does not know how to constructively criticize. Expects perfection. Does not recognize or compliment a job well done. Discourages creative thought and new ideas.
Sensitive to the effects of decisions on everyone involved. Emphasizes teamwork. Recognizes individuals and groups for contributions. Tries extra hard to relate to subordinates.	Totally focuses on self-promotion. Unenthusiastic. Cannot communicate vision or ideas.
Listens to thoughts and ideas of subordinates. Does not antagonize, but offers criticism. Brings harmony to historically battling departments. Does not just sit in office but goes out into the field.	Is not people-oriented; shows lack of interest; is not forceful enough; has no vision and/or way to implement a vision.
Recognizes a good job and how to do a better job. Notes problems or flaws created.	Communicates through the combination of yelling, waving and pointing of hands, and a dissatisfied look on his or her face. When something does go right, says, "That's not bad, but just make sure you don't do this." In essence, speaks in negative terms only. A true believer in theory X, but does not even know it.
Treats coworkers as human beings, as people rather than just another cog. Asks for input and thoughts on problems; allows subordinates to spend time on projects of their choice. Does not point a finger to place blame, but says, "The problem cannot be undone—what can be done to prevent it in the future?"	

Leaders come in all sizes, shapes, and colors. Although leadership has been exhaustively studied, we still are able to make only some generalizations about its process and attributes. Every person who has responsibility for other people has a leadership role to play. The style of leadership depends on the leader, those being led, and the environment. In general, some of the key characteristics of successful leaders are known.

By drawing on Warren Bennis' ideas, we define project leaders as those people who do the right thing (selecting the objectives, goals, and strategies) and project managers as those who do things right (building the project team and making it work). A person who manages a project should be both a leader and a manager, developing competencies in the management of *attention, meaning, trust,* and *self.*

Discussion Questions

1. Discuss the various definitions of leadership. What traits embody these definitions?

2. What are some of the approaches used in researching leadership? How do these differ?

3. Why has leadership been so difficult to define?

4. Leadership style should not necessarily be consistent in all activities. Explain.

5. Discuss some of the personal characteristics of successful project leaders.

6. What is the difference between leadership and management? What characterizes each?

7. Discuss the fundamental roles of a project manager's leadership position. How do these roles interact?

8. What is meant by *management of attention, management of meaning, management of trust,* and *management of self?*

9. Discuss the four themes that are often evident in organizations with effective leaders.

10. How can project managers establish a network among project stakeholders? Why is this network so important?

11. Discuss the participatory approach to project management. What assumptions define participative management?

12. Discuss some of the characteristics of successful leadership that are documented in the literature.

User Checklist

1. How does your organization define leadership? What traits characterize successful leaders in your organization? Explain.

2. How does your organization build leaders? Are young professionals given the opportunity to learn project management and leadership?

3. What style do leaders of your organization use? Is this style effective? Why or why not?

4. Do the project managers of your organization change their leadership styles to fit various activities? How?

5. Do the managers in your organization understand the difference between leadership and management? Do they develop skills in both areas? Explain.

6. Do project managers in your organization demonstrate competencies in management of attention, meaning, trust, and self? Why or why not?

7. Are the four themes, which are evident in organizations with effective leaders, evident in your organization? Explain.

8. Do the project managers in your organization form networks with project stakeholders? How?

9. What participatory approaches to management are used in your organization? Are these effective leadership tools? Explain.

10. Which of the core dimensions for effective project management are apparent in the leaders of your organization?

11. Where do the project managers and other managers of your organization fall in Table 16-1?

12. How would you judge the overall effectiveness of the leadership in your organization? What could be done to improve the leadership process?

17

Project
Communications

*"Good, the more communicated, more
abundant grows."*
JOHN MILTON, 1608–1674
Paradise Lost

The dictionary defines *communication* as the process by which information is exchanged between individuals through a common system of symbols, signs, or behavior.[1] The importance of communications to the individual engaged in management is singled out by Peter Drucker, who has stated that the ability to communicate heads the list of criteria for success. He notes that one's effectiveness depends on the ability to reach others through the spoken or written word when working in large organizations, and this ability to communicate is perhaps the most important of all the skills an individual can possess.[2]

A survey of U.S. corporations by the *Harvard Business Review* gives some insight into the ability to communicate as a factor in promotability.[3] A portion of this study consisted of a listing of personal attributes and their importance in promotion. Technical skill based on experience placed fourth from the bottom in the list of 22 attributes. Other attributes, such as ambition, maturity, capacity for hard work, ability to make sound decisions, getting things done with and through people,

---

[1] *Webster's New Collegiate Dictionary* (Springfield, Mass.: G. & C. Merriam Company, 1977), p. 228.

[2] Peter F. Drucker, "How to Be an Employee," *Fortune,* May 1952, p. 126.

[3] "What Helps or Harms Productivity," *Harvard Business Review,* January 1964.

flexibility, and confidence, all ranked high. Ability to communicate was at the top of the list.

In project management, the importance of communication is keynoted by Sievert, who says:

> A high percentage of the frictions, frustrations and inefficiencies in our working relationships is traceable to poor communication. In almost every case, the misinterpretation of a design drawing, a misunderstood change order, a missed delivery date or a failure to execute instructions is the result of a breakdown in communication.[4]

Communication Problems

Poor communication involving an error in or misinterpretation of a design drawing can reverberate through a project. One of the most notorious of such errors and subsequent reverberations was on the Diablo Canyon nuclear power plant project in San Luis Obispo, California.[5] One critical part of this project is presented below. The result of breakdown in communications on this project should be apparent to the reader.

On September 22, 1981, the Pacific Gas & Electric Company (PG&E) received its low-power testing license from the Nuclear Regulatory Commission (NRC) for the Diablo Canyon nuclear plant. After 13 years of planning, design, and construction, PG&E expected to begin commercial operation of the plant. This was not to be. On September 27, 1981, PG&E discovered that a serious error had been made which subsequently has been referred to as the "mirror-image error." To better understand the events which led to the mirror-image error and other errors, it is necessary to go back at least four years.[6]

On March 8, 1977, PG&E transmitted unverified, unlabeled, handwritten sketches of the Unit 2 containment geometry to Blume Associates in place of Unit 1 data. The diagrams were not labeled, but Blume correctly interpreted that the sketches were for Unit 2. However, Blume personnel believed Units 1 and 2 were aligned in the same way. That is, Blume assumed that both units had all compo-

---

[4] Richard W. Sievert, Jr., "Communication: An Important Construction Tool," *Project Management Journal,* December 1986, p. 77.

[5] California Public Utilities Commission, Public Staff Division, *Diablo Canyon Rate Case,* vol. 1, *Background, Diablo Canyon Project History,* Prepared Testimony of Bruce Deberry (Public Staff Division), March 1978, pp. 25–27.

[6] U.S. Nuclear Regulatory Commission, Order Suspending License, CLI-81-30, November 19, 1981, PSD Exhibit no. 10,033.

nents facing the same direction. Blume then performed its seismic analysis for Unit 1 on this basis. Blume then returned the information from this analysis to PG&E labeled "Unit 1," when in fact the analysis was really applicable to Unit 2, not Unit 1. PG&E accepted the analysis as representing Unit 1, and knowing that the units were "mirror-image" units, flipped the diagrams to be applicable to the mirror-image unit, Unit 2. In truth, the data were now applicable to Unit 1, not Unit 2. As a result, the seismic analysis for both units was incorrect.[7] This error went undetected for over 4½ years until it was discovered by a PG&E engineer while reviewing various drawings related to the plant.

The events that followed the initial discovery and reporting of this error became increasingly broad in scope and effect. After the initial report of the design error on September 27, 1981, PG&E informed the NRC on October 9, 1981, that both Units 1 and 2 had been designed incorrectly.[8] PG&E committed to the NRC staff to postpone fuel loading and to reanalyze a limited sample of the seismic design of the plant.

The initial review was performed by Robert Cloud Associates, who indicated that the design problems were more pervasive than first thought.[9] The results of this review were orally presented to the NRC at a meeting on November 3, 1981, and in a written report on November 18, 1981. In the Cloud analysis, additional design errors had been discovered.[10] In response, the NRC staff conducted special inspections at the offices of both PG&E and Blume and found that PG&E's quality assurance program did not effectively control the review and approval of design information passed between PG&E and Blume. The investigation also discovered that the design work by Blume had not been covered by a quality assurance program prior to July 12, 1978.[11]

In response to these findings, the NRC commissioners on November 18, 1981, issued an order suspending the low-power license for Diablo

---

[7] B. H. Faulkenberry, et al., Related Report of Seismic Related Errors at DCNPP, Units 1 & 2, U.S. NRC, Region V, NUREG-0862, Issue 1, November 1981, PSD Exhibit no. 10,034.

[8] Letters from Crane to Engelken, October 12, 1981, and November 5, 1981, PSD Exhibit no. 10,035.

[9] R. L. Cloud Associates, Inc., "Preliminary Report, Seismic Reverification Program," November 21, 1981, PSD Exhibit no. 10,036.

[10] Ibid.

[11] NRC Inspection Reports 50-275/81-29 and 50-323/81-18, "Special Inspection of Seismic Related Errors at DC, Units 1 & 2," PSD Exhibit no. 10,037.

Canyon Unit 2 pending satisfactory completion of certain actions, including an independent design verification program (IDVP).[12] This order found that, contrary to PG&E's statements in its operating license application, Diablo might not have been properly designed and violations of the NRC's regulations might have occurred. The NRC indicated that had this information been available previously, the license would not have been issued.[13]

The IDVP was a massive effort. The Bechtel Corporation was hired by PG&E to manage the DVP and complete the plant. The Public Staff Division of the California Public Utilities Commission recommended that its review of the prudence of design and construction of the Diablo Canyon Project that $2.484 billion be disallowed as unreasonable costs on the project due to mirror-image and other design errors and the design verification program that followed during 1981 to 1985.[14]

Project managers and professionals often fail to recognize that communication on a project takes many forms: verbal in-group and individual exchanges of information, and documentation such as design drawings, reports, contracts, work orders, and the like. Lack of quality assurance and control in engineering documentation creates the opportunity for errors by those who use the documentation in their work, as in the situations demonstrated by the Diablo Canyon Project.

A former CEO of an automobile manufacturing enterprise, recalling his failed efforts to upgrade the company's manufacturing capabilities by using project management techniques, felt that his major failure was in not doing a better job of communicating with the people in the organization. His failure to communicate made it impossible for the people to share his vision for the company. The people did not understand—or appreciate—why the organization was being torn apart and realigned, why certain plants had been targeted for closing, or why other changes were underway. He lamented that his inability to communicate caused him to be way out ahead of the people in the company in trying to institute change—but of course since his people were still at the bottom, trying to decide whether or not to go along with the change, the change was not effectively carried out on a timely basis.

---

[12]Order Suspending License, CLI-81-30 dated November 19, 1981, PSD Exhibit no. 10,033.

[13]NRC Letter, Denton to Furbush, November 19, 1981, PSD Exhibit no. 10,038.

[14]Executive Summary, Review of the Costs of PG&E Diablo Canyon Nuclear Power Plant Project and Recommendations on the Amount of Costs Reasonable for PG&E to Recover from Its Customers, by the Diablo Canyon Tear, Public Staff Division, California Public Utilities Commission, San Francisco, May 14, 1987, p. 14.

Information

During the communication process information is shared—information which is needed to make and implement decisions. In the retailing business, Wal-Mart's outstanding management is keyed to information. Samuel Moore Walton, one of the great showmen of retailing, was applying such concepts as a flat organization, empowerment, and gain sharing long before anyone used those terms. He shared information right down to single-store results with the "associates," as Wal-Mart called its employees. Profit sharing, equal to 5 to 6 percent of an associate's earnings, extends to the lowest levels.

Sam Walton had an insatiable hunger for information which in turn facilitated the quick decision making typical of the Wal-Mart culture. Managers gather information from Monday to Thursday, exchange ideas on Friday and Saturday, and implement decisions in the store on Monday.

Walton often spoke with genuine admiration for his competitors—he knew them intimately and copied their best ideas.[15]

The Process of Communication

In this chapter some basic ideas will be presented to bring attention to the role that the art of communication plays in the management of projects. We will also discuss some things that can be done to improve communication within the project team.

A project manager uses communication more than any other force in the project environment to ensure that team members work together on project problems and opportunities. The means and channels of information include

- Plans
- Policies
- Procedures
- Objectives
- Goals
- Strategies
- Organizational structure
- Linear responsibility charts
- Leader and follower style

---

[15]Bill Saporito, "What Sam Walton Taught America," *Fortune,* May 4, 1992, pp. 104–106.

- Meetings
- Letters
- Telephone calls
- Small group interaction
- Example set by the project manager

The above partial list strongly suggests that an important function of the project manager is to manage the process of communications with the project stakeholders. However, to manage the communications process, one must understand the nature of that process.

Communication is the process by which information is exchanged between individuals through a common system of symbols, signs, or behavior. People communicate with each other by three principal means: by an actual physical touch, such as a tap on the shoulder, a pat on the back, or the ritualistic expression of the handshake; by visible movements of some portions of their bodies, such as the pointing of a finger, the wink of an eye, a smile, a nod, or a grimace; and by the use of symbols, spoken or portrayed, which have some meaning based on experience.

Most present-day failures in communication can be traced to misunderstandings of the symbols that play an important part in the process of human communication. Such misunderstandings come about largely because of our inadequacies in creating, transmitting, and receiving these symbols, both written and spoken. People on a project team will readily recognize the value that symbols have in communicating phenomena in the engineering disciplines. Unfortunately the symbols that are used in communication in the management discipline are not so precise in their meaning.

Words and combinations of words give us more difficulty in communicating than other kinds of visual symbols. Take the word *manage* as an example. The *American Heritage Dictionary of the English Language*[16] defines *manage* as follows:

> 1. To direct or control the use of; handle, wield, or use (a tool, machine, or weapon). 2. To exert control over; make submissive to one's authority, discipline, or persuasion. 3. To direct or administer (the affairs of an organization, estate, household, or business). 4. To contrive or arrange; succeed in doing or accomplishing, especially with difficulty: *I'll manage to come on Friday—intr.* 1. To direct, supervise, or carry on business affairs; perform the duties of a manager. 2. To carry on; get along: *I don't know how they manage without him.*

---

[16] Boston: Houghton Mifflin, 1976, p. 792.

The term *management* is defined as

> 1. The act, manner, or practice of managing, handling, or controlling something. 2. The person or persons who manage a business establishment, organization or institution. 3. Skill in managing; executive ability.

The real meaning of words—or symbols—depends primarily on how the reader or listener perceives them. A word such as *management* would have one meaning for a corporate executive and another meaning for a union executive. The meaning would depend on the image that the word holds for the individual. Such meaning is something we have inside ourselves. Words and phrases that an individual uses may not evoke the same image in someone else's mind; knowing this, one should be as specific as possible in using words. Assuming that everyone knows what you are talking about is usually a poor assumption. Lewis Carroll's way of hinting at the dilemma of spoken communication points out how many of us feel about our use of the spoken word in our communication attempts: "When I use a word," Humpty Dumpty said in rather a scornful tone, "it means just what I choose it to mean—neither more nor less."[17]

Some writers have used models in explaining the communication process. For example, Gibson, Ivancevich, and Donnelly use the model depicted in Fig. 17.1. The elements of their model include

Source—the originator of the communication

Encoder—the oral or written symbols used to transmit the message

Message—what the source hopes to communicate

Channel—the medium used to transmit the message

---

[17]Lewis Carroll, *Alice's Adventures in Wonderland and Through the Looking Glass*, 4th printing (New York: Macmillan & Co., 1966).

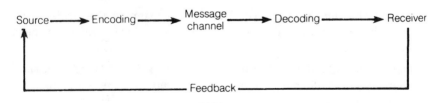

.... = Noise

Source: James L. Gibson, John M. Ivancevich, and James H. Donnelly, Jr., *Organizations, Structure, Processes, Behavior,* (Dallas, Tex.: 1973), Business Publications, 166.

Figure 17.1 A communications model.

Decoder—interpretation of the message by receiver

Receiver—recipient for whom the message is intended

Feedback—information used to determine the fidelity of the message

Noise—anything that distorts, distracts, misunderstands, or interferes with the communication process

The model shows the elements involved in the communication process. A project manager should realize that communication is the capstone of the management functions of planning, organizing, motivating, directing, and controlling; without effective communications these management functions cannot be carried out adequately.

Informal Communication

The above model portrays the formal communication that is carried out usually through the organization portrayed by the traditional organizational chart and by the linear responsibility chart. But there also is an *informal organization.* Membership in this informal organization is dependent on common ties, such as friendship, kinship, social status, etc. The need for an informal as well as a formal organization lies in both the psychological and the social needs of human beings and their desire to accomplish personal and organizational objectives. People join informal groups at their place of work for social contact, companionship, emotional support, and such things of value coming out of a particular community to which an individual belongs.[18]

What can the project manager do about the communications within the informal organization? His or her interpersonal style of management will probably have some effect on these informal communications. We offer a few suggestions in this matter:

- Accept the notion of informal communication in the project and what such communication can do and not do for enhancing project effectiveness.

- Find ways of getting feedback from the informal organization. Identify the "informal leaders," and spend time listening to what they have to say.

- Use these informal leaders as a source for testing technical approaches, ideas, strategies, administrative actions, reorganiza-

---

[18] Ross A. Webber, *Management* (Homewood, Ill.: Irwin, 1975), chap. 21, for a thorough discussion of groups and informal organization.

tions, and other things whose acceptance by the members of the project team is required for success.

- Recognize that much of the cultural ambience of the project is reflected in the attitudes and behavior of people in the informal organization. Insofar as possible, work with the informal organization in support of organizational purposes.[19]

Listening

Good listening is a skill that some people have and others lack. To become a good listener, a person must work at developing this skill by studying good listening practices and applying them to his or her own conscious program of self-development.

The importance of listening is underscored graphically by a Sperry advertisement that appeared in the *Wall Street Journal.* The ad read, in part, "It's about time we learned how to listen....[There's] the problem of people not knowing how to listen. Most of us spend about half our waking hours listening. Yet research studies show that we retain only 25 percent of what we listen to....Because listening is the one communication skill we're never really taught..."[20]

A project is tied together by its system of communications. Perceptive project managers are discovering that communication hinges on both the spoken word and the ability to listen to what the other person is saying. Often members of the project team overlook listening. It is the most important link in the project communications, and it is usually the weakest one. Even with good listening, retention is a problem. Right after we listen to someone talk, we remember only about half of what has been heard. Even after we have learned something, we tend to forget from one-half to one-third of it within 8 hours. Part of the problem of poor listening is a lack of training in listening skills. Yet experience demonstrates that if one is a careful listener, one starts getting some answers. Also there are some emotionally based reasons for not ignoring the need to develop better listening skills:

- Listening may uncover some unexpected problems; it is more comfortable not to listen, to ignore unsavory news that might make the project manager fearful of the project's status.

---

[19] Some of the material in the two preceding sections has been paraphrased from D. I. Cleland and D. F. Kocaoglu, *Engineering Management* (New York: McGraw-Hill, 1981), pp. 124–125.

[20] *Wall Street Journal,* September 11, 1979, p. 11.

- Team members may withhold bad news in the futile hope that the problem will work itself out.

- People, managers included, really do not want to tell a superior bad news. This probably accounts for the fact that bad news simply does not flow uphill in organizations. If the manager communicates in any way that he or she does not want to listen to bad news, there will be no bad news to listen to.

- People really don't want to listen to anything that is contrary to their preconceived ideas or prejudices.

- People can think faster than they can listen. In conversation, particularly heated ones, we tend to race ahead, thinking through a response, and in so doing we lose touch with what the speaker is saying.

- For some reason people listen to get the "facts" and miss the main idea or ideas of what the speaker is saying.

- We mentally turn off what we do not want to hear—our emotions act as aural filters.

- When someone says what we really want to hear, we are "all ears."

- When we hear something that opposes our deeply rooted preconceived notions, our brains become involved in planning a rebuttal or a response intended to put down or put the speaker on the defensive.

It is much easier and more comfortable to talk down to subordinates than it is to talk up to superiors. Conversely, it is much easier to listen to superiors (because we have to) than to subordinates (because we may feel that we do not really have to talk to them). Often we do so only to be polite.

Project communication—including listening—is carried out with project professionals, work package managers, functional managers, general managers, service managers, customers, subcontractors, and other stakeholders. The building and maintenance of alliance with these stakeholders require that avenues be opened so that messages can flow. Perhaps the most obvious and effective method is the human chain of people talking to people. The human chain has potential, but often it does not work for these reasons:

- Without good listeners, people do not talk freely and there is not an effective flow of communications.

- Only one bad listener is required to impair the flow of communication.

- There may be a flow of messages, but they can be distorted because of noise along the communication network.

The first step to improve the flow of communication among the stakeholders must be taken by the project manager, who must listen to everything and must set an example by letting the project stakeholders know that they will be listened to with empathy. When the stakeholders feel the need to talk, one remedy is to be a nondirective and nonjudgmental listener. The project manager hears, tries to understand but above all during the oral discourse refrains from interjecting personal thoughts or indicating disapproval by speech, manner, or gestures. It requires discipline to be a nondirective listener; this discipline is attained primarily through practice. Project managers can be in a position of power. There is the danger that they will wield that power by speaking, when in fact being an effective listener will help them to find out things that are causing problems for the project. The discovery of a problem, such as a cost overrun on a segment of the project, requires the right kind of communication skills. Nonverbal communication skills play an important role here, often expressed in the management style of the project manager and the senior managers of the organization. Davis has commented on the role of communication and its relationship to management style in encouraging frankness and integrity in the management of a project.[21]

Listening can be disturbing, for it may uncover problems and cast doubt about an existing strategy. Consider the ill-fated space shuttle Challenger that was destroyed on January 28, 1986.

In the aftermath of the accident, the presidential commission chaired by William Rogers conducted a wide-ranging investigation of the accident and of NASA decision making leading up to the accident.[22] While the immediate attention was directed at the cause of the accident, the commission soon expanded the focus of the investigation from equipment to NASA management decision making.

In the hearings, a significant amount of information was made public which showed that the engineering staffs of NASA and the Morton Thiokol Corporation (prime contractor for the solid fuel rocket booster) expressed doubts about both the design of and the effects of cold weather on the O-ring seals. Similar concerns had been expressed by Rockwell International Corporation's engineers and management (the builders of the shuttle orbiter) about the effects of cold and ice on other elements of the shuttle system. NASA and Morton Thiokol reports have since surfaced which document a suspected problem with the seals dating back over 8 years prior to the ill-fated launch.

---

[21] Sievert, op. cit.

[22] *Report of the Presidential Commission on the Space Shuttle Challenger Accident,* Washington, D.C., June 6, 1986.

The Rogers commission concluded that sufficient evidence had existed to postpone that Challenger launch, and that a critical problem existed with the design of the seals. Testimony was presented which indicated that NASA middle managers either disregarded or did not give sufficient credence to the warnings of contractors and engineers. Furthermore, higher levels of NASA managers, who had responsibility for the final decision to launch, were not even informed of the significant technical concerns which had been expressed. Thus, the commission concluded that there were serious flaws in the managerial decision-making and communication process and that safety concerns were deemphasized in favor of preserving the flight schedule. If more effective communication had existed on that program, perhaps the accident could have been prevented. One thing is clear—the key managers on that program were not good listeners. Perhaps they did not want to be.

Sometimes it is more comfortable not to listen, to ignore those subtle hints that might indicate a problem. For example, in the interest of completing a project quickly, a project owner may choose not to hear the conceptual estimator's claim that the cost of implementing the project design may not meet the budget constraints. Eager to proceed with the project, the owner may choose not to evaluate why the project costs may exceed the budget. A burning desire to complete the project may blind the owner to the possibility that the overall project may not be economically feasible.[23]

The principal reasons why communication on a project can be a problem for the project manager are as follows:

- People withhold information on a problem in the hope that the problem will go away.

- Team members are reluctant to share information which might be critical to the success of the project. They want to protect their territory and perhaps their jobs.

- The project manager maintains one-way contact with the team members, speaking but neglecting to listen. He or she issues orders, gives briefings, submits direction for contract changes, but fails to seek feedback to see if everyone understands and is committed to what is going on.

- The project review meetings, which should maximize the two-way flow of information, turn out to be one-person shows, with the project manager talking, not listening. If the functional and work package managers practice the same style, one can imagine the lack of communication on the project.

---

[23] Sievert, op. cit.

- If the people, at whatever level on the project, do not understand the communication process, then faulty communication is bound to exist.

Nonverbal Communication

A part of communication that is all too often ignored is the subtle hidden messages that people send out through nonverbal means.

As we consider nonverbal communication, a whole series of physical gestures come to mind: facial expressions, nodding, hand and body movements, eye movements, etc. Those of us who have visited the modern version of a burlesque theater would surely recognize the value of nonverbal communications in certain situations.

It would be difficult to portray nonverbal communication as formal or informal, since it depends on the context in which it is carried out. All of what we say, or do, and our style of listening play a role in our communication which is subject to interpretation by others. Even a failure to act is a way of communication.

Porter divides nonverbal communication into four categories:

- *Physical.* The personal type of communication, including facial expressions, tone of voice, sense of touch, sense of smell, and body motions.

- *Aesthetic.* Creative expressions, such as playing instrumental music, dancing, painting, and sculpturing.

- *Signs.* Mechanical communication, such as the use of signal flags, the 21-gun salute, horns, and sirens.

- *Symbolic.* Religious, status, or ego-building symbols.[24]

Team leaders need to be aware of nonverbal communication. By observing the nonverbal cues leaders can have insight into the success they are having in interacting with the team members. Team members display attitudes and feelings through nonverbal communication. If the project leader and the team members are aware of the physical gestures in communication, the chances are improved for having an open, honest team that can deal with conflict in a forthright manner.

Regardless of your position in the project team, it is important to develop an appreciation of the uses and limitations of nonverbal communication. Being aware of the possibility of what nonverbal cues can

---

[24] George W. Porter, "Non-Verbal Communications," *Training and Development Journal,* June 1969, pp. 3–8. Copyright © 1969, *Training and Development Journal,* American Society for Training and Development. Reprinted with permission. All rights reserved.

transmit can keep the project team working toward more effective understanding of what the project team is really saying.

For example, a project director in a huge aerospace company called a meeting of higher management people who supported his research project. He wanted them to fund development of a new project internally. Early in the meeting, as he began to outline the sizable costs involved, he sensed their disapproval from facial expressions and body postures. His intuition told him that if they were asked to make an explicit decision on the project, it would be negative. So he changed his line of argument and began stressing the possibilities for external rather than internal funding of the project. And he assiduously avoided asking for a funding decision at that time.[25]

Our physical actions, dress, manner, and language all communicate things to others about us. The project manager's interactions with the project stakeholders are affected by what they behold in her or his imagery, physical setting, and body language—and by what the project manager learns about them through their actions.

Written Communications

In project management, written communications include proposals, reports, plans, policies, procedures, letters, memoranda, and other forms of transmitting information. Writing effectively is an art and a skill, to be practiced at all times. Writing is a highly developed and very complicated part of communication. All people on a project team work at writing something to convey meaning to the reader. To serve this purpose, the message must be easily understood when it is quickly read. A well-written document reflects the writer's knowledge of the subject. The message is simple, clear, and direct.

The field of writing is so huge that we have neither the space nor the time to put much together on this subject. All professionals and managers should be able to find ample readings and courses on how to overcome their writing deficiencies. In this chapter we have provided only a few key suggestions on how to improve the writing deficiencies all too common in project management documentation.

The most important question that the project people can ask themselves is, Have we written our message clearly? There is nothing more important to a project team than being understood. A message should be easy to understand and informative.

Project proposals are one of the most important communication tools. Reports run a close second in importance. A proposal or report which uses simple, understandable language and uses tables, bar

---

[25]Michael B. McCaskey, "The Hidden Messages Managers Send," *Harvard Business Review,* November-December 1979, p. 145.

charts, pie charts, and graphs effectively will be more understandable to readers than one filled with technical jargon, vague concepts, and ambiguous language.

Effective writing depends on adequate preparation, based on selecting, analyzing, and organizing ideas required to communicate the intended message. Many processes have been suggested for preparing a written document; we have found the following steps useful:

First, think through the ideas you want to express in the written document. Build a "model" of the message in your mind. Do not start serious writing until you have a reasonably final model of what you want to say. On major documents such as reports, plans, and proposals, this step requires the project manager to work closely with the project team in "getting their arms around" the problem or opportunity.

Second, establish the basic purpose of the message. What are the general and specific purposes? Is the general purpose to direct, inform, question, or persuade? The specific purpose may be obvious or require thought and analysis. It is important that you take adequate time to define the specific purpose clearly; otherwise, it may be difficult to transmit a clear message to the intended receiver. The basic purpose of the message can be clarified in the next step.

Third, collect and analyze the qualitative and quantitative database of facts and assumptions bearing on the purposes of the message. Depending on the purpose of the message, detailed analysis may be required.

Fourth, organize the material into topics and subtopics in some logical sequence. Examine the way the material hangs together: Does the grouping make sense? Is the sequencing proper? If not, rework.

Fifth, prepare the first draft of the message. For short messages, this should be easy. For longer messages, including letters, papers, reports, and so on, this will require considerable effort. Concentrate on one section of the draft at a time and revise as required; do not try to write the entire message and then revise it in its entirety. After each section is finished, sit back and reflect on how it all fits together. Then set the first draft aside and let it "incubate" before beginning the first revision. Ask yourself these questions:

- Is it objective?
- Is it logical?
- Are there any fallacies in the reasoning behind the message?
- Did you say what you intended?
- Is there too much (not enough) detail?
- Does the main text of the message flow smoothly in a clear and logical manner?

Sixth, check out the message for acceptable grammar, spelling, punctuation, format, numbering, abbreviations, and the use of the right words and phrases.

Seventh, if the message is a report, does it follow this conventional structure?

I. Summary

II. Introduction

III. Discussion

IV. Observations, conclusions, recommendations

Finally, send the message. If you have carried out these steps diligently, the chances are very good that the receiver will get the message.

Project Meetings

The effectiveness of the meetings that the project team joins will tell a good deal about the sensitivity of the project manager to communications. Most meetings are poorly conceived and run; managers and professionals dislike meetings, particularly if the meetings are called by someone else. All would agree that well-run meetings are an effective focus around which the project can be managed. Many important matters on a project can be resolved by the project manager's working individually with the team members by telephone, conversation with individuals, or a brief ad hoc meeting with several team members. There is, however, value in getting all the team members together at scheduled times to talk and listen about the project.

Purpose

Project meetings serve several important functions:[26]

The meeting helps to define the major team players and the project. Those attending belong to the project team and other stakeholders; those who are absent do not.

The meeting provides an opportunity to revise, update, and add to the store of knowledge that the team possesses. This knowledge includes facts, perceptions, experience, judgment, and folklore. The information that the team has acquired separately or in smaller meetings is important to the cohesiveness and strength of the team's

---

[26] These functions are paraphrased from Antony Jay, "How to Run a Meeting," *Harvard Business Review,* March-April 1976, pp. 120–134.

role of knowing the cost, schedule, and technical performance status of the project.

Meetings can help the team members know where the individual parts fit into the general collective aim of the group, and where individual success can contribute to team success.

A meeting also helps team members to become and remain committed to the project. By participating in decisions affecting the project team members, they will feel an obligation to accept the decision even though they may have argued against it during the team meeting. Many times opposition to a project decision arises out of not being consulted rather than the decision itself. Then, too, a project team decision is much harder to challenge than a decision by an individual.

A project team meeting may be the only time where the team actually exists and works as a group and the only time that the project leader has visibility as the project manager leading the team.

A meeting is a status arena, one place for team members to play out their roles. A meeting may be the only time when members get the chance to find out their relative standing on the team.

Finally, a meeting provides the collective opportunity to pull together all the information on the project to see what action should be taken and to provide information on an individual work package.

By its nature, the project management process requires many meetings. Successful meetings do not just happen; many meetings suffer from

- Domination of the discussions by certain vocal members.
- The lack of an agenda around which to focus the discussions; consequently the discussions ramble.
- Domination of the discussion by the chairperson of the meeting, who fails to draw out the more reticent participants.
- The lack of firm starting and stopping times.
- People reading or talking among themselves, distracting others, and becoming nonparticipants in what is going on in the meeting.
- Avoidance of the meeting because it is emotionally upsetting to some team members.

How to manage project meetings

It is believed that project managers spend at least 90 percent of their time communicating with team members, superiors, peers, colleagues, stakeholders, and others who have—or believe they have—a vested interest in the project. The increasing use of project management, particularly in the context of international work, has posed new challenges for communicating about the project. Video conferencing is a recent innovation that promises to expand the ability of the project team to better communicate.

The ability to communicate during project meetings is an important attribute for the project manager and other team members.

A project meeting can be productive. It is an efficient way to share information, obtain immediate feedback on issues or questions, or clarify an unclear point. Meetings can save time that would be spent otherwise sending and answering memoranda, making telephone calls, or waiting for inquiries. By far the greatest value of a meeting is to bring collective judgment to project problems and opportunities.

The chairperson of the meeting has the responsibility to plan, host, and lead the meeting to establish the proper climate. That climate and the feeling conveyed to the participants will have a great impact on the outcome of the meeting. The chairperson must guide, stimulate, clarify, control, summarize, and evaluate the outcome in terms of the meeting objective, keeping in mind her or his responsibility for managing the project.

A meeting, even a conference with another person, is a managerial activity and can be looked at from the standpoint of the management functions of planning, organizing, and controlling. Using these management functions as a guide, we can suggest a strategy to prepare for and conduct a meeting. Planning and organizing a meeting consist of several actions, which include

- Determining the objective, or expected output, of the meeting
- Preparing the agenda
- Selecting and inviting the participants
- Determining the timing and physical arrangements
- Considering matters of protocol such as seating, introduction of newcomers, notification of attendees, etc.
- Preparing and distributing materials required for participant study

A key question to consider when you are planning a meeting is simply this: Is this meeting really necessary? In this context Jay has noted: "The most important question you should ask is: 'What is this meeting intended to achieve?' You can ask it in different ways—'What would be the likely consequences of not holding it?' 'When it is over, how shall I judge whether it was a success or a failure?'"[27]

Often the need for a meeting can be eliminated by judicious analysis of a problem before people are called together to seek some solution. A

---

[27] Ibid., p. 47.

practical process to reduce the number of meetings is to prepare a brief, informal memorandum to yourself that addresses these questions:

1. What is the issue (specific problem or opportunity) for which the meeting should be held? Many times meetings are held without any definition of what the output of the meeting will be.

2. What are the facts? Problems or opportunities do not exist in an information vacuum. There are some facts that bear on the situation, that cause the problem or suggest the opportunity.

3. What are the potential alternatives or solutions—and the associated costs and benefits that relate to these alternatives? Even a cursory thought about alternatives can prove useful in deciding whether a meeting should be held.

4. What specific recommendations can be proposed to deal with the problem or opportunity at this time, and could be suggested to the meeting participants?

5. What will happen if the meeting is not held?

Answering all these questions should help you find a solution and possibly eliminate the need for the meeting. Even a project team member who wishes to meet with the project manager will find that trying to answer these questions will reduce the frequency with which he or she needs to consult with the team leader.

Part of the planning for a meeting is a plan for the organization of the meeting. Motivating, leading, and controlling the meeting are the chairperson's responsibility. Given the agenda as a standard, the activities to be carried out by the meeting leader include the following:

- Seeking points of agreement or disagreement
- Limiting discussion
- Encouraging all to participate
- Periodically summarizing points of agreement or disagreement
- Identifying action items to be investigated by individual members
- Adhering to time limits for starting, stopping, and dealing with agenda items
- Reinforcing the objective and expected outcome of the meeting
- Encouraging and controlling disagreements
- Taking time during the meeting to assess how well things are going and what might be done to improve the effectiveness of the discussion
- Making sure each agenda item has a time allocation

- Providing for all participants to express their ideas and recommendations without interrupting or degrading their comments
- Listening to everything
- Playing down nonrelevant issues, perceptions, and personal speculations as soon as possible, before they can become disruptive
- Stopping the discussion and redirecting the meeting as needed
- Always being patient
- Making the decisions that the meeting is to bring into focus

One of the clearest signals that the chairperson is not doing the job is that he or she does most of the talking. The chairperson's greatest influence stems from the participants' perception of his or her commitment to the objectives of the meeting and skill and efficiency in helping the participants in meeting that objective.

If minutes are to be kept of the meeting (certainly recommended during the project planning, organizing, and evaluating meetings), then brevity is desirable. The minutes should include these facts:

- Times started and ended, date, place of meeting, and list of participants with their project role
- Agenda items discussed and decisions reached or held for further study
- Enumeration of action items and person(s) responsible for follow-up and reporting back to project team
- Time, date, place, and instructions for the next meeting

Meetings are an essential process of management. Depending on how they are run, they can improve or impair communications, promote or discourage cooperation, encourage or discourage people. The value of an effective meeting is that it can serve as a cornerstone for successful team building and for planning and evaluating progress on the project, as well as a communications link between the project stakeholders.

Technology is changing the way we communicate.

The Role of Technology

Teleconferencing is a growing use of technology to facilitate the management of a project, particularly a project where the key team members are geographically separated. Some project managers have found that teleconferencing is a useful substitute for business travel. When teleconferencing is used in lieu of face-to-face meetings, there tends to be far less socializing and chitchatting before the meeting starts, and the participants tend to stick with the agenda better.

Electronic mail has become a medium to unite people rather than through meetings and paperwork. Electronic mail has gained increasing acceptance as a substitute for regular mail, memoranda, and other means of written and verbal communication. Since E-Mail saves time and storage space and is much faster than regular written communication, it is, if properly used, a means of increasing productivity.

Another technological application is the electronic bulletin boards. An electronic bulletin board enables a message originator to post a message on the "board" so that anyone connected with the computer network can see it. Readers can read the message and then express their opinions by posting their own messages.

Groupware—computer software explicitly designed to support the collective work of teams—can facilitate the discussions carried out in project teams and accomplish the project work in much less time than needed to have team members attend meetings. In one case at Boeing Company, a team composed of engineers, designers, machinists, and manufacturing managers used Team Focus software from IBM to design a standardized control system for complex machine tools in several plants. Normally, such a job would have required more than a year—with electronic meetings it was done in 35 days.

At IBM the development of the 9370 mainframe computer was carried out through organizational networking. The objective was to develop, build, and get the complex machine to market quickly with minimal use of the corporate hierarchy. Many IBM people collaborated from the research laboratories, manufacturing plants, suppliers, marketing groups, and distribution centers around the world. The project team members were linked by electronic mail, teleconferencing, and other communications channels into ad hoc project teams, multidisciplinary conferences, and the like.[28]

Consider that the typical manager spends somewhere between 30 and 70 percent of the day in meetings. Even in the best-run meetings you seldom get all the latent best ideas out of people; some people remain shy, feel they are juniors in the meeting, feel intimidated, or are just too polite to say anything that might be adversarial or might challenge a superior. Then, too, research has shown that 20 percent of the people in a meeting do 80 percent of the talking.

In electronic meetings comments can be kept anonymous. This can be a powerful incentive to speak out.

Groupware is helping teams to function more efficiently and can help to move the company toward a more team-focused organization. Groupware, when properly used, can improve the quality and productivity of meetings. A team of people can reach a genuine consensus;

---

[28] Fred V. Guterl, "Goodbye Old Matrix," *Business Month,* February 1989, pp. 32–38.

members become more committed and feel more a part of the substantive process of what is going on in the team electronic meeting.

The strategy seems to be to use Groupware to integrate people into team-based organizations. It can be used for any type of project that requires groups of people to work together, as in product-process design teams engaged in simultaneous engineering. When a dramatic change in the market requires immediate and coordinated strategies to develop a countervailing strategy, group computing can achieve a consensus, even when people are geographically separated, in much less time. A strategic planning meeting that used to take 2 days can be done in 3 or 4 hours. When group computing is used, it is a "nondiscriminating" meeting—you don't know if the messages are coming from juniors, seniors, men, women, minority persons, or those people who have vested interests in what is being discussed. The technology of group computing makes people equal not in terms of power but in terms of being heard.

There are drawbacks: The verbal cues that can indicate how a person feels about an issue are lacking. Without the "eyeball-to-eyeball" contact, people's attention can wander. By putting so much on the electronic networks, management can learn a lot more about what is going on in the organization and how people are feeling. For some people this could be viewed as an invasion of personal privacy. Whatever the shortcomings, group computing can open new avenues for productivity and consensus building in the organization. As computers become smaller, electronic meetings can be held anywhere— wherever you have your computer. All this could lead to drastic population dispersal—keep in mind that our cities and the transportation to those cities—have been built so that people can *physically* work together. Now, with electronic meetings people can get together and *communicate intellectually* through the computers. A lesson to consider: In the future when you go on vacation, do not take your computer with you![29]

Communication Links

In the most general sense, the project manager needs to maintain communication links with all the project stakeholders. However, certain stakeholders require direct and ongoing communication:

- Customers (owners, users)
- Project team members

---

[29] David Kirkpatrick, "Here Comes the Payoff from PCs," *Fortune*, March 23, 1992, pp. 93–102.

- General managers
- Functional managers
- Regulatory agencies
- Subcontractors

Communication with all these stakeholders is important; the customer stands out as the most important of all.

There are a few key objectives in communicating with the customer that the project manager and the project team should keep in mind:

- Never surprise the customer. Keep the customer informed of anything that has affected or could affect the schedule, cost, or technical performance objectives of the project.

- Don't depend on formal reports to keep the customer fully informed. An excellent practice is for the project manager to keep in touch on a regular basis by telephone and visits with the customer. During these periods any items of progress or lack thereof can be brought to the customer's attention. If a problem has developed on the project, let the customer know even if a solution is not apparent. The customer will appreciate this news and might be able to help in designing a solution.

- Always follow up any customer question or concern with an action item, with someone designated as the action person to follow up and report back to the project manager. When an answer or solution is available, inform the customer. During the interim keep the customer informed of the progress.

- Remember that the customer has to be happy with the project's progress and its results. Build your customer communication philosophy around this objective.

Management of the project team depends so much on information and communication—and knowledge flows through people who are dealing with the different technologies needed to bring the project objectives into focus. Given the knowledge, skills, and attitudes of the project team, the willingness of team members to engage in ongoing conversation about the project is necessary to keep everyone informed of the project's status. Also an important benefit is that this bonds the team together. Conversation is important within the team itself but also with the project stakeholders who are external to the team's organization. Customers, suppliers, regulators, local community leaders, and other important stakeholders have to be engaged in continuous conversation to bond them to the project as well as keep them advised of what is going on and how their interests are being affected and are likely to be affected by the project itself. Keeping the project stakeholders informed at all times can do much to reduce the fear that they might have of the compromise of their stakes in the project. Conversation also helps to build trust and project team loyalty.

Information and conversation do much to penetrate the organizational and disciplinary boundaries that exist in any project. The larger the project, the greater the likelihood that there will be more complex boundaries.

Summary

Good communication and good project management are matched pairs in the successful completion of a project. A project manager gets the project done through people. To do this, effective communication is a must. The most effective communication is two-way between the sender and the receiver. Both understand and accept the message that is transmitted. If the message has not been understood, communication has not really taken place.

Communication is both formal and informal. Verbal communication and nonverbal communication play roles in getting your message across. Listening is an important communication skill—and a skill that all of us need to improve.

Project meetings are opportunities to improve the flow of communication on a project. By using the management functions of planning, organizing, motivation, directing, and control as reference points, the efficacy of the project meetings can be improved.

Communication should be carried out on an ongoing basis with all the stakeholders so that their roles in the project can be understood and accounted for in the management of the project.

Close communication from the start helps members of the project team understand how to deal with the different objectives of their various departments. This communication also helps the project leader understand enough of the team member's language and the technological nature of the work to do a better job of leading and managing the team. Building better bonds of communication also helps to facilitate more effective interaction among the specialists. The best way to transfer technology is through "people links" or face-to-face transfer of information. Close communication also is necessary to keep continual consultations and face-to-face status reports, so that members know what is going on and what is needed to keep members informed about priorities and resources. Information is at the heart of the process of making and implementing decisions in the management of project resources. Without adequate and relevant information, the management process cannot be carried out properly. Once available, this information has to be communicated to the people who need it. These people include the managers and professionals in the enterprise, the professionals on the project team, the suppliers, customers, regulatory agencies—indeed, with anyone who sees the enterprise as providing something of value to a person or persons.

In organizations that have failed, the lack of information or inadequate information is often at the heart of those failures. To manage without adequate and relevant information is like flying blind, with unknown mountains ahead!

Discussion Questions

1. Explain why the ability to communicate is among the most often cited attributes of successful project managers.

2. Describe a project management situation from your work or school experience. What communication problems affected the project? How?

3. What are some of the means by which information is communicated on a project? In what kinds of situations are each of these most effective?

4. Define communication in terms of the elements in the communication process. Define each of the elements.

5. Listening is often the most important aspect of good communication. Why is this factor often ignored? What can managers do to increase their listening skills?

6. Discuss nonverbal communication. How can a manager use an understanding of nonverbal communication in determining what project team members are really saying?

7. Describe some of the important steps in the preparation of a written document. What role do written documents play in the communication process?

8. Why are team meetings important for project communications? What steps can a project manager take in order to hold effective meetings?

9. What planning must be done in order to ensure an effective meeting process?

10. How might technology improve the effectiveness of communication in the management of a project?

11. What are some of the communication links that a project manager must control? What can be done to manage these links?

12. What are some of the other things that management can do to ensure good communication throughout the organization?

User Checklist

1. How would you judge the ability of the project managers in your organization with respect to communications? Explain.

2. What kinds of communication problems are often experienced on projects within your organization? How are these problems usually managed?

3. What methods do the project managers in your organization use to communicate information? Are the methods used usually effective for the particular situation? Why or why not?

4. Do the project managers of your organization listen to the problems and suggestions of project team members? How can they improve their listening skills?

5. What nonverbal communications are often used by project team members? Do project managers recognize and interpret nonverbal communications? Explain.

6. Are the written documents (policies, reports, etc.) from project managers effective at presenting information? What is lacking in these written reports? What can be done to improve their effectiveness?

7. How effective is the communication process during project team meetings? Do project leaders usually control project meetings? Explain.

8. How often are team meetings held? Do project team members understand the purpose of team meetings and their roles in the meetings? Why or why not?

9. Are project team meetings planned and organized ahead of time? Why or why not?

10. Has the organization fully exploited the use of technology to improve communications in the management of the project?

11. Do project managers manage the various communication links within and external to the organization? What are some of these links?

12. How would you judge the overall effectiveness of the communication process in your organization? How can the process be improved?

18

Working with Project Teams[1]

"A community is like a ship; every one ought
to be prepared to take the helm."
HENRIK IBSEN, 1828–1906
An Enemy of the People

The Hughes Electronics factory "High Bay" in El Segundo near Los Angeles International Airport might appear unusual by traditional norms of manufacturing. There are no assembly lines, no conveyor belts, and no grinding machine tools. Workers gather around a half-dozen shiny objects which create a "Star Wars" ambience. High Bay is where Hughes finishes satellites before launching them into space. Most of the satellites are old-fashioned telecommunication relays that will handle international calls. But the star of High Bay is a 14-foot cube, a so-called body-stabilized satellite model HS-601. Hughes hopes that this product will transform the television industry.

Hughes, a subsidiary of General Motors, is joining the communications revolution. Hughes will market direct broadcast satellite (DBS) services via 150 channels of movies, cable TV programs, and sporting events directly to anyone in the United States or Canada with a special 18-inch satellite dish and decoder, initially priced at $700.

The project began 8 years ago, when the Federal Communications Commission (FCC) set aside part of the radio spectrum for TV programs. But digital compression was not invented then, and satellites were more primitive. Hughes delayed the start of the system develop-

---

[1]This chapter was written by Hans J. Thamhain, Associate Professor of Management at Bentley College in Waltham, Massachusetts. He has held engineering and project management positions with GTE, General Electric, Westinghouse, and ITT. Dr. Thamhain is well known for his research and writings in project management, which include four books and 70 journal articles. He conducts training programs and consults in all phases of project and technology management worldwide.

ment until 1991 when the technology was more advanced; it had a chance to observe other competitors, such as Rupert Murdoch's Sky Broadcasting in Europe and Hutchison Whampoa of Hong Kong broadcasting into Asia.

By the end of 1993, the first 6000-pound DBS, almost completed, is crammed with stuff: power amplifiers, radio-wave propagators, titanium fuel tanks, navigational gear, explosive charges for deploying solar panels, azure-blue glass solar cells, thruster jets, antennas. Workers have just attached the solar panels. The anticipation in the room is palpable. The combination of great stakes, exotic technology, and painstaking effort by many people, culminating in a single event that may bring the instantaneous and total disaster of launch failure—three of the 58 Ariane launches so far have failed—is what makes satellite building the most tension-laden manufacturing industry in the world.

Pulling together a handful of technological breakthroughs has brought Hughes to the edge of success. In the world's first major application of video digital compression technology, Hughes will at least quadruple the capacity of satellite transponders. A transponder receives a radio signal from an earth station and then rebroadcasts it on a designated frequency. Since the signals will be digital, the TV-top decoder boxes will be able to translate them into nearly flawless sound and image as long as the signals are discernible when they reach the earth, even if they are weak. Much of the intelligence in the Hughes system will live atop each subscriber's TV. Housed in the decoder box will be a special chip that decompresses the signal and translates it into sound and image. The box also has a slot for a "smart card" with subscriber information on a embedded chip and an outlet for plugging in a telephone line.

The big question for Hughes: How long does it have before the cable TV and telephone giants build megasystems that will make 150 channels seem like chicken feed? Paramount Pictures video division President Robert Klingensmith thinks Hughes will have enough time to make a big profit. He says, "They're years ahead of what's going to be available on any electronic superhighway."[2]

The Project Environment of the 1990s

The complexities involved in the organization and management of the Hughes DBS project team are quite common in today's project environment. As indicated here, the team effort often spans organizational lines, including an intricate matrix of assigned personnel,

---

[2]This project situation has been excerpted from a report by Andrew Kupfer, *Fortune,* August 23, 1993, pp. 90–98.

support groups, subcontractors, vendors, partners, government agencies, and customer organizations. Uncertainties and risks introduced by technological, economic, political, social, and regulatory factors are always present and can be an enormous challenge to organizing and managing the project teams. The need for building effective linkages among the various team factions and support groups is yet another challenge which involves broad-scale team building toward interorganizational alliances and cooperation. Because of these complexities and uncertainties in many cases traditional forms of hierarchical team structure and leadership are not effective and are being replaced by self-directed, self-managed organizational paradigms. Often the project manager becomes a social architect who facilitates the work process and provides overall project leadership. Typical managerial responsibilities and activities of today's project team leaders are summarized in Table 18.1.

An Increased Focus on Multifunctional Teamwork

Teamwork is not a new idea. The basic concepts of organizing and managing teams go back in history to biblical times. In fact, work teams have long been considered an effective device to enhance organizational effectiveness (Dyer, 1977). Since the discovery of the importance of social phenomena in the classic Hawthorne studies (Roethlingsberger and Dickerson, 1939), management theorists and practitioners have tried to enhance group identity and cohesion in the workplace. Indeed, much of the human relations movement that occurred in the decades following Hawthorne is based on a group concept. McGregor's (1960) theory Y, for example, spells out the criteria for an effective work group, and Likert (1961) called his highest form of management the *participative group,* or system 4.

In today's more complex multinational and technologically sophisticated environment, the group has reemerged in importance in the form of project teams. The management practices apply principles of interpersonal and group dynamics to create and guide project teams successfully. Especially with the emergence of contemporary organizations, such as the matrix, traditional bureaucratic hierarchies declined and horizontally oriented teams and work units became increasingly important to effective project management. These teams became the conduit for transferring information, technology, and work concepts across functional lines quickly, predictably, and within given resource constraints. Because of their potential for producing economic advantages, work teams and their development have been studied by many. Yet prior to 1960, most of these studies focused just on the behavior of the team members, with limited

TABLE 18.1   Responsibilities and Challenges of Project Team Leaders

- Defining and negotiating the appropriate human resources for the project team
- Bringing together the right mix of competent people which will develop into a team
- Integrating individuals with diverse skills and attitudes into a unified work group with unified focus
- Dealing with support department values, managements, and priorities
- Directing multifunctional work teams across organizational lines with little formal authority
- Maintaining project direction and control without stifling innovation and creativity
- Coordinating and integrating the various task group activities into a complete system
- Fostering a professionally stimulating work environment where people are motivated to work effectively toward established project objectives
- Maintaining leadership at each task group in spite of often informal organizational structures and control systems
- Coping with changing technologies, requirements, and priorities while maintaining project focus and team unity
- Dealing with power struggle and conflict
- Dealing with technical complexities in an integrated multidisciplinary framework
- Building lines of communication among task teams as well as to upper management and the project sponsor or customer
- Keeping upper management involved, interested, and supportive
- Sustaining high individual efforts and commitment to established objectives
- Encouraging innovative risk taking without jeopardizing fundamental project goals
- Providing or influencing equitable and fair rewards to individual team members
- Building the specific skills needed in the particular task team
- Facilitating team decision making
- Providing an organizational framework to unify the team
- Providing overall project leadership in an often loosely structured, temporary team environment

attention given to the organizational environment and team leadership. While the qualities of the *individuals* and their interaction within the team are crucial elements in the teamwork process (Bennis and Shepard, 1956; Likert, 1961), they represent only part of the overall organization and management system which influences team performance. Since 1960 an increasing number of studies have broadened the understanding of the teamwork process (Tichy and Urlich, 1984; Walton, 1985; Dumaine, 1991). These more recent studies show the enormous breadth and depth of subsystems and variables involved in the organization, development, and management of a high-performing work team. These variables include planning, organizing, training, organizational structure, nature and complexity of task, senior management support, leadership, and socioeconomic variables, just to name the most popular ones. Even further, researchers such as Fisher (1993), Dumaine (1991), Roberts (1988), Drucker (1985), Peters and Waterman (1987), Moss Kanter (1989), Quinn (1979), and Thamhain (1990) have emphasized the nonlinear, intricate, often chaotic, and random nature of teamwork, which involves all facets of the organization, its members, and environment. Typical examples of such contemporary teams range from dedicated venture groups, often called *skunk works,* to product development teams, acquisition efforts, process action teams, and political election campaigns. For these kinds of highly multifunctional nonlinear processes, researchers stress the need for strong integration and orchestration of cross-functional activities, linking the various work groups into a unified project team that focuses energy and integrates all subtasks toward desired results. While these realities hold for most team efforts in today's work environment, they are especially pronounced for efforts which are associated with risk, uncertainty, creativity, and team diversity such as high-technology and/or multinational projects. These are also the work environments that first departed from the traditional hierarchical team structure and tried the virtual and self-directed concepts, which are discussed later in this chapter.

The team life cycle

Team management spans the complete project life cycle, not just a particular phase. For example, the Hughes DBS product team integrates activities ranging from recognition of an opportunity to product research, feasibility analysis, development and engineering, transferring technology to manufacturing and the market, product distribution, and field service. That work may also involve bid proposals, licensing, subcontracting, acquisitions, and offshore manufacturing. In addition, the team leaders may operate in a matrix environment with power and resource sharing, multiple accountability, and limited control over support services, budgets, and schedules.

Given these realities, it is not surprising that many business leaders and project managers are greatly concerned about their organization's ability to perform effectively as a unified work team. The principal challenge is to transform an ad hoc collection of people, assigned to a particular task, into a coherent, integrated work group.

Characteristics of a High-Performing Project Team

The characteristics of a project team and its ultimate performance depend on many factors which are related to both people and structural issues. Obviously, each organization has its own way to measure and express performance of a project team. However, in spite of the existing cultural and philosophical differences, there seems to be a general agreement among members on certain factors which are included in the characteristics of a successful project team.

Recent field studies suggest a simple framework for organizing the complex array of performance-related variables into four specific categories.

Task-related variables affect specific task outcome such as the ability to produce quality results on time and within budget, innovative performance, and willingness to change.

People-related variables affect the inner workings of the team and include good communications, high involvement, capacity to resolve conflict, mutual trust, and commitment to project objectives.

Leadership variables are associated with the various leadership positions within the project team. These positions can be created formally, such as the appointment of project managers and task leaders, or can emerge dynamically within the work process as a result of individually developed power bases, based on expertise, trust, respect, credibility, friendship, and empathy. Typical leadership characteristics include the ability to organize and direct the task, facilitate group decision making, motivate, assist in conflict and problem resolutions, and foster a work environment which satisfies the professional and personal needs of the team members (Thamhain and Wilemon, 1987).

Organizational variables such as overall organizational climate, command-control-authority structure, policies, procedures, regulations, and regional cultures, values, and economic conditions. All these variables are likely to be interrelated in a complex, intricate form (Thamhain and Gemmill, 1974; Thamhain, 1993).

It is interesting to note that managers describing the characteristics of an effective, high-performing project team not only focus on task-related skills for producing technical results on time and on budget but also stress especially the people and leadership-related qualities. The significance of grouping and categorizing team performance variables is seen in three areas:

1. It provides a model for demanding the factors which are critical to high team performance in a particular project environment.

2. It provides a framework for diagnosing and stimulating team-building activities.

3. The team performance variable might be useful in benchmarking the team's characteristics against the "norm" of high-performing teams, hence providing the basis for self-assessment and continuous improvement.

Taken together, within an integrated team, members enjoy their group association and derive much of their personal and professional satisfaction from the interaction with other team members. Specifically, some of the more important characteristics of a fully integrated team are as follows:

- Satisfaction of individual needs
- Shared interests
- Strong sense of belonging
- Pride and enjoyment in group activity
- Commitment to team objectives
- High trust, low conflict
- Ease with interdependence
- High degree of group interaction, effective communications
- Strong performance norms and results orientation
- Ability to encourage the development of team members
- Ability to interface with other organizations

The existence of work groups is a simple fact of organizational life. Creating a climate and culture conducive to high-performance, quality teamwork involves multifaceted management challenges which increase with the complexities of the project and its organizational environment.

Team Building for Today's Project Activities

Team building is important for many activities. It is especially crucial in a project-oriented work environment where complex multidisciplinary activities require the integration of many functional specialties and support groups. To manage these multifunctional activities, it is necessary for the managers and their task leaders to cross organizational lines and deal with resource personnel over whom they have little or no formal authority. Yet there is another set of challenges in the contemporary nature of project organizations with their horizontal and vertical lines of communication and control, their resource sharings among projects and task teams, multiple reporting relationships to several bosses, and dual accountabilities.

To manage projects effectively in such a dynamic environment, task leaders must understand the interaction of organizational and behavioral variables in order to foster a climate conducive to multidisciplinary team building. Such a team must innovatively transform a set of technical objectives and requirements into specific products or services that compete favorably in the marketplace.

Building effective task teams is one of the prime responsibilities of project managers. Team building involves a whole spectrum of management skills required to identify, commit, and integrate various task groups from traditional functional organizations into a multidisciplinary task management system. This process has been known for centuries. However, it becomes more complex and requires more specialized management skills as bureaucratic hierarchies decline and horizontally oriented teams and work units evolve. Starting with the evolution of formal project organizations in the 1960s, managers in various organizational settings have expressed increasing concern with and interest in the concepts and practices of multidisciplinary team building. Responding to this interest, many field studies[3] have been conducted, investigating work group dynamics and criteria for building effective, high-performing project teams. These studies have contributed to the theoretical and practical understanding of team building and form the basis for the discussion of the fundamental concepts in this chapter.

Team building is an ongoing process that requires leadership skills and an understanding of the organization, its interfaces, authority and power structures, and motivational factors. This process is particularly crucial in certain project situations, such as

- Establishing a new program
- Transferring technology
- Improving project-client relationships
- Organizing for a bid proposal
- Integrating new project personnel
- Resolving interfunctional problems
- Working toward major milestone
- Reorganizing mergers and acquisitions

---

[3] See "Bibliography" for works by J. J. Aquilino, J. D. Aram, and C. P. Morgan; S. Atkins and A. Katcher; L. Bennington, J. L. Hayes, D. S. Hopkins, F. E. Katz, R. Likert, and D. L. Wilemon; and H. J. Thamhain, B. Dumaine, K. Fisher, and A. Grove.

- Transitioning the project into a new activity phase
- Revitalizing on organization

Team building is defined as the process of taking a collection of individuals with different needs, backgrounds, and expertise and transforming them into an integrated, effective work unit. In this transformation process, the goals and energies of individual contributors merge and support the objectives of the team.

Today, team building is considered by many management practitioners and researchers as one of the most critical leadership qualities that determine the performance and success of multidisciplinary efforts. The outcome of these projects critically depends on carefully orchestrated group efforts, requiring the coordination and integration of many task specialists in a dynamic work environment with complex organizational interfaces. Therefore, it is not surprising to find a strong emphasis on teamwork and team-building practice among today's managers, a trend which is expected to continue and most likely intensify for years to come.

A Simple Model

The characteristics of a project team and its ultimate performance depend on many factors. Using a systems approach, Fig. 18.1 provides a simple model for organizing and analyzing these factors. It defines two sets of variables which influence the team's characteristics and its ultimate performance: (1) environmental factors, such as working conditions, job content, resources, and organizational support factors, and (2) leadership style. Both variables determine the drivers of and barri-

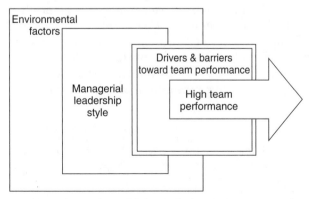

Figure 18.1 A simple model for analyzing project team performance.

ers to a desirable team and therefore influence the team's characteristics and its ultimate performance. All of these variables are likely to be interrelated in a complex, intricate form. However, using the systems approach allows researchers and management practitioners to break down the complexity of the process and to analyze its components. It can further help in identifying the drivers of and barriers to transforming resources into specific results under the influence of managerial, organizational, and other environmental factors.

Measuring project team performance

Obviously, each organization has its own way to measure and express performance of a project team. However, in spite of the existing cultural and philosophical differences, there seems to be a general agreement among managers on certain factors[4] which are included in the characteristics of a successful project team:

1. Technical project success according to agreed-on objectives

2. On-time performance

3. On-budget performance (staying within resource limitations)

Furthermore, over 60 percent of those who identified these three measures ranked them in the above order.

When describing the characteristics of an effective, high-performing project team, managers stress consistently that a high-performing team not only produces technical results on time and on budget, but also is characterized by specific job and people-related qualities, as shown in Table 18.2. In fact, field research shows a statistically strong association between the above team qualities and team performance at a confidence level of $p = 95$ percent or better.[5]

The significance of determining team performance characteristics lies in two areas. First, it offers some clues as to what an effective team environment looks like. This can stimulate management thoughts and activities for effective team building. Second, the results allow us to define measures of an effective team environment for benchmarking and further research on organization devel-

---

[4] In fact, over 90% of the project managers interviewed during a recent survey mentioned these factors as among the most important criteria of team performance. H. J. Thamhain and G. R. Gemmill, "Influence Styles of Project Managers: Some Project Performance Correlates," *Academy of Management Journal*, June 1974.

[5] Ibid. Specifically, a Kendall-tau rank-order correlation model was used. These measures yielded an average association of $\tau = .37$. Moreover, there appears to be a strong agreement between managers and project team members on the importance of these characteristics, as measured via a Kruskal-Wallis analysis of variance at a confidence level of $p = 95$ percent.

TABLE 18.2   Characteristics of High-Performing Project Teams

Task-related qualities	People-related qualities
■ Committed to the project	■ High involvement, work interest, and energy
■ Result-oriented attitude	■ Capacity to solve conflict
■ Innovativeness and creativity	■ Good communication
■ Willingness to change	■ High need for achievement
■ Concern for quality	■ Good team spirit
■ Ability to predict trends	■ Mutual trust
■ Ability to integrate	■ Self-development of team members
■ Ability to anticipate problems and react early	■ Effective organizational interfacing
■ Synergism	

opment efforts, such as defining drivers of and barriers to team performance.

Drivers of and barriers to high team performance

Additional management insight has been gained by investigating drivers of and barriers to high performance. Drivers are positive factors associated with the project environment, such as interesting work and good project direction. These factors are perceived as enhancing team effectiveness, and they correlate positively with team performance. Barriers are negative factors, such as unclear objectives and insufficient resources, that are perceived as impeding team performance and statistically correlate negatively with performance.

Studies by Gemmill, Thamhain, and Wilemon into work group dynamics clearly show significant correlations and interdependencies among work environment factors and team performance. These studies indicate that high team performance involves four primary factors: managerial leadership, job content, personal goals and objectives, and work environment and organizational support. The actual correlation of 60 influence factors to the project team characteristics and performance provided some interesting insight into the strength and effect of these factors. One important finding was that only 12 of the 60 influence factors were found to be statistically significant.[6] All

---

[6] Kendall-tau rank-order correlation was used to measure the association between these variables. Statistical significance was defined at a confidence level of 95 percent or better.

other factors seem to be much less important to high team performance. Specifically, the six drivers that have the strongest positive association to protect team performance are

1. Professionally interesting and stimulating work
2. Recognition of accomplishment
3. Experienced engineering management personnel
4. Proper technical direction and leadership
5. Qualified project team personnel
6. Professional growth potential

while the strongest barriers to protect team performance are

1. Unclear project objectives and directions
2. Insufficient resources
3. Power struggle and conflict
4. Uninvolved, disintegrated upper management
5. Poor job security
6. Shifting goals and priorities

It is interesting to note that the six drivers not only correlated favorably to the direct measures of high project team performance, such as the technical success and on-time and on-budget performance, but also were associated positively with the 13 indirect measures of team performance, ranging from commitment to creativity, quality, change orientation, and needs for achievement. The complete listing of the 16 performance measures is shown in Fig. 18.2. The six barriers have exactly the opposite effect. These findings provide some quantitative support to previous field studies by Thamhain and Wilemon.

What we find consistently is that successful organizations pay attention to the human side. They seem to be effective in fostering a work environment conducive to innovative, creative work, where people find the assignments challenging, leading to recognition and professional growth. Such a professionally stimulating environment also seems to lower communication barriers and conflict and to enhance the desire of personnel to succeed. Further, this seems to increase organizational awareness of and ability to respond to changing project requirements.

A winning team also appears to have good leadership. That is, management understands the factors crucial to success. Managers are action-oriented, provide the needed resources, properly direct the

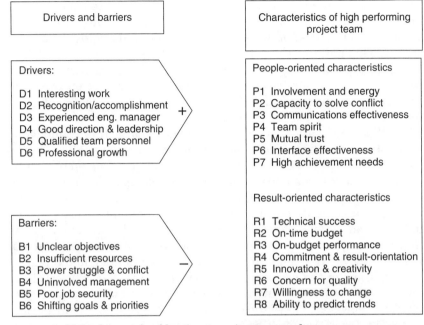

Drivers and barriers	Characteristics of high performing project team

Drivers:

D1 Interesting work
D2 Recognition/accomplishment
D3 Experienced eng. manager
D4 Good direction & leadership
D5 Qualified team personnel
D6 Professional growth

People-oriented characteristics

P1 Involvement and energy
P2 Capacity to solve conflict
P3 Communications effectiveness
P4 Team spirit
P5 Mutual trust
P6 Interface effectiveness
P7 High achievement needs

Result-oriented characteristics

R1 Technical success
R2 On-time budget
R3 On-budget performance
R4 Commitment & result-orientation
R5 Innovation & creativity
R6 Concern for quality
R7 Willingness to change
R8 Ability to predict trends

Barriers:

B1 Unclear objectives
B2 Insufficient resources
B3 Power struggle & conflict
B4 Uninvolved management
B5 Poor job security
B6 Shifting goals & priorities

Figure 18.2 Major drivers of and barriers to project team performance.

implementation of the project plan, and help in the identification and resolution of problems in early stages. Taken together, the findings support three propositions:

First, the degree of project success seems to be primarily determined by the strength of six driving forces and six barriers which are related to leadership, job content, personal needs, and the general work environment.

Second, the strongest driver of project success is a professionally stimulating team environment, characterized by interesting and challenging work, visibility and recognition for achievements, growth potential, and good project leadership.

Third, a professionally stimulating team environment also leads to low perceived conflict, high commitment, highly involved personnel, good communications, an orientation to change, innovation, and on-time, on-budget performance.

To be effective in organizing and directing a project team, the leader must not only recognize the potential drivers and barriers but also know when in the life cycle of the project they are most likely to occur. The effective project leader takes preventive actions early in the project life cycle and fosters a work environment that is conducive to team building as an ongoing process.

The effective team builder is usually a social architect who understands the interaction of organizational and behavioral variables and can foster a climate of active participation and minimal dysfunctional conflict. This requires carefully developed skills in leadership, administration, organization, and technical expertise. It further requires the project leader's ability to involve top management, to ensure organizational visibility, resource availability, and overall support for the new project throughout its life cycle.

It is this organizational culture which adds yet another challenge to project team building. The new team members are usually selected from hierarchically organized functional resource departments led by strong individuals who often foster internal competition rather than cooperation. In fact, even at the contributor level, many of the highly innovative and creative people are highly individualistically oriented and often admit their aversion to cooperation. The challenge to the project manager is to integrate these individuals into a team that can produce innovative results in a systematic, coordinated, and integrated way. Many of the problems that occur during the formation of the new project team or during its life cycle are normal and often predictable. However, they present barriers to effective team performance. The problems must be quickly identified and dealt with.[7]

Organizing the New Project Team

Too often the project manager, under pressure to start producing, rushes into organizing the project team without establishing the proper organizational framework. While initially the prime focus is on staffing, the program manager cannot effectively attract and hold quality people until certain organizational pillars are in place. At a minimum, the basic project organization and various tasks must be defined before the recruiting effort can start.

These pillars are necessary not only to communicate the project requirements, responsibilities, and relationships to team members, but also to manage the anxiety which usually develops during team formation. This anxiety is normal and predictable. It is a barrier, however, to getting the team quickly focused on the task.

This anxiety may come from several sources. For example, if the team members have never worked with the project leader, they may be concerned with the leader's style and its effect on them. In a different vein, team members may be concerned about the nature of the

---

[7]The research on team characteristics and drivers versus barriers is based on a field study by H. J. Thamhain and D. Wilemon, "A High-Performing Engineering Project Team," *IEEE Transaction of Engineering Management,* May 1987.

project and whether it will match their professional interests and capabilities. Other team members may be concerned about whether the project will be helpful to their career aspirations. Furthermore, team members can be anxious about life- or work-style disruptions. As one project manager remarked, "Moving a team member's desk from one side of the room to the other can sometimes be as traumatic as moving someone from Chicago to Manila to build a power plant."[8] As the quote suggests, seemingly minor changes can result in sudden anxiety among team members.

Another common concern among newly formed teams is whether there will be an equitable distribution of the workload among team members and whether each member is capable of pulling his or her own weight. In some newly formed teams, members not only have to do their own work but also must train others. Within reason this is bearable, necessary, and often expected. However, when it becomes excessive, anxiety increases and morale can plummet.

Make functional ties work for you

It is a mistaken belief that strong ties of team members to the functional organization are bad for effective program management and should be eliminated. To the contrary, loyalty to both the project and the functional organization is a natural, desirable, and often very necessary condition for project success. For example, in the most common of all project organizations, the matrix, the program office gives operational directions to the program personnel and is responsible for the budget and schedule, while the functional organization provides technical guidance and personnel administration. Both the program manager and the functional managers must understand this process and perform accordingly, or else severe jurisdictional conflicts can develop.

Structure your organization

The keys to successfully building a new project organization are clearly defined and communicated responsibilities and organizational relationships. The tools for systematically describing the project organization come, in fact, from conventional management practices:

- *Charter of the program or project organization.* The charter of the program office clearly describes the business mission and scope, broad responsibilities, authorities, organizational structure, inter-

---

[8] H. J. Thamhain and D. Wilemon, "Skill Requirements of Engineering Project Manager," *Proceedings of the 26th Engineering Management Conference,* 1978.

faces, and reporting relationship of the program organization. The charter should be revised for each new program. For small projects a simple half-page statement may be sufficient, while larger programs usually require a formal charter supported by standardized company policies on project management.

- *Project organization chart.* Regardless of the specific organizational structure and the terminology used, a simple organizational chart should define the major reporting and authority relationships. These relationships can be further clarified in a policy directive.

- *Responsibility matrix.* This chart defines the interdisciplinary task responsibilities—who is responsible for what. The responsibility matrix not only covers activities within the project organization, but also defines the functional relationship with support units, subcontractors, and committees. In a simpler format, a task roster can be used to just list project tasks and corresponding responsible personnel.

- *Job description.* If not already in existence, a job description should be developed for all key project personnel, such as the program managers, system project managers, hardware project managers, task managers, project engineers, plan coordinators, and so on. Job descriptions usually are generic and hence portable from one project to the next. Job descriptions are modular building blocks which form the framework for staffing a project organization. A job description includes the reporting relationship, responsibilities, duties, and typical qualifications.

Define the project

It is seldom a problem to define the technical components of the project. Project personnel usually are very competent in their technical areas. They also enjoy the technical content of the project. Yet, this is only one of the four segments of the project management system that must be defined, at least in principle, before staffing can begin, as show in Table 18.3.

Regardless of how vague and preliminary these project segments are at the beginning, the initial description will help in recruiting the appropriate personnel and eliciting commitment to the preestablished parameters of technical performance, schedule, and budget. The core team should be formed prior to finalizing of the project plan and contractual arrangements. This will provide the project management team with the opportunity to participate in tradeoff discussions and customer negotiations, leading to technical confidence and commitment of all parties involved.

**TABLE 18.3   Segments of the
Project Management System to Be
Defined before Staffing Begins**

Segment 1: The work

---

1. Overall specifications
2. Requirements document
3. Statement of work
4. System block diagram
5. Work breakdown structure
6. List of deliverables

Segment 2: Timing

---

1. Master schedule
2. Milestone chart
3. Network
4. Critical path analysis

Segment 3: Resources

---

1. Budget
2. Resource plan

Segment 4: Responsibilities

---

1. Task matrix
2. Project/task roster
3. Project charter
4. Work packages

Staff your project

Staffing the project organization is the first major milestone during the project formation phase. Because of the pressures on the project manager to produce, staffing is often done hastily and without properly defining the basic project work to be performed. The results are often personnel poorly matched to the job requirements, conflict, low morale, suboptimum decision making, and, in the end, poor project performance. The comment of a project section leader who was pressed into quick staffing actions is indicative of these potential problems: "How can you interview task managers when you cannot show them what the job involves and how their responsibilities tie in with the rest of the project?"

Therefore only after the project organization and the tasks are defined in principle can project leaders at various levels start to interview candidates. These interviews should always be conducted one-to-one. The interview process normally has five facets which are often interrelated, as shown in Table 18.4.

TABLE 18.4   Facets of the Interview Process

1. Informing the candidate about the assignments

- What are the objectives for the project?
- Who will be involved and why?
- What are the structures of the project organization and its interfaces?
- What is the importance of the project to the overall organization or work unit, including short- or long-range impact?
- Why was the team member selected and assigned to the project?
- What role will he or she perform?
- What are the team member's specific responsibilities and expectations?
- What rewards might be forthcoming if the project is completed successfully?
- Candidly, what problems and constraints are likely to be encountered?
- What are the "rules of the road" that will be followed in managing the project, such as regular status review meetings?
- What challenges and recognition is the project likely to provide?
- Why is the team concept important to success, and how should it work?

2. Determining skills and expertise

- Probe related experience; expand from resume.
- Probe candidate's aptitude relevant to project environment: technology involved, engineering tools and techniques, markets and customer involvement, and product applications.
- Probe into the program management skills needed. Use current project examples: "How would you handle this situation...?" Probe leadership, technical expertise, planning and control, administrative skills, and so on.

3. Determining interests and team compatibility

- What are the professional interests and objectives of this candidate?
- How does the candidate manage and work with others?
- How does the candidate feel about sharing authority, working for two bosses, or dealing with personnel across functional lines with little or no formal authority?
- What suggestions does the candidate have for achieving success?

4. Persuading to join project team

- Explain specific rewards for joining the team, such as financial, professional growth, recognition, visibility, work challenge, and potential for advancement.

5. Negotiating terms and commitments

- Check candidate's willingness to join team.
- Negotiate conditions for joining: salary; hired, signed, or transferred; performance reviews; and criteria.
- Elicit candidate's commitment to established project objectives and modus operandi.
- Secure final agreement.

Suggestions for Handling the Newly Formed Project Team

During its formation, the project group is just a collection of individuals who have been selected for their skills and capabilities as collectively needed to perform the upcoming project task. However, to be successful, the individual efforts must be integrated. Even more demanding, these individuals have to work together as a team to produce innovative results which fit together to form an integrated new system as conceptualized in the project plan.

Initially, many problems prevent the project group from performing as a team. While these problems are normal and often predictable, they present barriers to effective team performance. The problems, therefore, must be quickly identified and dealt with. The following list presents typical problems which occur just after a project team formation:

- Confusion
- Responsibilities unclear
- Channels of authority ambiguous
- Work distribution load uneven
- Assignment unclear
- Communication channels unclear
- Overall project goals unclear
- Mistrust
- Personal objectives unrelated to project
- Measures of personal performance unclear
- Commitment to project plan lacking
- Team spirit lacking
- Project direction and leadership insufficient
- Power struggle and conflict

Certain steps taken early in the life of the team can help the project leader to identify the specific problems and deal with them effectively. These steps also may be preventive measures which eliminate the potential for these problems to develop in the first place.

The assignment should be clear

Although the overall task assignment, its scope, and objectives might have been discussed during the initial sign-on of the person to the project, it takes additional effort and involvement for new team members to feel comfortable with the assignment. The thorough understanding of the task requirements comes usually with the intense personal involvement of the new members with the project team. Such involvement can be enhanced by assigning the new member to an action-oriented task that requires team involvement and creates visibility, such as a requirements analysis, an interface specification, or producibility study. In addition, any committee-type activity, presentation, or data gathering will help to involve the new team member. It also will enable that person to better understand the specific task and her or his role in the overall team effort.

New team members must feel professionally comfortable

The initial anxieties and lack of trust and confidence are serious barriers to team performance. New team members should be properly introduced to the group and their roles, strengths, and criticality to the project explained. Providing opportunities for early results allows the leader to give recognition for professional accomplishments, which will stimulate the individual's desire for the project work and build confidence, trust, and credibility within the group.

Team organization should be clear

Project team structures often are considered very "organic" and inconsistent with formal chain-of-command principles. However, individual task responsibility, accountability, and organizational interface relations should be clearly explained to all team members. A simple work breakdown structure or task matrix, together with some discussion, can facilitate a clear understanding of the team structure, even one with a highly unconventional format.

Locate team members in one place

Members of the newly formed team should be closely located to facilitate communications and the development of a team spirit. Locating the project team in one office area is the ideal situation. However, this may be impractical, especially if team members share their time with other projects or if the assignment is only for a short time. Regularly scheduled meetings are recommended as soon as the new project team is being formed. These meetings are particularly important where team members are geographically separated and do not see each other on a day-to-day basis.

Provide a proper team environment

It is crucial for management to provide the proper environment for the project to function effectively. Here the project leader needs to tell management at the onset of the program what resources are needed. The project manager's relationship with senior management support is critically affected by his or her credibility and the visibility and priority of the project.

Manage

Especially during the initial stages of team formation, it is important for the project leader to keep a close eye on the team and its activities to detect problems early and to correct them. The project manager can also influence the climate of the work environment by her or his own actions. The manager's concern for project team members, ability to integrate personal goals and needs of project personnel with the project objectives, and ability to create personal enthusiasm for the work itself can foster a climate which is high on motivation, work involvement, and resulting project performance.

Team Building as an Ongoing Process

While proper attention to team building is crucial during the early phases of a project, it is a never-ending process. The project manager is continually monitoring team performance to see what corrective action may be needed to prevent or correct problems. Several barometers provide good clues of potential team dysfunction. First, noticeable changes in performance levels for the team and/or for individual team members always should be followed up. Such changes can be symptomatic of more serious problems, such as conflict, lack of work integration, communication problems, and unclear objectives. Second, the project leader and team members want to be aware of the changing energy level in various team members. This, too, may signal more serious problems or that the team is tired and stressed. Sometimes changing the work pace, taking time off, or setting short-term targets can serve as a means to reenergize team members. More serious cases, however, can call for more drastic measures, such as reappraising project objectives and/or the means to achieve them. Third, verbal and nonverbal clues from team members may be a source of information about team functioning. It is important to hear their needs and concerns (verbal clues) and to observe how they act in carrying out their responsibilities (nonverbal clues). Finally, deregulatory behavior of one team member toward another can be a signal that a problem within the team warrants action.

It is highly recommended that project leaders hold regular meetings to evaluate overall team performance and deal with team functioning problems. The focus of these meetings can be directed toward

"What are we doing well as a team?" and "What areas need our team's attention?" This approach often brings positive surprises in that the total team will be informed of progress in diverse project areas, such as a breakthrough in the technology department, a subsystem schedule met ahead of the original target, or a positive change in the client's behavior toward the project. After the positive issues have been discussed, attention should be devoted to areas needing team attention. The purpose of this part of the review session is to focus on real or potential problem areas. The meeting leader should ask each team member for his or her observations on these issues. Then an open discussion should be held to ascertain how significant the problems really are. Assumptions should, of course, be separated from the facts of each situation. Next, assignments should be agreed upon for how to best handle these problems. Finally, a plan for follow-up should be developed. The process should result in a better overall performance and promote a feeling of team participation and high morale. Over the life of a project the problems encountered by the project team are likely to change, and as the old problems are identified and solved, new ones will emerge.

Social scientists generally agree that there are several indicators of effective and ineffective teams. At any point in the life of the team, the project manager should be aware of certain effectiveness-ineffectiveness indicators which are summarized in Table 18.5. As we go through this decade, we anticipate important developments in team building. These developments will lead to higher performance levels, increased morale, and a pervasive commitment to final results that can withstand almost any kind of adversity. It is especially this individual and collective ownership and commitment which characterize the self-directed team. These are the qualities which are often essential for producing innovative results within given resource constraints, typical for today's complex project situations associated with technology, risk, and uncertainty.

Recommendations for Effective Team Management

Leading a project team in today's vastly complex organizational and business environment involves multifaceted management challenges and sophisticated skills. The recommendations advanced here reflect the realities of this new environment where project managers have to cross organizational, national, and cultural boundaries and work with people over whom they have little or no formal control. Alliances and collaborative ventures have forced project managers to focus more on cross-boundary relationships, negotiations, delegation, and commit-

TABLE 18.5   Project Team Characteristics: Effective versus Ineffective

Likely characteristics of effective team	Likely characteristics of ineffective team
+ High performance and task efficiency	− Low performance
+ Innovative/creative behavior	− Activity-oriented
+ Committed, results-oriented	− Low level of involvement and enthusiasm
+ Professional objectives of team members coincide with project requirements	− Low commitment to project objectives
+ Technically successful	− Unclear project objectives and fluid commitment levels from key participants
+ On-time, on-budget performance	
+ Team members highly interdependent, interface effectively	− Schedule and budget slips
+ Capacity for conflict resolution, but conflict encouraged when it can lead to beneficial results	− Uninvolved management
	− Anxieties and insecurities
+ Communicates effectively	− Unproductive gamesmanship, manipulation of others, hidden feelings, conflict avoided at all costs
+ High trust levels	
+ High achievement needs	− Confusion, conflict, inefficiency
	− Subtle sabotage, fear, disinterest, or foot dragging
+ Results-oriented	
+ Interested in membership self-development	− Frequent surprises
	− Quality problems
+ High energy levels and enthusiasm	− Cliques, collusion, isolating members
+ High morale	
+ Change-oriented	− Image problems (credibility)
	− Lethargic, unresponsive

ment, rather than on establishing formal command and control systems.

The project leader must foster an environment where team members can work together across organizational and national boundaries in a flatter and leaner company which is more flexible and responsive to quality and time-to-market forces. To be effective in such a team environment, the leader must create an ambience where people are professionally satisfied, are involved, have mutual trust, and can communicate well with each other. The more effective the project leader is in stimulating the drivers of effective team performance (Fig. 18.2), the more effective the manager can be in developing the membership and the higher the quality and candor in sharing ideas and approaches.

Furthermore, the greater the team spirit, trust, and quality of information exchange among team members, the more likely the team will be able to develop effective decision-making processes, make individual and group commitments, focus on problem solving, and develop self-enforcing, self-correcting project controls. These are the characteristics of an effective and productive project team.

Managing the process

This final section summarizes the established criteria for effective team management in the format of specific recommendations. These recommendations should help project leaders and managers responsible for the integration of multidisciplinary tasks in their complex efforts of building high-performing project teams in a multinational environment.

Barriers

Project managers must understand the various barriers to team development and build a work environment conducive to the team's motivational needs. Specifically, management should watch out for the following barriers:

- Unclear objectives
- Insufficient resources and unclear funding
- Role conflict and power struggle
- Uninvolved and unsupportive management
- Poor job security
- Shifting goals and priorities

Project objectives

The project objectives and their importance to the organization should be clear to all personnel involved with the project. Senior management can help develop a "priority image" and communicate the basic project parameters and management guidelines.

Management commitment

A project manager must continuously update and involve management to refuel its interests in and commitments to the new project. Breaking the project into smaller phases and being able to produce short-range results frequently seem to be important to this refueling process.

Image building

Building a favorable image for the project, in terms of high priority, interesting work, importance to the organization, high visibility, and potential for professional rewards, is crucial to the ability to attract and hold high-quality people. It is also a pervasive process which fosters a climate of active participation at all levels; it helps to unify the new project team and minimize dysfunctional conflict.

Leadership

Leadership positions should be carefully defined and staffed at the beginning of a new program. Key project personnel selection is the joint responsibility of the project manager and functional management. The credibility of project leaders among team members, with senior management, and with the program sponsor is crucial to the leader's ability to manage multidisciplinary activities effectively across functional lines. One-on-one interviews are recommended for explaining the scope and project requirements as well as the management philosophy, organizational structure, and rewards.

Planning

Effective planning early in the project life cycle will have a favorable impact on the work environment and team effectiveness. This is especially so because project managers have to integrate various tasks across many functional lines. Proper planning, however, means more than just generating the required pieces of paper. It requires the participation of the entire project team, including support departments, subcontractors, and management. These planning activities, which can be performed in a special project phase such as requirements analysis, product feasibility assessment, or product/project definition, usually have a number of side benefits besides generating a comprehensive road map for the upcoming program. They stimulate interest, foster understanding of requirements, develop commitment, and unify the team.

Involvement

One of the side benefits of proper project planning is the involvement of personnel at all organizational levels. Project managers should encourage such an involvement, at least with their key personnel, especially during the project definition phases. This involvement will lead to a better understanding of the task requirements, stimulate interest, help unify the team, and ultimately lead to commitment to the project plan regarding technical performance, timing, and budgets.

Project staffing

All project assignments should be negotiated individually with each prospective team member. Each task leader should be responsible for staffing her or his own task team. Where dual reporting relationships are involved, staffing should be conducted jointly by the two managers. The assignment interview should include a clear discussion of the specific task, outcome, timing, responsibilities, reporting relationships, potential rewards, and importance of the project to the company. Task assignments should be made only if the candidate's ability is a reasonable match to the position requirements and if the candidate shows a healthy degree of interest in the project.

Team structure

Management must define the basic team structure and operating concepts early during the project formation phase. The project plan, task matrix, project charter, and policy are the principal tools. It is the responsibility of the project manager to communicate the organizational design and to ensure that all parties understand the overall and interdisciplinary project objectives. Clear and frequent communication with senior management and the new project sponsor becomes critically important. Status review meetings can be used for feedback.

Team-building sessions

The project manager should conduct team-building sessions throughout the project life cycle. An especially intense effort might be needed during the team formation stage. The team should be brought together in a relaxed atmosphere to discuss such questions as these:

- How are we operating as a team?
- What is our strength?
- Where can we improve?
- What steps are needed to initiate the desired change?
- What problems and issues are we likely to face in the future?
- Which of these can be avoided by taking appropriate action now?
- How can we "dangerproof" the team?

Team commitment

Project managers should determine whether team members lack commitment early in the life of the project and attempt to change possible negative views toward the project. Since insecurity often is a major reason for lack of commitment, managers should try to determine why insecurity exists and then work on reducing the team members' fears. Conflict with other team members may be another reason for lack of commitment. It is important for the project leader to intervene and mediate the conflict quickly. Finally, if a team member's professional interests lie elsewhere, the project leader should examine ways to satisfy part of the team member's interests by bringing personal and project goals into perspective.

Senior management support

It is critically important for senior management to provide the proper environment for the project team to function effectively. The project leader needs to tell management at the outset of the program what resources are needed. The project manager's relationship with senior management and ability to develop senior management support is critically affected by his or her credibility, visibility, and priority image of the project.

Organization development specialists

Project leaders should watch for changes in performance on an ongoing basis. If they observe performance problems, the problems should be dealt with quickly. If the project manager has access to internal or external organization development specialists, they can help diagnose team problems and assist the team in dealing with the identified problems. These specialists also can bring fresh ideas and perspectives to difficult and sometimes emotionally complex situations.

Problem avoidance

Project leaders should focus their efforts on problem avoidance. That is, the project leader, through experience, should recognize potential problems and conflicts before their onset and deal with them before they become big and their solutions consume a lot of time and effort.

A Final Note

In summary, effective team building is a critical determinant of project success. Building the team is one of the prime responsibilities of the project manager. Effective team building increases productivity. Team building involves a whole spectrum of management skills to identify, commit, and integrate the various personnel from different functional organizations into a single task group. In many project-oriented organizations, team building is a shared responsibility between the functional and/or resource managers and the project manager, who often reports to a different organization with a different superior.

To be effective, the project manager must provide an atmosphere conducive to teamwork. There are four major considerations in the integration of people from many disciplines into an effective team: creating a professionally stimulating work environment, good program leadership, providing qualified personnel, and providing a technically and organizationally stable environment. The project leader must foster an environment where team members are professionally satisfied, and involved, and have mutual trust. The more effectively project leaders develop team membership, the higher is the quality of information exchanged and the greater the candor of team members. It is this professionally stimulating involvement that also has a pervasive effect on the team's ability to cope with change and conflict and leads to innovative performance. By contrast, when a member does not feel part of the team and does not trust others, information will not be shared willingly or openly.

Furthermore, the greater the team spirit, trust, and quality of information exchange among team members, the more likely the team will be able to develop effective decision-making processes, make individual and group commitments, focus on problem solving, and develop self-enforcing, self-correcting project controls. These are the characteristics of an effective and productive project team. Such a team usually requires a minimum of supervision and coaching, but operates in a self-directed mode.

Over the next decade we anticipate important developments in team building which will lead to higher performance levels, increased morale, and a pervasive commitment to final results. This chapter should help both the professional in the field of project management as well as the scholar who studies contemporary organizational concepts to understand the intricate relationships among the elements of organizational behavior. Success will require long-term changes in managerial thinking and leadership style and will depend on the managers' ability to adapt to the increasingly global business topology.

Discussion Questions

1. What kinds of questions can project managers ask in order to analyze the major challenges of building multifunctional project teams? How can these questions be answered?

2. What are some of the characteristics of a fully integrated team? What factors indicate integration of a project team?

3. Give a definition for *team building*. Why is this such an important concept for today's managers?

4. In what project situations is team building most critical? Why?

5. What are some of the systems variables that influence project team characteristics?

6. Discuss the three major characteristics of successful projects. How are these interrelated?

7. List and discuss some of the task- and people-related qualities of successful project teams.

8. Discuss the importance of a project manager's understanding of the drivers of and barriers to team performance.

9. Do you accept the two propositions related to project success given in the chapter? Explain.

10. Discuss the importance of establishing basic objectives and an organizational framework before staffing a project. What are some of the tools for accomplishing this?

11. Describe the staffing phase of a project. What steps are necessary? Explain.

12. Why must team building be an ongoing process? Discuss the importance of regular review meetings for ongoing team building.

13. What are the characteristics of a self-directed, self-managed team? As a project manager, how can you promote such a team performance?

User Checklist

1. How are the major challenges of building project teams being addressed in your organization? Explain.

2. Do teams in your organization exhibit any of the characteristics of a fully integrated team? How?

3. What steps do the project managers of your organization take to facilitate team building? In what project situations is the process of team building used?

4. Are the majority of your projects completed on time, within budget, and with technical performance objectives met? If not, how are these failures related to the effectiveness of the project team?

5. Do the managers of your organization understand the drivers of the barriers to high team performance? Why or why not?

6. Which of the six strongest drivers or six strongest barriers are evident on current projects within your organization? Explain.

7. What do project managers within your organization do to promote the various drivers of high team performance? Are these methods successful? Explain.

8. Are objectives and an organizational framework established before projects are staffed? Why or why not?

9. Describe the staffing procedure used on projects in your organization. Is the procedure effective? How can it be improved?

10. What structure is used on projects in your organization? Are functional ties effective?

11. What tools does your organization use for establishing and describing the project organization? What other tools could be used?

12. Describe ongoing team building efforts in your organization. How can this process be improved?

13. How can you develop team leadership skills?

Bibliography

1. Adams, J. R., and N. S. Kirchof: "A Training Technique for Developing Project Managers," *Project Management Quarterly,* March 1983.
2. Aquilino, J. J.: "Multi-skilled Work Teams: Productivity Benefits," *California Management Review,* Summer 1977.
3. Aram, J. D., and C. P. Morgan: "Role of Project Team Collaboration in R&D Performance," *Management Science,* June 1976.
4. Atkins, S., and A. Katcher: "Getting Your Team in Tune," *Nation's Business,* March 1975.
5. Baler, K. H.: "The Hows and Whys of Teambuilding," *Engineering Management Review,* December 1985.
6. Bennington, L.: "The Team Approach to Project Management," *Management Review,* vol. 61, January 1972.
7. Bennis, Warren G., and Herbert A. Shepard: "A Theory of Group Development," *Human Relations,* no. 9, pp. 415–437, 1956.
8. Carzo, R., Jr.: "Some Effects of Organization Structure on Group Effectiveness," *Administrative Science Quarterly,* March 1963.
9. Conover, W. J.: *Practical Nonparametric Statistics* (New York: Wiley, 1971).
10. Diliddo, B. A., P. C. James, and H. J. Dietrich: "Managing R&D Creatively: B. F. Goodrich's Approach," *Management Review,* July 1981.
11. Drucker, Peter F.: *Innovation and Entrepreneurship* (New York: Harper, 1985).
12. Dumaine, Brian: "The Bureaucracy Buster," *Fortune,* June 17, 1991.
13. Dyer, W. G.: *Team Building: Issues and Alternatives* (Reading, Mass.: Addison-Wesley, 1977).
14. Ely, D. D.: "Team Building for Creativity," *Personnel,* April 1975.
15. Fisher, Kimball: *Leading Self-Directed Work Teams* (New York: McGraw-Hill, 1993).
16. Foster, R. N.: "A Call for Vision in Managing Technology," *McKinsy Quarterly,* Summer 1982.
17. Grove, Andrew: *High Output Management* (New York: Random House, 1983).
18. Jewell, Linda N., and H. Joseph Reitz: *Group Effectiveness in Organizations* (Glenville, Ill.: Scott, Foresman, 1981).
19. Likert, R.: *New Patterns of Management* (New York: McGraw-Hill, 1961).
20. McGregor, D.: *The Human Side of Enterprise* (New York: McGraw-Hill, 1960).
21. Moss Kanter, Rosabeth: "The New Managerial Work," *Harvard Business Review,* November-December 1989.
22. Ouchi, William G.: *Theory Z* (Reading, Mass.: Addison-Wesley, 1981).
23. Peters, Thomas J., and Robert H. Waterman: *In Search of Excellence* (New York: Harper & Row, 1987).
24. Quinn, James Brian: "Technological Innovation, Entrepreneurship and Strategy," *Sloan Management Review,* vol. 20, no. 3, Spring 1979, pp. 19–30.

25. Roberts, Edward: "Managing Inventions and Innovation," *Technology Management,* vol. 31, no. 1, January-February 1988, pp. 11–30.
26. Roethlingsberger, F., and W. Dickerson: *Management and the Worker* (Cambridge, Mass.: Harvard University Press, 1939).
27. Senge, Peter: *The Fifth Discipline: The Art and Practice of the Learning Organization* (New York: Doubleday/Currency, 1990).
28. Thamhain, H. J.: "Managing Engineers Effectively," *IEEE Transactions on Engineering Management,* August 1983.
29. ——: "Building High Performing Engineering Project Teams," *IEEE Transactions on Engineering Management,* vol. 34, no. 3, August 1987.
30. ——: "Managing Technologically Innovative Team Efforts towards New Product Success," *Journal of Product Innovation Management,* vol. 7, no. 1, March 1990, pp. 5–18.
31. ——: "Skill Developments for Project Managers," *Project Management Journal,* vol. 22, no. 3, September 1991.
32. ——: "Developing Engineering Program Management Skills," chap. 22 in D. Kacaoglu (ed.), *Handbook: Management of R&D and Engineering* (New York: Wiley, 1992).
33. ——: *Engineering Management: Managing Effectively in Technology-Based Organizations* (New York: Wiley, 1992b).
34. ——: "Effective Leadership Style for Managing Project Teams," chap. 22 in P. C. Dinsmore (ed.), *Handbook of Program and Project Management* (New York: AMA-COM, 1993).
35. ——, and G. R. Gemmill: "Influence Styles of Project Managers: Some Project Performance Correlates," *Academy of Management Journal,* June 1974.
36. ——, and D. L. Wilemon: "Leadership, Conflict and Project Management Effectiveness," *Executive Bookshelf on Generating Technological Innovations, Sloan Management Review,* Fall 1987.
37. Tichy, Noel, and David Ulrich: "The Leadership Challenge—Call for the Transformational Leader," *Sloan Management Review,* Fall 1984, pp. 59–68.
38. Walton, Richard: "From Control to Commitment in the Workplace," *Harvard Business Review,* March-April 1985.

The Cultural Elements

19

Continuous Improvement through Projects

"...everything is in constant motion and every change seems an improvement."
ALEXIS DE TOCQUEVILLE, 1805–1859

Continuous improvement of products, services, and organizational processes is becoming the hallmark for success in the global marketplace. Yet there still remains the opportunity for major technological breakthroughs—even of the transistor, jet engine, or computer magnitude. On balance, however, the predominant competitive advantage will be gained by a company's ability to provide a cultural ambience where creativity leads to innovation followed by continuing small improvements in the organizational products and processes required to deliver improved products and services that provide value to the customer.

The reader might properly ask, Why is the topic of continuous improvement dealt with in a book about project management? The answer lies in the strategic management responsibilities of the senior executives of the enterprise. Continuous improvement covers the design, development, and implementation of many small innovations in the products and processes making up the organization. Senior managers who are concerned with maintaining the competitiveness of their enterprise have little choice but to pursue a strategy of continuous improvement—a strategy that should encompass elements of the organization. The realities of global competition offer no alternatives: Either compete by being able to offer customers improved products and services, or go out of business. Senior managers have the residual responsibility to prepare the enterprise for its future. This book has repeatedly made the point that projects are building blocks in the design and execution of organizational strategies. Projects which have as their objective bringing continuous improvement to products and processes are an important block in preparing the enterprise for its competitive future. Indeed, senior managers have little choice: Either provide for a stream of projects directed to bringing about continuous improvement in the enterprise, or prepare to cease to exist. Competitors will not allow you to maintain a competitive edge for long in products and services. They will develop their own continuous improvement projects and move ahead of the complacent status-quo-directed enterprise.

Given the inevitability of continuous improvement in competitor offerings, a chapter that ties together continuous improvement and project management is a needed addition to this work. As you peruse this chapter, consider this question: How does the use of project management facilitate a continuous improvement strategy in the enterprise?

Survival through Change

Competitive survival requires that the company develop the ability to pursue an extended and prolonged strategy of continuous improvement. Unceasing action must be underway to raise the quality and productivity of the organizational processes which will lead to improved products and services. Undesirable situations and strategies in the enterprise that negatively affect a strategy of continuous improvement need to be reevaluated. Everything has to be done better. Change has to be managed for the continuous betterment of the enterprise through a strategy of adding something worthy to that which already exists. One senior industry executive has noted that the result of many small improvements is the surest way, in most industries, to increase competitive advantage. Through such continuous improvement, and the attitude required to assume the risks of such improvement, enhanced competition is realized, and the stakeholders—customers, suppliers, employees, creditors, and so forth—find increasing value in continuing an association with the enterprise.

Continuous improvement can take many forms. Increasing the efficiency of current operations through better utilization of assets is one way. Developing strategies that result in greater effectiveness—doing the right thing—is another way of realizing continuous improvement. A common base of continuous improvement through the use of state-of-the-art technology in organizational processes ultimately improves the products and services offered by the enterprise. Caution is required to make sure that the introduction of technology is consistent with all the systems that will be impacted by that technology.

By using project teams as the organizational design alternative for working continuous improvement in the organization, an interdisciplinary perspective of the need and remedial strategy for continuous improvement can be provided. Such interdisciplinary teams provide an ambience where there is a high probability that all facets of the problem or opportunity will be exposed and considered by the team. In the operation of such teams, a viewpoint by one team member is likely to cause a reaction by another team member, who would not have reacted if there had not been the stimulus provided by work in the team situation. In the material that follows, examples are given of how continuous improvement through projects has been achieved.

- At the Motorola cellular phone business, a plantwide team was formed to improve the manufacturing environment for circuit boards for phones. The team tested various antistatic packages used to move boards along the assembly line and determined that a clamshell-shaped package was the best. The change in the board helped boost quality and keep Motorola ahead of its rivals. At Levi Strauss and at Sara Lee, corporations have created teams of 30 to 50 workers that make an entire garment. Operators within each team move between machines to eliminate bottlenecks. The teams, not the engineers or supervisors, decide on how to set up the line. Levi Strauss & Company began to convert its U.S. plants, and each plant now can make a bundle of 30 jeans in 7 hours from start to finish instead of the 6 days it often took under the old method, where bundles often got stuck at different stages of the manufacturing process. At the Levi Strauss, 432-employee plant in Blue Ridge, Georgia, which converted to teams in the spring of 1992, an immediate improvement in quality was realized.

- General Electric Company has initiated the concept of a "workout" where interdisciplinary teams work at improving productivity through eliminating wasteful paperwork, duplication, unnecessary approvals, and other bureaucratic impediments to efficiency and productivity. At the company's Schenectady turbine plant, a team effort under workout strategy has improved productivity beyond anything that was ever envisioned. In the steam turbine bucket machinery center, teams of hourly employees now operate, without supervision, a $420 million new milling machine that the team members have selected, tested, and approved for purchase. The cycle time for the operation has dropped 80 percent. CEO Jack Welch has stated: "It is embarrassing to reflect that for probably 80 or 90 years we've been dictating equipment needs and managing people who knew how to do things much better and faster than we did."[1]

- A manufacturer, as part of a new manufacturing strategy, established a project team with the objective of making one of its key plants a model for high-capacity, manufacturing efficiency and round-the-clock operation. Several key subobjectives had to be met to attain the overall project objectives:

1. Hire, train, and deploy a third shift of workers to meet the round-the-clock objective.
2. Develop a master schedule to provide maintenance support in between the rotating shift of production operation.
3. Assess, design, install, and check out increased automation of the production process.
4. Develop and implement just-in-time (JIT) inventory management policy and procedures to include transport of finished products on an accelerated schedule.
5. Conduct a feasibility study for the development of flexible manufacturing systems to deal with an anticipated future mix of new product models, fewer parts, and more standardized assembly procedures.
6. Study the advantages of using product-process design teams in the context of concurrent engineering to facilitate the development of coordinated "systems" changes needed to meet the plant's objectives for a new manufacturing strategy.

- GE's electric motors division was in trouble in 1987. The division's revenues had fallen by 7 percent since 1984 to $710 million. Return on sales was less than 2 percent versus an average of 6 percent at other GE units. To improve chances for profitability improvement, workers accepted an 11 percent cut in pay and passed up scheduled raises of $1.30 an hour. The pay cuts saved $425 million a year, and the other plant closing eliminated 1000 jobs—but productivity plummeted and worker morale fell drastically. To remake the division, several strategies for modern manufacturing techniques were undertaken: just-in-time inventory, quality control, design for manufacture, and the establishment of teams of seven to eight workers who rotated tasks and made oper-

---

[1]John F. Welch, Jr., chairman of the board and chief executive officer, *1991 Annual Report*, General Electric Company, pp. 1–5.

ational decisions about how work should be done. Productivity gains have been above moderate, says a GE official.[2]

To stay competitive, Boeing Company needs to reduce the cost of building a plane by no less than 25 to 30 percent. Turning the company into an efficient manufacturer is an awesome challenge that CEO Shrontz faces. Overcoming the hierarchical orientation of the company and reinventing the company in the way it designs and builds its customized, high-quality products are a challenge that has to be met. Cost savings realized through the continuous improvement process teams can be used to substantially lower prices and fund the innovations needed to reduce customers' maintenance and fuel costs. Improvements underway include

- Reduction of inventory costs through just-in-time strategies
- Reduction of the time required to manufacture a plan from more than a year to just 6 months
- Cutting engineering hours
- Eliminating raw material waste
- Minimizing expensive tooling
- Use of concurrent engineering during the design phase of new products
- Empowerment of product design teams to approve or alter a design change
- Use of computer-aided design[3]

Continuous improvement springs from the creative act leading to improvements—the introduction of something new in the organization's products and processes. Creative thought is required which, properly formulated and implemented, leads to acts of change in the enterprise. "New blood" is introduced to the organization, providing for a change to be developed and introduced into products, services, and processes.

Management Innovation Again

Innovation has been studied primarily in the context of product-process innovation. Ray Stata, writing in the *Sloan Management*

---

[2]Aaron Bernstein, "GE's Hard Lesson: Pay Cuts Can Backfire," *Business Week,* August 10, 1992.

[3]Shawn Tully, "Can Boeing Reinvent Itself?" *Fortune,* March 18, 1993, pp. 66–73.

Review, offers a refreshing view of innovation in the context of management innovation. In this section in the material that follows, his viewpoints are paraphrased and augmented.[4]

Innovation is usually thought of in the context of product-process innovation. The opportunities for innovation go beyond just products and processes—the key to progress in companies also rests with *management innovation.* Japan's success and rise to an industrial power are based on management innovation, not technological innovation in the traditional sense. Management innovation comes about through the use of management technology.

Systems thinking and dynamics can be used to solve complex problems in organizations. The combination of individual and group learning means that organizational learning also takes place. The rate at which individuals and organizations learn is one key sustainable competitive advantage. This is so because

- Organizational learning occurs through shared insights, knowledge, and mental models.

- Organizations can learn only as rapidly as the weakest link in the organizational membership.

- Learning builds on past knowledge and experience—on memory. Organizational mechanisms such as policies, strategies, plans, and procedures are used as means to retain organizational learning.

Systems thinking is required—the recognition that a change in one part of the organization will have impact throughout the organizational system. A basic characteristic of a system is the delay time between cause and effect, such as when an order is received and when the finished products are shipped. Another example is the time between the start of the design of a product and when that design is finished and committed to manufacturing. Anything that can be done in the decision process to motivate a systems viewpoint and to reduce the time delay in the linkages of the system will raise the chances of improvements in products and processes.

In the design of any system, such as a planning system, the process that people go through is just as valuable as the output. When a task force is appointed to do strategic planning for the organization, the output of the objectives, goals, and strategies of the organization is valuable. Another valuable "product" of the planning process is the learning, both individual and collective, enjoyed by the people work-

---

[4]Ray Stata, "Organizational Learning—The Key to Management Innovation," *Sloan Management Review,* Spring 1989, pp. 63–74.

ing together on a project team to understand and carry out the development of objectives, goals, and strategies. For example, at Analog Devices, Inc., strategic planning was initiated through the appointment of 15 corporatewide product, market, and technology task teams that pulled together 150 professionals. These teams worked for 12 months to come up with nine imperatives for improvement through change to include specific recommendations for how to bring about these changes. The professionals serving on these teams acquired an understanding of corporate beliefs and assumptions that had served the company well in the past. A significant outcome that became clear to both senior managers and project team members was the need to coordinate technological development across divisions and to centralize certain aspects of manufacturing. The need to better coordinate product planning to capitalize on the company's strengths became clear to the people engaged in this planning effort.

Other project teams were formed in the company to consider strategies to reduce the percentage of orders shipped late. The use of a team approach in dealing with this problem and other problems was helpful in improving interdepartment communication and helped to get people to think about problems and issues in an interdisciplinary and objective fashion as well as subjectively and politically. The teams facilitated the abandonment of parochial departmental thinking—to separate the vital few problems from the trivial many—and focus organizational resources on solving them. Indeed teamwork was elevated to a virtue in the culture of Analog Devices, Inc.

In order to carry forth the advantages gained from teamwork, openness, and objective thinking, these attributes were included in the company's performance appraisal process and in the criteria for hiring and promotion. The company found that the best way to introduce knowledge and modify behavior is by working with small teams that have the power and wherewithal to bring about change.

Management innovation is an important part of industrial competitiveness, and it will surely become even more of a factor in the future. Management innovation requires new knowledge and skills, new technology, and then the means for the technological transfer of that innovation to the management community. The bottom-line question is this: Are the United States and U.S. companies investing enough in management innovation? We may not be doing so, and the large sums that are being put into product-process development will not produce anywhere near their full potential if we do not put resources into the innovation of management. We need better management concepts, processes, and tools to better help companies be more effective in realizing a payoff in the innovations they develop in products and supporting organizational processes.

If we broaden the concepts of innovation and technology to management, then the need for collaborative research is important. A partnership between academia and business suggests that the following characteristics of research should prove useful:

- Focus on critical management problems.
- Develop and disseminate new learning tools and methods.
- Test tools and methods in practice.
- Provide cross-organizational learning.
- Use a cross-disciplinary approach.
- Provide cooperative education opportunities for students.

Ray Stata's viewpoint of the need for *management innovation,* which is interpreted as innovation in how managerial functions of planning, organizing, directing, and control are carried out, has great appeal for continuing improvement through the use of projects.[5]

Continuous Improvement in Productivity

Increases in manufacturing productivity can come about through the innovation of small changes leading to continuous improvement. In the United States, manufacturing productivity increases between 1982 and 1990 have been impressive—rising at a 4.5 percent annual rate. The rate was 3.9 percent from 1980 to 1990, but it was the best decade-long performance in the entire post-World War II period, not far behind Japan's 5.5 percent per year pace from 1979 to 1989, and better than Germany's 2 percent.[6]

How did these increases come about? We "worked smarter," closed obsolete plants, downsized and restructured organizations, trained employees, got more worker involvement through the use of self-autonomous teams, improved management of manufacturing, developed total quality management processes, eliminated waste, and gained the leverage of updated equipment.

To maintain the growth in productivity, U.S. manufacturers will have to keep the same pace of a broad continuous improvement strategy across the board for all hardware, software, and the utilization of people. Continuous improvement in *process* technology will be a must.

Productivity improvements through continuous improvement proj-

---

[5] Ibid., pp. 63–64.

[6] Joseph Spiers, "A Coming Surge in Capital Spending," *Fortune,* April 22, 1991, pp. 113–119.

ects are coming in the office. These improvements are what is behind many of the layoffs, with office staff getting leaner and more productive. The jobs that are being cut in offices will likely be permanent—the jobs will not come back when the recession is over. Improved technology in offices has replaced people, and the offices will be more productive with leaner payrolls.

Demand will grow for information and computer specialists not doing routine administration, but doing creative design work that leads to better, more timely information for managers and professionals. More office people will truly be involved in doing "knowledge work," leading to continued improvements in quality and productivity.[7]

Creativity and innovation precede continuous improvements in products and services. Formal market research plays a less significant role than is usually believed on the part of the innovator in positioning the firm for future competition. Hewlett-Packard is said to have rejected a McKinsey analysis that claimed an absence of market demand for their calculator. Likewise, Sony's founders did not believe in market research—how do you research a market for a product that does not currently exist?[8] Some writers have claimed that the United States is as innovative as ever. Nevertheless, some suggestions are paraphrased and augmented from *Fortune* magazine on how to facilitate continuous improvement:

- Avoid protecting short-term profit to the detriment of long-term innovation.

- Use a company strategy that encourages both incremental improvement and "breakthrough" innovative strategies.

- Get interest rates down and provide for a reduction in capital gains taxes.

- Recognize that innovation is a process that must be managed through the use of all employees and all the resources of the enterprise. (This can be facilitated through the use of project teams.)

- Dismiss the popular view that creativity and innovation are mysterious, divinely inspired miracles. Most come from long, hard work immersed in the product-process technology that is improved.

- Accept the notion that only about 1 of every 20 to 30 new product ideas becomes a successful product; 1 of 10 to 16 becomes a "hit."

---

[7] Esther Dyson, "Job Losses Are Mounting: Good News?" *Forbes,* March 2, 1992, p. 104.

[8] R. S. Rosenbloom and M. A. Cusumano, "Technological Pioneering and Competitive Advantage: The Birth of the VCR Industry," *California Management Review,* vol. 29, no. 4, Summer 1987.

This means that failure in innovation should not be punished—the effort should be rewarded.

■ Foster a corporate culture that sustains and rewards innovation, even that which fails, for out of such failures will ultimately come successes.

■ Use concurrent engineering to foster innovation, leading to earlier commercialization of products and better performance of organizational processes.

■ Work closely with the customer—lead that customer. In satisfying the customers' needs, watch for how all organizational processes can be improved. A good starting point is to do benchmarking against the competitors and other industry best performers.

■ Encourage all employees to adopt a professional reading program. Not only will they pick up ideas that can lead to innovation, but also they will gain insight into how the parts of the organization and the disciplines will fit together to form a useful synergy in products and processes.

■ Avoid the inevitable delayers, debaters, coordinators, and others who fear change and are comfortable with the status quo. These plodders can kill creativity and innovation in the best-managed organizations.

■ Take risks—get the product reasonably well designed, and get to the marketplace ahead of the competitors. Then develop a rigorous strategy of continuous improvement of products and strategies to keep ahead of the customer. Once a market base is established and the customers have accepted the product, then fine-tuning of the product can be done during the follow-on strategy of continuous improvement.[9]

Once an innovative strategy is undertaken for product-process change through the use of project teams, there is an unending struggle to keep up a continuous improvement posture. There is little rest, even for the innovative person and organization. Competition will always be relentless.

Product Quality through Projects

The drive for improvement in product quality has resulted in U.S. manufacturers catching up with the Japanese. But new dimensions

---

[9]Paraphrased in part from Brian Dumaine, "Closing the Innovation Gap," *Fortune,* December 2, 1991, pp. 56–62.

and applications of total quality improvement are happening. U.S. carmakers are getting their quality up to the level of the Japanese cars, but the Japanese are expanding their concept of quality to a new concept called "miryokukteki hinshitsu"—translated to English, it means "things gone right." By entering the second phase of quality, the "personality" of the car is dictating additional quality improvements. The Japanese believe that quality in automobiles is now taken for granted and that in a defect-free product it is the fine touches that will impress consumers. Many of these fine touches have a technological base, such as:

- Computer-driven hydraulics to cushion jolts

- Equal pressure for stereo buttons, door locks, and turn-signal levers

- Electronically activated, liquid-filled engine mounts that dissipate engine vibration when the car is idling

- Aluminum body and suspension which improve performance by slashing weight

- Air bags

- Seat belts that use pressurized gas to cinch tightly automatically in a crash

- Windshield wipers tuned to speed up as the car accelerates

- Electronically adjustable suspension

- Other sundry performance goals

The Japanese do much better at replacing models of cars than U.S. manufacturers do. Detroit replaces old models an average of every 8 years. Ford averages a glacial 9.5 years versus 4.5 for all Japanese carmakers and just 4 years for Honda. This gives the Japanese more chances to get things going right. Simultaneous engineering (or concurrent engineering), in which suppliers, designers, engineers, manufacturing experts, and other disciplines develop a car jointly, accounts for much of Japan's ability to replace its models sooner than Detroit. Concurrent engineering is discussed in Chap. 1. In the past year Japan's U.S. automobile market share has jumped 3 points; some believe that Japan's share in the near future will have another 3-point jump. In part, these increases have come about because of the variety of incremental advances of product technology and the many varieties that Japanese manufacturers are able to offer.[10]

---

[10]David Woodruff et al., "A New Era for Auto Quality," *Business Week,* October 22, 1990, pp. 82–96.

Trendsetters

Innovation acts by entrepreneurs and companies have changed the way organizations function as well as the products they offer. There have been some notable change makers that set a new trend:

- Ray Kroc and his fast-food restaurants leading to McDonald's.
- Ted Turner, in CNN and UHF television, discovered satellites and changed the way the world gets its news.
- Federal Express.
- Alexander Graham Bell.
- The Mustang automobile.
- The Chrysler minivan.
- Hewlett-Packard's LaserJet printer.
- At GE Jack Welch and his vision of a less hierarchical company.

Once a trend has been set, the opportunity for continuous improvement is also set. Without continuous improvement, obsolescence is very real. Project teams can help to keep this from happening.

Change is necessary to survival—a trite statement, but one that is ignored by many people and organizations. Resistance to change is very real; and to bring about change, you have to have change champions—a role that can be admirably performed by project teams—adequate resources, and the commitment and support of senior management.[11]

Sometimes the act of continuous improvement can be as simple as changing the way people work. In research laboratories and in the professional work carried out by product design engineers, there will usually be found adequate opportunity for improvement through assessing how, and where, people spend their time. Studies show that researchers rarely spend more than one-quarter of their day in the laboratory, and design engineers work on design only 20 percent of the time. Alleviating the impediments can be as simple as drawing attention to them, to someone who can do something about them.

Historically the way to be competitive has been to concentrate on improving the *product* (the result) through continuous improvement, scrap and repair costs, 100 percent inspection, warranty costs, return of defective products, and assessment of complaint notices from customers, essentially concentrate on the results that the organization produces *after* the product or service has been delivered to the cus-

---

[11]John Huey, "Nothing Is Impossible," *Fortune,* September 23, 1991, pp. 133–139.

tomer. The *processes* that have been utilized in the producing of the product or services have not been given their proper due.

When the managers and professionals who want to improve the overall competitiveness through continuous improvement restrict their creative and innovative work to the *results* of the organization, they are neglecting a major source of improvement—the *processes* that are undertaken in the enterprise to produce the results. Such processes include product design, marketing, manufacturing, after-sales service, quality, supplier relationships, and finances. A willingness to explicitly study *product and process design and implementation* can provide enormous benefits to the enterprise if carried out effectively. When product-process design teams are utilized to *concurrently* consider all the organizational functions required in conceptualizing, making, and delivering a product or service to the customer, better competitiveness is realized. A product-process design project team provides for the integration of the many disciplinary considerations involved in meeting and exceeding the competition. Quality changes will happen in the marketplace—and the competitors will benchmark your products and your processes in their efforts to match and exceed your competitive products and services.

Focusing on the organizational processes needed to create and deliver quality products and services to the customer makes good sense. Improvement of organizational processes is needed. But in managing such improvement, the integrity of the products and services should not be forgotten.

New products brought about through supporting efficient organizational processes are at the center of global competition. Key strategies in the global marketplace include the development of high-quality products at lower cost and faster commercialization.

Product Integrity

Product integrity means that the product has more than just a basic functionality or performance character; it has additional characteristics which complement the customers' values and lifestyles. Industrial products match the existing work flows and production systems of the customer. Product integrity has two components: internal integrity and external integrity. *Internal integrity* refers to the unity between a product's function and its construction—the parts fit smoothly, the components match well, and the product works well—and the layout maximizes the available space. From an organizational viewpoint, product integrity means that a focus has been achieved through interdisciplinary project teams working with customers and suppliers. *External integrity* refers to the unity between the product's performance and the customers' expectations. Product integrity can be enhanced by having an organizational approach which provides focus and management to the product management activities to include how people do their work, the way decisions are made, the effectiveness of information flow and use, and the way that supplier and customer considerations are integrated into both the management of the project and the technical aspect of the product.[12]

Most people in the enterprise work in the manufacturing or operations side of the business. Improvement in manufacturing systems technology has become a key global competitive consideration.

Continuous Improvement in Manufacturing

Continuous improvement through the introduction of technology to an organization has to be done with great care. Despite the billions of dollars that General Motors invested in factory robots in the United States, GM failed to take into consideration the human issues that would arise as the result of introduction of automated factory systems in its plants. The company had to slow down the start-up of its automated factories until the workers were ready and trained to assume their roles in the production systems. Even though GM invested in advanced manufacturing systems to improve productivity, reduce costs, and improve quality, the company's eroding domestic market share was not saved.

Automobile manufacturers must move to "lean manufacturing" strategies and techniques that were developed in Japan. This was made clear in a 5-year study of the automobile industry by the International Motor Vehicle Program at the Massachusetts Institute of Technology (MIT). This study showed that the techniques of lean manufacturing developed in Japan have made traditional mass-production methods as obsolete as the Model T. In lean manufacturing, teams of skilled workers use flexible manufacturing systems to produce customized products of endless variety to exacting quality standards, quickly, and at low cost. In Europe, carmakers have concentrated too much on improving the efficiency of mass-production techniques—the enhancement of an existing technology whose time has passed.

The Japanese system of lean manufacturing helps manufacturers make cars with fewer defects, in smaller spaces, with workers who are better trained and who work with less absenteeism. According to the MIT study done in 1989, the Japanese take 16.8 hours on average to produce a car, the Americans require 25.1 hours, and the European

---

[12]Kim B. Clark and Takahiro Fjuimoto, "The Power of Product Integrity," *Harvard Business Review,* November-December 1990, pp. 107–118.

manufacturers require 36.2 hours. More striking is the difference in product development time. The Japanese can design, develop, and deliver an entirely new car in 46 months, using an average of 1.7 million hours of engineering effort. The Europeans and Americans take about 60 months and use 3.0 million engineering hours. Even more challenging, Japan's competitive advantage in the automobile industry is accelerating. Even in automobile components, the Japanese are ahead of the rest of the world. Japanese producers have higher productivity and product quality and faster design-development-delivery cycles. They also achieve more product variety at a lower cost.

European manufacturers face the challenge of raising their productivity and quality standards to maintain global competitiveness. To do this, they have to evolve quickly away from traditional mass production toward flexible, lean manufacturing systems. This will require the embracing of project teams, self-directed teams, just-in-time inventory management, and other techniques of lean manufacturing.[13]

Continuous improvement in the automobile industry led by the Japanese manufacturers has caught the attention of automakers in Europe. Competitive survival will require these manufacturers to change, not only through a continuous improvement strategy, but through more radical change.

Change is underway in European automobile plants. These automakers are struggling to meld local workers and Japanese manufacturing and management techniques. This change is not without pain. Automobile manufacturing executives have taken longer to understand that the new innovations will not work without radical shifts in labor relations. Japanese management techniques such as just-in-time inventory management and total quality management are complex and require careful consideration of the human issues involved as well as close employee cooperation. Some experts have questioned whether such techniques will work in a contentious country such as France. But to meet competition, the work culture in France and other European countries will have to change. The major impact will be on labor relations. In the use of modern manufacturing and automation, workers have to abandon their narrow job classifications and learn more jobs, solve problems, and work in less predictable and programmed ways. Customers demand a greater variety of products and options. This means complex, harder jobs for employees. After decades of working in traditional ways, workers in Europe are having difficulty accepting the new philosophy.

---

[13] Paraphrased from Christopher Knowlton, "Can Europe Compete?" *Fortune,* December 2, 1991, pp. 147–153.

To compete, European companies will have to downsize and restructure. Older, big factories will have to be closed, and new, smaller ones set up to use modern management concepts. Workers will have to be closely screened to ensure that they have the aptitude and the right values to work in production teams, quality improvement teams, product-process design project teams, and such innovative organizational design alternatives as are being used in the modern factory. The opportunities for project management have never been better.[14]

Change is difficult in all organizations. The challenge for small and midsized companies is particularly critical since these companies often lack the resources to adequately cope with the needed change. Financial resources are scarce. Continued legislation that puts additional administrative burdens on these companies ties up managerial and professional time. Many of these small enterprises are poorly capitalized.

Manufacturing Philosophies

A manufacturing management philosophy for continuous improvement means many things. It means that truly a systems viewpoint has to be taken in the seeking of improvement in the products and processes of the enterprise. Total quality management, just-in-time inventory, flexible manufacturing systems, and other innovative techniques have to be integrated as a way of life in continuous improvement in manufacturing. All the organization's people have to be involved in the process, and the message has to get across that the improvement is not just another program but is a set of related programs and projects working together. The formation of project teams to study and make recommendations for improvement not only brings in the multifunctional nature of the change, but gets people involved at different levels and from different functions, which sends an important message to the organization of the systems nature of the changes.

Some basic principles for continuously improving manufacturing processes include the following:

- Reduce the number of parts by combining or eliminating them.

- Minimize assembly surfaces, and ensure that all processes are on one surface and completed before moving on to the next one.

---

[14]Paraphrased from E. S. Browning, "Europe's Auto Makers Struggle to Meld Local Workers and Japanese Techniques," *Wall Street Journal,* November 22, 1991.

- Design for top-down assembly, thus gaining the advantage of gravity and reducing the number of clamps and fixtures.

- Improve assembly access by increasing unobstructed vision and ensuring adequate clearance for standard tooling.

- Maximize parts compliance by providing adequate grooves, guide surfaces, and specifications for marrying parts. This can reduce misalignments and poor quality.

- Maximize part symmetry, which makes parts handling easier. If symmetry is not possible, then design in whatever asymmetry or alignment features are possible.

- Make effective use of rigid-parts design rather than flexible ones. Rigid parts are easier to handle. Provide adequate surfaces for mechanical gripping, and design in barriers to tangling, nesting, or interlocking which take time to correct.

- Minimize, or avoid, separate fasteners. By using standard fasteners into components, such as snap-fits, the assembly process can be simplified.

- Provide self-locking parts such as tabs, indentations, or projections on mating parts to identify them and their orientation through final assembly.

- Move toward modular design for common functional requirements and standard interfaces for easy interchangeability of modules. This will improve testing and service on the product, provide more options, and offer faster, continuous improvement of the product.[15]

Computer-integrated manufacturing (CIM)

CIM has become a key strategy in improving U.S. competitiveness. The decision to introduce CIM into manufacturing operation can improve efficiency and reduce product costs. But CIM by itself will not ensure competitive success. Customers have to buy the products; competitors will be trying to beat you out in the marketplace. Order entry procedures have to be effective; sales and sales promotion take on new significance. Customers may require financing, and the work force may see CIM as a threat. The use of CIM has to be blended into other functions and activities of the enterprise—thus a decision to implement CIM has potential reverberations throughout the company. Responsibility for the development of a CIM strategy is not limited to manufacturing; it encompasses

---

[15]Paraphrased from Theresa R. Walter, "Design for Manufacture and Assembly," *Industry Week*, September 4, 1989, p. 82.

all functional elements of the business. The enterprise's functional and specialized areas have to interact through project teams in answering the questions about the CIM strategy: How will that strategy affect our business? What are its short- and long-term results? What will be done with extra production time? How will the improvement in manufacturing productivity affect the rest of the business? What forces are developing in the marketplace that have a potential influence on our manufacturing strategies? If new products are developed, how will the manufacture of those products be changed by our current strategy in CIM? These are a few of the questions that have to be answered in considering the use of CIM.

Market needs and customer-use considerations have to be evaluated. What will be the cost of shared resources and overhead allocations? How does the mission of the information system change? How will manufacturing deal with shorter runs of more specialized products?

The introduction of CIM is a strategic decision that affects all business activities, a decision whose impact will be felt across the traditional functional lines of the enterprise and will extend to suppliers, customers, regulatory bodies, local communities, and unions, to name a few. CIM implies that decisions concerning what you make, how you make it, where it will be made, and how the products will be supported have to be made in unison and in harmony. CIM should come out of the development of systems-strategic project planning in the enterprise—basically as part of a broader business strategy. Thus CIM does not just lower manufacturing costs, it is part of a larger business strategy that has to be compatible with globally changing technologies, competitive realities, and unforgiving markets. It is difficult to imagine CIM without the catalyst of project management.

Just-in-time manufacturing (JIT)

JIT manufacturing is revolutionary in the way that inventories are managed in today's organizations. The improvement in manufacturing technology through the use of JIT strategies has created systems changes. JIT concepts and processes have been adequately described in the literature. There is the opportunity in organizations to take JIT manufacturing beyond the manufacturing plant to other situations in the enterprise. Billesback and Schniederjans have suggested the application of JIT techniques to the administrative activities of the enterprise. The following section, paraphrased from these authors, provides a refreshing opportunity for the transfer of JIT technology.

Consider the application of the JIT concept to administrative activities. Administrative activities are any activities *not* related to the production of goods: scheduling, billing, order entry, accounting, plant maintenance, and financial tasks, to name a few. Manufacturing activities include such things as assembling a component, stamping, welding, milling, sanding, grinding, and cutting metal; transporting work-in-process is also considered a manufacturing activity.

Think of JIT as a philosophy for the elimination of all waste in administrative activities. Waste does not add value to the product. Some activities simply add cost to the product or process.

Storing, moving, expediting, scheduling, and inspection soon reach diminishing returns in adding value, as do stacking, filing, mailing, transmitting, "rush ordering," routing, and proofing.

Some project-directed strategies that can be employed to improve administrative just-in-time (AJIT) techniques include the following:

- Provide employees with time for identifying problems and solutions to improve productivity.

- Improve layout to facilitate flow of work.

- Locate workers whose work is related close together.

- Allow workers to see total of work to be performed insofar as possible.

- Look for barriers to communication.

- Specialized and quality training and performance help to reduce waste.

- Consider standardization of activities and pooling of responsibility for similar activities.

- Use worker-centered total quality management.

- Trace performance to a specific individual.

- Decentralize authority to make the appropriate decisions.

- Monitor the process from start to finish to see what factors slow down or halt the processes.

- Reduce the number of workers until the processes slow down or come to a halt.

- Look for extra workers, procedures, policies, processes, and backup equipment that mask organizational weaknesses.

- Consider a better grouping of related organizational functions and processes.

- Look for bureaucratic structure or processes that stifle information flows, decision making, and orderly procedures or create lethargy in the flow of work.

- Provide for an organizational design (steering committee) to facilitate the AJIT techniques review and facilitate the transfer of processing technology.

- And the bottom line—use cross-functional project teams to seek improvement.[16]

JIT philosophies and techniques can extend from the purchases of components and materials throughout the entire manufacturing process and out to the customer to include after-sales services to customers. Within organizations there are many different forms of "inventory" to include: information, housekeeping supplies, time, equipment, machine and equipment time, material—indeed any resource that can provide value to organizational products and processes. Strategies can be employed to reduce the amount of inventory required to support the organization. USAir dealt with this kind of opportunity through the organizational design of a project team in a very explicit way.

Reduction of inventory was the reason that the CEO of USAir gave for standardizing the interiors of aircraft in the fleet. The postmerger fleet of the airline had 5 colors of seat belts, 5 colors of curtains, 16 colors of seat covers, and 3 different kinds of carpet. The company was stocking 180 different seat covers, which proved too costly from an inventory standpoint. Furthermore, the requirements of nine types of aircraft, each with varying shapes of seat backs and bottoms, with some having in-arm food trays, different shaped window seats, and so on, added complexity to the inventory management challenge for the airline. Planners at USAir worked with designers and suppliers on selecting patterns and colors for the redone aircraft fleet, keeping in mind the need for a corporate identity and ease of care and management of the inventory.[17]

Continuous Improvements: The Connections

In his book *Connections,* James Burke acquaints the reader with some of the forces that have caused changes in the past, examining eight innovations which have markedly influenced the way we live.[18] These innovations are the atomic bomb, telephone, computer, production-line system of manufacture, aircraft, plastics, guided rocket, and television. He explains how closely connected events extending from the ancient world to the present have been influenced by technology and have, in turn, influenced future events of technology.

---

[16]Thomas J. Billesback and Marc J. Schniederjans, "Applicability of Just-in-Time Techniques in Administration," *Production and Inventory Management Journal,* Third quarter 1989, pp. 40–44.

[17]*USAir Magazine,* October 1991, p. 7.

[18]James Burke, *Connections* (Boston: Little, Brown, 1978).

A *connection* is the condition of being joined—a relationship expressed in some union which relates and links associated technology. For example, manufacturing systems technology has relevant subsystems of hardware, software, people, culture, products, processes, and so forth. A change in any of these subsystems will have reverberations throughout any given manufacturing system.

It is no different when one pursues a strategy of continuous improvement through the use of projects; many relevant subsystems will be connected. In the material that follows, a few of these connections are described.

The common denominator of continuous improvement is technology. As an example, consider the technology of a simple product such as a diaper. Kimberly-Clark product developers envisioned the concept of disposable training pants, a cross between absorbable diapers and underwear. After incurring over $12 million development costs in 1987, the company kept its scientists working on the concept. The result: Huggies Pull-Ups, a fast, competitive seller. This innovative product is expected to reach sales of $500 million a year, even though the unit price is about twice the price of standard baby diapers but about half the promotion costs. Pull-Ups are enormously profitable.

The development of this product came from the use of a project team of managers and professionals who focused on using innovation from the company laboratories rather than acquisitions to acquire a new, competitive product. The product worked in laboratory tests. By assuming the risk of going immediately to full-scale commercial production with four new machines at the company's Paris, Texas, diaper plant, and by reducing manufacturing and marketing steps, Kimberly-Clark got the product to market 50 percent faster than past products.[19]

Of course, continuous improvement is needed in all industries. Some additional examples follow.

Airlines

The airlines today are seeing most challenging times. Some of the older airlines have gone into bankruptcy and then liquidation. But others have done well. One profitable airline is Southwest Airlines. The reasons for this airline's success can be attributed to the continuous improvement of its service. The reasons for this success include

- It adopted a conservative financial strategy.

---

[19]Alecia Swasy, "Kimberly-Clark Bets, Wins on Innovation," *Wall Street Journal,* November 22, 1991.

- It has a philosophy of managing so that the company will do well in bad times.
- Spending is not allowed to get out of control.
- It has a unique niche among U.S. airlines. It is the nation's only high-frequency, short-distance, low-fare airline. It has not allowed success to move it from its niche.
- A city is "attacked with a lot of flights."
- It views the competition as the automobile.
- Southwest has the industry's lowest costs. It uses only one aircraft, the Boeing 737, and saves on training, maintenance, and inventory.
- It has the fastest gate turnaround.
- Southwest offers peanuts and drinks, but no meals. There is no assigned seating. Southwest does not subscribe to any centralized reservation system, and does not transfer baggage to other carriers.
- Employees are unionized.
- There are flexible work rules. Pilots and crews clean up the airplane after each flight, then cleaning crews come in at night.
- In training, the emphasis is on attitudes.[20]

Restaurants

Taco Bell, a successful company in the fast-food business, has pursued a successful strategy of continuous improvement. In an overall market that has seen flat to declining sales, growth at Taco Bell has expanded by over 60 percent. Profits have grown by well over 26 percent per year, compared with under 6 percent annually at McDonald's. Taco Bell has been able to cut prices for its core menus by over 25 percent. Why? The key elements of Taco Bell's strategy include the following:

- The simple premise is that customers value the food, the service, and the physical appearance of a restaurant, and that is all.
- Everything that helps the company to deliver value to customers along these dimensions deserves reinforcement and managerial support. Everything else is not value-added overhead.
- Every role in the corporation was evaluated in terms of its ability to create value.

---

[20] Subrata N. Chakravarty, "Hit 'em Hardest with the Mostest," *Forbes,* September 16, 1991, pp. 48–54.

- The stores are staffed with talented, motivated people supplied with timely, accurate information on how the store is doing.

- There is a minimum number of supervisors because of the empowerment of people in the stores.

- Span of control has gone from one supervisor for every 5-plus stores in 1988 to one for every 20-plus stores today.

- Supervisors are coaches and facilitators, rather than agents of direction and control.

- New information systems were installed to raise quality and sales and to monitor mistakes.

- Restaurant managers are freed from more than 15 hours of nonproductive work each week.

- The company collects real-time performance data on costs, employees, and customer satisfaction.

- Fresh, tasty food is served in clean surroundings, and subcontracts the work of preparing the food.

- Taco Bell's people concentrate on the customer. At McDonald's, the back room (the production site) becomes more complex—as new items such as pizza and fresh muffins are added, the manufacturing becomes more complex.

- More than 15 hours of back-room labor per day is eliminated.

- People are shifted from the back room to serving customers.

- Job descriptions focus on customer service.

- Employees are carefully chosen based on values and attitudes toward responsibility, teamwork, and other themes that have been measured to correlate with successful service. Detailed interviews with prospective employees are conducted.

- Store managers are required to spend at least half of their time developing the capabilities of their employees.

- Everyone receives training in communication, performance measurement, team building, coaching, and people empowerment.

- Employee morale is measured, and actions are taken to improve that morale.

- The bottom line is that Taco Bell has redefined the service business.

McDonald's has focused on more of the same—more advertising, more promotion, more new products, more new locations—but more of the same does not work anymore.

Building trucks

In the truck engine business, competition from overseas has created problems for U.S. manufacturers. Detroit Diesel, a mainstay producer of diesel engines, got into difficulties in its new model 92 series heavy-truck engine. Too many shortcuts in design had been taken, too much coddling of model 92 during preproduction tests, poor fuel mileage, and engines that failed on the road put the company into grave difficulties. In the plant, the company was faced with over 2000 grievances that had been filed during the personnel cuts made during layoffs and buyout restructuring. A new CEO took over the leadership of the company and brought about an impressive turnaround.

Review of the strategies which facilitated the turnaround of Detroit Diesel, brought from General Motors in 1988 by Roger Penske, indicates plenty of continuous improvement through project teamwork and effort. Key attitudes at Detroit Diesel include "Manage your business, manage your job, most importantly manage your personal life." The company's share of heavy-truck engine sales exploded to 23 percent in the first half of 1991, from 3.2 percent in 1987. In addition, the company won the race to develop the first methanol-fuel heavy vehicle to meet California and federal clean-air standards. Arch rival Cummins Engine Company, wallowing in red ink, cut its dividend and payroll; Detroit Diesel ($1.2 billion business) is profitable and hiring more workers. How? What happened by way of continuous improvement?

- There is a new ownership and entire operating philosophy and style.
- The focus is on people and customers.
- There is ceaseless salesmanship by the CEO.
- The decision process is fast-paced ($5 million training and fitness center and new cafeteria).
- Sample engines are given away.
- There is a close working relationship with the unions.
- Factory tours are available for dealers and customers.
- There are mass meetings with workers to answer questions.
- The CEO meets regularly with union leaders and small groups of workers.
- New hires spend a week in the factory being tested on their own time to qualify for employment.
- Profit sharing is a productivity goal.
- Workers who miss more than 5 days a year get smaller paychecks.

The difference goes to the workers who have worked, so absenteeism is way down.

- Detroit Diesel slashed 25 percent of its white-collar work force.
- Speed is the hallmark of managing.[21]

Summary

To be competitive today, a company has to practice continuous improvement and be nimble in responding to changes in markets and in the technology of products and processes. Two potential strategies exist for companies to pursue in advancing the technologies of their products and processes: (1) continuous improvement of the products and services that are offered and (2) a push for a "breakthrough" in technology of products and processes. Both strategies are facilitated by the use of project management techniques. Which strategy to pursue depends on the resources available to the organization and the amount of risk that the managers are willing to assume. To do nothing means obsolescence and ultimate dissolution.

The leader of an enterprise that wishes to introduce and eventually institutionalize continuous improvement in the culture of the organization can follow the following general ideas of how such improvements can be designed and implemented by the use of project teams:

First, recognize that any meaningful innovation must come from many sources. Innovation is not the sole capability of the managers in the enterprise. Rather, the talent for innovation is widely distributed among the members. How willing these members are to suggest areas for improvement depends to a large degree on how they perceive the cultural ambience of the environment, how that ambience rewards improvement suggestions, and how forgiveness is provided for those who try to improve but make an occasional mistake.

If people see and accept the use of project management as an organizational strategy for dealing with continuous improvement, it has a better chance of happening.

People will act according to what they believe is expected of them. If they know—and feel—that they are expected to pursue continuous improvement in their work, they will act accordingly. Conversely, if the general perception is that "business as usual" is the way of doing things, then people will react in just this way: While they may do their jobs, they will not offer suggestions to improve products and organizational processes.

---

[21] Joseph B. White, "How Detroit Diesel, out from under GM, Turned Around Fast," *Wall Street Journal,* August 8, 1991.

Continuous improvement successes should be noted and publicized throughout the organization. Those people who were responsible for creating and implementing the improvements should be recognized and rewarded. Improvements can be used to communicate to everyone that "the way we do things around here" is indeed to keep relentlessly improving everything we do. And the status quo is a sure step to lack of competitiveness—a lack which surely leads to loss of markets and jobs.

Provide the training and tools required to give people an edge in seeing ways of improving the products and services they provide to both external and internal customers. The use of statistical quality control, the use of computers, how to build and maintain information systems, how to lead and serve on a project team, and how to find and review data of all kinds are some of the basic capabilities that people require to be able to see through the curtains of "business as usual" and sense the opportunity for improvement.

Get people involved on project teams to benchmark their competitors as well as the best performers in related industries. Determine why these organizations have been excellent in offering improved products and services through improved organizational processes. Send some of the people to visit these performers and have them come back and conduct briefings for members of their peer groups on what they saw and learned—and what these performers were doing to keep the record of continuous improvement active and moving ahead.

Finally, get the message across to all the people that continuous improvement is really a strategy on how to manage change through project management in the enterprise. Tell them that it is much better to manage your own change through continuous improvement than to have a competitor manage your change.

For most companies the pursuit of continuous improvement in products and processes is the most realistic strategy. This requires a full acceptance of the need to use "strategic thinking" and project management in the management of the enterprise and to strategically manage the organization as if the future mattered.

Discussion Questions

1. What does a philosophy of continuous improvement mean?
2. Why should senior managers be concerned about the process of continuous improvement?
3. It has been said that global competitiveness and continuous improvement are relentlessly linked. Why does such a linkage exist?
4. What are some of the forms that continuous improvement can take on in an enterprise?

5. Why does the use of project teams as an organizational design for continuous improvement make sense?

6. If project teams are not used as an organizational design for continuous improvement, what alternative organizational designs might be used?

7. What are some of the common themes of continuous improvement that can be deduced from a perusal of the examples given in the chapter?

8. What are some of the opportunities for continuous improvement to be found in the area of management innovation?

9. What are some of the benefits to be realized from continuous improvement in productivity and quality considerations?

10. Which companies have set high standards in the area of continuous improvement?

11. What are some of the key gains for continuous improvement in manufacturing? Are there any opportunities for the "technology transfer" of these gains to service-related enterprises?

12. In this chapter the notion of the connections involved in continuous improvement is given. What is meant by these connections, and what are some examples?

User Checklist

1. Does the company have any philosophy and strategy of continuous improvement? If not, why not?

2. Is the climate in the company compatible to the development of a deliberate strategy for the design and implementation of continuous improvement initiatives?

3. After a perusal of the examples given in this chapter of organizations that have pursued a strategy of continuous improvement, are there any areas where such a strategy might be developed for your company?

4. What challenges does the company currently face that suggest the need for continuous improvement leading to increased productivity and quality?

5. Are there opportunities in your company for the use of alternative teams for continuing improvement initiatives?

6. What might be learned if the senior management of the company were willing to appoint a project team to examine the opportunities for continuing improvement in manufacturing?

7. Are there any attitudinal issues that might mitigate against the development and implementation of successful continuous improvement initiatives in the company?

8. What are the major strategic and operational issues facing the company at present? Given these issues, would a strategy of continuous improvement initiatives hold any promise for producing positive results for the enterprise?

9. Are there any opportunities for administrative just-in-time improvements in the company? Why or why not?

10. What might be the outcome if each of the major functions within the enterprise were examined to see what specific opportunities might exist for designing and launching a continuous improvement strategy?

11. Are any of the company's competitors using continuous improvement initiatives in their organizational strategy? If so, could any of these initiatives be benchmarked to gain insight into the competitor's advantages?

12. The only thing that is permanent today is *change*. Furthermore, any company's strategy in products and organizational processes is aging. Given these conditions, do the senior managers of the enterprise possess the leadership qualities to cope with change through the development and implementation of continuous improvement strategies?

20

Cultural Considerations in Project Management[1]

"A corporation's culture can be its major strength when it is consistent with its strategies."

In other chapters of this book, we have presented the concepts of project and team management. This chapter develops the concept of an organizational culture as the ambience within which project management exists.

Culture is a set of refined behaviors that people have and strive toward in their society. Culture, according to anthropologist E. B. Taylor, includes the totality of knowledge, belief, art, morals, law, custom, and the other capabilities and habits acquired by individuals as members of a society.[2]

Anthropologists have long used the concept of culture in describing primitive societies. Modern sociologists have borrowed this anthropological concept of culture and used it to describe a way of life of a people. Here, the term is used to describe the synergistic set of shared ideas and beliefs that is associated with a way of life in an organization.

The interest in a company's culture is illustrated by efforts underway at DuPont Company. DuPont is trying to create a new culture

---

[1]This chapter contains substantial material from the author's article, "The Cultural Ambience of Project Management—Another Look," *Project Management Journal,* June 1988, pp. 49–56.

[2]Paraphrased from E. B. Taylor, *The Origins of Culture* (New York: Harper & Row, 1958), 1st ed. published in 1871).

driven by profits, not just research prowess. The new chairman, Edgar S. Woolard, Jr., recognizes that the company takes too long to convert research into products that can benefit customers. The company is trying to restructure a "bloated bureaucracy." About 30 percent of its research budget, or more than $400 million a year, is being shifted toward speeding new products to customers. A "skunk works" antidote is being tried by several DuPont departments to speed the new-product process. These departments have created small, interdisciplinary project teams to field all new-product ideas. These teams include research, manufacturing, and sales representatives. DuPont is also working more closely with customers.

Another problem being addressed at DuPont is how to reduce the debugging of a new product after the product is launched. Interdisciplinary teams are working to think through how to prevent such debugging after product delivery.

The emphasis is being shifted from only product development to improving the processes used to manufacture new products. The potential savings—and resultant products—from improving manufacturing at DuPont at more than 100 plants worldwide are huge. At the polymers division, 60 percent of the research budget is being spent on improving processing and only 40 percent on new products. A few years ago, 70 percent of the budget went to products and only 30 percent to processing.

One of DuPont's plants, located in Wilmington, Delaware, has gained productivity improvements, some of which have come from involving workers in the process. To encourage the workers to think about improvements, the plant manager gives cost figures on any of the operations down to the newest worker on a maintenance team. More discipline is coming in the manner in which projects are approved. Research managers say that they think a lot harder before approving projects without an obvious payoff.

But still there remains a strong commitment to fundamental research at the senior management level of the company.[3]

The Nature of an Organizational Culture

An organizational culture is the environment of beliefs, customs, knowledge, practices, and conventionalized behavior of a particular social group. Every organization, every corporation has its distinct character. People make organizations work, and the culture of the corporation ties the people together, giving them meaning and a set of

---

[3] Scott McMurray, "Changing a Culture: DuPont Tries to Make Its Research Wizardry Serve the Bottom Line," *Wall Street Journal,* March 27, 1992.

principles and standards to live and work by. Arnold and Capella remind us that achieving the right kind of corporate culture is critical and that businesses are human institutions.[4] One author has defined organizational culture as

> The pattern of basic assumptions that a given group has invented, discovered, or developed in learning to cope with its problems of external adaptation and internal integration, and that have worked well enough to be considered valid, and, therefore, to be taught to new members as the correct way to perceive, think, and feel in relation to those problems.[5]

A given group is described as a set of people who have been together long enough to have shared significant problems, solved those problems, observed the effects of the solutions, and taken in new members.[6] Project teams in the life cycle of a project meet the definition of a "given group" and therefore can be seen as developing a distinct culture, one that is influenced by the culture of the organization to which the team belongs.

Corporate culture may be reflected in the key slogans put forth by an organization such as General Electric's "Progress is our most important product" or Dupont's "Better things for better living through chemistry" or IBM's "IBM means service," or the 3M Company's "Never kill a new product idea." These slogans can set the tone for the entire corporation. Or a corporate culture may be altered by a structural change in the organization. In some organizations such as Hewlett-Packard, General Electric, and 3M, the crucial parts of the organization are kept small to encourage the personal touch in an environment of spirited teamwork.

Corporate culture usually is explained in terms of organizational values and beliefs and the behavior of members of the corporation. In the corporate setting, the value orientation and leadership example set by senior managers greatly influence employee behavior.

But a cultural unit has many subcultures: the company, the work group, and the project teams. Together these also help to determine individual behavior. Managerial behavior is affected by the culture in which the manager operates. This culture in turn is reflected in the subordinate elements of the organization. Culture influences manage-

---

[4]D. R. Arnold and L. M. Capella, "Corporate Culture and the Marketing Concept: A Diagnostic Instrument for Utilities," *Public Utilities Fortnightly,* October 17, 1985, pp. 32–38.

[5]Reprinted from Edgar H. Schein, "Coming to a New Awareness of Organizational Culture," *Sloan Management Review,* Winter 1984, p. 3, by permission of the publisher. Copyright © 1984 by the Sloan Management Review Association. All rights reserved.

[6]Ibid., p. 5.

rial philosophy which in turn affects the organizational philosophy. The organizational culture can be affected by the lack of a management philosophy on which plans, policies, procedures, guidelines, rules, and basic values important to the growth and survival of the organization are based.

A culture can be analyzed by examining the organization's technology, manner, visible or audible behavior patterns, and documents such as charters, plans, policies, and procedures, as well as its organizational structure, leadership style, and the individual and collective roles played in the organization.

Examples of Corporate Culture

Values, the basic concepts and beliefs of an organization that often are reflected in the documentation of a corporation, contribute to the heart of the corporate culture. For example, at Harnischfeger Engineers, Inc., the attitude toward project management is communicated in a project management mission statement:

> Professional management for projects through eminently qualified personnel, using state-of-the-art project management techniques—resulting in satisfied customers and achieving Harnischfeger Engineers' profit objectives.

This mission is printed on a business-size card with a statement of the company's project management strategy on the reverse side:

- *To ensure* that realistic achievable schedules and cost estimates are developed for projects.

- *To ensure* effective communications and rapport with HEI Management and project-related groups within and outside the company.

- *To coordinate* technical support groups to ensure optimum installation sequencing and acceptance testing of project systems and components.

- *To complete* projects on schedule, within budget, and in compliance with technical and other specifications.

Such a card, and the clear message it conveys, has obvious value in influencing the corporate culture and communicating the corporate philosophy to project stakeholders.

Motorola, Inc., a giant organization, is much more nimble than other large corporations like General Motors, IBM, and Westinghouse Electric Corporation. In part, Motorola's nimbleness comes from its ability to change, to foster a participative culture, and to use teams as a way to organize workers and professionals to do productive, quality-driven work. It has an elaborate corporate culture that kindles rather than stifles conflict and dissent, finds promising but neglected projects, and generates a constant flow of information and innovation from thousands of small teams which are held to quantifiable goals.

Intelligence gathering in Motorola is done through a department that has as its mission the reporting of the latest technological developments, gleaned from conferences, journals, rumors, and such. Intelligence gained from many sources helps to build "technology roadmaps" that assess where breakthroughs are likely to occur and how these breakthroughs can be integrated into new products and processes. The culture of conflict helps to quickly identify and fix mistakes, unmasks and eliminates weak or illogical efforts, and keeps senior managers abreast of problems and opportunities in the marketplace. But sometimes the conflict leads to missed opportunities. As described in the *Wall Street Journal,*

> In 1986, a chip team in Austin, Texas, designed a new high-speed workstation microprocessor called the 88000, many times more powerful than Motorola's by now successful 68000 line. But the 68000 project group lobbied against the new chip and tried to persuade customers to ignore it. The conflict led to delays and to a critical decision by a potential customer, Sun Microsystems, Inc., to design its own chip after initially leaning toward the 88000. Sun's design is now the brains for its market-leading workstations. Motorola officials have conceded that 88000 was late to market and that "jealousy" was a factor.[7]

Traditional managers—bureaucrats—may fight more for their turf than for what is right for the enterprise. This fighting slows decision making and prevents people from trying anything new. These turf battles contributed to IBM missing the early markets for laptop computers, notebook computers, and workstations. IBM also sat back and procrastinated while competitors exploited mail-order distribution of personal computers. Even in more mature product lines, IBM came months late to the market—a failure to capitalize on what concurrent engineering can do for commercializing products sooner. Part of IBM's current problems came out of their early success in the 1980s, when the company had so many successes that the managers began to lose touch with competitive realities. With the success of the 1980s, IBM's culture became complacent, and the "...measure of success became how high someone could rise in the company. The highest compliment someone could pay a rising star

---

[7]G. Christian Hill and Ken Yamada, "Staying Power," *Wall Street Journal,* December 12, 1992.

was: 'He's good with foils'—the transparencies used on overhead projects in all IBM meetings. Foils became such a part of the culture that senior executives started having projectors built into their beautiful rosewood desks."[8]

McDonnell Douglas Corporation provides another interesting example of how senior executives influence an organization's culture. There, senior executives encouraged workers and managers to form cells to set their own productivity goals, with some managers even moving their desks onto the factory floor to strengthen their roles as cell members. These cells are used to facilitate participative management. Participative management is one of the five maxims that act as keys to the corporate culture of the company. The other four maxims are strategic management, human resources management, ethical decision making, and quality/productivity.[9]

In *The Soul of a New Machine* (New York: Avon, 1981), Tracy Kidder characterizes Tom West's primary role as protecting his team from organizational conflicts that could impede the team's progress in the computer design-and-build task. West feels that protecting the team is particularly important in situations where dominant cultural values (e.g., competition, or rules and regulations, etc.) may interfere with accomplishing the project team's goals.

Duke Power Company has managed its nuclear power plant projects effectively and has avoided the cost overruns that have been experienced by many other utilities. This success is attributable to an excellent strategic and project management process inseparable from and executed within a supportive corporate culture having these distinguishing features:

- Tight control of construction with little dependence on outsiders
- An in-house engineering and construction staff
- Procurement mostly through a subsidiary
- Clear-cut responsibility for problems—no outside engineering firms, consultants, or contractors with which to share the blame
- Operation of the company by engineers with hands-on experience
- Hiring and promoting of local talent with local community ties in areas where labor unions are weak
- Utilization of computer tracking for flexible job assignments to obviate idleness

---

[8] Paul B. Carroll, "The Failures of Central Planning at IBM," *Wall Street Journal,* January 28, 1993.

[9] Colin Leinster, "The Odd Couple at McDonnell Douglas," *Fortune,* June 22, 1987, pp. 120–126.

- Internal competition among plants and departments to counter any trends toward mediocrity[10]

Morty Lefkoe, president of a consulting firm that specializes in helping corporations reshape their cultures, believes that the most common cause of failure of mergers is a "clash of corporate culture."[11] He further believes that

- Behavior in an organization is determined more by its culture than by directives from its managers or any other factor.

- It is almost impossible to implement any strategy that is inconsistent with an organization's culture.

- Culture has a greater impact on a company's success than anything management can do.

Project teams face diverse cultures, shared cultures, evolving cultures as these teams work in complex, multifaceted, global project teams. The ambience in which these teams work is complex; unique assumptions about behavior from diverse cultural groups compound the challenge. The project team becomes a focus around which multiple, overlapping cultural forces operate. Team members maintain ties to their parent organizational cultures as well as participate in the amalgamated culture of the project team itself. The projects to develop new products at Airbus Industries have become something of a model of high-technology multinational cooperation. The organizational culture found in the projects to develop new aircraft and supporting systems transcends nationalities.

An organization's culture can impact its effectiveness. Two researchers have found a relationship between culture and long-term economic performance. These researchers have also documented the cultural traits that successful companies share.[12]

Cultural Features

An organization's culture consists of shared explicit and implicit agreements among organizational members as to what is important in behavior, as well as attitudes expressed in values, beliefs, standards, and social and management practices. The culture that is developed and becomes characteristic of an organization affects strategic planning and implementation, project management, and all else.

---

[10]Ed Bean, "Going It Alone," *Wall Street Journal,* October 17, 1984.

[11]*Fortune,* July 20, 1987, p. 113.

[12]John P. Kotter and James L. Heskett, *Corporate Culture and Performance* (New York: Free Press, 1992).

It is possible to identify common cultural features that positively and negatively influence the practice of management and the conduct of technical affairs in an organization. Such cultural features develop out of and are influenced by

- The management leadership-and-follower style practiced by key managers and professionals
- The example set by leaders of the organization
- The attitudes displayed and communicated by key managers in their management of the organization
- The managerial and professional competencies
- The assumptions held by key managers and professionals
- The organizational plans, policies, procedures, rules, and strategies
- The political, legal, social, technological, and economic systems with which the members of an organization interface
- The perceived and/or actual characteristics of the organization
- Quality and quantity of the resources (human and nonhuman) consumed in the pursuit of the organization's mission, objectives, goals, and strategies
- The knowledge, skills, and experiences of members of the organization
- Communication patterns
- Formal and informal roles

The policies of an organization reflect its overall cultural climate. Two examples of how this climate can positively affect a project are seen in the approaches taken by the Florida Power and Light Company and the Arizona Power Service Company on their respective nuclear plants. Florida Power and Light established a special office in Bethesda, Maryland, near NRC headquarters and staffed it with engineers to facilitate exchange of information with the NRC during the St. Lucie unit 2 nuclear plant licensing process. Senior management of Arizona Power Service established the following policies concerning the NRC:

> Don't treat NRC as an adversary; NRC is not here to bother us—they see many more plants than the licensee sees; inform NRC of what we (APS) are doing and keep everything up front; and nuclear safety is more important than schedule.[13]

---

[13]U.S. Nuclear Regulatory Commission (NUREG-1055), *Improving Quality and Assurance of Quality in the Design and Construction of Nuclear Power Plants*, Washington, May 1984, pp. 3–21.

This type of corporate attitude prompted the following conclusion from the NRC:

> A characteristic of the projects that had not experienced quality problems was a constructive working relationship with and understanding of the NRC.[14]

In the projects studied by NRC there appeared to be a direct correlation between the project's success and the utility's view of NRC requirements. More successful utilities tended to view NRC requirements as a minimum level of performance, not maximum, and they strove to achieve increasingly higher, self-imposed goals. This attitude covered all aspects of the project, including quality and quality assurance.

The Project Culture

Each project has a distinct culture reflecting in part a universal culture found in all projects. Some insight into this universal culture can be found in what follows.

The project team is an organizational entity devoted to the integration of specialized knowledge for a common purpose: the delivery of the project results on time and within budget to support organizational strategies. The project team must be organized for creativity and innovation to emerge and grow; the team must be organized as a force for *continuous improvement and constant change* in positioning the enterprise for dealing with its changing products/services and processes in a changing global marketplace. Appointment and empowerment of a project team are an explicit recognition that creativity and innovation to bring about change in products/services and organizational processes are both possible and essential to organizational survival.

Every organization has to provide for the means to maintain surveillance over the real and potential changes in its environment— and then it has to design the means for the organization to manage the change needed to remain competitive. What this means is that the organization has to have the discipline to abandon those products/services and processes that are currently successful, and to provide the means for an orderly, disciplined, and systems strategy to develop new organizational initiatives in those products and services provided to customers, and in the organizational processes by which those initiatives come forth. Several strategies are needed to bring a project focus to the management of change in the enterprise: First,

---

[14] Ibid.

enhance the organizational culture so that people at all levels and in all specialities are encouraged to bring forth ideas for improvement in their areas of responsibilities. Second, develop an organizational culture that seeks to abandon that which has been successful through the continuous improvement of existing products/services and processes. Third, become a "learning" organization through the explicit recognition that all organizational members will have to retrain and relearn new technologies to escape obsolescence. Fourth, organize the enterprise's resources so that explicit opportunity is available to bring an organizational focus (a project focus) to the development and implementation of new organizational initiatives that will bring forth new products/services and processes. Fifth, provide a strategic management capability by which organizational leadership is proactive in providing the resources, the vision, and the discipline to strategically manage the future through the use of product and process projects.

The project team—a "body of companions"—dedicated to the creation of something that does not currently exist in the enterprise provides for a way of decentralizing the organization of resources to deal with change. The team members represent those different specialities needed to create value to satisfy the needed change in products/services and processes. The nature of the task needed to bring about the change determines the organizational membership on the "body of companions." The organizational membership in turn influences the culture of the project team—and, to a certain extent, that of the participating stakeholders as well. Since each member of the project team comes from specialized areas of the enterprise and represents parochial areas of expertise, the objectives, goals, and strategies of the project team must be unequivocal—crystal-clear to all the project stakeholders. Only focused project objectives, goals, and strategies will hold the team together and enable it to create something that does not currently exist in the enterprise, in an efficient and effective manner.

The project team is comprised of knowledgeable people, who must be led and not supervised or managed in the traditional sense. Team loyalty is obtained by providing members with the opportunity to put their knowledge to use; the team is an organization of knowledgeable peers and equals, colleagues and associates who are bonded together by the focus of the team to create and innovate continuous improvement in organizational products and processes. Project teams are clearly not an organization of "supervisors and bosses" or any form of the traditional supervisor-subordinate relationship that has been characteristic of traditional organizations. How do you "boss" knowledgeable workers? It cannot be done—if attempted, the team members will find ways of leaving the team to seek more motivational environments. Yet there still remains the need for someone to make decisions on behalf of the team after a participative and consensus process actively seeking the knowledgeable expertise of the team members is carried out. The project leader who makes decisions on behalf of the project team has to be willing to be held accountable for those key decisions coming out of the project team's deliberation. The project leader has to inspire the team, provide the means for a vision to be developed for the team, provide the team with the resources needed to do the job, seek participation and consensus on key project problems and opportunities, and provide the means for the team's performance to be evaluated on an ongoing basis during the life of the project. Projects and cultures change. But sometimes people do not want to change.

Why Change?

Individual and group behavior in an organization is controlled as much by the basic relationship that people have in the organizational culture as by anything else. It includes organizational policies and procedures, and how perceptions, rules, and expected behavior are carried out.

Businesses are organized to exploit the profitability of their products and services. The process of innovation can help improve that profitability. But there is a larger dimension of innovation—the abandonment of old ways and the creation of new products, services, and organizational processes needed to bring something new to the customers. To innovate means to challenge the existing order, the prevailing viewpoint, and to assume the risk and uncertainties and the enmity of those who wish to preserve the status quo—those who encourage the traditional viewpoint, who postpone evaluating existing strategies, who tolerate mediocrity and even failure because of a fear of what change might bring. We have a litany of old saws that serve to protect us and rationalize the status quo.

Don't rock the boat.

The way to get along is to go along.

Why change?

I'm only a couple of years from retirement.

What we are doing now is good enough.

I like things the way they are.

The good old days were the best days.

Innovation cannot be fostered in the same way that improvement in organizational efficiencies can be fostered. This is a mistake that many managers make. Managers have to run an efficient business, make a profit, and at the same time provide for the *concurrent* development of new products, services, and organizational processes.

Responses of managers in their attempts at remaining competitive include the following.

- Do nothing, with the hope that the traditional products and services offered will be adequate.

- Respond with defensive strategies of cutting costs, reducing the number of products and even product lines, and emphasize the most profitable products and services.

- Make innovation a way of life in the organization, and energize and empower every member of the enterprise to look for new and better ways of doing things—both in doing things for the internal customers and in providing products and services to outside customers.

- Work at building a culture which encourages and rewards creativity and innovation from the highest to the lowest levels of the organization.

- Have senior management provide a leadership model in encouraging creativity and innovation, and tune the organizational management and cultural systems to make innovation a way of life—to be accepted by everyone at every level in the enterprise. Everyone in the organization is protected from any criticism of any sort for brainstorming and being on a constant quest for new ways of working and serving the organization.

The Constancy of Change

Corporations and other types of organizations are seeing the beginning of the end for doing business under the traditional "command and control" philosophy. Organizational hierarchies with explicit chains of command are being redesigned and realigned. Managers in organizations today are seeing their traditional roles being challenged. An article in *Fortune* magazine brought into focus some of the current changes affecting managers and their roles. According to *Fortune,* call these new nonmanagers "...sponsors, facilitators—anything but the M word. They're helping their companies and advancing their careers by turning old management practices upside down."[15]

Rapid change and the demands of organizational stakeholders to include customers, suppliers, workers, unions, local communities, and such vested groups have helped to change the role of managers to one of being able to provide an organizational context in which decisions are made and executed through a "consensus and consent" management style rather than the traditional—and antiquated—command-and-control model. Organizational structures are becoming flatter,

---

[15] "The Non-Manager Managers," *Fortune,* February 22, 1993, pp. 80–83.

and many "middle managers" have found their supervisory roles and the jobs in gathering, processing, and transmitting of information becoming superfluous—partly through the emergence of computers and more sophisticated information systems. Challenges from stakeholder groups, such as institutional investors, have started a trend of greater involvement by outside directors who want corporate managers to be more responsive to stakeholders and less responsive to some internal, traditional order of managing the company. Managers in the future will likely see continued changes in their roles, motivated by pressures from key stakeholders through the board of directors, and from the workers who can—and will—-contribute to the management of the enterprise.

The new nonmanagers who are emerging will be called something different than managers. New titles are coming forth such as leader, facilitator, coach, sponsor, mentor, adviser—titles which suggest a role far from the traditional command-and-control model now becoming obsolete.

The evolving theory and practice of project management have played a major role in demonstrating that a management philosophy of consensus and consent is workable and is more in tune with what people want in today's organizations. Organizations that have used project management over many years have seen a subtle change in attitudes about what managers should be responsible for—and what form their exercise of authority has taken. Project managers who have had to operate in the context of the matrix organizational design have had to develop strength in their exercise of de facto authority since many times their de jure or legal delegation of authority has been insufficient to get the job done.

Project Management Actions

In a very real sense of the word, project managers have to be *change managers,* and at the same time participate with other organizational managers in designing and facilitating a culture that brings out the best in people.

Project Strategies

The project manager who is able to function as a project leader along with the other managers (leaders) of the parent organization is responsible for arranging the conditions conducive to a creative and disciplined culture supportive of project teamwork. Certain actions can help to develop and maintain such a culture.

First, design and implement an ongoing disciplined approach in planning, organization, and control of the *project management system.*

This is a fundamental first so that team members have a model to use in managing the project. This is one of the first task-related actions to let people know where they stand and what is expected of them on the project team.

Also, provide as much leeway as possible for the project team members to try new ways of getting their jobs done. This includes the encouragement of experimentation without fear of reprisals if mistakes are made.

Give team members a reasonable amount of attention through project reviews, strategy meetings, and checking in on a regular basis to see how things are going. Too much attention can be counterproductive and might be interpreted as meddling. Too little attention might be construed as disinterest on the part of the project manager.

Make sure the members of the team understand in specific terms their authority, responsibility, and accountability so that they know what's expected of them on their work package. If team members know their assigned work packages, there is less likelihood that they will become overburdened with the minute details of their jobs. Creativity requires the opportunity to reflect on the totality of the job being done. If members are too busy with details, it's easy for them to miss the big picture.

Give project team members part ownership in the decisions affecting the project. When the team members know that their opinions are valued on project matters, their self-confidence is bolstered and the chances for creative thinking are enhanced. By encouraging participation in decision making on the project, the general culture of the project team will be improved. When team members see their work on the project work packages as challenging and the goals as realistic, they are more likely to exhibit creative behavior and be happier in their work.

Maintain proper oversight of the project. A project manager is not a supervisor in the usual sense of the word, although such person should have "supervision" of the project, should know where the total project stands, and should know where the project stands on cost, schedule, and technical performance at all times. The project manager maintains oversight of the project by watching and directing the major activities and course of action of the team. Most team members who have maximized their creative potential would prefer a low level of oversight by the project manager. The oversight effort should be focused on those activities most directed to achieving project results.

Encourage the use of creative brainstorming approaches to solve the many unstructured problems that arise during the project's life cycle. Many different types of unstructured solutions will be needed to solve these problems. The use of a single routine problem-solving approach would be inappropriate since such an approach too often assumes there is one "best and correct" solution. Projects create something new. Innovation and creativity are musts to deal with something so new.

Provide timely feedback to the project team. In this way, the project manager will encourage open communication in the project's culture. If the team members sense that key information is being withheld or that the project leader is less than candid with them, dissatisfaction and disenchantment could result, thus adversely affecting the project culture. If feedback is provided too late for the team members to make adjustments, the project could suffer and the individuals could be discouraged.

Provide the resources and support to get the job done. This is another fundamental and positive contribution that the project manager can and must make to the project culture. Adequate resources are required to do the job and to facilitate a creative and innovative culture. A shortage of resources may allow people to use their innovative and creative skills, but in the long run adequate resources are needed to ensure a supportive culture.

Finally, recognize the key "people-related" cultural factors and utilize them. These people-related factors include

- Rewarding useful ideas
- Encouraging candid expression of ideas
- Promptly following up on team and member concerns
- Assisting in idea development
- Accepting different ideas—listening to that team member who is "marching to a different drummer"
- Encouraging risk taking
- Providing opportunities for professional growth and broadening experiences on the project
- Encouraging interaction with the project stakeholders so that there is an appreciation by the team members of the project's breadth and depth

The Trust Factor

A key challenge to the project leader is to manage the team members and the other project stakeholders, so one of the key characteristics in the team's culture is *trust*—a security that one feels concerning the integrity, ability, and character of people associated with the project. To trust is to have confidence in the abilities and personalities of the team. To trust the team is to feel that team members will be responsive and responsible in the making and implementing of decisions affecting the team, the project, and the other stakeholders. Trust must exist between the team and higher management, and these managers must have a vision of how the project fits into the larger goals and objectives of the enterprise.

Trust is a condition in a relationship that takes years to develop, and then it can be damaged or destroyed by a single act of imprudence. Trust is easy to violate; it requires that members of the project team "open up" to each other and let each other know "where they stand." Trust is particularly challenging to develop and maintain on a project team, where people from different disciplines have to pull together for the common project goals and projects. Jack Welch, CEO of General Electric, has said in GE's 1991 annual report that the corporation will be built on mutual trust and respect and that "trust and respect take years to build and no time at all to destroy." The bottom line of trust is that a person's word is his or her bond.

By becoming sensitive to the importance of these factors, the project manager can enhance the positive aspects of the culture.

Culture and Project Extensions

Sometimes projects are extended even when they might better be abandoned. These unwise extensions often are caused by the cultural factors present in the parent organization and on the project team. Managers who have had track records of success will hang on to a near losing or fatal project simply because they are used to winning and don't want the project to fail. With such an attitude, resources will be poured into the project to make it work out. Also, people tend to see what supports their beliefs, even to the point of biasing cost and schedule estimates to support their view. Investing more resources in the project is perceived as a preferable alternative to admitting failure. To fail would be to admit to others that the project could not be handled; hanging on in the face of mounting project losses seems to make more sense. When a person has become a project champion, it's easy to rationalize the defense of that project despite growing concerns about its feasibility and eventual outcome. Social and cultural pressures also tend to encourage managerial persistence to "stay the course" and to "stick to your guns"—to exhibit strong leadership.

Administrative inertia also can occur when the cancellation of the project and the divestment of resources that would follow are perceived as politically threatening. Institutionalization of the project in the organization's strategy can be another powerful persuader for continuance. Indeed, an organization can become so enamored of a project that the costs of terminating it are perceived as much greater than a persistent continuation even though the project's linkage with the organization's strategic purpose has become spurious. Managers concerned with projects should be aware of the psychological, social, and cultural forces that can influence their viewpoint and can hamper their rational judgment on when it's best to "pull the plug" on the project.[16]

Influencing the Team's Culture

A project manager can help to develop a supportive culture for the team through the team building process. Mower and Wilemon describe team building as a process aimed at developing a team's task competencies (meeting goals, objectives, and targets) and interpersonal competencies (resolving conflicts, listening, and building trust). According to them, an effective team culture teaches members to develop these competencies fully through a series of team phases in order to reach a level of sustained high performance. Table 20.1 portrays qualities teams need to develop in order to become effective and perform at a sustained high level.[17]

What can the culture do for the project team? Several writers have noted the following:

- Culture creates social ideals which help to guide behavior.[18]

- Culture sends messages to insiders and outsiders about what the organization stands for.[19]

- Culture helps to align individual and organizational goals and values.[20]

- Culture serves to control, monitor, and process beliefs and behavior in the organization.[21]

The Culture of Successful Teams

In Table 20.2, Tuman identifies the key characteristics of successful teams. The culture in which a project team works is discernible to a

[16] Material in this section has been drawn from Barry M. Staw and Jerry Ross, "Knowing When to Pull the Plug," *Harvard Business Review,* March-April 1987, pp. 68–74.

[17] Ibid., p. 377. The overall concept of team building is discussed in chap. 18.

[18] M. R. Louis, "Organization as Cultural Bearing Milieux," in L. R. Pondy et al. (eds.) *Organizational Symbolism,* vol. 1: *Monographs in Organizational Behavior and Industrial Relations* (Greenwich, Conn.: Jai Press, 1983), pp. 39–54.

[19] T. C. Dandridge, "Symbols' Function and Use," in L. R. Pondy et al. (eds.), *Organizational Symbolism,* vol. 1: *Monographs in Organizational Behavior and Industrial Relations* (Greenwich, Conn.: Jai Press, 1983) pp. 69–79.

[20] R. Harrison, "Strategies for a New Age," *Human Resource Management,* vol. 22, no. 3, Fall 1983, pp. 209–235.

[21] A. L. Wilkins, "Organizational Stories as Symbols," in L. R. Pondy et al. (eds.), *Organizational symbolism,* vol. 1: *Monographs in Organizational Behavior and Industrial Relations* (Greenwich, Conn.: Jai Press, 1983), pp. 81–92.

TABLE 20.1   Characteristics of Effective and Ineffective Teams

Key variables	Ineffective teams	Effective teams
Goals	Goals unstated or unclear.	Goals are clear and accepted.
Roles	Individual responsibilities are unclear.	Responsibilities are clear and change as needed.
Conflict	Conflict is suppressed, producing destructive attitudes and behaviors.	Conflict is managed openly and accepted as a vital part of team development.
Learning	Team learning is minimal.	Learning is valued and captured.
Leadership	One person is seen as the leader. Other people stuck in roles.	Leadership is seen as a shared responsibility.
Performance	Lack of concern for performance—objectives are not met.	Performance, satisfaction, and growth are valued and achieved.
Communication	Communication is guarded and restricted.	Communication is clear, open and energetic.
Processes	Team processes emerge which may impede team progress.	Team processes are "invented"—which ensure alignment with team objectives.
People	Team members' personal and professional needs are ignored.	Individual goals are blended with team objectives.
Power	Many team members feel powerless. Power inequities cause an uneven desire to contribute.	Team members feel powerful—each one's contribution is valued and sought.

SOURCE: J. Mower and D. Wilemon, "Team Building in a Technical Environment," in D. Kocaoglo (ed.), *Handbook of Technology Management,* forthcoming.

perceptive, seasoned outsider. Tuman cites the experiences of such seasoned project managers:

> I can walk onto any project site anywhere in the world and within a short time tell you if that project is going to be a winner. It's easy; I just look at the people, what they are doing and how they are doing it. If the project people look determined, confident, enthusiastic, and busy, it's a good bet that you've got a winning team. If the people respect each other, help each other and things seem to be getting done with a minimum amount of confusion, then you can be fairly certain that they have their act together and they will pull it off without much strain.[22]

Another veteran project manager put it this way:

---

[22]J. Tuman, Jr., *Success Modeling: A Technique for Building a Winning Project Team,* paper presented at the Project Management Institute 1986 Seminar/Symposium, Montreal, September 1986, p. 97.

TABLE 20.2   Characteristics of Successful Project Teams

Characteristics of the team	Characteristics of the team leader	Characteristics of team members
■ *High performance*—Team members consistently work hard and display a high level of interest, dedication and motivation in the project, its members and its goal.	■ Should be comfortable in an environment of high uncertainty.	■ Have the ability to get up to speed quickly and adjust to changing conditions.
■ *Well organized*—Roles, responsibilities, authority and information flow are well defined and understood by all; furthermore, there is little or no conflict relative to project procedures and administration.	■ Should be problem oriented (technical, administrative, schedule and cost); and gain satisfaction from solving problems.	■ Have endurance and drive; high energy. ■ Even temperament and consistent performance. ■ Personally well organized. ■ Optimistic view of things.
■ *Well planned*—The project has clearly defined objectives and well established plans, schedules, budgets and monitoring and reporting systems.	■ Should have a positive outlook and the ability to display enthusiasm, energy, and a "can-do" attitude. ■ Should have experience and knowledge of the *organization,* the *industry,* the *technology,* the *management principles* and *methodologies,* and *systems* and *procedures* related to the project.	■ Keep interest in own personal development and growth. ■ Stability in personal life.
■ *Good team interdependency*—Team members are committed to project goals and objectives, display high levels of trust and foster an environment which provides for good communications and information flow.	■ Should have the skill to apply experience and knowledge to project requirements and problems.	

SOURCE: J. Tuman, Jr., *Success Modeling: A Technique for Building a Winning Project Team,* paper presented at the Project Management Institute 1986 Seminar/Symposium, September 1986, p. 97.

The real test is the first major problem or screw up. Look at how the team reacts. If they tackled the problem together like professionals, each working hard and contributing the best of what he has to offer, then you have a team that can't be beat. However, if they take sides, look for the fall guy, worry about fixing blame, then you have a bunch that is done for. In the high stakes, high stress environment that we work in, we all win together, or we all fail together. There can be no super stars and there can be no individual casualties.[23]

Meredith Willson's "The Music Man" told the story of a midwestern salesman who went from one small town to another, selling the need for a boys' band—and, ultimately, the musical instruments and uniforms that went along with it. Unhampered by musical knowledge, the music man held out a vision for the community of River City and succeeded in his sale. More conventional salesmen could not understand his success, insisting that "you gotta know the territory!"

But in one sense, Professor Harold Hill did know the territory; he understood boys, civic pride, the dangers of the pool hall, and the heart of Marian the librarian. And, after all, the "Professor" was selling not a product or a service, but a dream.[24]

Somehow the project manager has to sell a dream—the project's objectives—to the project team and in so doing help to facilitate a supportive, successful project management culture.

Conflict

When people are working together, circumstances are ripe for controversy, disagreement, opposition, and intellectual struggles as team members pursue their individual and collective roles on the team. How this inevitable conflict is dealt with will impact the project and organizational culture.

Conflict is an inevitable force to be contended with in any organizational effort. On a project team composed of people with different specialist skills, the opportunity for conflict is ready-made. Disagreements over the use of functional input to the project can occur; people who are fluent in a functional specialty can have problems in being able to communicate with other functional specialists who have their functional parochialism and beliefs. Interpersonal conflict—where people don't want to get along because of personal prejudices, ethics, morals, value systems, and the like—can be a basis for ongoing conflict.

Conflict, which can be guided into the substantive issues such as the design approach on the product, can be healthy if the resolution of conflict teaches everyone something about how to deal with and participate in the resolution of the conflict. Conflicts that result from

---

[23]Ibid.

[24]Adapted from N. R. Horton, "You Gotta Know the Territory," *American Management Association*, April 1987, p. 3.

poor communication, lack of understanding of team objectives and goals, organizational politics, and the like are dysfunctional and should be dealt with in a forthright manner. Dealing with any conflict involves elements of confrontation—when the confrontation can be directed to the substantial problem of opportunity—and away from the interpersonal dynamics. There will be a greater likelihood of resolution of the conflict when everyone wins something—if only that means having had the opportunity to be heard and to have her or his opinions adequately assessed.

Conflict will also be present, and the identification of the conflict, putting it into the substantive context of the project, and seeking resolution at the lowest level in the project team can be satisfactory to all concerned. Compromise is usually needed in the resolution of a conflict, and the chances for compromise are increased when the conflict is identified as soon as possible. Once identified, the conflict should be brought out into the open and resolution processes can be undertaken. Once it has surfaced, there are different ways to deal with conflict, ranging from unilateral action on the part of a manager, to full debate and analysis by the project team. Procrastination in hopes that it will go away is sometimes a conflict resolution strategy. Conflicts seldom go away—the issues just remain out of sight and mind, to come up again when the chances for a successful resolution are not so good. When the conflict is dealt with on a timely basis through a mutual assessment and compromise, the cultural ambience of the project team is likely to be enhanced.

During the formative phases of the project team, an important issue should be raised: How will we deal with and resolve conflicts on this team? By getting members of the team to talk about how they would like to deal with the inevitable conflicts, there is a greater chance that the conflicts will be properly managed and resolved. Conflicts that are successfully resolved at lower levels of the team are, in general, the way to go. Senior management involvement should be infrequent in part because the senior managers would not be familiar with the details of the conflict. Only when the team is unable to resolve the conflict or the conflict has higher implications in the organization should senior management become involved.

Summary

More than ever, the rewards in the future will go to managers who make some contribution to the organization, and not to those who master bureaucracy and have people "work for them." Ability to work as a contributing team member will be vital. Leadership of a project team which creates something of value that did not previously exist will be a critical skill at all levels of a much more austere organizational hierarchy than has existed in the past.

The basis of a person's authority, however, will come from knowledge, skill, personal effectiveness, and attitudes more than from the legitimacy of an organizational position. Understanding and managing the organizational and project team culture will be part of the formula for success.

The cultural ambience of an organization using project management is subtle, yet very real. In the project-driven organization, the attitudes, values, beliefs, and management systems tend to become more participative and democratic. Every project has its distinct culture, and the project manager can—and must—strive to influence that culture to be supportive of both project and organizational purposes.

Senior management must recognize the importance of the cultural ambience of the organization and the role that the organizational culture can have in facilitating effective management of the project.

Discussion Questions

1. Define culture in terms of its use in describing an organization.

2. How do organizational beliefs and values affect corporate culture? How do senior managers' values and beliefs influence employee behavior?

3. What kinds of corporate documentation can assist in understanding the culture of an organization? How?

4. Describe an organization from your work or school experience. What was its culture like? Explain.

5. How is the project management culture exhibited in organizations? Explain.

6. Discuss some of the factors that influence cultural features. What role does each factor play in defining culture?

7. Discuss some of the cultural factors that affect teamwork. How can management develop an effective team? What people-related factors must be considered?

8. In addition to the project team culture, what other cultures must the project manager be concerned about? Why?

9. What can culture do for the project team in terms of meeting individual as well as organizational goals? Explain.

10. What are some of the cultural characteristics of successful teams?

11. How can the project team's management of the first major problem help the project manager assess the potential of the team? Explain.

12. Discuss the importance of the role of project culture in the overall effectiveness of the project.

User Checklist

1. Define the culture of your organization.

2. What senior management values and beliefs have affected the definition of culture in your organization? How?

3. What corporate documentation exists that has influenced the culture of your organization? Explain.

4. Define the culture of the various projects within your organization. Do project cultures differ from the overall organizational culture? Why or why not?

5. What features (such as leader-and-follower style) have influenced the culture of your organization? How?

6. Do project managers pay enough attention to individual members of the project team? How has this affected the operating culture?

7. What factors play a role in the creation of effective teamwork in your organization? What inhibits teamwork?

8. What other cultures must project managers understand? Do the project managers of your organization interact effectively with the various cultures that they encounter? Why or why not?

9. Does the project culture in your organization combine individual and organizational goals? Why or why not?

10. Compare some of the successful and not so successful projects within your organization. What were the cultural characteristics of these projects? Explain.

11. How do project team members handle conflict on the project? What does this indicate about the effectiveness of the project team? Why?

12. Do the project and senior managers of your organization understand the importance of the role of culture in the overall success of a project? Why or why not?

Index

Index note: The *f.* after a page number refers to a table; the *t.* to a table.

ABOUT THE AUTHOR

Dr. David I. Cleland is the Ernest E. Roth Professor and Professor of Engineering Management in the Department of Industrial Engineering at the University of Pittsburgh. He is a Fellow of the Project Management Institute and consults on project management for industrial, government, military, and educational organizations. Recognized as one of the leading authorities in the field of project management, he is the author/editor of 25 books, including the award-winning *Systems Analysis and Project Management* and *Project Management Handbook*, as well as two new titles, *Military Project Management Handbook* and *Global Project Management Handbook*, both available from McGraw-Hill.